POWER
IN THE
ORGANISATION

POWER
IN THE
ORGANISATION

The Discourse of Power
in Managerial Praxis

Philippe Daudi

Basil Blackwell

90231

© Philippe Daudi, 1986

First published 1986
Basil Blackwell Ltd
180 Cowley Road, Oxford OX4 1JF, UK

Basil Blackwell Inc.
432 Park Avenue South, Suite 1503
New York, NY 10016, USA

British Library Cataloguing in Publication Data
Daudi, Philippe
    Power in the organisation: the discourse of
    power in managerial praxis.
    1. Management   2. Power (Social sciences)
    I. Title   II. Makt, diskurs och handling. *English*
    658.4   HD38

    ISBN 0-631-15086-2

Library of Congress Cataloging in Publication Data
Daudi, Philippe.
    Power in the organisation.
    Bibliography: p.
    Includes index.
    1. Management. 2. Organization. 3. Power (Social
    sciences) I. Title.
    HD31.D23. 1986   658.4'09   86-1025
    ISBN 0-631-15086-2

Typeset by Columns of Reading
Printed in Great Britain by
T.J. Press, Padstow, Cornwall

Contents

Preface

As soon as I began to study power I was impressed by the way in which the discourse of power in many sub-disciplines of the social sciences was handled: it was sometimes present and sometimes absent; it also frequently changed shape as a result of new fashions or the use of different languages. Within the particular field of organisation theory there has been increasing interest in the subject. Notions such as influence strategies, coalitions, bargaining, authority and politics have been abundantly debated in a variety of discourses obeying different and sometimes contradictory assumptions. No coherent body was to be found, but rather a discontinuous discourse with all the marks of ambiguity which characterise human affairs, which yet claimed to be true. Thus it gradually became apparent that large portions of theories on organisations are rootless in the sense that they are unaware of the philosophical nature of the very problems which they raise. In this book I attempt to reconcile the philosophical nature of the problems raised by power with its organisational context, in theory and in praxis. In trying to do so my journey perhaps followed an unconventional track. From Nietzsche I learned that one must dig deeply because down below it is not always hell. From Foucault, whom I had the privilege to meet on several occasions in Le Collège de France in Paris, I learned that the important thing in research is curiosity. Not the one which 'seeks to assimilate what is conventional to know, but the one which makes us take a deconstructive stance'. I also learned from him that it is essential for one's intellectual health to constantly explore new modes of thinking and new ways of looking at the world.

Compiling this book has taken a long time, and also many combined efforts and contributions from different people and institutions. To name a few of them would be unfair; there are so many who contributed so much: my gratitude to all of them. One special acknowledgement, though, to Lena Andersson, who devotedly achieved the heroic act of typing and retyping the manuscript the required number of times. The present text is an elaboration of a previous version in Swedish in 1984.

Introduction

The thesis for which I shall argue in this work is that our present knowledge and conception of power rest upon a rudimentary understanding of the phenomenon and upon arbitrary assumptions as to its nature. We conceptualise the phenomenon of power in a *primitive* manner, treating it as if it were a thing, an attribute, or a concrete reality. As researchers of power, we aim our analysis directly at the phenomenon itself, with the purpose of grasping it, assigning it a value and axiomatising it. We produce a *discourse*[1] of power in which the fundamental assumptions derive from the ideological and cultural heritage of the western world. We shall conquer and subjugate nature, rule over the laws of physics and *have* power over things. This mentality is also expressed in our desire to treat people in the same way as we have learnt to treat things. We see each other as instruments to mould and manoeuvre as if people also were things. Power is thus conceptualised by the primitive discourse as if it were a concrete means by which to govern and dominate; a means to be *owned* and which should be understood, studied and used as such. Apart from the pseudo-knowledge which results from this conceptualisation, the primitive discourse also produces and spreads a distinctive conception as to what power is: a mentality *dictating* the way in which one should relate to power. This mentality and this idea of power is then evident in organisations. As organisational members, our way of relating to others, whether we may be superiors or subordinates, derives from a mode of thought in which power, as an attribute and as a *coercive* means of domination, control and repression, is a central ingredient. The primitive discourse is not, however, satisfied with the mere dissemination of this notion of power; it also justifies and substantiates it via its procedures of knowledge production: researchers of power base their studies on this conception while organisational members act with this very conception in their minds in their interactions.

In spite of the fact that people in organisations have apparently internalised the conceptualisation generated by the primitive discourse of

1

power, however, the models of the discourse seem neither to be able to provide satisfactory explanations of the ways in which power is manifested, nor of the meaning which it has for the intra-organisational processes. The reason for this is that the primitive discourse seems to consider power as an anomaly, a pathology, or, in other words, as a dysfunction in organisations: a pathology which disturbs the harmony, equilibrium and balance of what are assumed to be rational systems. The reductionist approach of the primitive discourse is another factor contributing to the low explanatory potential of the models at hand: power (or its manifestations) is rooted out of its organisational context and reduced to *frozen* facts, disengaged from the events giving the meaning. The main reason for the inadequacy of the traditional models, however, is that the primitive discourse is based, as indeed are other discourses constituting the way we think in the western world, upon principles of exclusions as regards its formation, development, reproduction and dissemination. But what we see here is a paradox: it is precisely those dimensions that are excluded from and regarded as external to the discourse which are meaningful for the actors involved in power relations. Power is made manifest by the actions of the actors which are merely a reflection of their interpretations of the notion of power – the same notion that is produced and dictated by the primitive discourse: power as a coercive means of domination, control and repression. Meanwhile, at the same time as the discourse constructs models as to how people are assumed – and *ought* – to behave, these very people continue, 'incorrigibly', to act quite regardless of the models.

Even if the organisational members do not act exactly as is presumed by the models, they do still conceptualise power in accordance with the notions dictated by the primitive discourse, which in turn has its roots in our ideology and culture. One implication which this conceptualisation has for the organisation is that superiors tend to ignore (or at any rate, act as if they ignored) the fact that the relationship which they have with their subordinates is one of interdependency. They 'exercise' a *coercive power* in their interactions with subordinates, the primary purpose of which is the control and prediction of their behaviour as well as the contraction of their space of action. This is experienced by subordinates as a repressive and arbitrary exercise of power against which they then try to protect themselves by developing *contra-coercive* strategies. While the first exercise 'their' coercive power, the second develop contra-coercive mechanisms of protection which take the shape of various strategical actions. This often results in a vicious circle. Among the 'antagonists' a spirit of low trust may prevail; while in the organisation *negative dynamics* may develop, accompanied by *losses of energy* since attention is channelled into pseudo-activities, into intrigues and various attempts to contract each other's space of action. This state of affairs has negative implications for the intra-organisational processes. The essence of the argument is thus that the conceptualisation of the primitive discourse produces a particular view and a mentality as to the way in which power should be understood and studied, on the one hand, and the way in which it is interpreted by organisational members, on the other. This interpretation constitutes the base which shapes the actions and interaction between members; which means that the way in which people view and perceive the phenomenon of power is apparently a central ingredient in the development of intra-organisational processes. It also implies that the phenomenon of power is an essential, if not central, mechanism of regulation in organisations.

My approach to the formulation of this argument has to a large degree been through a comprehensive study of the literature on the subject, but it has also to some extent been influenced by the empirical experiences that are presented in Chapters One and Two. The ideas have gradually emerged and taken shape in connection with the discourse of power and its praxis inasmuch as they reflect, on a general level, that which I deem to be the core of the problem of power, both on the theoretical and on the empirical levels. In this sense the *thesis* argued for could be said to express a problem of research. It is meant to point to the shortcomings of the discourse of power and to the effects thereof. The formulation of this *thesis* would not have been possible, however, without first having thoroughly examined these shortcomings and thereafter having developed special methods by means of which the phenomenon of power could be studied.

In the following pages I shall present and discuss the various phases leading up to the specific formulation of the research problem. My interest in the phenomenon of power began to materialise in connection with my studies of organisational theory and other contiguous subjects,[2] particularly that of the philosophy of action. I had naturally considered the concept of power earlier, but until then not in any specific manner. It is astonishing how little attention has been paid in traditional organisation theory to such an important phenomenon as that of power. It seems, none the less, that power (or at least the idea of power) was invariably present in these theories, even if only implicitly and often in the form of vague assumptions, the meaning of which was left to the divination of the reader. The older management theories (see note 2), and their principles of organisations and management (Berg and Daudi, 1982), make no particular or explicit statements about power, yet in these principles[3] one can perceive a certain willingness to deal specifically with the problem of power in organisations and with its distribution as regards the right to decide in various matters. Parallel to my growing interest in the philosophy of action, I began to search for those particular trends in organisation theory having some connection with this philosophy. The idea that there exists a dichotomy between the various ways of looking at action in society was suggested by Silverman (1968): the transcendental and immanent models. The first model implies that action is a reflection of the needs of the system as a whole (systemic perspective), whereas the second relates action to the meaning which it has for the actors against the background of their interactions with others. Silverman (1970) further developed the idea of this dichotomy to denote the systemic perspective of the structural functionalists (transcendental model), on the one hand, and, on the other hand, the perspective which emanates from the actions of the actors (immanent model). Other researchers had, however, used 'the immanent model' before Silverman, if only implicitly, in order to demonstrate the significance of the mechanisms of interaction for intra-organisational processes (Eisenstadt, 1965; Crozier, 1964). Yet in both Crozier's (1964) and Silverman's (1970) work, and also in Cohen's (1970) – the last-mentioned argues for the explanatory potential of the action perspective when showing how changes can be seen as direct consequences of the actors' interactions – a theme began to appear; namely that of the strategical character of the actions of organisational members. It should be noted, none the less, that this theme had been latent in many older classical works,[4] even if it had not been studied in an explicit and specific manner. I continued my search via the theme of strategical action and 're-discovered' the tendency within organisation theory that emphasises the specific rationality governing the strategies and interactions of the actor (e.g. Crozier, 1964). In this search I came across the literature concerning *strategic interaction* including, amongst other classics in this field, Goffman, who wonders:

> Whenever students of the human scene have considered the dealings individuals have with one another, the issue of calculation has arisen: When a respectable motive is given for action, are we to suspect an ulterior one? When an individual supports a promise or threat with a convincing display of emotional expression, are we to believe him? When an individual seems carried away by feeling is he intentionally acting this way in order to create an effect? When someone responds to us in a particular way, are we to see this as a spontaneous reaction to the situation or a result of his having canvassed all other possible responses before deciding this one was the most advantageous? And whether or not we have such concerns, ought we to be worried about the individual believing that we have them? (Goffman, 1969: 85)

The ideas expressed in this type of literature seem to show some similarities with those argued for in game theory.[5] The concept of power here is often treated in an explicit manner. With few exceptions – e.g. in

Schelling (1960) – the formulation of the concept has in these theories taken the shape of highly developed mathematical models, having no foundations nor relevance to the empirical reality (Harsanyi, 1962a,b) other than as a source of nourishment for the debates of the researchers.

Elsewhere in game theory, interesting contributions are to be found in which human interaction is conceptualised as a game. Long (1958), for example, sees the organisation (or a certain 'community') as an 'ecology of games'. He maintains that the actors are involved in various games (or in game-like situations) in which each and everyone is striving, according to his/her own capacity, to win strategies. Walton and McKersie (1965: 2) regard human behaviour as 'a set of instrumental acts which can be more or less intelligently conceived and more or less expertly excented'. Their attention is devoted to identifying those strategies that are used by the actors in their negotiations, and relating these to the goals after which the actors strive. This type of game theory in particular has influenced many researchers of power from different disciplines: political scientists, sociologists, psychologists, and even power researchers with an orientation to business administration.[6] In exploring these theoretical fields, the importance of the concept became apparent, not only for the understanding of intra-organisational processes (from the point of view of the researcher), but also for the way in which the members of organisations interpret the situations which they experience, and the ways in which they interact with others.

The task then became one of mapping out the relationship between the theme of the strategical character of the actions taken by the actors, on the one hand, and the theme of power as an important phenomenon in organisations, on the other. It became increasingly apparent to me that this link was not, apart from a few single exceptions to which I will return shortly, self-evident in the literature. Statements have been made about the first theme, as likewise they have been made about the second, but without any noteworthy connection between the two. Theoretically speaking, this connection seemed entirely natural to me. Having read about the repeated failures of the attempts made by organisational theorists to reproduce organisational reality by means of rationally designed systems, models, and hybrid metaphors,[7] I became convinced that this assumed 'best way' was not appropriate for the understanding of intra-organisational processes. My concept of the organisation was (although this concept has, to a certain extent, been modified since then) that of a fabricated and artificial solution (Gouldner, 1965; Crozier, 1964; Sainsaulieu, 1965; Elger, 1975; Silverman and Jones, 1976) to the problems arising as a result of collective actions: i.e. those actions implying an interaction and integration of different individuals, groups or coalitions having various interests and diverging orientations. Ideas about action, interaction and strategy have indeed been expressed, but, as mentioned earlier, more as something which ought to be taken into consideration in organisational studies than as actual, applied concepts. Silverman was perhaps one of the first to appreciate the value of the action perspective for the understanding and analysis of the complex world of the organisations.[8] His discussions seem to me to be essential, not because I use them to support my own argument, but rather because they have played an important part in the formulation and definition of my research problem since the time when I first became interested in the concept of power. Having given a general review of the discourse on organisations, Silverman suggests an alternative way of studying organisations: the action frame of reference. Of interest here is his argument that the perspective of action, interaction and strategy does indeed describe actual organisational conditions. In arguing thus, he also demonstrates the advantage of perspective, as an analytical concept, over the traditional approach:

> The theme that has underlain this discussion is that of the social world in a continuous process of definition and re-definition through the *motivated interaction* of men. In particular the following aspects of this interaction have been stressed:
>
> 1) The nature of the attachment by the actors to any existing norms is shaped by the orientations that they bring to the situations (especially taken-for-granted worldviews) and by their subsequent experience of the situation itself. The actor's definition of his condition is therefore an *emergent* characteristic which is continually reshaped by his experiences.
> 2) When this subjective view is expressed in action one may speak of the use of tactics or *strategy*. By so doing, we catch the purposive nature of social action. Most strategies seem to be defensive but this may be because action that is defined as aggressive may not be acceptable in cultures where tradition and 'playing the game' are still quite important.
> 3) When subjective views become institutionalized, one may speak of the emergence of rules of the game towards which actors orient themselves. Which views become institutionalized depends upon several factors including:
>   a – The already existing world-taken-for-granted of the participants
>   b – The ends they pursue and the degree of attachment to the existing pattern that this implies
>   c – The strategies they perceive to be available to them and the resources they can call upon to attain their ends
>   d – The actions in which they engage and their ability to convince others of the legitimacy of these acts.
>
> (My italics except for emergent) (Silverman 1970: 212–213)

Silverman goes on to say that neither a pure 'strategic model' nor a pure 'games model' can provide satisfactory explanations as to the complexities of social life. In combination with the action perspective, however, they enable us to see more clearly with regard to social interaction of people in organisations. Furthermore, the concept of power in organisations has been considered, among others, by Giddens (1976, 1979), Crozier and Friedberg (1977) and Wrong (1979), in terms of the strategies and actions of the actors.[9] While Giddens argues that the concept of power 'is logically tied to the notion of action', and Wrong insists upon the relational dimension of power, Crozier and Friedberg argue for the necessity to proceed from the concept of power in the analysis of organisations. Of interest in their work is their combination of various aspects of the 'games model' with aspects of the 'strategic model' to form a conceptualisation of intra-organisational processes as structured games in which power holds a predominant position.

For Crozier and Friedberg, organisations are artificial constructs based on various assumptions concerning human behaviour which are neither given nor self-evident. For an organisation to be able to function properly, a certain measure of trust, loyalty and responsibility among organisational members is a necessary requirement. These conditions are undermined, however, due to the frequently opposing interests for which the members strive. The overwhelming and perhaps impossible task of the organisation (as an artificial construct) is then to unite the diverging interests of the members and to bring them to a point in which they will cooperate in the pursuit of a common interest. This problem is, according to Crozier and Friedberg, a fundamental dilemma[10] which could be said to characterise all human action. The way out of this dilemma, they continue, is not the creation of even more 'ought to be models' (note 7). These have proven to be incapable of giving a just representation of the complexity of the organisational world, or of serving as a set of criteria against which the intra-organisational processes are to be adjusted. Crozier and Friedberg argue that one should first rethink the entire subject matter and conceptualise the idea of organisation in completely new terms. It was via this theoretical path, concerning which I have attempted to give a brief description above, that I was to arrive at the discourse on power. This description is not exhaustive, however, as it presents only a very general idea of my reflections on the research problem taken up for consideration in this work. It does not depict the research problem in its entirety with all its hazards. It has been my intention, however, to concentrate this part of the introduction on the research problem *per se*.

The discourse on power is, in effect, *ad infinitum*, since the question of power with its various aspects – the distribution of resources, politics, justice, and morals, to name but a few – has been a constant object of attention, interest and deliberation since the beginning of time. I have presented, in a previous publication (Daudi, 1980), a brief review of discussions relating to power conducted by various writers in different eras: from the first Hebrew prophets, Amos, Isaiah and Micah, to the current debates between elitists and pluralists and the implications of social ideals on the conceptualisation of organisations and the distribution of power.[11] The dating of the origin of power (Nietzsche 1887–1964) as a concept and as a subject of debate has proven to be an impossible task. Lenski (1966), for example, maintains that the problem of the distribution of power has existed since the emergence of *homo sapiens*. We know, or at least think we know, that hierarchies and social inequalities have existed since the primitive communities of the Stone Age up until the complex industrial societies of today, even if the forms assumed and the degree of extremity have varied extensively. Beyond this, it could be said that the discourse of power that emerged constituted an ongoing dualism between two opposing perspectives (Daudi, 1980: 19): a conservative and a radical perspective. From the conservative point of view, power is conceptualised as the exercise of a necessary and legitimate authority. On the radical side it is conceptualised as a means whereby human potential is misused and oppressed. That which is common to both perspectives is the idea of power as a means of control and thus also as a coercive means of dominance and repression. It is also conceptualised as an attribute, something to be owned, which polarises the positions of those who are in possession of it against those who are not. There is also a tendency to identify it with the state, with institutionalised order and with authority.

What does the discourse on organisations have to say about the phenomenon of power? I shall consider this question in detail in Chapters Four to Six. Until then I shall refer only to those dimensions which may illuminate the essence of the problem of research. In recent years new and challenging perspectives have been developed in the discourse on organisations with regard to both the organisation as a phenomenon and the methodological study thereof. Research findings in another context (Berg and Daudi, 1982, part II: 312 ff.) have shown that new trends have emerged in which it is indicated that organisations are now being conceptualised (or at least there is an ambition to do so) as complex, multidimensional entities rather than as simple formalised systems. It could thus be said that organisation theorists are thinking more in terms of action, culture and symbolism, and social rationality (logic of action) than in terms of behaviour, instrumentality and mechanistic logics. There is then, methodologically speaking, a transformation from simple to multi-faceted, sophisticated analyses of data-gathering procedures, from neutral to committal ones and from the mere collection of facts to a search for meaning. Many of the rituals, smoke-screens and taboos found in the traditional discourse of organisations have been demystified. The taboo of *authority* was intensively studied during the 1960s and 1970s, but power in these studies has, for the most part, been equated with the positions given by the hierarchical structure. Naturally, there are many cases in which the concept of power has been studied *per se* (for example, Krupp, 1961; Mechanic, 1962; Emerson, 1962; Blau, 1964; Perrow, 1970; Pettigrew, 1973; Clegg, 1975). None the less, research on power does not seem to have followed a line of development as fruitful as that followed by the rest of organisational research carried out today. The concept of power is, according to Crozier and Friedberg (1977), probably one of the most important and last remaining taboos in organisational research, and its study is a necessity for the understanding of organised action.

The fact that the concept of power is often reduced to – and implicitly equated with – authority, influence, decision-making, etc., is a matter of some significance in this context. Power has, empirically speaking, for example, been conceived of as a *determining* variable in local decisions (Dahl, 1961; Polsby, 1963) or else as the decisive factor in the distribution of resources (material, non-material and symbolic resources) within the framework of social stratification system (Lenski, 1966; Keller, 1963; Parsons, 1956; Heller, 1969; Parkin, 1971). In the majority of these studies, power is conceptualised as a measurable *taken-for-granted* attribute. There have been attempts in studies more specifically focused upon organisations to evade the taken-for-granted mentality and to consider power as a *dependent variable* (Perrow, 1963, 1970; Gasparini, 1976; Abell, 1975; Butler, 1976; Hickson et al., 1971). As a dependent[12] variable, however, power has been regarded either as a result of deviations from the structure of authority (Clegg, 1975) of the organisation, or as a product of external circumstances, such as the demands of the market or the pressure of the legal macro-environment (Child, 1969). Although the systems theorists may not explicitly reduce power to authority and decision-making (Cyert and March, 1963), pluralist participation in organisational processes (French and Raven, 1959; Fox, 1966), or the contingent strategies or organisations (Hickson et al., 1971), they still tend to base their studies of power conflicts in organisations on the assumption of an ideal equilibrium. In their analyses of competitive and conflicting demands for influence in the organisation the pluralists, for example, proceed from the assumption of an ideal state in which power is equally distributed, and where each and everyone respects the rules of the game. This ideal state, according to the pluralists, is presumed to guarantee equilibrium and requires balance in the system. This simply takes for granted that which most requires explanation. A pseudo-knowledge of power is subsequently produced which cannot possibly lead to an understanding of the nature of the phenomenon and its manifestations in organised action, nor of the consequences which it may have for the latter. But power is neither an attribute, nor a dependent variable, nor yet the product of a structure of authority. It cannot be discussed in terms of determining–determined, nor in terms of causality. Neither is it a concrete object to be grasped, measured and axiomatised (Foucault, 1976a). To analyse power as an object *per se*, or to explain it away by reducing it to something else, does *not* facilitate study, but rather serves to inhibit our understanding. Power yet seems to be one of the unknown dimensions in the life of organisations. A review of the discourse on power would reveal just how little we actually know about the subject. This has already been confirmed by a number of authors who have devoted attention to the study of power (Giddens, 1976, 1979; Crozier, 1973; Crozier and Friedberg, 1977; Gustafsson, 1979; Clegg and Dunkerley, 1980, etc.) and who maintain that there exists no unequivocal theory nor any empirically operationalisable models of power. As I see it, the problem does not merely lie in the inadequacy of the instruments, methods and procedures used in the study of power, but also in the ideological and cultural values from which our conceptualisation of power as a coercive means of dominance, control and repression emanates (Foucault, 1971a,b, 1976a). This mode of thought seems to have permeated the discourse of power since its very earliest phases (note 11). One could say, metaphorically, that it is as if the current discourse of power were merely reproducing a debate which could have taken place between the Hebrew prophet Micah and the Hindu priests (The Law of Manus). It is *as though* the discourse of power has developed horizontally in the form of a circle, rather than vertically in the form of a spiral, and that our knowledge of power today, generally speaking, does not seem to differ noticeably from that of antiquity. Neither do our frames of reference and methods of analysis differ very much. The 'monks' of the discourse of power ascend and descend the stairs of knowledge without ever reaching a higher level.

The problem

The problem dealt with is thus embedded, as I have tried to show, within the framework of a broader perspective or, in other words, an original structure in which power is conceptualised as a coercive means of dominance, control and repression. Since the problem could then be considered as multidimensional I shall consider these levels in some detail further on in the text. But first a general presentation.

(a) At the first level we can see that power is treated *as if* it were an attribute and as a concrete physical reality. Analysis here is aimed directly at the concept of power *per se*, and indicators which are quantifiable and axiomatisable are regarded as being of central importance, implying that which is decisive for being the mechanisms of power is being overlooked. This means that one of the dimensions of the problem is that of the incompleteness, and in some cases even inadequacy, of the theoretical assumptions and the methods for empirical investigations of the discourse of power.

(b) The second level is that the knowledge produced about the phenomenon of power is incoherent, fragmentary and vague, not only as far as the theoretical knowledge is concerned, but also, and perhaps especially, so far as the empirical manifestations of power are concerned.

(c) The third level is that the discourse of power, with its basis in the original conceptualisation of power and its discursive rules of formation, produces, and even dictates, a certain way of conceptualising power: not only how it should be understood and studied by scholars, but also how it is to be interpreted by groups and individuals in everyday situations in organisations. On the other hand, although the 'producers' of the discourse of power and the individuals involved in power relations share a common ideological basis for their conceptualisation of power,[13] the *a priori* models of the former do not seem to provide satisfactory explanations for the actual actions taken by the latter in their relations of power. The problem here is that whereas the discourse of power – in order to be constituted as a discourse – is governed in its formation by principles of exclusion, and is thus forced to reduce manifestations of power to *frozen* facts, disengaged from the empirical reality in which they have a meaning, the individuals still continue to act in this very empirical reality against the background of their interpretations of it (and the interpretation of the meaning which power has for them in this empirical reality).

(d) The fourth and last level of this research problem is that of the frequent reduction of the concept of power in the discourse of organisations to a variable of secondary importance which is, at the most, sparingly referred to in the last instance in order to elucidate parts of a certain process (e.g. the decision process) or else it is considered as an anomaly, or a dysfunction which disturbs the ideal of a desirable harmony and state of equilibrium in the system. In other cases the phenomenon of power is reduced to a dependent variable which is intimately connected to the structure of authority in the organisation. In some cases the concept of power is not even mentioned in the discourse. This may be due either to the proclamation of the concept as a taboo, or to the assumption that it has already been taken up for consideration when, in fact, one has been discussing something else, such as authority, influence, or hierarchical positions.

The purpose

The time has come, now that the problem of research has been specified, to give a presentation of the purpose of this work. Obviously this must be seen in the light of the thesis which has been formulated. As I have mentioned earlier, the thesis gives utterance both to the problem of research and to the purpose of the study. This purpose then denotes what this study attempts to achieve and the procedures – empirical, methodological and theoretical – used in this pursuit. In the first instance the purpose is to conduct a discussion which emphasises the need for an alternative conceptualisation of power; secondly, to try to develop alternative methods and procedures for the study of power; and thirdly, to contribute with knowledge as to the ways in which power is *de facto* manifested empirically, given the alternative conceptualisation. The purpose could also be envisaged as a process[14] reflecting the various stages of which it is constituted.

(a) An important step in this process is to discuss and critically analyse the rules of formation of the primitive discourse of power (Foucault, 1969), along with the conditions which make it possible, and its development. I shall do this by developing and applying a system of concepts inspired by the work of Foucault.[15] Such an examination would entail a study of the procedures of exclusion and a discussion of the ways in which that which is excluded from the discourse, and which is thereby defined as pertaining to its *outer* territory, and the procedures of exclusion *per se* are in fact decisive factors in the development of the discourse. It is also implied hereby that, in order to emerge, the discourse must delimit its territory, i.e. it must state what can be considered as belonging to the discourse and what should remain outside. The identity of the discourse is defined more by its outer than by its inner territory (Foucault, 1961). The paradox here is that it is precisely those dimensions which are discarded by and excluded from the primitive discourse of power that seem to be the intrinsic bearers of an explanatory potential as regards the empirical manifestations of power.

(b) A further step in the process is that of using a case study to illustrate the effects of the primitive conceptualisation of power on intra-organisational processes, and to examine the explanatory value of the models of the primitive discourse in confrontation with the empirical manifestations of power. This will lead us to the attempt to identify that which handicaps the models, and relate this to the discursive rules of formation and to the original conceptualisation of power.

(c) A third step is to develop and suggest an alternative conceptual way of regarding the phenomenon of power in organisations. The aim here is to present a frame of reference which could not only alleviate the studies of power, but which could also illuminate certain dimensions in organisations, focusing particularly on the impact of the phenomenon of power in the latter.

(d) The last step goes beyond the primitive discourse of power and its implications for organisational theory. The discussion here is aimed at the original, basic conceptions and mechanisms within which the discourse of power is embedded and wherein it has its roots. With the help of Foucault and a number of other thinkers we will take a closer look at the multiplicity of the discourse in different fields of knowledge.[16] The discourses of rationality, surveillance, punishment and normalisation in the western world show how the mechanisms of power have been articulated as complex, political and strategical relations since the Middle Ages; power → knowledge; knowledge → power. At this level the discussion could be seen as a step towards the demystification of many of our *a priori* assumptions as to how power ought to be conceptualised. My ambitions in this respect are modest and I have no illusions as to the difficulty of, so to speak, stepping out of one's own ideology in order to be able to see through it. In fact I regard this task as being nearly impossible. This impossibility perhaps originates from what could be called the paradox of knowledge. Our overall ideology dictates, both directly and indirectly, that which our discourses have to say about power. This ideology is mediated in different forms and can be found on different levels. It is with us from the cradle to the grave; in the family, in education, in research, in daily life, in the mass media, in politics . . . it shapes our thoughts. Saussure used to say: 'It is not I who speaks French, but rather French which speaks through me.' A paraphrase of Saussure could read: 'We are the eyes of our ideology, we see through it, but can we see it?' But it is perhaps not so much a point of seeing one's ideology as perceiving that it is through this ideology that one sees what one sees. The principal aim in speaking of the discourse on power in terms of demystification is to draw attention to the fact that the discourse does not rest upon absolute and universal truths, but rather upon a fragile basis with a considerable measure of arbitrariness (Foucault, 1966). The question as to whether a discourse is true or false is of little interest. The question as to its legitimation is, however, elucidatory as regards the mechanisms governing its formation. The discourse on power is not, in effect, about power; rather, it *produces* power. A discourse produces its object, multiplies it and thereby grows stronger itself. To speak of the demystification of the *discourse on power* is to become aware of, and to draw attention to, the *power of discourse*, i.e. that power which holds us prisoner of our own discourses.

The purpose which I have formulated, and the process leading to its fulfilment, implies a quest for ideas, concepts, and statements that are external to the primitive discourse of power and to the discourse of organisation. It is a matter here not only of the methodological procedures which I have chosen to use in the study of power, but also of the theoretical reflections which might eventually lead to the articulation of an alternative conceptual framework for the study of the phenomenon of power. The process as a whole will be reflected in the logics of the present work, while its various phases will be taken up for detailed consideration in the respective chapters.

The empirical part of this work consists of one case study. This could cause problems in other contexts – if, for example, one's purpose were to test hypotheses and verify statements and assumptions (note 14). Neither of these constitute my purpose, which is to observe, understand and possibly to describe and interpret the ways in which power is manifested in organisations. This purpose cannot, to my mind, by fulfilled in any other way than by means of deep case studies. The more numerous the studies one chooses to carry out, however, the less likely they are to be of any depth, which implies that one never risks getting close enough to the phenomenon that one wishes to study. At least two crucial factors were decisive for my choice of one case: (a) the necessity of considering the research problem in depth and (b) the possibility of 'access' to relevant information that was given to me when I came into contact with the case. These two reasons are interdependent, and both are necessary and sufficient *per se* to motivate the choice of one case. This will be further discussed in Chapter Two. A further aspect to which I would like to draw attention here is that, due to the wealth of detail in the case, different readers will find in it different sets of problems and different problematical aspects. My discussion will be limited, however, to the problem specified on these pages.

The logic of the present work

This refers to the particular construction which characterises the work along with the ways in which the different parts relate to each other. So far, in this introduction I have tried to convey to the reader a notion of the breadth and complexity of the problem concerning the conceptualisation, the study, the understanding and the interpretation of the phenomenon of power. I have insisted upon the paradoxality of this problem and argued for the need to develop an alternative conceptual framework for the study of the phenomenon of power, while simultaneously drawing attention to the epistemological difficulties involved in such an enterprise. The various dimensions of the problem of research upon which I have commented in the thesis argued for here are interrelated and contained, so to speak, within each other. This spans over problems, ranging from the original conceptualisation of power on an ideological and cultural level to the effect of this conceptualisation on the intra-organisational processes at a practical level. Considering the nature of the problem, I find it justifiable to move after this introduction directly to the case study. The reader will then become acquainted with the concretisation of the problem before gradually approaching its epistemological source.

The first section of this work (Part One) is constituted by the case study and by some considerations, on the level of the theory of science, which are relevant to the problem of research at hand. This section consists of three chapters. In the first two chapters I shall describe the actual problem upon which the forthcoming discussion will be based. The character of the empirical report demands some commentary. The case is entitled: 'Chronicle of a Removal Foretold', and it consists of two acts, corresponding to Chapters One and Two respectively.

Due to the way in which the case is constructed and presented, the reader is given a reasonable opportunity to acquaint himself, under almost the same conditions as those of the author, with the actual course of events. I say 'almost' since this course of events was on ongoing process during the period of data-gathering. This implies that through my interactions and close contact with the actors involved I have had, so to speak, front-row tickets to the grandstand. In this sense my interpretation of the process is sure to differ from that of the reader due to the fact that it has been complemented by the experience gained during my journey through the course of events. The reader of a book of travel can hardly see the same colours, smell the same scents, and hear the same music as the author has seen, smelt and heard and which he might try to communicate through his text. The reader of a case study is thus limited when it comes to making his own interpretations. Cries of protest might go up from those who would assert that the description should be neutral so as to allow for a neutral and unbiased interpretation. I am inclined to agree that interpretations may be neutral and/or unbiased, but fail to see what a neutral description (in a case study) would look like. The matter of neutral descriptions is seldom mentioned by authors who have devoted attention to case study methodology (Cicourel, 1964). They do insist, however, upon the suitability of the methods used in the studies of processes and complex social situations. But how can this complexity be justly represented? Barthes (1964) maintains that a neutral description annihilates and distorts the richness and diversity of reality. A good text, he continues, is one in which a total picture is conveyed. One does not have the same experience when reading the text of a play as one would if one were to see it performed. A good text, according to Barthes, is one which combines both the text of the play and a description of its representation. This is easier said than done. However, my endeavour has been to give as good a picture as possible of the situations experienced as meaningful by the actors involved, and of which the process as a whole has been constituted. This picture reflects the contextual situation. It also reflects the standpoints taken by the actors in confrontation with various problems and situations; describes the network of relationships which exists and develops among the actors; shows which interests are involved and illustrates which of these are in opposition to each other; serves as a background against which the intentions, motives and strategies of the actors may become visible; and describes the enactment of the actions and the ways in which the reactions are articulated and expressed. Moreover, the picture renders perceptible the actors' own experiences of situations, including their feelings of frustration and anxiety, of joy and involvement. It also reproduces the atmosphere which prevails during the entire course of events.

In Chapter One the first act is presented. It contains the latent prerequisites for the enactment of the second act. I begin with the presentation of the broad background so as gradually to conduct the discussion towards a narrower perspective: the actual process of removal. We then become acquainted with a number of people who partake, either consciously or unconsciously, in the development of the source of events in the second act. The idea is to render perceptible the ponderings of the actors and the mentality that gradually emerges, takes shape and grows, establishes itself and, finally, takes control.

In Chapter Two the second act is presented. Here the enactment of the actual process takes place, its different phases are described, the actors are personified and my role in the course of events is accounted for. This act emphasises the intra-organisational processes against the background of the intentions, strategies and actions of the actors involved.

It seems justifiable, before continuing with this presentation, to mention some essential methodological aspects of this work. The method applied in this work is what one could call a 'multi-level method'. Depending upon the particular purposes which they fulfil, these levels will be introduced in three different contexts: in the Introduction and in Chapters Two and Three.

Note on method

This method is constituted by *four* separate, yet interrelated, dimensions. The first dimension refers to the perspective and the analytical instruments

considered during the empirical part of the research: *the logic of action.*[17]
The second dimension refers to the data-gathering process and is
composed of the following stages: the choice of the object of study; the
problems of access to information; the research design; the carrying out of
interviews; access to important documents of relevance to the object
studied; the evaluation, control, processing, classification and presentation
of the data: *fieldwork.* The third dimension refers to various aspects of the
theory of science and raises questions which have come to light during the
empirical work: *generating knowledge.* The fourth and last dimension
refers to certain methodological and theoretical problems of an entirely
different nature, namely conceptual instruments with which the primitive
discourse of power is analysed; *the theory of discourse.*

The second dimension, that of 'fieldwork', is of a practical nature and
should thus be integrated in the empirical description. Accordingly, it is
treated in the actual case study and especially in the second act, i.e. in
Chapter Two. This integration is particularly important when working
with deep case studies and when the situation is such that the process of
data-collection runs parallel to the development of the course of events.

I shall discuss the third and fourth dimensions, 'generating knowledge'
and 'theory of discourse', in Chapter Three. It could be said that
'generating knowledge' is retrospective, whereas 'theory of discourse' is
prospective. The discussion referring to the theory of science and the
generating of knowledge would not have been significant to the reader had
I treated them before the case study, since this discussion is intimately
related to the problems that arose during the empirical work. This does
not imply, however, that this discussion is so specific and case-related that
it cannot be applied elsewhere. Effort has been made to transfer it from a
specific to a general level.

The discussion referring to 'the theory of discourse' is prospective in the
sense that it constitutes a methodological frame of reference which is then
applied to examine the rules of formation and the procedures of exclusion
of the primitive discourse of power. It is primarily based upon the
archaeological and genealogical methods of Foucault and Nietzsche.

Let us now turn to a brief discussion of the first method dimension: the
logic of action. This concept focuses on two aspects, both of which are
relevant in the studies of social systems. The one aspect is primarily
concerned with *intentions* and the ways in which these are put into *action*,
whereas the other aspect has to do with perspectives of the actors and the
researchers. From the actor's perspective it is a matter of identifying and
distinguishing the interests and preferences from means and methods used
in the pursuit of the intentional results. The same goes for the researcher's
perspective. In the latter case, however, it is a question of reconstructing
the perspective of the organisational actors. For the researcher the starting

point is thus the observation of the organisational praxis and of the manifest goals and interests of the actor as they appear from his own perspective. This implies, methodologically speaking, that the researcher strives to identify the *strategical and tactical methods*, used by various actors in the pursuit of special interests and orientations which characterise and influence intra-organisational processes.

Interests and orientations refer to the intentions and desired outcomes formulated by actors, groups or coalitions. The implementation in action or the fulfilment, in some other way, of these intentions is not too important. What is more important is that for the actor the intentions still exist (or have existed) as a desired future condition. These intentions need not necessarily be articulated as (or in) a formal process; they could as easily be formulated consciously or unconsciously, individually and collectively.

The strategies and tactical methods of the actors are related to their interests and orientations. These may not always lead to the desired results, but what is significant is that they are consciously chosen. The mobilisation of resources and the active involvement in particular strategies is based upon the choices which the actors make in the pursuit of desired ends.

The logic of action may also refer to the rationality which the researcher may reconstruct from his own observation and which he believes to be the motives for the actions taken by the organisational actors, groups or coalitions. These principles and rationalities govern certain patterns of action in the sense that the organisational members organise their strategies, intentions and actions around them. The concept of the logic of action seems useful as an analytical tool in situations in which it is necessary for the researcher to distinguish between two important aspects: (a) the personal interests and orientations of the actor as he himself defines them; and (b) as a group or a coalition defines them. The concept is also useful when distinguishing between these definitions and that which the researcher can observe and register himself by means, for example, of interviews, analyses, and interpretations, as well as by participation in the situation. In fact, the concept represents a broad spectrum of various fields: social, economical and political. The politics of organisation are manifested in the way in which the actors concretise and implement their intentions in actions. It is the task of the researcher to reconstruct and chart the politics of organisation by means of observation and analysis. These (politics of organisation) are constituted within and manifested through the strategies and actual methods used by actors, groups or coalitions when attempting to force their logic of action onto the organisation as a whole, or parts of it.

The logic of action as described here should not be seen from a purely phenomenological perspective. From this perspective, the mapping of any particular organisational phenomenon would be reduced to the narrow meaning which it has for the actors experiencing it (e.g. Schutz, 1962). Apart from the fact that it is nearly impossible to describe another person's experiences, it is conceivable that we, as researchers, might possibly have other intentions with the study of a particular phenomenon than those experiencing and constituting this phenomenon. The concept could none the less be regarded as an application of a *limited phenomenology*. The advantage is that it permits a differentiation between the intentions, strategies and actions of the organisational members, on the one hand, and the outcome of the process, on the other. In other words it permits a differentiation between the former and the observed and actual, implemented logic of action.

Instead of logic of action, one could speak of *the logic of the logic of action* to denote those actions which seem to be governed by 'their own logic' and which lead to outcomes that differ from those desired by the acting individuals. This notion refers, then, to those actions whose logic goes beyond – and develops independently of – the intentions and rationalities of the acting individuals.

The second section of this work (Part Two) consists of four chapters. In Chapter Four, 'Power, politics and action in organisations', the political dimensions of organisations are emphasised as primary in the understanding of intra-organisational processes. This chapter should be seen as the reflection of the *état d'esprit* which is prevalent in the continued discussion.

Chapter Five, 'The discourse of power and organisation', constitutes the main part of the analysis and discussion. The primitive discourse of power is examined from a theoretical point of view, and its statements and models are discussed in the light of the case study. With this in mind, a generation of an alternative power conceptualisation is then attempted.

In Chapter Six, 'The genealogy of power in organisations', the argument presented is based on, and further develops, 'the theory of discourse' along with the conceptualisation presented in Chapter Five. I specially emphasise the procedures of exclusions of the primitive discourse of power. This chapter ends with the summary and concretisation of the findings of this study. Finally, questions are raised concerning the origin and demystification of the primitive discourse of power, thus preparing for the argument in the next chapter.

In Chapter Seven, 'The discourse of power or the power of discourse', I will argue that discourses of power – or indeed of other objects of knowledge – in fact create their objects, expand and develop and, in the end, normatively dictate what the object *ought* to be. From *the discourse of power* we will turn our attention to *the power of discourse*, and see how it shapes and reshapes mentalities and conceptions, and how it normalises actions. The specific relationship between power and knowledge and the interplay between these two notions is examined. The final argument concerns the meaning and the dilemma of the possible demystification of the discourse. Does this demystification necessarily imply that one has to step out of the discourse? Is this possible? And, if it were, or even if we only believed it to be, would we not just be reproducing a 'new' discourse? Perhaps we are doomed to construct discourses about discourses.

PART ONE

The Discursive Praxis

CHAPTER 1

Chronicle of a Transfer Foretold

Act I

An idea is born, grows and becomes self-evident

The beginning of the end of a loop

A large elegant room with heavy draperies in the windows. At one end of the room there is an inviting group of sofa and armchairs in dark red leather and a sofa table in traditional style. Opposite the suite there is a majestic writing desk in the same style. The writing desk is tidy, nothing disturbs its harmony. At the other end of the room six gentlemen are sitting around an oval conference table. The gentlemen's discussion is low-keyed. They seem to be in agreement. The room as a whole conveys a mixed feeling of security and anguish. The man sitting at the short end of the table looks around with satisfaction. Everyone sitting at the table nods. A decision has been taken. The man thanks the gentlemen for their understanding and cordiality, then casts a glance at the agenda which is in a file on the table in front of him and announces soberly, 'Let us proceed to the next matter'.

One of the gentlemen seconds this proposal and hands out a memorandum to all those present. The man is M. Ziegler. He is vice managing director of W, a unit within Goliat Inc. The memorandum concerns a small unit (an ex-independent company) within W. The unit is called L, and Ziegler comments on the memorandum as follows:

> The results of the unit have improved considerably, but an economic recession could drastically change the situation. The goal will thus be to strive to minimize the risk of future losses and at the same time retain the know-how and the unique products. A probable solution is to transfer the unit [. . .] and to purchase certain services externally. A coordination of the sales departments of L and ES is also considered to be valuable. The sale of the premises in [. . .] would also imply liberation of capital (from the minutes of the Board meeting, 29 August 1980).

The board of W listen to what Ziegler has to say. They have confidence in him. It is decided that as managing director, Ziegler would be assigned the task of proceeding in accordance with the memorandum. The draft of the minutes is approved, and the meeting drawn to a close. It is Friday 29 August 1980.

When Ziegler leaves the room shortly afterwards he is not dissatisfied with the decision. He likes to see it as a phase in the extensive reorganisation of W which he has in mind. Already he has begun to realise that the organisational form with which he has been working since 1978–79 was no longer tenable. The organisation must be rendered more effective. He has managed to improve the results but it is now necessary for him to see to it that W would expand on the Swedish market. This is the primary goal. To attain it, he thinks, he must reorganise, rationalise and gather everything under one roof. Then it would be a matter of making oneself known on the foreign market. His attention is entirely devoted to these goals.

RETROSPECT

I shall begin this retrospect by trying to convey a feeling of perspective, a perspective of a size and complexity that is often experienced as problematical by those whom I shall describe and who are the participants in the process. Some of them are aware of this perspective and either feel proud of 'belonging' to a large, powerful organisation, or very small and insignificant for the same reason. Others do their best to ignore it. In both cases the big giant is present.

Goliat Inc. is a large multi-national corporation which has a turnover of approximately 4500 Mkr (Mkr = million Swedish crowns; 10.95 kr = £1 sterling at time of publication) and employs roughly 14,700 people, 6000 of whom are in Sweden. The business of the corporation is divided into four principal areas of business which I shall henceforth refer to as Groups A, B, C and D.

The long-term goal of the corporation is to attain a relatively high return (15% before taxes on total capital with an average inflation of 10%). The stated intentions are to attain this goal primarily by means of a concentration of the input within, in the first instance, Groups A and B. It is held, at the level of the corporation, that the possibility of attaining this goal, and of subsequently retaining the same level, is dependent both on the development of the results and on the growth of capital. Thus there is to be an expansion within all the divisions of the corporation, but on condition that this leads both to profitability and financial stability. In recent years there has been a prioritisation of large investments (during 1980, for example, the fixed asset investment amounted to 574 Mkr, i.e.

fully 13% of the sales of the corporate). This is seen as reinforcement of the strategical positions and is preferred to the short-term increase of returns which would be implied by a lower level of investment. The returns, and even the claims for these, vary in the different areas of business of the corporation depending on differences in market conditions, growth rates and capital intensity. This means that one finds it natural to demand a higher return in Groups A and B, since they have a larger fixed asset capital than do C or D, whose capital is largely working capital. This demand could, to a certain extent, be met with during 1980 due to Group A, which stands for the greater part of fixed assets, showing a return of 15%.

A brief presentation of each area of business follows. Apart from interviews, various documents such as annual reports and company descriptions have been used as source material. The presentation is very brief and is merely intended to give an idea of the background within which the process takes place. I deliberately begin the account with Group D and end it with A, so as to connect with the course of events which I shall describe, and which takes place within A.

Group D

This group comprises a group of four Swedish and seven foreign companies. The group was founded in the autumn of 1980 and entails a concentration and development of the activity of this group. The invoicing of the group for 1980 amounted to 480 Mkr, which constitutes approximately 10% of the total invoicing of the corporate.

The products are primarily manufactured in Sweden, from where they are exported to a number of countries in Western Europe. Selling, in most of these countries, is managed by the corporate's own subsidiary companies. During 1980 the Swedish market absorbed 50% of the total sales.

Group C

This group was founded in 1980 around the companies who, from 1979 onwards, were included in Goliat Inc.'s industrial group. These were then supplemented during 1980 with units from an older division in Group A, as well as units from Group D.

This group comprises some ten firms which are characterised by high technology, and whose diverse activities are seen as being advantageous from the point of view of risk-spreading. The group is regarded as having financial stability.

The purpose of the establishment of Group C was to increase the possibilities of faster growth for the constituent units as well as to facilitate external financing. The invoicing of the group amounted in 1980 to 538 Mkr and constitutes 12% of the total invoicing of the corporate. The group as a whole is expansive and competitive, and its possibilities of growth are deemed to be foremost in continued efforts on the international market.

Group B

This group consists of only one firm, but this is one of the world's largest within its field. It is a multinational firm and, apart from being active in Scandinavia, is active in the rest of Europe and in America. The firm was acquired by Goliat Inc. in 1978. Its invoicing for 1980 amounted to 959 Mkr, which constitutes 21% of the total invoicing of the corporate.

The course of events, the development of which we shall soon follow, takes place in Group A. For this reason I shall describe this group somewhat more extensively than the others.

Group A

During the spring of 1980 several of the equipment firms in Group A were transferred to Group C. The activity of Group A was then specialised so as to embrace the production and marketing of particularly closely related products to be used industrially and medically, along with equipment and expendable items for processes whose fields of usage embrace virtually the whole of the engineering industry. The invoicing of the group amounted in 1980 to 2454 Mkr, which constitutes 53% of the total invoicing of the corporate.

Group A's products consist of two main categories. One of these is constituted by a base product which is produced in a number of different varieties and which, together with related products and services, stands for 75% of the total invoicing of the group. The other category involves *S-*activity which, in turn, is divided into *GS* and *ES* activities, and which comprise the remainder of the invoicing.

The demand for base products runs parallel to the industrial growth as a whole, since nearly all industry consumes this type of product to some extent. Furthermore, the need seems to be influenced by the extent to which Group A and its rivals are capable of finding new fields of application for the products.

The world market for the base product and its different variants is valued at approximately 25 billion crowns, a third of which relates to Western Europe, a third to the United States and a third to the rest of the world. The group works in 21 countries in Western Europe and in Latin America, as well as in the United States. The total market in these countries amounts to approximately 20 Mkr, of which Group A has roughly 10%. The group is regarded as one of the world's largest suppliers of base products. One of the most important characteristics of this group is the necessity of working on local markets since the production must, due to the economic factors of technology and transport, be performed in the proximity of the client. This implies that the strength of the group depends on how well one manages to establish oneself in each particular market. At the same time, demand and growth are based only on each particular market. Thus the group must be able to evaluate, in each geographic market or region, the possibilities of development for the product, and also to rate the production capacity, product-mix and distributive system in an optimal fashion. This is difficult since it presupposes a comprehensive knowledge of the local market – the present and future needs of the customers as well as the potential for new applications. In any case it is held, within Group A, that the extensive international spreading of the business entails significant risk-spreading advantages. The spread of risks and flexibility is further increased by the large number of customers which the group serves. At present (1980–81), the base products and the processes based thereupon are sold to roughly 400,000 customers. The engineering industry, including the shipbuilding industry and the motor industry, absorbs half of these sales. Large consumers are also to be found within the chemical industry and the building industry, as well as within public health. No category of customer represents more than 25% of the sales, and no single customer attains the mark of 1%.

On the world market the group competes with six other international firms for market shares. Local producers are only to be found in a handful of countries, among them Norway, Denmark, Mexico and Japan. The United States holds a unique position, with a combination of large and small regional and local suppliers together with all the international firms. Apart from Group A, one of the six large firms is French, two are American, one British and two German.

Group A and the French and British firms were internationalised at an early stage. Expansion of the French firm followed the extension of the French colonial empire and then entered into Italy, Japan and the United States. The British firm worked in countries that had connections with the British Empire, while Group A could enter a number of countries throughout the world. All this was carried out in accordance with a 'gentlemen's agreement'. The two American companies began to take an interest in Europe 15–20 years ago, but 80% of the sales of these firms today still take place in the United States. The activity of the two German firms is primarily in Germany. Internationally speaking, Group A is in fifth place. This position was not improved or reinforced until the 1970s when the corporation invested in base products which gradually came to be concentrated in Group A. At the same time the restructuring of the corporation was initiated so as to give organisational support to the concentration plans.

S-activity

Fully 20% or 550 Mkr of Group A's total invoicing during 1980 concerned S-activity. This S-activity embraces equipment and expendable items for important processes within the steel and engineering industry. The economic recession within these sectors in the middle of the 1970s led to a minimisation of the market for S-products, but towards the end of 1979 and during 1980 the situation improved both in Sweden and in most Western European countries, mostly due to the fact that new technology, better suited to the ongoing development within the engineering industry, had developed.

Today the production and marketing of Group A's S-equipment is primarily located in the subsidiary of W which has its head office in southern Sweden.

The establishment of W

W was established in 1978 in connection with the incorporation of the then S-division in Goliat Inc. into Group A. At that time, much of the production of ES-products was reduced, since these, due to short series and a failing market, could not be made profitable. At the same time there was an intensification of efforts to produce an effective product programme which would correspond to the demands of the market.

The S-activity is, as mentioned earlier, divided into GS and ES. Goliat Inc. was in this business for slightly more than 70 years, but in Sweden the corporation was regarded as being more specialised in GS than in ES equipment. ES-processes, however, demand more advanced equipment than do GS, and Goliat Inc. did not specifically have this. Moreover, there are rivals who have managed to specialise over the years in just ES products and, to Goliat Inc., GS-products are closer related to the base product in Group A. Goliat Inc. was therefore not very interested in ES. At the same time, there was an obviously rising demand for ES, but Goliat Inc. was unable to participate in the race. This situation remained unaltered until the middle of the 1970s.

At that time there was no Group A, but rather a division-like construction which consisted of a number of independent firms. These were an S-firm in Stockholm, a GS-firm in southern Sweden, a factory in Finland, a firm in England, one in Germany, a Swedish sales organisation and a number of other so-called supply units which were later to be transferred to Group C when Group A was established.

The idea of independent units was not very successful. The various firms were torn by internal disputes and the results deteriorated markedly. The sales organisations complained of the poor quality of the products, the long delivery delays and the extensive production costs of the supply units. Inversely, the latter complained of the former's poor marketing efforts and their general incompetence. In the middle of this family row it began to be realised where the S-market was heading. It was recognised that it was no longer possible to sell components, but that it was necessary to deliver 'process know-how'. Customers have to be visited, the working process analysed together with them, and package solutions suggested. However, this demanded qualifications which were not available. What could be done in a situation where the corporation, by tradition, chose to acquire appropriate objects for its growth? At the time, the object lay near at hand. We know now that in the old construction there was an S-firm in Stockholm. This firm handles *ES*-products with regard to both production and selling. The production gradually became a problem, since it could not keep pace with the development. The market became increasingly demanding but was experienced as failing, and series became increasingly shorter and at the same time less profitable. Production was laid down. However, the sale of contract-produced *ES*-products continued. A search for possible producers showed that there were a few who seemed to have understood what was wanted on the market. There was one in Finland, one in Denmark and one in Sweden. After some test orders the Swedish producer was selected. Good conditions for cooperation were established between the manager of the S-firm in Stockholm, G. Faiblén, and the Swedish producer. The producer constructed virtually any kind of machine within the *ES*-process. Sometimes he would do this from drawings, and many times merely on the basis of verbal and written problem descriptions. The machines were then delivered to everyone's satisfaction, not least in terms of price.

The idea of having such fine qualifications within the division gradually began to take shape in Faiblén's mind. He thought that his position would thus be decidedly reinforced. He believed that the Swedish producer had a potential for development which fell right in line with the development of the S-market. He knew that it would become more and more difficult for his firm to assert itself on this market in the future if its competence was not improved. He also believed that something worthwhile could be made of the small Swedish producer, bearing in mind the resources of Goliat Inc. Investments in new plants could be made, new premises could be built, and new staff could be employed and trained.

THE ESTABLISHMENT OF *L*

L was the small Swedish producer which Faiblén had in mind: a typical example of a firm started by one man, an entrepreneur with good ideas, knowledge and imagination – an entrepreneur who sees a pattern somewhere and who succeeds in combining seemingly vastly different elements, thereby arriving at an idea or a product which perfectly matches existing problems and needs in praxis. B. Andersson was such a man.

During the late 1960s and early 1970s, Andersson worked in the family-owned firm, Anderssons Mekaniska, situated in southern Sweden. The business primarily concerned conventional *ES*-products. Andersson was very inventive. He had ideas and vision which were often based on the problems of the customers with whom he had frequent and good contact.

The customers felt that they could speak to him. He could understand their technical problems and could often come up with intelligent solutions. One day in the spring of 1972 one of the customers came to him with a complex problem which demanded a radical solution. The customer had a workshop and normally worked with conventional *ES*-equipment. This time it was a matter of a 'construction' which simply could not be put together in any normal way. It demanded a machine which could, so to speak, do all the work, or at least facilitate it considerably. The machine needed to be manoeuvrable in a specific way: it needed to be able to lift, lower, twist and turn whatever it was that was being built at that moment. It also had to be controllable from a certain distance. This was particularly important, because when working with conventional *ES*-equipment there is close contact with various dangerous substances: this entails necessary precautions and safeguards. Apart from these important working environ-mental considerations, the conventional process also implied time losses and a severe limitation on what could, on the whole, be done. The problem which the customer had put forward was in no way foreign to Andersson. Work on the project was initiated. The result was successful. This was the beginning of a new enterprise. Andersson acted quickly; he probed the market and found that there was a latent need for his product. With the help of an engineer, he started production. The news spread and interest in Andersson's machines increased. The constantly travelling and exploring salesmen within this branch contributed to the spreading of the news, and even began to order machines on behalf of their firms, which were then sold to their customers.

One of these salesmen, S. Malisman, was at that time specially connected to Anderssons Mekaniska. He had known the father a long time and he got on well with him. He himself worked for a relatively small producer on the Swedish market. Thirty years in the branch had given him a certain feeling for the technology within this field and, above all, an 'accurate' vision with regard to tendencies of development. He used to discuss his ideas with the engineers in his firm. One of them began a sketch of something that had been expressed vaguely by Malisman. It was never to become more than the sketch of an idea, but Malisman kept it with him. In 1967 it happened that one of Goliat Inc.'s rivals in the S-business bought up the firm where Malisman worked, and closed it down. Malisman refused to stay with the firm and accepted a job offered to him by one of the American competitors in a subsidiary firm in Scandinavia.

When Andersson began to consider his project, Malisman's drawings lay near at hand since he quite often came to Anderssons Mekaniska for a visit. The drawings were not exhaustive. they were no solutions as such, but might rather be seen as the embryo of an idea which, for that matter, Andersson also had. What was important in this context was the connection and the cooperation between Malisman and Andersson. Andersson produced one machine after the other. Even large firms, including Goliat Inc., via the S-firm in Stockholm, were on the order list. The large purchasers asked for the basic components used in the machines to bear their trademarks. Andersson satisfied all demands. The machines were painted in different colours, and different trademarks were attached. Andersson was 'extremely skilful' in all fields. 'He provided all of us with machines', said Malisman.

In 1974 the business became so comprehensive and interesting that Andersson felt the need to go his own way. He found his own premises and employed engineers. But then events moved too quickly.

Goliat Inc.'s acquisition of L

Andersson became feverish with success. In that same year he bought a plot and began to build large modern premises. New workers were employed, including draftsmen and fitters. At the turn of the year 1975–76 the company moved into the new premises. There turned out to be too many investments at the same time. The financial situation suddenly became worse. Rumours of Andersson's difficulties spread quickly, and soon there were several buyers on the doorstep, including the largest and the most powerful companies in the industry. Andersson did not like the idea of selling what he himself had built up, but the project still fascinated him. He began to think of new possibilities of development, but resources were insufficient. It was at this moment that G. Faiblén, the managing director of the S-firm, came forward and persuaded him to sell to Goliat Inc. He would have access to virtually unlimited resources and would remain in charge of L. The business would be developed and the capacity increased. The future of his 22 employees would be secured. These were good perspectives, thought Andersson. Moreover, he had confidence in Faiblén and allowed himself to be convinced. Faiblén thought that at last his firm would get the know-how and the unique products necessary for a more effective performance on the market. Although the S-firm was merely a sales organisation within the division, the idea of gaining direct control over a unique production unit was very attractive in Faiblén's eyes. He took up the matter with the supervisory board of the division who had the formal authorisation to take investment decisions of this size.

The duel

The reader will recall that there was a GS-company in southern Sweden in the old division-like construction. No doubt the reader will also remember M. Ziegler from W's board meeting on 29 August 1980, and that W was established in 1978. In the spring of 1976 Ziegler was the managing director of the GS-firm in southern Sweden. It was a production unit, a so-called supply unit which provided the sales organisation, i.e. the S-firm in Stockholm, with GS-equipment. Ziegler had long been active in this branch, that is for approximately 10 years. He had also begun to realise that there were strong tendencies in the market indicating a mechanisation of the S-process. He was anxious to supplement his production unit and to give it a leading role in the S-business. Furthermore, he was convinced that it was probably the only chance he had of expanding and perhaps becoming larger and more important than the other units. Ziegler took a lively interest in the initiation by Faiblén of official contacts with L. It was not difficult for him to participate, more or less, in the process of acquisition as he had, in fact, the technical qualifications and he was the manager of the production unit. The problem was that they were both interested in L.

To Faiblén it was obvious that he could incorporate L into his S-firm since he had taken the time to familiarise himself with L's products, he possessed knowledge of the market and he could easily orientate L in the best conceivable way thanks to his daily contacts with the customers. He believed that L needed to be developed, and that the only way to do this was by a constant and direct contact with the market. In addition to this, Faiblén was also technically interested in spite of the fact that he was now only dealing with selling. Moreover, he suspected ulterior motives behind the actions of Zeigler, whose unit, even if it was a production unit, was in no way related to L as a product.

Ziegler asserted that he, in his GS-firm, had the capacity necessary to manage the L-firm. First there was the proximity: L is also situated in southern Sweden. Secondly, he could handle L's administration more effectively than the S-firm. L would be relieved of this burden and concentrate on the improvement of its know-how. Furthermore, he could also, when necessary, supply *L* with technical assistance.

Ziegler was strong and could assert himself. Faiblén had difficulties in giving up the idea of an *L* within his *S*-firm. The tug-of-war ended up in a compromise: *L* would be incorporated in the *GS*-firm but the sale of *L*'s products on the Swedish market would be the exclusive concern of the *S*-firm. The *GS*-firm would handle exports. This is what happened when the acquisition became a fact in August 1976.

The weakening of L

After the acquisition, an agreement was made with Andersson. He would remain in the firm for the next few years, continuing with largely the same functions as he had performed earlier, with an emphasis on marketing. The new management wanted to produce results relatively quickly. Andersson had nothing against this and suggested the employment of a salesman who would be commissioned to travel around and visit customers. Both Ziegler and Faiblén were against this since it did not really fit in with the construction. *GS* plus *L* were, after all, supply units, while the *S*-firm had sales exclusively. A compromise was reached. The new salesman would follow up the customers who were to be introduced to him by the *S*-firm. Andersson naturally thought of Malisman, the old family friend. He had just been bought up for the second time by the same firm, and he found this deplorable. The situation was such that the firm that had bought up the first company to employ him, and had closed it down, had now bought up the American subsidiary company where he had been given new employment and also closed it down. Malisman was convinced that he was persecuted. It was he whom the 'buying firm' were after, he thought. He would never work for them. He accepted Andersson's offer and was employed in *L* at roughly the same time as the acquisition took place: 15th August 1976.

Everyone was convinced that the problem was solved. Time passed, but no miracle occurred. On the contrary, sales decreased. In other words *L* had sold more when Andersson had done everything himself. It seemed strange to Ziegler that sales should deteriorate now that the firm had been relieved of the pressure of all the administrative work. The firm was now managed by the 15-man-strong effective sales corps of the *S*-firm. Moreover, the firm now had its own salesman who, under the supervision of the *S*-firm, would follow up any customer who might be hard to convince. Ziegler was confused, Faiblén was glad, and Andersson began to direct his thoughts elsewhere. Finally he resigned at the beginning of the spring of 1977.

Shortly in advance, Andersson had sent out some distress signals. He could not recognise L any more. The firm was suddenly tied up left, right and centre with other firms within the corporation. He saw this as a definite burden rather than as a supply of resources as efforts had been made to convince him. Naturally his plans to resign worried Ziegler, who notified his closest colleagues and announced that L was now in need of a new local manager. He assumed that in all probability it was just this function that, if rightly fulfilled, would improve the situation, particularly now that Andersson would be leaving L.

L gets a local manager

In the summer of 1977, L. Abrahamsson was one of Ziegler's assistants. Two years previously he had worked in a large engineering firm. He recalled with delight the time when he and a colleague had been assigned the task of building a complicated machine. They had only a drawing, and approximate indications as to the required functions, to go by. They worked together with the project, which took a relatively long time. In this way they grew to know and to respect each other, particularly since they succeeded in the end, against all odds, in building the problematic machine. They were, in fact, even highly praised for their work. Shortly after this Abrahamsson moved to southern Sweden and was employed in the S-company as a development engineer. He thought that his old colleague would be perfectly suited to the position of local manager in L. After having consulted and received the go-ahead from Ziegler, he phoned up his ex-colleague and asked him if he wished to be local manager for a small firm with great development potential. Perdfelt accepted this offer gratefully. He was eager for a change of environment. This, he thought, was an excellent opportunity, which would also, no doubt, be the introduction to higher and more interesting opportunities. Perdfelt entered into service on 1 June 1977.

The deterioration of L's situation

Perdfelt entered his position as local manager responsible for production. The selling was managed by the S-firm according to the agreement between Faiblén and Ziegler; but the salesmen in the S-firm had no feeling for the technologically advanced ES-equipment produced by L. They could not read a drawing or discuss customers' problems in technical terms. In addition to this, as early as the days of Andersson some standard productions of this mechanised S-equipment had been worked out. The standard products were produced in a number of different variants. When Perdfelt started in L, a high level of competence in producing these standard products had already been attained. The management – that is, Ziegler – believed in the possibilities of expansion on the basis of precisely these standard products. Ziegler was convinced that these products had great development potential and that business would flourish, bearing in mind the resources which could be made available by Goliat Inc. At that time Ziegler had definite plans to develop and expand the activities in *L*. Plots situated behind the present factory had already been bought for building purposes.

In reality, however, things turned out differently. Apart from the clumsy sales construction the market was beginning to change. The customers appreciated the standard products, but their problems were specific. They needed special solutions, sometimes in the form of modified standard products, and at other times in the form of tailor-made products. This meant that Perdfelt and the group in *L* had great difficulties. Today they are as skilled at special products as they are at standard products, but at that time it was a nightmare. The customers made enormous demands and required special solutions. There were often calculation mistakes of the product cost. The finished product proved to be more expensive than its selling price. Moreover, the first two to three years (1977–79) necessarily became learning years. Mistakes were often made in the actual construction, which meant that a considerable amount of complementary work, such as servicing, was necessary. The proportion of standard products, which had initially constituted approximately 75% of the volume of activity, decreased until it fell below 50%. The major part of the activity today consists of producing special products, approximately 60–70%. There were many reasons for the decline of the standard products. One of these is, paradoxically, that these products are conducive to satisfactory working conditions and can be said to facilitate the work considerably. However, this quality is very difficult to quantify in economic terms. It is thus not possible to present a profitability calculation to the customer. This means that this type of product is not very high on the lists of priorities of the customers with regard to investments. A special installation is, on the other hand, something which is born directly from the needs of the customer. A profitability calculation for a specially adapted product is thus easier to make and, moreover, easier for the customer to understand. The products that are at issue here are expensive ones. In fact they could rather be said to be investment projects. A standard model costs roughly 70,000 kr, and a special model may cost roughly 500,000 kr. This implies that the buyer who orders conventional GS-products costing between 100 and 1000 kr each is, in all probability, not the same as the one who takes investment decisions of the magnitude mentioned above. Thus the sellers from the *S*-firm did not always meet the right man.

It took a long time for Ziegler to discover all of this. Towards the end of 1977 he was fully aware that he had made errors in his judgements, and that the compromise with the S-firm was unrealistic. He disregarded the problem with the standard and special products, and concentrated his energy on the sales organisation. He asserted within his firm and at division level that a sales corps of the type to be found in the S-firm was not qualified to sell the assortment in question. What was needed, he argued, was for the designer of the equipment to go to the customer himself; but he could not do anything about this just then. Everyone was stuck in the old construction and they all blamed each other. There were all kinds of problems, including rather poor results. At the corporation's management level, serious consideration began to be given to doing something about the situation. It was in this context that the old S-division was incorporated within Group A. S-activity, which constitutes nearly 20% of Group A's total invoicing, was concentrated on the places which had the know-how, or profitability, or both. This meant two units in South America and the remaining unit being established around the GS-firm in southern Sweden. Ziegler, who this time also had a good hand, then became the managing director for the new unit, W. The year was 1978. During this time the sales in L fell: from 3500 Mkr in 1976 to 3043 Mkr in 1978.

W IN FOCUS

Thus W was established in the autumn of 1978 and was commissioned to manage a number of units that were spread throughout Sweden. Ziegler's ideal was, and is, to gather all activities under one roof; to concentrate all activity to the old GS-firm in southern Sweden. This proved to be a difficult process which is still ongoing.

Today W employs approximately 500 people and has a turnover of roughly 170 Mkr. It is composed of a number of units that are run as profit centres. It was important for Ziegler to be able to measure exactly the results of each of these units.

The ES-unit is mainly located in southern Sweden. The ES-unit's goal is simple: to build up a competitive assortment and to be profitable. ES sells directly to the world market and, by means of the sales organisation in Sweden, to the Swedish market. L is subordinate to the ES-unit.

The GS-unit is also located in southern Sweden, apart from one production unit in Finland. Beyond this the GS-unit is the same as the old GS-firm. This unit was given the same tasks as the ES-unit. Further, there are the following:

(a) a sales organisation in Germany,
(b) a sales organisation in Britain,
(c) a sales organisation in Sweden with the head office in Stockholm and regional offices elsewhere in the country,
(d) an engineering unit which was located in Stockholm the first two years after the establishment of W, but which has now been closed down.

All of these units are supported by two connected departments: administration and logistics.

If one were to look at W from the point of view of localisation, then it would be seen that the production, apart from the factory in Finland and the L-unit, is to be found in southern Sweden in the old GS-firm. The Finnish factory is actually incorporated in the Finnish company, Goliat Inc., Finland, but is controlled by Ziegler from W.

This means that, within Goliat Inc., the Finnish factory is regarded as a part of W. As far as the sales organisations are concerned the British firm functions as a subsidiary, whereas the German firm has a special character. The revenue of the German firm is entirely constituted by the commission obtained for the mediation of sales. The commission is meant to cover all the expenses of the German firm. It should preferably also produce positive results. According to Ziegler, the advantage of this construction is, among other things, that it is possible to negotiate with the tax authorities in advance as to which rate of commission is to be paid to the firms.

I have spoken of the production units, the sales organisations in Britain and Germany, the supporting organisations, administration and logistics, but not of the sales organisation in Sweden. The reader will recall the old S-firm in Stockholm and G. Faiblén. The irony of destiny brought the old antagonists together again. This time too they would fight, but not with the same weapons. Faiblén and his S-firm were now subordinate to Ziegler and his W. The S-firm had become W's juridical subsidiary in Sweden. It is a sales organisation, the task of which is to sell W's S-products, both GS and ES, on the Swedish market; just as in the good old days when the former S-firm sold the former GS-firm's products. But this time there was a difference in that now it was W, through Ziegler, who had the say. Shortly after the establishment of W, Ziegler had intended to relieve the Swedish sales organisation of all of its administrative burdens so that it could specialise on sales. The organisation was relieved of the pressure of activities such as book-keeping, accounting, administration, stock-keeping, and purchasing. These activities were centralised in W. As has been mentioned previously, however, Ziegler wanted every department or unit within W to produce measurable, and positive, results. This implied that the Swedish sales organisation had to pay a sum as compensation to the subsidiary for its administrative services.

W had undergone organisational changes since its establishment. Although these may not always have been profound, they have nevertheless been sufficient for members to regard them as a constantly ongoing process.

Let us, for the time being, leave the description of W aside. It is obvious that a full close-up picture would demand much more information and numerous discussions, in addition to further explanations of various relations.

It is now time to go on with the story; later we shall have occasion to proceed with this retrospection and to find the supplementary pieces of the puzzle.

THE REORGANISING

I shall begin this section with a brief summary of what has happened since the acquisition of L by Goliat Inc. Group A, of which L is today a part, was established in 1978 in connection with a comprehensive restructuring which affected the whole corporation. Before this there was an old division, the S-division, which contained all the units that today are included in W, as well as some units abroad. The S-firm was one of these units. It was primarily a sales organisation which bought equipment from the various supply units and then sold them elsewhere. Difficult problems, such as non-customer-adapted products and prices that are too high, are intrinsic in this type of construction. I drew attention to these problems earlier in the text. G. Faiblén was the managing director of the S-firm and it was he who first came into contact with L. It was also he who, with the idea of incorporating the unique products and interesting know-how of L, saw a possibility for Goliat Inc.'s S-activity. As L expanded, the firm was confronted with financial problems. B. Andersson, the founder of L, was thinking of selling and there were many large firms who wanted to buy. He got on well with Faiblén and discussions of acquisition were initiated. Another unit within the S-division, the GS-firm, produced and sold GS-equipment via the S-firm. The managing director of the GS-firm, M. Ziegler, also saw the opportunity of incorporating L into his own business. The tug-of-war as to who was to take over L broke out. Ziegler won. L was incorporated in the GS-firm and its products were to be sold via the GS-firm. Ziegler hoped for visible progress, but the sales of L declined. Together with the specific problems of L, the situation for most of the units within the S-division deteriorated. Lively discussions as to who should be held responsible for the poor results started up. Most people blamed the organisational arrangements with the supply–sales organisations. In 1978 the corporation had had enough. The S-division was taken apart. The units abroad, with their local production and know-how, were to remain independent in so far as they were directly connected to the then newly established larger group, Group A. The rest of the units were gathered under the same roof with the *GS*-firm as their base in southern Sweden. This was to become *W*. The *S*-firm was also subordinated to *W*. This meant that Ziegler became Faiblén's boss. A problem arose, however: the *S*-firm was subordinated to *W*, not as a sales department, but as its juridical subsidiary. This implied, among other things, that the organisational arrangements in *W* were the same as those in the *S*-division, and from which one had hoped to escape. We shall return to this problem later on. As the reader will understand, however, Faiblén was not satisfied with this solution. He therefore resigned from Goliat Inc. soon after the establishment of *W* and started his own business. Meanwhile, the founder of *L*, Andersson, had resigned and a new local manager, Perdfelt, had been appointed.

Let us now resume the thread from where we left off shortly before the close-up section of *W*. After *L*'s establishment, Ziegler began trying to cut costs, wherever he was able, and as much as possible. He was aware that the root of the problem was in the ineffective sales organisation, but there was nothing he could do about it at the time. Thus, he concentrated on eliminating double functions, rationalising production, rendering the stock-keeping more effective and shortening delivery delays, at least to some extent. One result here was that 1979 was a year with a slight improvement in the results of *W* as a whole. However, these improvements were not to be found in each of the units *per se*. *L*, for example, for which there had been such high hopes, ran at a loss. The turnover had increased compared with that in 1978 and reached approximately 6 Mkr, yet there was a decline in the result to roughly 300,000 kr. This was due to a large extent to changes in the market structure that had come about as a result of the demand for special instalments rather than standard instalments. This situation was experienced in *L* as being very troublesome indeed, since a grasp of this area of business had not yet been acquired. Furthermore, Perdfelt, *L*'s local manager, preferred to work with standard products. He began to feel increasingly frustrated. This was not what he had been expecting. Abrahamsson, the manager of *ES* within *W*, who had brought him from his previous employment, had promised something else. He had painted the picture of a small firm with fantastic development prospects. He had given him the impression that significant resources would be put at his disposal for the implementation of bold development plans. Instead, Perdfelt was made scapegoat when sales declined, or when he made errors in calculations on tenders for installations which he had never before constructed. He began to blame Malisman and the sales organisation. Malisman, in turn, blamed Perdfelt.

He claimed that the local manager lacked the necessary technical competence.

At the beginning of 1980 a state of general confusion prevailed on the various levels of W. To Ziegler, a change of direction from the negative trend which had been indicated by the annual results of 1979 was of vital importance. Instructions were handed out to all the units, and various measures were taken in different parts of W. We shall concentrate, in this account, on the ES-units within which L is incorporated.

Abrahamsson, the manager of ES, was responsible for the results of L. He was worried about L's situation and tried to remedy the problem on the basis of the conditions existing at the time. In March–April 1980 he drew up a five-year plan for L's development. The plan was intended for the period of 1981–85.

From March–April 1980 onwards a pattern began to emerge. The pattern which was gradually to be more and more concretised so as finally to lead to MBL (Medbestämmande lagen – the Act on Employee Participation in Decision-making) negotiations about the transfer of L. The pattern may be divided into four phases, the first of which leads us back to the starting point of this narrative: W's board meeting on 19 August 1980. The account of these phases is based upon numerous interviews with the parties concerned, and upon various documents, often confidential ones, such as internal memoranda and reports, minutes and letters. Ethical considerations have unfortunately led to the narrative at times seeming somewhat colourless since I have been forced either to delete or to disguise a number of elements to protect the anonymity of the company and its staff.

PHASE I – A PATTERN EMERGES

The five-year plan

When Abrahamsson prepared and sent off his five-year plan for L to Ziegler, Perdfelt and Malisman in April 1980, the idea of a prospective transfer of L had not entered his mind.

Abrahamsson's point of departure was the fact that the analysis of the annual results of the previous year had shown that the production of special equipment gave poor returns for the business due to considerable differences in calculation, and due to the fact that the relation between the cost of production and the selling price on standard equipment had not been satisfactorily followed up. For the period stated he recommends:

(a) manage own production for standard and standard-special, and try to buy special equipment;

(b) invest in resources for development on the standard assortment;
(c) introduce more support to, or sell more directly from, *L* on our principal markets.

(L. Abrahamsson's five-year plan)

Moreover he stresses that the market is characterised by low profitability and an unstructured production process. Nevertheless, he holds that there is probably a potential volume growth of approximately 10% per year during the period (1981–85), due to the marked interest in the environment and ergonomics.

Abrahamsson's report reveals some optimism with regard to the development possibilities of *L*, and underlines that *L* is one of the four larger producers of standard equipment in Scandinavia. *L*'s market share on standard is estimated to be Sweden, 40–50%; Norway, 25%; Denmark, 10%; other markets, roughly 3%. Furthermore, he gives some sales and market-strategical guidelines to be followed during the period. These guidelines are that:

(a) the products are to be sold directly from *L* or via specially trained salesmen in the firms;
(b) Goliat Inc.'s firms are to function as commission-based 'sleuth-hounds';
(c) the *S*-firm is to be offered the standard assortment in its own colours;
(d) an integration with the *ES*-units' market organisation on the European market is foreseen during the period.

(L. Abrahamsson's five-year plan)

The Scandinavian market, which is regarded as Goliat Inc.'s domestic market, will, as has been said in the plan, 'be strongly covered directly from *L*'. The German market has a good potential and it will be covered at the same time as reinforcement of the local office is foreseen. The British market has also indicated a certain potential for *L*'s products, but sales via the British company have not proved to be very successful. An active support or direct sales from *L* will be planned for the period. The other markets will be covered by the *ES*-unit's market organisation, and be watched over by the other firms in Group A.

The production resources are not considered to be in need of investment, except for the stock resources. This is due to recommendations to buy special equipment or to produce each item with the help of contract workers rather than manufacture it with existing resources. The number of productive hours during the period referred to is estimated to remain unaltered. Capacity utilisation is expected to level out with the help of a certain measure of special production for *W*'s account. Abrahamsson does not feel that staff should be increased during the period with the exception of the employment of two salesmen, one in 1982 and the other in 1983. Product development is also discussed in the plans. The investments primarily concern the development of standard products and amount to approximately 100,000 kr per year up until 1985.

It can be seen from this five-year plan that confidence was placed in the development possibilities of *L* in its existing structure, and that a doubling of the turnover would be fully possible towards the end of the period. Table 1.1 shows the planned sales development per market, as well as totally, and table 1.2 shows the sales development per product group.

It is possible to see, with reference to Abrahamsson's five-year plan, that there was no intention at the beginning of Phase I, when the plan was drawn up, of rooting *L* out of its environment and of incorporating it into W. This was also evident in the many conversations which I had with the actors on various levels. Everyone was simply firmly convinced that *L* would develop undisturbed, and that this development would depend on

TABLE 1.1   *L*'s sales development per market ('000 kr), drawn up on the basis of the five-year plan

Market	1980	1981	1982	1983	1984	1985
Sweden	3,700	4,230	4,720	5,375	6,155	7,020
Norway	700	800	936	1,090	1,251	1,437
Denmark	750	860	988	1,137	1,367	1,500
UK	600	800	1,500	1,850	2,200	2,500
Germany	550	900	1,250	1,800	2,000	2,500
Other	700	860	965	1,065	1,180	1,318
Total	7,000	8,450	10,350	12,317	14,353	16,275
Volume increase (%)		+10.7	+12.2	+9.2	+6.4	+3.5

TABLE 1.2   *L*'s sales development per product group ('000 kr), drawn up on the basis of the five-year plan

Product group	1980	1981	1982	1983	1984	1985
Standard	2,500	3,150	3,926	4,696	5,464	6,194
Standard-special	1,200	1,577	1,991	2,562	3,005	3,416
Special	2,250	2,590	3,230	3,739	4,308	4,905
Total	5,950	7,317	9,147	10,997	12,777	14,515

TABLE 1.3 *L*'s results ('000 kr), drawn up on the basis of the five-year plan

	1980	1981	1982	1983	1984	1985
Turnover	7,000	8,454	10,332	12,317	14,343	16,285
Income	1,826	2,066	2,451	2,904	3,344	3,786
Costs	1,203	1,420	1,780	2,200	2,500	2,720
Results	523	646	671	704	844	1,066

the retainment of *L*'s distinctive character as a small unit with its own identity. Table 1.3 shows *L*'s planned development results.

Ziegler's reflections

Ziegler did not like the plan since he did not like the uncertainty. At that time, the spring of 1980, *W*'s results were not very impressive, and Ziegler did not want to take any risks. It was, in his opinion, merely a matter of trying to increase the sales and reduce the expenses. As has been mentioned earlier, all the units were assigned various tasks in this direction. We shall now take a closer look at *L*'s destiny.

L's assortment is divided into two product groups: standard and special. The idea of having standard products was that it was possible, with relatively little trouble, to sell products according to price lists.

> Originally we thought we'd be able to deliver this kind of thing in exactly the same way as we'd delivered other components, but as it turned out, it wasn't that simple. Instead, it became obvious that we had to go to the customer, tell him how to use the product, speak to him of its advantages; and help him motivate the investment. Often the machine would need to be modified. There will be an almost tailor-made product. (M. Ziegler)

This implies, among other things, that the sale of a standard product takes almost as long a time as that of a special one, which, in turn, leads to the immobilisation of capital for a longer period than would normally have been necessary.

Neither is the other section of the assortment, that of special products, entirely free from complication. Rather the opposite prevails.

> This section implies the building of customer-adapted solutions. Lately we've noticed that we have to go to the customer frequently and repeatedly. At the same time we have to know how these products can be adapted so as to be able to offer technical solutions to the customer. What's most important here is that the period of decision from the time when the customer begins to

decide until he actually buys is always a relatively long one. If, then, it's also a special solution, it'll take even longer until it's delivered. (M. Ziegler)

Looking more closely at Ziegler's argument, we find that sometimes it could take up to a year from the time when the customer first became interested until the delivery of the product. Apart from the tying up of capital, Ziegler was also worried about the problem of capacity utilisation.

The composition of the staff in L is as follows:

Manager	1	
Construction	2	
Sales	4	
Economy	1	
Foreman	1	
Storeman	1	10
Electric plant	3	
Mechanical workshop	7	10

The first ten are affiliated to SIF (Svenska Industritjänstemannaförbundet – the Swedish Industrial Salaried Employees' Association), while the others are employed in accordance with a collective agreement in 'Metall'. Both groups, the manual and the non-manual workers, are paid monthly. According to Ziegler the workshop is scaled for a certain production capacity, approximately 15,000 hours per year. Some temporary solutions have been tried, such as making standard products and buying special products from sub-suppliers. None the less, the firm remains responsible for the functioning of the products. This means that some tests and adjustments must always be done. This particular solution had the opposite effect and contributed rather to the capacity utilisation becoming increasingly uneven.

We have come up against a heavy fluctuation of the capacity utilization in this group [L], especially in the workshop. When there is a trade boom we don't have enough time. The increased demand for the products, added to the long time it takes to bring home components and everything else that is needed, means that we don't have time to deliver. Then we end up in a situation of buying up and we begin to build and assemble, but gradually the demand decreases and we land up in a recession. There we stand without any orders and can do no more than drive the finished products off to storage. Then it takes a while before we can get started again. This costs a lot of money. After all, it's a matter of 10 men in the workshop and 10 office employees, plus the machines. It then becomes impossible to reduce further our fixed organization. It's a small business and that's the problem. (M. Ziegler)

Ziegler has even wondered whether it would not be wiser to close down the business since it is not profitable; but other forces in both L and W have held with conviction that the unit can be made profitable with the help of further sales efforts and investments in product development. Although Ziegler did agree to this he resolved to find another way to produce a capacity utilisation which, at the level of the budget, would correspond to the dimensions of the workshop and thus imply lower hourly costs.

> We have pondered over the extent of the value of L for Goliat Inc. We have found that L's activity is supplementary to the ES-unit and that the S-process with the customer is, as a whole, becoming more and more mechanized. We also know that the use of robots is spreading more and more and that L is extremely proficient at producing dirigible machines. Thus, we've realized that we could find, with our products, combined with the robots and the advanced ES-apparatus, the niche where we could be strong. To cut a long story short, we believe that L's knowledge suits and supplements the total S-activity of Goliat Inc. (M. Ziegler)

The idea of alleviating the problem of capacity utilisation by means of a transfer of the entire activity to southern Sweden and incorporating it within W began to take shape in Ziegler's mind. L's turnover for the year 1979 was approximately 5.6 Mkr and it was expected to amount to approximately 7 Mkr in 1980, which meant a considerable improvement. But Ziegler, who had fixed ideas about the variation of demand and the settlement of capacity utilisation, did not believe in a continued boom and gave no greater credibility to Abrahamsson's five-year plan. He was 'convinced' that if L was allowed to continue on its path undisturbed, then one could expect, broadly speaking, to lose money every second year and to be on a level of $\pm$ 0 every other year. At the same time, he was aware of the difficulties implied in the eventuality of a transfer. He knew

> that lot up there, some miles from here, are very closely knit. Because after all they've worked alone, they stay together, they solve their problems together and they feel like a strong group. (M. Ziegler)

Against this background he gave instructions to find out, in the first instance, whether L was at all a competitive producer. He thought that perhaps it was not necessary to have a factory. All of the contract services, all of the production, could be acquired elsewhere on the basis of drawings that were owned, and according to particular specifications. A small work group was started with people from L under Abrahamsson's supervision. They got in touch with a number of firms and requested tenders for certain drawings. It was soon to be seen that the suggested prices were no better than *L*'s own production costs. Ziegler thought than that the only way out of this dilemma was to seriously take the step towards a transfer of *L*'s activity to *W*.

> If we're to stand for the production ourselves then we must minimize the risks of having high expenses in the trade boom. I can't sit here with the whole of *W* and try to save money in a certain area while going at a loss in another area. It just doesn't work. I must have a relatively acceptable profitability in all fields. That's why I ask people to investigate the possibilities of moving the factory here. The whole business, manual and non-manual workers, so as to attain the advantages of co-ordination in a larger business. I have the load of other production. This means that if I get too much to do then I can move people over from one business department where I have less to do and reinforce the overloaded section during the period that it's necessary. If this doesn't work then I would probably have somewhere else where I could use people. What I'd like to achieve is the transfer of people in *L*'s case, in the same way as I've done with the other workshops. (M. Ziegler)

Thus the process was initiated. Abrahamsson was given the task of investigating the matter. Shortly thereafter he presented a confidential report which was addressed to Ziegler only. The report is dated 13 August 1980 – four months after the optimistic five-year plan and two weeks before the decisive board meeting.

A hesitant report

For obvious reasons I cannot render the report in its integral form. What I shall do, however, is to bring to the fore those elements in the report that indicate a certain irritation on the part of the author, and which also shows that he experienced the situation as conflicting.

Abrahamsson stated that the business in *L* made a contribution, if only a small one, during the past twelve months, after having had a number of relatively weak years. He went on to say that the reason for this could most probably be sought in a good economic situation, and that Ziegler was probably right in his prognosis. He discussed the sales policy and noted that the sales via *L* Goliat Inc.'s firm, including the *S*-firm, 'have been an outright fiasco'. *L* needed more direct selling. He went on to emphasise that the sales potential tended to increase due to ergonomic and environmental characteristics of the products. He also wrote that other firms had recently begun to show an interest in *L*'s products, which he saw as an indication that other suppliers were falling away, and that serious firms regard the work equipment (*L*'s products) as a natural supplement to their product programme. He ended this section with the prediction that the growth of *L*'s products would be greater than the growth of the engineering industry, and that the plans he was making were actually pessimistic compared with what he really believed about the development. He held, in this context, that the annual budget of 1980 would be attained and that the volume of demand would not decrease. The question of the settlement of the capacity utilisation which had so bothered Ziegler, and which had been presented by him as the principal argument for the transfer, was carefully brushed aside by Abrahamsson, who believes that the settlement could be attained by the transfer of a certain amount of standard production from *W* to *L*. In one place he wrote that 'engineering workers would be needed and that these could be employed without an increase in fixed expenses and within the already existing buildings' within the foreseeable future. Thereafter certain propositions for the future development of the firm were outlined. It was written, among other things, that 'without consideration to fluctuations of the economic situation, a slow but even rise in the sales volume is foreseen'. Then the author of the report admitted that 'experience has shown that the products are sensitive to cyclical influences', and that 'the development of results is weak'. The first section of the report was brought to a close with the repetition of some general statements.

The second part of the report discussed, very briefly, 'the consolidation of *L* and *W* implicating the transfer of the *L* unit to *W*'s premises', and the positive and negative effects of the consolidation. The author of the report recommended that, if a decision for transfer were made, a detailed investigation ought to be carried out. The effects of the consolidation which could be seen as positive were that it enabled:

(1) the liberation of capital via the sale of real estate; (2) the reduction of fixed expenses in *L* due to the possibility of integration in *W*; (3) more flexible capacity within the whole in the form of reduced labour sensitivity; (4) the gathering of know-how; and (5) perhaps, in the future, the integration of marketing within *W*.

In connection with this Abrahamsson recommended that, to maintain activity, staff effectivity should not be immediately reduced. Efforts should be made, rather, to make resources available in *W*'s activity within stocks, finance, administration, production, planning and management. In the space of a year, he continued, the corresponding functions which today were a burden for *L* could be reduced by two or three men: 'from the point of view of results, a well-needed saving on the staff side'. The negative effects could be that: (1) professional workers resigned; (2) *L*'s identity as a company disappeared; and (3) difficulties could arise due to the process of production in *L* not being suited to *W*'s system.

The report is very abruptly brought to a close with the following short section concerning the time perspective of the transfer:

Election of board members
Informational duties
Planning of details in work groups
MBL – (the Act on Employee Participation in Decision-making)
Decision turn of the year 1980–81
Arrangements for the transfer

The end of the beginning of the loop

Two weeks later Ziegler sat in the large elegant room with the heavy draperies in the windows. The chairman of the board and a few of the members had already arrived, but they were still waiting for one member. Meanwhile, the conversation was friendly and relaxed and moved around earthly concerns. Ziegler took part in this social *causerie* for a while, and then went towards the majestic table upon which he laid his attaché case. He opened it and took out the memorandum he had compiled on the matter of the transfer of L to W's premises. He quietly read to himself the lines which he had underlined and which he intended to present to the board as a summarised commentary: the results of the unit have improved considerably, but an economic recession could drastically change the situation. The goal will thus be . . . (from the minutes of the board meeting 29 August 1980).

EPILOGUE

We have just come to the end of the beginning of a loop. In this narrative I have tried to bring to the fore the various archaeological findings that I made when looking for the original ideas which seemed, to my mind, to form the basis of the transfer idea.

We began in the room where W's board had their meeting. We saw how Ziegler, after having presented the matter of L's transfer, left the room. As we know, he was commissioned by the board to act in accordance with the memorandum which he himself had presented. But we never found out there how it was that he came into the room, and how the matter which he had with him had taken shape. To find out about this we went up the historical stream, so to speak, and at each significant event took a break to take a closer look at the findings.

We acquainted ourselves with Goliat Inc.'s architecture in general, and then 'went down' and looked at the old constructions that preceded the establishment of W. We saw how openings were made for communication with L, which we recognised from the memorandum and, in connection with this, we looked for L's origin. We arrived at the period of contact, witnessed the acquisition and the duel of the aspirants. We continued on our journey through the course of events which led to the establishment of W. We saw how L's situation gradually deteriorated and how other problems in W had become sedimented from older periods. Then we began to perceive the thought, the strategies and the actions which led to the board meeting. We followed the birth of the transfer idea, how it developed and how it gradually became an intention according to which to act and to be effected. Finally we took out the document with which Ziegler substantiated his memorandum at the board meeting – namely Abrahamsson's hesitant report. When we had come this far, only the escorting of Ziegler, to the room where we had met him for the first time, remained.

CHAPTER 2

Chronicle of a Transfer Foretold

Act II

The process enacted, the actors have their say, their intentions, motives, strategies and actions are clarified

INTRODUCTION

During the first act of the narrative we were able to see how the transfer, as an idea, was born, had grown and had become self-evident.

Phase I, which finishes off the first act, shows how the transfer process is initiated and how the idea in the described actions is institutionalised and 'legalised'.

In the second act the actual process takes place, the various actors have their say, and I shall account for my journey through the course of events and for the transformation of my role. The focal point of this act lies in the organisation of the process against the background of the intentions, motives, strategies and actions of the actors involved. This second act consists of two different episodes:

(a) The first episode begins with Phase II and ends with the introduction of Phase IV. This episode is a reconstruction of the course of events.
(b) The second episode, on the other hand, is not a reconstruction. The introduction of Phase IV is the point when I enter into the course of events. This means that the description in the second episode is based on my participation in the process and the subsequent implications thereof.

Thus I shall begin this part of the narrative by accounting for the way in which I came into contact with the process. After this I shall recall the events by way of retrospect so as to tie up with the first act.

This is of special importance since I first came into contact with this process when it had already 'begun'. What I shall try to do is lead the reader along the same path as I travelled myself.

EPISODE I

The search of empirics

At the turn of the year 1980–81 I got in touch with SAF (the Swedish Employers' Confederation) department in Malmoe and, in particular, with the Metal Trades Employers' Association. This is the largest of the trade associations within SAF. My aim was to gain insight into the ideology that is expressed in SAF's actions via their representatives (ombudsmen) when they enter an organisation as the representatives of the employers, i.e. as a party in the case, and in so doing, try to help solve the internal disputes of the firm.

As a step in the then planned investigation to map out how the actions were organised within the association against the background of 'SAF's ideology', it was meaningful for me to partake in the daily praxis of these ombudsmen. Their work begins when a firm cannot solve its disputes internally and conflicts are experienced which, in effect, set employer up against employee. There are local unions within the firms such as staff unions or union branches with whom the employer negotiates. When an agreement cannot be reached it is usual for central parties or ombudsmen to then be summoned from the trade associations concerned. The disputes may be solved either by means of locally reinforced negotiations or by means of central negotiations. In certain cases the dispute may be of such a nature that it is necessary to go to an appeal court: the Labour Court. During the last decade the work of the ombudsman has grown increasingly difficult, but at the same time more valuable as a consequence of the complexity of the many laws concerning the situation in the labour market. As examples of these laws one might mention the employment security legislation, the law of participation in decision-making, and vacation laws. In addition to this the collective agreements become increasingly complicated. The likelihood that the sole trading companies and the local unions have of translating all these regulations, and of applying them to specific cases, is very limited. The ombudsmen, who stand apart from the rest because of their acquaintance with the regulations, and who gain experience by going from case to case, make a valuable contribution in this context.

At the same time their role, and the access which they gain to the affairs of the firms, together with the confidence which the management has for them, is the source of a very strong position. I am primarily thinking of their potential as creators of public opinion, or as catalysts for and reinforcers of a certain mentality. They see how various conflicts arise and how they may be solved. They have a firm opinion as to how things ought to be. They often express their personal opinions to managers, and talk about their experience of many other cases. They frequently confirm the conceptions (perhaps prejudices) of the management, thereby providing an indirect support for the management position. From another angle they are regarded with hostility and scepticism by the employees and their representatives. Even though the latter may not have anything to which they can point directly, they are very conscious of an ideological implication hidden behind the ombudsman's role of mediator in his conduct and performance in contexts of dispute. The employees in *L* clearly expressed their suspicion of these missionaries. They held that the role of the ombudsman was to maintain a ritual, the purpose of which was to delude the employees and to convince them of the pseudo-goodwill of the employers; a goodwill in which they in no way believed, since, as they said, 'the management gets what it wants in the end'.

The connection with the case

I wished to learn more about the way an ideology or philosophy is put into operation and entered into praxis by participating in the mediatory work in firms. I presented my wish to one of the ombudsmen, who was at first doubtful that I, as an outsider, would ever be accepted by the antagonists. After a few discussions, however, we agreed to make an attempt. He would look for a 'neutral' case, ask the other party concerned if I could join them, and then consider the possibility of my participation in other cases.

My first case was, indeed, rather neutral. It was a middle-sized firm in southern Scania which was intending to carry out minor rationalisations in production and administration. The employees had via the local unions opposed this intended rationalisation, and after a few rounds had arrived at locally reinforced negotiations. It was at this point that the ombudsman and I came to the firm. It was soon to be revealed that the initiator of the opposition, the chairman of the local union, had left the firm some weeks previously for the simple reason that he had been given a better-paid function in another firm. The ombudsman presumably knew this, and this was most probably why he took the risk of allowing me to be present. We sat at the negotiating table but there were no negotiations. Everyone noted with relief that the initiator was missing. It was also affirmed that in reality none of the employees were actually opposed to the rationalisations at issue. The union chairman had been the one to push the question, and there was no-one else who had either the energy or the will to contradict. Everyone seemed to be in agreement. The matter was withdrawn and everyone shook hands. It was a neutral case. The ombudsman was satisfied and, probably due to the positive atmosphere, decided that I could 'tour' with him on condition that I remained as neutral as possible. We looked at the timetable and decided that I was to partake in one case per week. We chose four cases which seemed to be interesting, in terms of the nature of the problem and in terms of the size of the firm. This meant that we would be touring together for a month, although not all the time, since the ombudsman sometimes had three or four cases per week in his appointment diary. I preferred to be selective, partly for the above-mentioned reasons, and partly to have time to be able to process the material from one case before going on to the next. We also decided that, after the first four-week period, we would sit down and evaluate the collected experience. We would then decide about our continued cooperation.

By this time it was March 1981 and we had been through three cases of moderate interest. On 14 April we arrived at a small firm in a small town in Scania. The first impression came from the building itself, which was well designed, brightly painted and generally gave a good impression. A few people were already seated in the conference room. They greeted me politely and said that my presence was not in the least disturbing; on the contrary, they were glad that an outsider could see 'this show'. From the discussions I gathered that the people present were waiting for someone from another firm: the owning firm. While we sat and waited the discussion was at its liveliest. It concerned the previous meeting and how they had been tricked. One person also spoke of numerous documents that were missing and which were obviously being 'withheld by Them'. There was indignation over the 'disgusting' conduct of the other side, and a firm resolution that 'now that everything has been disclosed, things will certainly not be allowed to go the same way in the future. We'll show we're not that stupid'. Although I was confused, I became increasingly interested. A short while later two gentlemen arrived with severe expressions on their faces. They were the firm's representatives. The lively discussion turned into silent whispers, and attitudes stiffened. It felt as if each one of the people present was preparing for battle.

The small firm that was in question here is *L*. The general atmosphere which I encountered on arriving at the firm for the first time was decisive in my continued work with *L*. At this stage I already knew that it was a matter of the transfer of the business of *L* to the principal place of production in *W* in another town some miles away. I knew that negotiations were held, but not how they were held, i.e. how the inner processes appeared and which direction these gave to the development of the course of events. I was later to find out that the two gentlemen who arrived late were Abrahamsson, the manager of the *ES*-business, and

Kolinsky, the production manager, both of whom were active in W and represented the employers *vis-à-vis* L's employees. Also present were three employees from L, a representative from the local department of the Industrial Employees' Association, and one from the metal workers trade union. L's local manager, Perdfelt, was also present as secretary and keeper of the minutes, which may well have had the effect of neutralising him as a potential party (a holder of opinions) in the context.

The part of the process which, in my classification of the data, corresponds to the fourth phase, was initiated when the meeting was opened. Due to narrative technical reasons I find it meaningful to forestall the chronology, and instead reproduce the course of events in the order in which they became significant to me. I have noted, earlier on in the text, that Phase IV serves as the introduction to the second episode, which is when I entered into the course of events. Thus before going further and connecting chronologically to Phase II (which introduces the first episode in the second act and which is a reconstruction of the events), we must begin with Phase IV.

PHASE IV – GENERAL CONFUSION (FIRST SECTION)

The meeting was opened in a state of general confusion. To my great surprise they began to discuss the minutes of the previous meeting. The minutes had not been approved by the employees, i.e. the representative of the Industrial Employees' Association and of the metal workers' trade union. The minutes concerned were distributed, and a heated debate began. Its purpose was to investigate whether the minutes really did give a just reflection of the situation. It is of interest here to reproduce the essence of these minutes with particular emphasis on the disputed points.

The minutes at issue had been kept at a meeting held on 27 March 1981. The people present at that meeting were the same as the participants of the meeting of 14 April, and Perdfelt had been secretary then, as also he was now. Abrahamsson had suggested the following, which was approved:

(a) Account of background and development during Goliat Inc.'s period of ownership.
(b) Account of the establishment of W and its goals.
(c) The motives of the firm (W) for the transfer of the business.

Thereafter he announced that:

> We have a good comprehension of our position. We have built up production and market organizations, W was established in 1978 with the

goal of gathering the S-resources of Goliat Inc. to southern Sweden. Since then units have been transferred from Gothenburg and Stockholm. Furthermore, restructuring and investments have been made in production equipment and the warehouse.

The goal of the firm within the framework of W's endeavours is to incorporate the activity of L with other activities in southern Sweden, thereby accomplishing a levelling-out of employment, less sensitivity to cyclical changes along with the possibility of coordination effects. All those who are today employed in L are offered continued employment in W.

The minutes continue with a couple of justifying phrases to maintain that:

We intend for the unit of production in L to be coordinated with the production department in W as well as for the marketing unit to be added to W's marketing department (the one that manages GS-products).

It is also evident in the minutes that both the union representatives were troubled by the situation of employment in W's factories. Rumours had been spread that L was in the process of introducing a short working week, which invalidated the argument that the transfer of L's activities to W would increase the level of employment for L's personnel.

In reply to the question posed by the metal workers' trade union representative, Kolinsky informed that:

A short-time week will be introduced during the period May–September 1981 with the intention of reducing the tying-up of capital in the production supply and in the storage of finished products. After the short-time week has been effected we reckon that production and sales capacity will be at the usual level.

The same representative of the employees, and still according to the minutes of the meeting on 27 March 1981, wondered why the union had not been informed when the investigation of the transfer was initiated in the autumn of 1980. Afterwards I learned that the investigation mentioned was that to which I have referred in Act I as Abrahamsson's report, along with an investigation which initiated on 9 September 1980 and to which I shall return later on in the text. In answer to this question Abrahamsson replied that 'The investigating group was appointed by the staff at L and was not intended to investigate the eventuality of a transfer.'

The other representative of the employees from the Industrial Employees' Association had several questions in mind; he asked, among other things, 'why the alternative presented by the staff had not been taken into account'. Abrahamsson replied that:

The proposition does not fulfil the goal of W to gather the resources of the company in southern Sweden and neither does it contribute to the stabilizing of L's business.

Abrahamsson promised that the proposition put forward by the staff would be further considered. The minutes ended with a few commentaries on the annual accounts for 1980, along with the promise that the minutes from all of the meetings of investigation would be handed over. It was established that at the next meeting – the meeting at which I was present – the content of the minutes of the previous meeting would be the object of negotiation.

We were thus sitting there, people were speaking without taking heed of each other, and no-one missed an opportunity to show aggression. Abrahamsson emphasised time and again that the minutes from 27 March had to be checked and signed by the employee's representatives. They, in turn, asserted that this could not be done and that some additions and comments first had to be made. The ombudsman tried to mediate, but it was a short-lived attempt. He was firmly requested to keep a respectable distance, since he had not been present on 27 March and thus could not make a constructive contribution. In the end it was agreed to comment on and criticise some points of the minutes. Among other things, it was written that 'the employees' representative sees it as a necessity that they ought to have participated in the investigation initiated by W for the transfer of the business'. It was also written that 'the employee party sees the whole affair as a very strange machinery of negotiation', especially when Abrahamsson, in reply to the question as to why the alternative of the staff had not been considered, said that 'it was irrelevant'. This caused a certain tension, but Abrahamsson seemed eager for the minutes to be checked and signed by the two union representatives. They signed and I wondered whether negotiations about the transfer itself would begin or whether discussions about the manner of negotiating, and what was written or not written in the minutes, would continue. I had a strong feeling that Abrahamsson had the same question in mind just then. He looked unhappy. Rightly enough, discussion began on what could appropriately be written in the minutes of the meeting taking place.

The atmosphere was strained and confused, and everyone wanted to make sure that 'this time the minutes must correspond to what has been said at the meeting'. The employees' representative insisted that it would be explicitly written, among other things, that the alternative to the transfer put forward by L's staff ought to be carefully considered, and that it was believed that the transfer decision had, more or less, already been taken by the firm (W) before negotiations had been requested in the matter. He also wanted it entered in the minutes that the employees' representatives demanded the breakdown of the negotiations, and that they intended to come back with the demand for negotiation with regard to the right to claim damages for breach of the Employee Participation in Decision-making Act § 11. Perdfelt promised to arrange minutes which would be true to the meeting, and to send them to the parties concerned for checking and signing. The meeting was then closed. Afterwards I went from room to room and spoke to the employees. Not only were they willing to speak their minds, but they seemed to *want* to do so. It was an openness accompanied by a feeling of anguish. For them I seemed to serve as a kind of safety valve. I found out that the employees in *L* had heard about the transfer for the first time in the autumn of 1980. This was in connection with the task assigned to them by *W*'s management of appointing a group for the investigation of the possibilities of transferring the business from *L* to W. When I spoke to them they were disappointed and thought that *W*'s conduct was 'unfair'. 'They're out to deceive us', they said, 'but we won't give up'.

As I went through the collected data, I grew to be more and more interested in the case. Of all of the firms that I had visited with the ombudsman, and the meetings I had participated in together with him, *L*'s meeting was the one that had impressed me the most. The commitment of the participants revealed what might be called a great depth of intention. It was obvious that what was at stake was of great significance for the individuals involved. The roles and attitudes were vividly marked and the various tactical features were sometimes very clear. It was also apparent that knowledge of the various dimensions of the object of negotiation were not equally distributed. While one person was surprised by the insight of another into the matter at issue, the latter would be equally surprised by the former's prejudices. On several occasions during the meeting, when the discussion came to a cul-de-sac, the participants were forced to take cover under their official roles. Abrahamsson called attention to the fact that, in spite of everything, he was still the manager; the employees' representatives frequently referred to the statute book and the employees demanded acknowledgement of their unique competence. Those who were present at the table gave the impression, by their conduct and arguments, that specific personal interests and diverging orientations were fundamental for the standpoints which they adopted. The nature of the meeting was more like a struggle between individuals than a negotiation. People marked out their positions or took on defensive attitudes. An accusatory tone prevailed and those involved seemed to harbour a fierce distrust of each other. Abrahamsson and Kolinsky were convinced that *L*'s employees had organised some kind of sabotage. The workers and the employees' representatives did not try to hide the facts that they thought that *W*'s representatives underestimated them, treated them as being insignificant, and thought that the decision was as good as taken. They also believed that W withheld the most important parts of the information with regard to this matter, and which constituted the fundamental and necessary knowledge which was essential for the conduct of negotiations.

I began to realise the value of being able to follow an ongoing process. An important decision was to be made and implemented, but no-one knew how or when. The decision entailed radical changes in the lives of the actors involved. It also entailed an activation of the deep internal organisational problems which . were clearly manifested. An ongoing process, compared with an entirely reconstructed case, is preferable for the following two reasons: The researcher learns from and about the process at the same time as it is in progress. By speaking with the people involved it is possible for him to know 'more' about the process than each one of them. It is also possible for him, to a 'greater' extent than those involved, to speculate on the development of the course of events. He may be surprised by a certain development, find confirmation for his predictions, or both. This is of particular importance for the researcher's acquisition of knowledge and deeper understanding of the problem. It also enables him to experience the process in the same way as the persons involved, or at least as some of them. This last point involves difficult methodological–ethical problems which will be treated separately in Chapter Three.

I decided, thus, to work with the case of L's transfer, and to follow it up until the decision was either implemented or abandoned, i.e. until the actual physical transfer had taken place or something entirely different had happened. A few days after the meeting in L on 14 April 1981, I had a conversation with the local manager, Perdfelt. I told him what the situation was and together we investigated my chances of following the course of events. This naturally meant that I must inform myself, either in advance or while working on the case, as to what had taken place before I was connected with it. Perdfelt did not show the slightest sign of discomfort in the face of the fact that an outsider would gain insight into a process which he himself experienced as rather infected. He was so worried and felt so powerless that instead he looked 'positively upon my supervision of the process', and felt that it could 'certainly bring some good to the antagonists and even to others who could perhaps learn something new from the process'. On 28 April I met Ziegler, W's manager, for the first time. He was well disposed and regarded my interest in the process with an almost philosophically elevated calm. None the less, I noticed that this was, in fact, a poorly concealed hope that he had of gaining confirmation, from an outsider, of the validity of his ideas. He gave a thorough account of the background of the whole affair, and explained quite openly that the ongoing negotiations were 'more a formality than anything serious to get hung up on'. He could well understand, he said, that *L*'s employees were indignant but, he continued, he had acted and would continue to act in exact accordance with the rules of the game. When I asked for more details of these rules, he recommended that I go to the ombudsman with whom he had conversed on occasion. This was the same ombudsman with whom I had 'toured'. He gave me permission to move freely in *W* and to collect data. He also agreed to see to it that I received copies of any documents concerning the case: correspondence, investigations, minutes, internal memoranda and various economic calculations. It was later to be discovered that there were certain important documents missing in the pile that I had received. I then supplemented my existing collection with documents from various sources: *L*'s staff had some, the local employee parties, SIF and Metall, had others. Perdfelt had a great deal of important correspondence, and Abrahamsson also had interesting documents. All of these documents will appear at one time or another in the narrative. I experienced this as particularly typical of this case in which every actor struggled to know a little more than the others. To withhold documents from others was a part of the game, and was experienced by those involved as an important tactical advantage. On this occasion Zeigler recommended that I also speak to Abrahamsson, who was Perdfelt's boss, and who was the one who was actually responsible for the transfer project. Abrahamsson was very sparing and careful with his utterances. He was also extremely suspicious and critical towards any kind of interference in the process. He held that it could only worsen the situation which he experienced as already being extremely difficult. 'The more one speaks of the matter with employees', he said, 'the more infected it becomes.' I assured him that I would be as discreet as possible and emphasised that my 'interference' might even facilitate the process somewhat. It was not until he understood that Ziegler had given me all information and provided me with numerous documents that he began to change his attitude. In the end he too told me how he experienced the problem, and I was allowed to move freely in the *ES*-department as well as in *L*.

The questions with which I was then confronted concerned what had happened before I was connected to the case: when did the process begin, which strategies were the most suitable for finding out as much as possible, which methodological approaches could produce the best results? Some of these questions have already been answered in Act I, and others will be elucidated henceforth. I am now following the same path in the text as the one I took during the process of the investigation. This implies that, as indicated earlier, I shall now resume the course of events starting with Phase II.

PHASE II – THE DILEMMA

At the end of the first act I spoke of how the idea to alleviate the problem of capacity utilisation by means of a transfer of the whole activity, and of incorporating it into *W*'s business, began to take shape in Ziegler's mind. I also spoke of the investigative report which Abrahamsson presented in August 1980, four months after the optimistic five-year plan and two weeks before the decisive board meeting.

A few days after this meeting Abrahamsson was given the task by Ziegler of appointing a group which would immediately set about investigating the needs for premises in connection with the transfer of *L*'s business. Abrahamsson found this task rather difficult. He was still dissatisfied with the slight credit which Ziegler had given his optimistic five-year plan. Furthermore, he felt inhibited from acting freely in the *L* affair, bearing in mind the special relation which he had with Perdfelt. The two had worked together in another company before one of them, Abrahamsson, was employed by Goliat Inc. A short while afterwards, when a local manager was needed in *L*, he thought of his old friend Perdfelt who gratefully accepted the job. Today, this friendship is no longer so self-evident.

Abrahamsson thought that he had to handle this task smoothly. In other words, he was prepared to evade the directives of Ziegler, and instead of taking the direct path, to try to fade the matter out as much as possible. On 9 September 1980 he was with *L*'s employees. He explained his version of the matter to them and said, among other things that:

> We're not going to discuss the transfer now, it's not a question of that. What we're going to look at rather are the conditions that exist for any future transfer. You, as experts, shall participate in the study of this possibility. (L. Abrahamsson)

It was the first time that the employees in *L* had officially heard of the transfer. This came as a shock for many of them despite the careful formulation. This came, moreover, just when *L* had begun to produce positive results for the first time in years. The level of optimism was rather high, and the possibility of a transfer was thus experienced as a hard blow below the belt. As well as the local manager, two of *L*'s employees were appointed to the investigatory group. Perdfelt had already begun to fear the worst. When the transfer discussions began he said it was already clear that there would be a great deal of opposition from the staff:

> It all came as a shock. We'd just managed to get above water when this

happened and we were virtually told that now you're not going to carry on with this any longer.

Personally, I felt it was a great pity that we wouldn't be allowed to keep up the fine trend that we'd begun to develop. I was very sad about this and wasn't at all enthusiastic about starting to work with the transfer question, which I believed to be very destructive for the business, instead of devoting ourselves to leading the firm onwards as we'd begun to do. (R. Perdfelt)

From my many conversations with L's employees when I tried to find out what had happened during the second phase, and how it was all experienced, I frequently had the impression that the atmosphere had at the time been very negative and loaded. This was due to the fact that it had never been said, from W's side, that 'We, the members of the board, have made a decision for the transfer to be put into effect'; instead it was always a matter of the possibility of a transfer. This meant that the employees, including Perdfelt, devoted considerable amounts of energy trying to find all kinds of arguments against a transfer. The atmosphere was negative since L's employees felt that the management in W was making plans for them without them knowing what these were about. They said: 'We simply felt very insecure. We felt that we were totally controlled by others.'

A relationship of opposition coupled with a mutual suspicion began to grow between W's management and L's employees. Both sides were occupied with attempts to find out what the opposite party was planning. The employees in L, for example, made several attempts to find out the intentions of W by gaining allies in the local unions in W. W's management tried to keep informed as to the 'plotting of the rebels' via Malisman in the first instance, whose loyalty to his colleagues in L was dubious. In the beginning Abrahamsson had attempted to use Perdfelt as a channel, but he soon realised that the latter was in a difficult position. He preferred, moreover, to see himself as belonging to the team of L's employees. I shall take up the question of how L's employees regarded him later on in the text. He was fully aware of his own difficulties when he said:

Personally, I was in a very difficult position. I'm assumed to represent the management of the firm here. At the same time, I feel like a part of the staff. In other words, there was an ambiguity to be taken into consideration which I experienced as extremely trying. I know that it is my duty to see to the interests of the company and the furthering and realization of the intentions of my employers. But in many cases these interests clash with my own conception of the situation and with my experience of the here and now and the way that I felt it should be. (R. Perdfelt)

In reality, and over and above that which has been expressed by Perdfelt here, there was the animosity and the bitter after-taste which characterised his relationship with Abrahamsson. Perdfelt felt that he had been deceived by his ex-colleague, and his doubts and fears seemed to be confirmed by the rate at which the course of events unfolded. Abrahamsson had never been satisfied with Perdfelt. He, too, had difficulties in expressing this. It is true that he did stress certain points such as the facts that he was not sufficiently market-oriented, that he had never succeeded in coming to an adequate agreement with Malisman for the coordination of the production and sales activities, and that he was not loyal with regard to his employer, W; while he never spoke openly of this, there were others who spoke more readily. Kolinsky, the production manager in W, was relatively new in the firm (1 May 1980) and not as historically burdened as the others. He related that:

> The process has undeniably been encumbered, and is still encumbered since L. Abrahamsson and R. Perdfelt are old friends. It must be difficult in certain situations; they have to be especially considerate towards each other. L. Abrahamsson has never been satisfied with R. Perdfelt, but such things are difficult to say. I think it might have been even worse if he'd employed someone else, but that's just a theory. Anyway, R. Perdfelt hasn't really fulfilled the expectations which he had of him. So I'm sure it's been difficult for L. Abrahamsson sometimes. Especially seeing that M. Ziegler has a completely different attitude, he's a bit more straightforward, a little bit harder. He merely tells L. Abrahamsson that now he has to do such and such with L and he must tell R. Perdfelt that this is how it has to be. And then naturally, L. Abrahamsson is stuck in the middle and thinks that it's 'hell'. This has meant that L. Abrahamsson, in order to avoid conflict situations, has beat a bit around the bush. He hasn't really dared to take hold of the situation in any forceful way. (B. Kolinsky)

Abrahamsson thus shifted balance from the one foot to the other in the same way as Perdfelt experienced his own ambiguity. While the one, driven by Ziegler – who did not wish to have anything to do with trivial things – attempted to obey orders, but implemented them with kid gloves, the other experienced a dividedness on different levels. He was forced to identify himself with L's employees, while at the same time he was reproached for this. He also saw in Abrahamsson's attitude a betrayal of his person. In his attempts to temper the whole affair, Abrahamsson had often withheld a part of the truth, but it would still emerge sooner or later. This added to the already prevalent suspicion, and contributed to the locking of positions right from the start.

This was the *état d'esprit* in which the investigative group started their work. We shall now go back to the investigation. What directives were given to the group? How did they work? And what conclusions did the group arrive at?

The investigation

The investigatory group was appointed on 9 September 1980; it consisted of the local manager, Perdfelt, and two of *L*'s employees. The group was given various directives, including the investigation of whether the physical conditions for working – such as the required floor area, the height of the roof, lifting possibilities and mechanical equipment – could be fulfilled on *W*'s premises. Within the framework of these preconditions, three alternatives were to be investigated:

1　Running the business according to a model that is as good or better than in the present premises.
2　A model where the activity is somewhat spread out, but where the production is primarily concentrated in one building, with staff concerned with production being in direct contact with the production rooms.
3　The activity being split up into several rooms which can be made available. The integration with various functions of *W* to as large an extent as possible.

It was also stipulated in the directives of the investigation that with any alternative adopted, efficiency would always be maintained.

The group, which felt no enthusiasm for this task, took their time before presenting the report. This was done on 4 December.

Meanwhile, Abrahamsson and Kolinsky took this opportunity to inform the representatives within *W* from 'Metall', SALF and SIF in accordance with the MBL (SALF – the Swedish Foremen's and Supervisors' Association). The minutes of that meeting reports, among other things, that:

> An investigatory group has been appointed in *L* with the task of examining the conditions for a transfer of the business [. . .]. The investigatory group is composed of two people appointed by the employees themselves plus the local manager [. . .] The directives of the investigation are based on the attainment of at least the same level of effectiveness of production in *W* as in *L* [. . .] If it is shown by the basic documents of the investigation that there is a good chance of implementing the transfer, then MBL negotiations will be taken up immediately.

The investigatory group made a thorough study of the three alternatives listed above and arrived at the conclusion that if these alternatives were to be put into practice, the result would be a marked deterioration of the business. Alternative 2 would mean, among other things, an isolation of the products from the market, which was considered to have a negative influence on efficiency. Alternative 3, which implies a total integration of *L*'s activity into *W*, was considered to lead to catastrophic consequences for the production of special equipment. The investigatory group concluded its report with a fourth alternative, which was not included in the directives, and which was presented 'as a desirable alternative where all the resources can be utilized in an effective manner'. Furthermore, the investigatory group emphasised that 'it is of vital importance that a decision as to *L*'s future be taken before the end of 1980'. It also pointed out the fact that the prevailing situation has created uncertainty and stress among the staff 'which naturally influences activity negatively'.

The fourth alternative recommended that *L*'s business not be moved and that a number of measures be taken to improve efficiency and the utilisation of the resources. A summary of the propositions put forward by the group reads as follows:

(a) The factory should be extended in accordance with the old plans from 1977.
(b) Investment should be made in processing machines for refining the products.
(c) These combined measures (along with a better layout of the workshop) would lead to a 25% rise in employment in the mechanical workshop. This in turn would imply a lowering of hourly costs and production costs, and contribute towards an improvement of the competitive position of *L*.
(d) An intensification of marketing measures in combination with lower production costs ought to bring about a higher turnover and high profitability.

The group's concluding commentary to alternative 4 pleaded against an eventual future decision taken by the management for the transfer of *L* and, in the form of a speech of defence, it held that:

> The existing staff of *L* has today experience and proficiency which must be highly esteemed in the context, and, furthermore, they have a 'feeling' for the firm which is expressed in moderate salary demands and in their loyalty which, in many cases, is extremely valuable to the firm. A business of *L*'s type which is based upon a very extensive customizing of the products (even the standard products) demands a great deal of flexibility in the organization and intimate cooperation between marketing and production. A split unit

would no doubt have a negative effect in this respect. Our rivals [...] are an example where one has taken the opposite path and founded a smaller separate unit for a similar business.

A transfer to [...] might have advantages since certain functions can be integrated in *W*'s organization, but since the nature of the business in *L* is unlike that of *W* in other respects it is questionable whether the advantages outweigh the disadvantages. (The investigatory group)

At the confused meeting of 14 April 1980, the representatives of the Industrial Employees Association wondered why the staff alternative referred to above was not taken into consideration. The development of the course of events is henceforth connected to this.

PHASE III – LEGITIMATION

Ziegler felt that *L*'s investigatory group took far too much time over their assignment. He believed it was Abrahamsson's fault. For one thing the group had not presented any encouraging suggestions with regard to the transfer, and for another they had taken three months to complete what was more like a speech of defence than an investigation. Ziegler could well understand that Abrahamsson considered the whole affair to be very troublesome and painful, but he still believed that 'now that the race is as good as run, one must begin to seriously work with the situation'.

> Instead, they [the investigatory group in *L*] wanted us to make additional investments in *L* and achieve additional rationalization gains. I said that these suggestions were all very well, but that we could apply them to *W* instead, since these measures would not solve the problem of the fluctuation in the workshops in *L* in any case. My saying this resulted in severe clashes. We had such problems that we couldn't even manage to keep common minutes of the meetings. Because the one party didn't even wish to discuss what the other party felt had already been discussed. (M. Ziegler)

The minutes referred to by Ziegler were those of the meeting of 14 April. There were, in fact, no formal minutes of that meeting; merely a draft. Attempts were made from all sides to compile the minutes, and all these failed.

Abrahamsson was given strict orders to go ahead with the process and accelerate its outcome. Rightly enough, he took care of the process and drew his own conclusions (although in accordance with the directives of Ziegler) of the report from the investigatory group:

> The report showed that the prerequisites necessary for a transfer did exist.

Then we brought the investigation to a close. Later we initiated an internal investigation within the firm here in W. The management of the firm discussed what the transfer would imply and how we would be able to organize it, before demanding MBL negotiations about the actual transfer. (L. Abrahamsson)

On 9 January 1981 Abrahamsson initiated an internal investigation. Notification of this was sent out to Perdfelt, Kolinsky and to one other person in W. The message stipulated that the investigation, which from the start was unbiased, showed that a transfer of L's business can be implemented. The investigation referred to here is the one that was done by L's group and which had come to entirely different conclusions. Abrahamsson's evaluation, however, which was clearly apparent in the message, was that the investigatory group had in fact arrived at a result which made it 'meaningful to carry out a detailed investigation with regard to the transfer according to alternative number two'. The goal of the internal investigation was, with an eye to the transfer in 1981, to state the costs and the consequences both in the short and long term. Among other principal questions to be treated were (a) investment needs within W for the total solution; (b) efficiency of production in L; (c) the organisational form (after the transfer); (d) sale of L's existing premises; (e) the physical transfer of L, time and method; (f) staff matters; and (g) the effect of the transfer on L's results in the short and long term. The members of this internal investigation group were Abrahamsson, Perdfelt, Kolinsky, plus one of his colleagues.

Typical of Phase III was that the work was carried out at rather high speed, and that it concentrated on only a few dimensions of the form of the process, without taking into consideration the content of the course of events. The thought of conducting a dialogue, for example, with those involved did not occur to anyone in the internal investigatory group.

The group had its first meeting on 13 January, with Kolinsky in charge. It was decided that the investigation would be completed on 1 March. Tasks were distributed among the members of the group in accordance with Abrahamsson's directives.

The second meeting took place on 23 January, and this time the tasks that had been performed, and those that had not yet been accomplished, were surveyed. A new list emerged, which contained the unsolved problems as well as some new ones, such as the integration of L in W from the organisational perspective and staff matters such as salaries, allowances for expenses, compensation and so forth. At the same meeting it was decided that Perdfelt was to inform L's employees, and that Kolinsky was to arrange an information meeting with the union in W.

The third meeting took place on 3 February. There it was asserted, according to the minutes of the meeting, that the transfer would take approximately four weeks, and that there would be a drop in production for about the same period. No measures would have to be taken since supply was dependent on the market situation, and 'besides, there are enough standard products in store. Tailor-made products can wait.' Questions such as the organisational form and staff matters must also wait. What was discussed, however, was the question of different alternatives with regard to premises and the resulting consequences. One of the alternatives would demand a high investment and would imply an unchanged production programme and an efficiency level that was acceptable. The second alternative would cost less but would mean that the product programme would have to be reduced. The first categories of products to be affected by this would be customer-adapted products. Information to *L*'s employees and to the union in *W* was postponed until later.

The fourth meeting took place three days later, on 6 February. It was to be a very short meeting with very concise minutes. A decision was taken to investigate further the two alternatives just mentioned. One already knew that the second alternative would imply a halving of the staff, since home production would be reduced while the purchased production would increase. The approximate business results for both of the alternatives remained to be seen, as did also the costs of the physical transfer.

A while later, on the same day as the fourth meeting took place, Kolinsky arranged a meeting with *W*'s local union. Those present were, apart from Kolinsky himself, two representatives of Metall, one of SALF and one of SIF. Kolinsky detailed the position of the investigatory work with regard to the activity of *L*. He spoke of the alternative mentioned above (the third meeting) which fulfilled the requirements of unchanged product programme with equivalent or better production resources, but which demanded relatively large investments. He also detailed the additional alternative which was being investigated, alternative 2, which implied a somewhat reduced product programme. This meant that parts of the product programme would be laid out for contract work. This alternative would entail considerably lower investment requirements. On this occasion the union representatives expressed their concern about market conditions and *L*'s sensitivity to cyclical changes. Of interest in this context is that this concern was a manifestation of the knowledge which the union representatives had received from *W*'s management with regard to the situation in *L*, which had been supplied to legitimate the transfer decision. In view of this the union representatives held that:

> if it is true that the situation of *L*'s products on the market is failing and that the employees in *L* are to move here to *W*, then we have every reason to be

apprehensive that our own and our comrades' employment might be affected.

At this stage a new dimension began to emerge in the process. *W*'s union representatives began to feel some opposition and suspicion with regard to the decision about *L*'s transfer. Not out of sympathy for *L*'s employees, but rather to 'save' themselves from what they conceived of as a threat to their interests. This meeting was closed in a generally negative atmosphere. The union representatives felt that they ought to have been informed, while Kolinsky began to realise that effecting the transfer process was not going to be as easy as all that. He also began to realise how *peu à peu* he had to take over Abrahamsson's responsibility in the affair. I mentioned in the first act, that in connection with the restructuring of *W* in the spring of 1980, a new production department had been established. Kolinsky was employed in connection with this in May 1980. I also mentioned that, being new to the job, he lacked the historical connection to the course of events with Goliat Inc. and *W*. In the beginning he acted in a relatively insensitive manner since he was, as he himself said, immune to the ongoing conflicts between the units in transformation. Now that he was acting in a more concrete way on the scene of the course of events, he began to experience the conflicting nature of the situation.

> When I appeared in this process together with L. Abrahamsson I didn't realize that it would be like this. Naturally, I had my doubts about what we were going to do, since many people who've been here for a long time said that it wouldn't work, one wouldn't be able to change anything. Being new, I had no historical perspectives on this matter, so I said that it had to work. Now, afterwards, I think that my attitude was used, in one way or another, to drive people on, so to speak, without knowing that I was doing so. (B. Kolinsky)

The fifth meeting took place on 25 February. Kolinsky was summoned to this meeting. On the day before, the 24th, he had decided, together with Abrahamsson, that from now on it would be a matter of two entirely new alternatives. One of them, it was assumed, could retain the existing product programme of *L*, and at least equivalent conditions of production after the transfer. The second would worsen the conditions of production somewhat. At the meeting it was simply stated that from now on it would be these two alternatives that were going to count.

I discovered, from a conversation that I was later to have with Ziegler, that he was very dissatisfied with the way in which this series of meetings had been handled. He held that far too much emphasis had been laid on the formal aspect of the transfer, or rather on some of its physical aspects.

He would have preferred it if discussions had been held parallel to this with *L*'s staff. To Ziegler it was important to take advantage of the 'good manpower and competency which *L*'s employees represent and possess'.

> I think that this lot in *L* have worked well during this time. When you speak to them like this, there are no problems. They work and they struggle. We must take advantage of this attitude and not waste time and resources discussing spray-booths and whether or not to have water taps in the workshop premises. (M. Ziegler)

Parallel to these activities that were in progress, and which were gradually to determine *L*'s destiny, Ziegler worked feverishly with *W* as a whole. The idea of a total reorganisation once again began to make itself felt. He believed that the business ought to be able to function much better than it did. The production units were screened off from the market units, a consequence remnant of the earlier structure. It was then that the old *S*-firm was subordinated to *W* as a juridical sales subsidiary. Eight months later Ziegler was to start up an extensive reorganisation which already, i.e. February 1981, was being prepared and was maturing. On 19 February, between the fourth and the fifth meetings, Ziegler gave a commentary to the board on *W*'s annual accounts for the whole of 1980. In the report Ziegler says that

> The *ES*-unit, which consists of *W*'s section as well as *L*, had sales of 27.1 Mkr for 1980. The result amounts to 1.4 Mkr, which is 0.4 Mkr better than the budget and 3.0 Mkr better than 1979. The improvement lies entirely in *W*'s section of the *ES*-business, whereas *L* has fallen below the budget result with 0.1 Mkr [. . .]. *L*'s sales amount to 7.1 Mkr, which is equal to the budget and 27% above the previous year. The contribution is, as before, higher than the budget and amounts per whole year to 23.3% against 19.5%. During the fourth quarter the unit has been debited with negative overhead variances of 0.2 Mkr as well as negative calculation variances of 0.1. The unit has not, therefore, given any surplus during the fourth quarter in spite of positive price variances. The result amounts per whole year to 0.2 Mkr against the budget 1.3 Mkr. Compared to the calculation of the third quarter this is a decline of 0.2 Mkr.

Perdfelt's dividedness

Perdfelt had been assigned the task of officially informing *L*'s staff. At that time he had become unsure of his position. Deep inside he felt solidarity with *L*'s personnel. At the same time he was reminded at every meeting with Abrahamsson and Kolinsky that he must act as *W*'s spokesman. He simply informed his staff after each meeting of the practical deliberations and discussions that had been held within the group in connection with various eventualities. He never spoke of the impressions that he had gained from Ziegler, on any occasion, nor from Abrahamsson and Kolinsky. These impressions clearly indicated that the management really did want to put the transfer into effect. For the staff, however, there was still hope.

> We have produced excellent results during 1980 and everything points to the first half of 1981 being equally good. We shall not produce a negative result at the end of this year. What we're asking for is to work in peace, without disturbances and suspicion. (L's staff)

For Perdfelt it was all in Ziegler's head; but he believed, or wanted to believe, that the decision depended on the results. He thought, like the staff, that 'now that we've shown good figures, the transfer will lose its current appeal'.

> He [M. Ziegler] has clearly strived to gather all of the activity to W and thus he also wanted L to move. I think that his overall goal is to gather all of the resources within W's premises [. . .]. There are many indications that this overall goal overshadows the rational deliberations. But M. Ziegler should have had to rethink his plans against the background of the fine figures that we've produced for 1980 and for the beginning of 1981. This should at least have made it more difficult for him to make the decision and shown him that the transfer is an unnecessary and difficult process. But instead he used our fine results to legitimise his intentions in a devilish formulation in a commentary on the annual accounts. (R. Perdfelt)

During this whole period Perdfelt tried to call the attention of the management to the way that he experienced the situation and to how he believed the staff at L were affected.

> I've told them, or at least I've tried to tell them, how this affects our activity negatively, how our working spirit is sinking and how we're beginning to feel pressurized. (R. Perdfelt)

But he had a strong feeling that they did not want to listen to him. Both Kolinsky and Abrahamsson, he said, could understand what he said intellectually but they screened themselves off emotionally. 'I reckon that they reason roughly like this; the less I know the better' (R. Perdfelt).

On the other hand Perdfelt believed, until the last moment, that something would happen to alter the plans for the transfer. During various conversations with Abrahamsson, who is subordinate to Ziegler, he realised that the former did not really share the opinions of the latter with regard to the transfer. He was simply not as convinced of the necessity of the transfer, Perdfelt said.

> But it seems as though he's also caught in the middle and feels that it's his duty to carry out the plans and intentions which come to him from above. I can understand that L. Abrahamsson has quite a difficult position with regard to myself, just as I have with regard to my staff. (R. Perdfelt)

At the same time, he felt that people on the middle levels (including himself), should have been able to influence it all. He reproached Abrahamsson for not having taken *L*'s side if it was true that he did not believe in the transfer. Shortly afterwards Perdfelt was exposed to the same criticism from the staff. They held that he was to a large extent to blame. They were deeply dissatisfied with his way of handling contact with the management and with his 'cowardly attitude' when it came to speaking 'on behalf of the staff'. On one occasion, one of *L*'s employees said:

> If I'd been local manager I would have stormed into *W*'s corridors like a raging elephant, slammed my fist on M. Ziegler's table and told him everything that we have to go around carrying within us here. Then I'm sure they would have listened.

At this stage one had already begun to realise, from *W*'s side, that Perdfelt was in a difficult situation. It could be seen that he had ended up in a tight corner and that he was partly to blame. According to both Kolinsky and Abrahamsson, he had gone wrong from the start in connection with the internal investigation.

> He doesn't even know which leg he wants to stand on. He doesn't know whether he wants to belong to this lot (*W*'s) or the staff in *L*. (B. Kolinsky)

But does this mean that they showed any kind of understanding of Perdfelt's situation? Everything pointed rather to the fact that his 'weak' character was exploited from *W*'s side to push the transfer question, and at the same time to legitimise the action, if necessary, in the face of *L*'s employees, by saying that 'Your local manager agrees with us.' This, indeed, he had never done even if he had suffered difficulties in asserting his standpoint.

Towards the end of February the situation in *L* was strained. A general feeling of uncertainty and insecurity prevailed. Numerous rumours circulated. *L*'s employees had no chance of getting anything confirmed. Ziegler had a feeling that this was the case and wanted to do something about it. On 6 March he came to *L* for the first time in the context of the process and held what, in his opinion, was supposed to be an informative discussion about the various possibilities for the continued activity of *L*. All he said was that he intended to demand MBL negotiations. This had a totally confusing effect on the employees. They had heard of the numerous investigations that were in progress. They had not thought that the process was so far advanced, and that the decision was as good as taken. The 'staff', they said, 'went around here for half a year without any kind of information whatsoever'. 'Totally ignorant of what was happening.' 'At the same time', they continued, 'when these investigations were initiated they ignited all kinds of imaginings. We began to think up all sorts of things', they said, 'and this was actually due to the simple fact that we hadn't been given any information or clear motives as to why these investigations had been initiated.' They knew, however, that the investigatory groups were given a number of alternatives to evaluate. They also knew that they themselves had worked out an alternative in the first investigatory group, and that this alternative recommended an investment in the continued activity of *L*. It was this alternative that had the greatest anchorage with the staff, and upon which they had laid down the most work. According to the staff, 'this alternative was not even received by the management in *W*'. 'They simply pretended that the alternative didn't exist.' 'And what'll happen now', *L*'s indignant employees held, was that 'they [M. Ziegler] come here and virtually say that there's no point in struggling.' 'You're going to move.' 'Then he took a pen' – this is still according to *L*'s employees – 'and drew on a pad what was supposed to be a negotiation pattern: local negotiations, difference of opinion, central negotiations, difference of opinion, Goliat Inc. – *W*, decides.' In retrospect, it is possible to see that this is what happened. But at that time the employees in *L* could not believe that was how it would be.

> The way we see it is that this shows that they [*W*] had a definite goal – this is how it's going to be. We feel that he should already have told us about this last autumn [August–September 1980, soon after the board meeting]. He ought to have told us about his intentions in straightforward language and not manipulated us in this way. Of course, if you ask him, why haven't you done it before, why haven't you come up to *L* and told people that they're going to be moved, then he probably would've answered – 'I couldn't do that since I had no grounds to believe it to be possible. The investigation wasn't ready yet.' In other words there's always a way of safeguarding oneself, but deep down this was manipulation. (*L*'s employees)

The employees were in a state of despair. They could not and did not want to understand the conduct of the management. They would have preferred it if management had at least shown some interest in them, and their alternative. They had expected management to ask them to clarify alternative 4 and to investigate it further. Now they were convinced that their alternative had been ignored simply because it was not in accordance with the intentions of the management.

The scapegoat

Stormy discussions arose among *L*'s employees. They experienced the situation as very serious and troublesome and tried to agree on a strategy. Then came the 'inevitable' conclusion that someone had be sacrificed – made scapegoat. Perdfelt suited this role perfectly. He was local manager and from the perspective of the employees he was the spokesman for the management of the firm. The fact that he did not see himself as such could not be taken seriously by the employees. 'He must have known about the transfer intentions', they said. 'At least he could have figured that out.' 'He was present at every turn of the investigation.' 'Or else he's not capable of putting two and two together and is paralysed', they said, 'and that doesn't make it any better.' 'In other words, it's his fault.'

Thus it seems that everyone was unhappy with Perdfelt, yet for different reasons: the difference being due to the fact that the employees had always been divided into two blocks. One consisted of the constructors and the workshop staff, and the other consisted of the salesmen, Malisman and his colleagues. These were not really bothered about the transfer. They were (and are) directly subordinate to Abrahamsson, their formal boss, and they were not interested in acting against him. Furthermore, their work involved a great deal of travelling, often over long distances. Thus for them it was of no importance whether they had *L* or *W* as their base. The employees in the first block had always looked upon Malisman and his colleagues with suspicion. They were experienced as deviants without any feeling for *L*'s identity and as 'lackeys' of the management in *W*.

> We never count on them [S. Malisman and his colleagues]. On the whole, we can never speak of our plans in their presence. It would get to L. Abrahamsson in no time. In fact, one could even say they're outright traitors.
> (*L*'s employees – block one or the 'loyal group')

This polarisation was to be further reinforced, and to a certain extent used by *W*'s management to play off one group against the other. Moreover the belief was held by Malisman and his colleagues, who had never agreed with Perdfelt, that he was useless as local manager, and this was reinforced. Not because he hadn't been able to do anything about the transfer, but because 'he is incompetent' (S. Malisman).

The dramatic part of all this is that one let the goat be the gardener. When W was to appoint R. Perdfelt as local manager, the rumour circulated that they would be getting a very competent person. When I met him I truly believed that he was a knowledgeable workshop man. But after a month I discovered that he's totally incompetent for the position which he occupies. He has nerves that creep on the surface and that just won't do in this job. (S. Malisman)

Malisman also thought that it was wrong of W's management to involve Perdfelt in the investigations. 'He can't handle the situation', said Malisman, 'either he says too much and excites people unnecessarily, or else he says nothing and allows speculations to circulate wildly.'

It is of interest in this context to recall that Malisman had professional contacts with L as early as the time of its founder, B. Andersson. He was given employment in L already in connection with its acquisition, and when Andersson left the company Malisman felt that he possessed the required qualities to be appointed as local manager.

Fighting, slander, criticism, polemics, suspicion, mobilising of prejudices, scapegoats, are some words which can be said to have characterised the situation in L when the MBL negotiations were initiated on 27 March 1981. During this meeting of 14 April 1981 (MBL negotiations) the participants devoted most of their time and energy to a stormy discussion of what had happened and been written (and not been written) at the previous meeting. But what did actually happen in connection with this meeting of 14 April? What line of development did the course of events take there? In order to answer these questions we must now return to Phase IV, and go through the events of the second part.

PHASE IV – CONFUSION AND MANIPULATION (SECOND SECTION)

Perdfelt had been the secretary at this meeting. He promised to keep minutes that were true to the meeting; but the employees' representatives who were dissatisfied with the contents of the minutes of the previous meeting (27 March) wanted to make sure that this time it would be explicitly written in the minutes that: (1) the alternative to the transfer presented by L's staff ought to be carefully considered, and (2) it seemed as though the decision to transfer had already been made by W before any negotiations had been entered in the matter. Furthermore, they requested that it be written in the minutes that the negotiations had broken down, and that they would return with a demand for negotiation with regard to damages for breach of MBL § 11.

All involved experienced this situation as very tedious. According to Perdfelt it was due to the management's flippant attitude that the negotiations had taken the form of a conflict and that general disagreement prevailed:

> Bit by bit, the negotiations broke down, and finally they broke down altogether. (R. Perdfelt)

According to Ziegler everything that happened was, as a whole, incomprehensible and unmotivated. He said that:

> When we felt that we were forced to present a concrete proposition, then we summoned to MBL-negotiations. It was then that these local authorities [the employees' representatives] experienced that we had not given them sufficient information. They refused to summon to MBL-negotiations and wanted first to have an information meeting. Then this meeting turned out to be an MBL-negotiation in any case, but during the whole process they refused to enter into detailed MBL-negotiations and evaluate the alternative of moving here [to W], because they claimed that we'd decided in advance to move the business here. It's obvious, as I said to them, that we wouldn't initiate an MBL-negotiation if we weren't sure that it was the best proposition. We don't simply go out and say: 'Let's think about moving the business here'. (M. Ziegler)

Surely it's enough, he said, that the staff themselves have been involved in the groundwork for the decision: they had participated in the investigation. They had also looked at the consequences and the savings that would be made compared to the existing situation. 'Why has it become like this', Ziegler wondered. 'Why did we have such great problems that we couldn't even manage to write common minutes for the meeting?'

For this is exactly what happened at the meeting of 14 April. There were no common minutes, no minutes at all. What there was, on the other hand, was a claim for damages.

> The union representatives have also started up an MBL-negotiation, § 12 or whatever it's called, because we hadn't given sufficient information in February. Now they're demanding damages. (M. Ziegler)

To Abrahamsson it all seemed like a farce. He felt that a situation that was as clear as daylight ought not to be made so complicated. The management of the firm discussed the matter internally, he said. They discussed what the transfer would imply, and how it would be shaped, before demanding MBL negotiations. The approach in such matters seemed clear to him. 'The first thing they do', he thought, 'is to gather some elementary information on the changes that are wanted and then simply to inform the union representative of these intentions.' The trade unions concerned in this case were Metall and SIF on a local level (in the district where L was located). In the firm L there are no local unions, only representatives; L is a too small unit. 'This', said Abrahamsson, 'made the picture even more complicated.'

> You don't speak with one party but with several of them representing different interests. What I mean is that the local union representatives in [...] have no knowledge of the current situation in L and yet they're the ones who sit and negotiate on their behalf. That negotiation went completely wrong. The union in [...] sued us quite simply because we hadn't followed MBL. They claimed damages. They maintain that I ought to have summoned them to the information meetings which I held each quarter with L. [...] First of all they got hung up on our having carried out the investigation in January/February without having informed them. But now they've withdrawn this accusation and instead got stuck on the general duty of information which we, from the management, have not fulfilled [...] so things just turned out wrong. We had two meetings [27 March and 14 April 1981] and we couldn't agree about what was going to be written in the minutes. (L. Abrahamsson)

Different strategies

Let us now try to take a closer look at the meaning of what both Ziegler and Abrahamsson said: 'We couldn't come to any agreement over what would be written in the minutes.' What is this about? Is it a matter of checking and signing some formulations or is it something more essential than that? To gain a better understanding of the situation we ought to examine the texts of the minutes; for there were two sets of minutes, and neither of them was checked and signed. First let us see how the local union representatives experienced the situation.

According to the Act on Employee Participation in Decision-making § 11 it is the duty of the employer to take the initiative for negotiations if he wishes to bring about changes in the business. This happened in this case. W's management got in touch with the local union representatives and demanded negotiations. The letter came on 11 March and the negotiation was to take place on 27 March 1981. Then, when everyone was sitting at the negotiating table, the union had no documentation of W's proposition (to transfer L). The praxis in this context is for the union to have access to the same documentation as the employer. This documentation was not accessible on the first occasion for negotiations. This meant that the actual negotiation did not take place until 14 April, when the union had received parts of the documentation of the decision, or 'the documents of intention'. 'It wasn't easy', the union said, 'to get this documentation.'

> There was a lot of talk about this. We received a small part, then it came out
> that there were additional papers in the matter which we had not received.
> We were obliged to fight for every single paper. Still we didn't get everything.
> (SIF and Metall's local union representatives)

According to the union, this was why there was not much to be discussed
on 27 March. However, after having gone through the acquired
documentation,

> . . . then [14 April] it was confirmed that the firm had already taken its
> decision so there was no reason to go on with MBL-negotiations. (SIF and
> Metall's local union representatives)

The union's view that the decision had been made in advance was clear
and unambiguous. The arguments they presented were numerous. For
example, they commented on the fact that in the minutes of the meeting on
27 March, the goal of the company (W) was to incorporate L into the
rest of the business on W's premises to even out employment, lessen
sensitivity to cyclical changes and increase the possibility of coordination
effects. The union regarded these reasons with scepticism. In the first place
they believed that this was definite proof that the company's goal of
transfer was already clear from the beginning. Secondly they believed that
W's representatives 'manipulated' the data when they spoke of the
levelling out of employment and the reduction of sensitivity to cyclical
changes.

> The argument of levelling out employment is a hoax. The fact that there are,
> today, difficulties in occupying the staff in W [. . .] is not without
> significance. Sensitivity to cyclical changes is not something which has been
> felt at L. There is plenty to do, and there would have been even more to do
> had they been given free hands. And then we have these investigations which
> were started as early as the autumn of 1980 and we feel that the union
> organizations ought already then to have been brought into the matter. (Local
> union representatives)

We know that in connection with the last point in the above quotation
Abrahamsson and Ziegler were of the opinion that this 'investigation was
appointed by the personnel in L and did not concern a transfer'. According
to the union, however, both they and the personnel ought to have
participated in the discussion from the very beginning, preferably at the
point when Ziegler was gathering arguments for these recommendations
for a transfer which he intended to present at the board meeting. The

union also made a detailed analysis of the internal investigations that were done in January and February (see Phase III). There it was confirmed that the details of the transfer were investigated and just about finished. Investment calculations had been done, workshop and office layout had been considered; they had even discussed the physical aspects of the transfer. In other words, as far as the union was concerned, the race had already been run and there was no reason to sit and argue in an MBL negotiation since . . .

> It is conducted on the conditions of the employers and, thus, we maintain that it is no negotiation. (Local union representatives)

What then are the alternatives? The union says that there were not any.

> . . . then one lets the employer decide, since that's how it'll be in the end anyway. But the point of the Act on Employee Participation in Decision-making is for the employees to have an influence in the taking of decisions within the firm. Here, all that can be said is that your opinions are of no interest whatsoever since they don't coincide with that which has been decided by Goliat Inc. There are many noteworthy details in what we have observed. On the 30th March 1981, an internal notification was handed out to the employees (in both W and L), in which it is written that: 'L is to be transferred to . . .'. We received this notification on the 2nd April. After having had the first sitting. What other explanation could there be to this than that we've been treated like playthings. (Local union representatives)

Rightly enough, the notification referred to by the union in the quotation above came to L on 30 March 1981, three days after the first negotiation and two weeks before the fateful meeting of 14 April when the negotiations broke down. The text in the notification is *de facto* edited in such a way that it contradicts W's argument of truly wanting to discuss the eventuality of a transfer during these two meetings of negotiation. The formulation of the text is as follows.

L MOVES TO [W'S TOWN]
L in [. . .], which today employs approximately 20 people, develops, produces and sells standard as well as special equipment for the *ES*-business. The unit was acquired by Goliat Inc. in 1976, and since 1979 has been included, organizationally speaking, in W's *ES*-department. The business has, in spite of a positive development, proved to be very sensitive to cyclical changes. Profitability has been poor. Internal investigation has shown that the assortment is of interest for W and, also, that our own production is competitive in comparison to how it would be if we were to buy the products from external producers; on the condition that we are able to

utilize the capacity of the business even during an economic recession. A transfer of *L*'s activity from [*L*'s town] to [*W*'s town] has been suggested by the management of *W* in order to minimize the risks of additional losses, increase the flexibility and, in addition to this, render possible future coordination, particularly on the office employees' side, with *W*'s other activities. The investigation shows that there is room on *W*'s premises, and that a modern business can be accomplished if certain investments are made, particularly with regard to lifting and handling. For this reason, those concerned among *L*'s staff were informed on the 6th of March that MBL-negotiations were to be initiated on the 27th of March. The aim of the firm with the MBL-negotiations is to be able to effectuate a transfer of the business to *W* before the end of the year. (Internal notification 2/81)

It is not difficult to understand that both *L*'s staff and the union resisted on 14 April and felt that there was nothing about which to negotiate. The editor of this notification is the personnel manager of *W*, and Ziegler is the responsible editor. This does not make things easier.

Manipulatory attempts

The time has come to examine the texts of the minutes from 14 April. At the end of the meeting Perdfelt had a draft of the minutes. Everyone wanted to go through what had been written, especially the union representatives. Perdfelt, who had every reason to believe that the minutes had this time been firmly established with all the parties, edited a text which he first sent to Abrahamsson for checking and signing, which were later to be sent to the union for the same reason. Below I shall take up only those paragraphs which were the objects of dispute and strife.

§ 3 The employees' representatives held that the information given to the staff on the 6/3/81 and the information pamphlet 2/81, together with the documentation handed over, clearly showed that the firm had taken the transfer decision before demanding MBL-negotiations in the matter. The firm's representatives resolutely denied that any decision had been made.

§ 4 The employees' representatives demanded that the negotiations be regarded as having broken down and will return with the demand for negotiation with regard to damages according to MBL § 10 for breach of MBL § 11, as well as negotiation in the issue of facts in accordance with MBL § 12.

§ 5 The documentation that was handed out by the firm was reviewed and it was noted then that the minutes from the investigatory meeting of the 4/12/80, among other things, were missing. Copies of these minutes were handed out.

(From the last version and unsigned minutes, 14 April 1981)

Abrahamsson, who received these minutes, refused to sign. He notified Perdfelt that something must be done, and some time later he phoned him and said that the minutes ought to be reformulated. It was then that the 'strange thing', as Perdfelt said, happened: Abrahamsson dictated new minutes over the telephone.

> How come you're dictating minutes which I'm assumed to have written? Then he [L. Abrahamsson] said that M. Ziegler and himself had come to an agreement with the union that this is what must be written. (R. Perdfelt)

Perdfelt found this very strange since Ziegler had not even been present at the negotiation. 'But', he thought, 'if both the parties involved are in agreement, then there's nothing else to be done but to obey orders. I then wrote what they had told me to write.' It read as follows:

§ 1 – Minutes checker . . .
§ 2 – Previous minutes from the 27th of March 1981 were reviewed.
§ 3 – L. Abrahamsson gave the employers' view of the proposition worked out by the staff in *L*.
§ 4 – The employees' representatives did not feel they could accept the transfer proposition.

The parties parted in disagreement and the local negotiations were brought to a close.
(Draft of minute 2 – dictated by L. Abrahamsson to R. Perdfelt)

Perdfelt sent the minutes to the union, as he had been told to do, and he was astonished when they replied that 'this was pure manipulation and that they'd never been in agreement with anyone about anything of the sort'. Ziegler had indeed attempted to pursuade the union to change the text of the minutes; but they had refused to align themselves with what they considered to be a settlement at the expense of *L*'s employees. To Ziegler it was important that it be written in the minutes that the parties had parted in disagreement; not that the negotiations had broken down. In this way it would have been possible to make the decision from *W*'s side and to implement it right away without having to go to central negotiations.

> Had we checked and signed these minutes then we would not have had the possibility of bringing this to central negotiations, because then we would have concluded, so to speak, the local negotiations, and already then left it to the employers to take their decision. It's quite remarkable that they act in this way. He [M. Ziegler] wasn't even present at the negotiations. (Local union representatives)

To Perdfelt this came as a 'shock'. The union sent the drafts of the minutes back to him together with the indignant comments to which I have just referred. Abrahamsson wanted Perdfelt at least to sign as keeper of the minutes. He refused to do so; instead he sent the dictated draft to Abrahamsson with the following accompanying letter.

> I'm very dubious about putting my name under the minutes, bearing in mind the way in which they came about. Had the parties been in agreement as to the formulation of the minutes then there would have been no question, but in this particular case the thought of signing minutes which do not recognize the very fact that the negotiations had broken down is disagreeable to me. To my mind this does not mean that I'm being disloyal, but rather that I suspect that the affair could be blown up and that I personally might be subjected to juridically unpleasant consequences. (R. Perdfelt's letter to L. Abrahamsson)

The lift dropped

When I asked Perdfelt to comment on these events, he said that to him it was morally impossible to edit and sign minutes which had been dictated to him by a superior who had not even been present at the meeting. 'This is contrary to my principles and my conviction', he said.

Perdfelt expressed these views in the presence of *W*'s management on several occasions. Their confidence in him decreased markedly. To them this was 'proof' that he did not have the interest of the firm in mind. He seemed to be on *L*'s employees and the union's side. When he expressed his desire no longer to participate in the negotiations which he experienced as unpleasant, the management made it easier for him by not demanding that he adopt any standpoint. He felt relieved not to have to participate any more. I am still not sure whether the initiative came from him or whether he was 'put aside' by the management because of his conduct with regard to the minutes. His version states that he had taken the initiative to make a retreat:

> [...] I have withdrawn from the negotiations and I have not been involved at all since then. The negotiations have subsequently gone above my head. But I still think that it was terrible of M. Ziegler to try to get the union to make a settlement over the minutes. I hadn't thought that of him. But it's the bitter truth. (R. Perdfelt)

This was the situation at the end of the fourth phase. Ziegler did not get things to go the way he wanted them. Now that negotiations had broken down he was forced to wait with the decision until the central negotiations had taken place. This would take another few months, a loss of time which W had hoped to avoid by using unorthodox methods. This procedure became generally known among L's employees, who became very indignant. Feelings were running high, and the remainder of the process took the form of a massive confrontation. 'Now we're going to be driven over', L's employees thought, 'but they're not going to get away with it so easily.' The question of damages was also to come into the picture at a later stage.

Here we put an end to Phase IV's second section and to the reconstructed part of the case.

EPISODE II

Introduction

The month of April was an eventful period. Positions were locked since L's employees had decided not to give up without a struggle. The employees' representatives had managed to act in such a way as to get the process to 'stretch over a longer horizon of time than had been expected'; the negotiations would eventually take place on a central level and the question of damages was a reality. Perdfelt was more ambivalent than ever, especially since he had now 'decided' no longer to participate in any discussion. The dividedness which he had felt previously was reinforced now that he had withdrawn from the formal dimension of the process. Abrahamsson was dissatisfied with the way in which the situation had developed. He partly reproached Perdfelt for what had happened and interpreted his conduct as incompetence. This he did more or less openly during the conversations which he and I had together. He was less open when he laid part of the blame on Ziegler who had 'forced' him to implement and to push various questions in this process, questions in which he himself did not believe. He said:

> I myself was not particularly convinced as to whether this [L's transfer] was the right decision from the beginning. Now, in retrospect, I think that it will be better from an economic point of view when they move here [to W]. M. Ziegler has always thought so and one could say he's managed to convince me. Moreover, in this matter it's me that has to act in a concrete manner and be confronted with people. But then I personally feel that there aren't so many facts to speak of in this process. It's more a matter of emotional problems, friction and blockages. (L. Abrahamsson)

Kolinsky had no greater problems with this. He was still somewhat on the outside in spite of his having participated in the various meetings. L was still formally subordinated to Abrahamsson's department. He participated as an expert in questions of production, and gave advice in connection with the coming integration of *L*. At the same time, on another level, discussions about a total reorganisation of *W* were in progress. Among other things, the possibility was discussed of subordinating *L* to Kolinsky's production department, thereby liberating Abrahamsson from his *L* problems. The latter, who had originally been a technician, was exclusively interested in marketing. It was a task which, for that matter, was deemed by the management to suit him perfectly. In other words, Kolinsky's participation in the process was by no means an accidental occurrence; it fell in line with the overall plans which were gradually to be implemented.

Ziegler seemed to govern over the whole affair with an elevated philosophical calm. He had people who managed the whole situation, people who, so to speak, fought on the battlefield, while he could devote his attention to less trivial matters which were yet of significance for the firm as a whole – namely the imminent total reorganisation.

At the same time other negotiations were in progress within *W*. Those concerning the introduction of a short-time week had already been initiated in February. This was a consequence of a combination of circumstances. Sales were not particularly flourishing, partly due to the paralysing construction to which I have referred in the first act of the case; the warehouse was overfilled. The board had given orders that something be done about the situation. Added to this was the fact that the organisation, or structural formation of the firm, was conducive to grave misunderstandings among the units. The orders made by the buying department were more a matter of routine than an answer to the needs of production. The production department, which had almost no contact with the marketing and sales personnel, belonged to an 'independent' juridicial subsidiary firm. The employees on logistics and stocks treated the orders they received in about the same way as one treats a budget request in circulation for comments at a government office. 'They have the dusty bureaucrat's culture', Kolinsky said, 'they don't even know what a customer looks like.' One of Kolinsky's tasks in this context was to computerise purchase and inventory procedures, a part of the extensive reorganisation. *L*'s employees regarded this with suspicion, since they held that their 'production is so special that it ought not to be programmed'. It is a matter of customised products which differ from each other and which demand that the producers have a certain amount of freedom of action as far as orders are concerned.

Negotiations about this short-time week finally were held. The intention was to introduce a short-time week which meant working three days a week from 30 April until 18 September, including the holiday month of July. The employees would be compensated, and during this period they would be given two days' training each week.

These negotiations were not directly connected with the process that I was studying. I had not, thus, in any active way attempted to participate in them. I had, however, got in touch with the local unions in W and attempted to find out how they, considering their own problems with the short-time week, regarded L's transfer. The answer was unanimous: 'We would readily have the work but not the men.' At the same time they knew that this was wishful thinking. Circumstances such as the legislation and the 'necessary' competence of L's employees, made the realisation of this wish an impossibility. This statement (and the event as such: the short-time week) is of interest from another perspective as it shows, in the first instance, that Ziegler's fundamental argument about the levelling out of employment lacked grounds in reality. In the second instance it explains the negligible support which the local unions in W were prepared to give to L's employees. At a later stage of the process, when the representatives of all the parties met around the negotiating table, it could be said that W's union representatives had a markedly aggressive attitude towards L's representatives who they experienced as 'troublemakers, spoilt brats'. I shall return to discuss these meetings later.

The author's participant observation

During the rest of April I pursued intensive activities so as to justify my presence among various groups and individuals who were participants in the process. I did this in several steps. (a) I confirmed with W's management, above all with Ziegler (vice managing director), that I would be able to move freely and participate in various activities that were relevant to the process. (b) I subsequently got into contact with all of the parties involved and investigated how they felt about the eventuality of my participation (by all the parties involved I mean Kolinsky, Abrahamsson, Perdfelt, L's employees, the local departments of the union from L's side and the local union in W). (c) I drew up a preliminary reconstruction of the course of events which I then presented to each one of the parties involved. The purpose of these lectures was to make sure that I had really reached (or received information about) all the individuals and groups who directly or indirectly had something to do with the process. I also wished to make sure that I had not missed anything in the process, such as a meeting, an investigation, or a document. Another purpose of the lectures was to acquire additional information by means of the discussions which followed each lecture and to have any possible misconceptions of mine rectified. A third purpose was simply to socialise among the groups and individuals with whom I would be spending quite a lot of time.

The attitudes of the parties

Ziegler saw in my interest the opportunity of having an outsider as a discussion partner who would also have some insight into the internal affairs of the firm. Apart from the concrete case of L, we discussed the extensive reorganisation, which occupied him at that stage. I noticed, during these discussions, that the transfer decision of L was seen as an integral part of an overall policy, which in turn was a consequence of the problems with which the whole of W was grappling. Indeed, these problems prompted an endeavour to attain rationalisations and coordination effects. The question was to what extent. What was more urgent, however, was the actual production in W and the relation between the production and the sales. L, as Ziegler has remarked on a certain occasion, was the fragment in the whole. Paradoxically, however, it is there that the energy was concentrated for almost two years.

Perdfelt and L's employees had a positive attitude towards my participation in the process for the simple reason, I think, that they saw in me someone who took an interest in their problems. No-one (from W) had devoted any time to investigating how they experienced the situation, what their interest was in the matter, how they worked and what they worked with, nor what significance the whole affair had for them. Abrahamsson, for example, had on some occasions said that 'the less one speaks with them about it [the transfer process] the better'. There were many others in W's management who were of the same opinion. L's employees were well aware of this and were quite dissatisfied. They interpreted this attitude as indifference. They believed that from W's side they were regarded as insignificant in all respects, even with regard to their professional competence. This was not true, however, since W had in all its investigations and meetings emphasised time and again the value of the competence which existed in L.

The local unions and the employees' representatives were more than willing for me to take a stand in this question. While the former wished to gain a hearing for their demands for damages, the latter wished to discuss and gain confirmation of their opinion that this ought from the start to have been a matter for W's employees. 'They are the most numerous and they have concrete problems with the short-time week.' These viewpoints, diverging orientations and different perspectives meant that the information which I was to receive was both rich and multi-faceted and, to a great extent, reflected the complexity which is characteristic of the whole process.

The documents

Towards the end of April I had two long conversations with Ziegler. We discussed various matters with regard to the extensive reorganisation, the actual transfer process and my participation in it. I expressed my desire to gain access to all the previously executed investigations, the minutes and the correspondence that existed. At the same time I tried to find out as much as possible about the background from which the transfer idea had been generated. Ziegler could not find the documents at issue at the time, but he promised to compile an account of the course of events and to send it to me together with the documents. Two weeks later I received a box which contained everything from internal memoranda to minutes of meetings and annual report commentaries. Most of these documents have been used in my description of the course of events until now. I was then to discover some gaps, as I have mentioned earlier, in my collection of documents. I made this discovery partly by making up my own composition, and partly during my various conversations with the parties involved. It seemed that different people had different kinds of documents. The employees' representatives, for example, had the various versions of the minutes from the meeting of 14 April; Abrahamsson had the reports from the first investigations and also some specific economic calculations concerning *L*'s profitability; Perdfelt had some letters and directives which originally came from Abrahamsson. I added to my collection of documents as time went on and as I advanced in the process and interacted with its participants.

At that time – towards the end of April – I knew that many things were going to happen, and that a large amount of documents would be prepared, written and become relevant. My problem was to gain access to these documents at the rate of their appearance. Ziegler offered a solution by giving me a pigeonhole with my name on it, in his secretary's office. She was asked to put a copy of all the incoming documents into my pigeonhole. I visited her regularly to fetch my 'post', and this gave me opportunity to gather information by speaking to people in *W* and check the validity of the information which I already had. It was a defective solution, however, since some documents were, so to speak, circulated unofficially. For example, it might be a matter of *L*'s internal documentation and the records of the course of events, or a matter of letters from *L*'s employees to the local union. Perdfelt took on the task of leaving me the copies of any documents there might be on each of the occasions when I visited *L*.

Each time I was given a document, I tried to find out the circumstances around it, the intentions which dictated the need for it, and any reactions which it might create.

The sojourn in L

Until the end of July I interacted intensively with the parties involved. I pursued in-depth interviews and had conversations on several occasions with groups and individuals whom I had identified as participants in the process. I thus decided to spend as much time in *L* as I could, and was permitted, in order to get as close as possible to the everyday life of *L*'s employees and their 'everyday' interpretations of the process. I imagine that such an interpretation would differ considerably from the interpretation that they would have given me had I only met them in a few single-interviewing situations. I wanted to avoid organised situational descriptions of the kind where the respondent reformulates his descriptions in relation to the interviewer and in relation to the actual experienced situation. Feelings were so loaded, and the conditions so tangible, that one or two interviews would not have sufficed for an understanding of the various dimensions of the process. It felt more meaningful instead to stay with *L*'s employees and, in the course of a few weeks, gradually work out a more complete situational description and interpretation.

Over and above my activity in *W*, I stayed for two to three days a week in *L*. My work there took on various forms. I was installed in the conference room, where I had my documents, notes, tape-recorder, and other material. I moved freely in the buildings and conversed with various people as time allowed. Afterwards I always returned to the conference room to dictate or to make notes of certain impressions and compile the information I had received. At the same time I learnt quite a lot about people's tasks and about the connection between the various operations in the work. Furthermore, I learnt about the relations that existed between different people, owing both to the nature of the work, and to more personal, unspoken rules.

These conversations unfolded in the light of the knowledge which I already had of the process and of the particular characteristics which I managed to sort out by reading and structuring the documents. During these conversations I attempted to gather the various dimensions which provided me with information as to how the parties involved experienced their respective situations. My attention was focused, in the first instance, on the following aspects.

(a) The actions of the actors as they were experienced and as they were carried out against the background of the possibilities, and the difficulties which emerged in the context of the transfer.

(b) The interrelations of the actors, the significance that these relations have for them, what they expect from these relations, the conflicts which arise and the possible solutions which are adopted.

(c) How the actors evaluate their relations to others, how they judge their situations, their activities and, in relation to this, the reasons they have to be satisfied or/and dissatisfied, their hopes and disappointments.

(d) How they regard the opportunities of action which they and others have.

A principal idea in these conversations, apart from those just mentioned, was to attempt to see how each actor conceived of the transfer process, and what differences and similarities might be found compared to the conceptions of others – in other words, the various actors' versions of what had happened. For me it was a matter of being able to see and understand the strategies behind the actions and interactions of the actors. After each conversation I made supplementary notes in a diary where I noted whom I had met, commentaries and impressions in connection with these meetings, which documents (if any) I had received and how these fitted in with the already acquired selection and similar details.

What I have attempted to convey here is, in the first instance, the perspective and the approach with which I have worked. I have purposely kept my description on a concrete level. No doubt a number of associations will arise on reading this text which might bring to mind questions such as participant observation and the objectivity of the researcher. These issues, and other ones, will be treated separately within the framework of a special theoretical–methodological discussion. Right now, however, it is meaningful to advance in the process. This will be done against the background of the newly acquired knowledge and in view of my presence in the course of events.

PHASE V – CENTRAL NEGOTIATIONS

One week after the decisive meeting of 14 April and the troublesome events associated with it, copies of two letters were left in my pigeonhole. One of these was from the representatives of the Metal Trade Union in *L*'s region and the other was from the representatives of the Salaried Employees' Association in the same region. Both of the letters were addressed to *L* and related that negotiations had broken down and that they were going to demand central negotiations. This gave me occasion to discuss, with the various parties, the way in which they experienced the conditions that were brought to the fore by the letters, and how they thought the events would develop.

Ziegler's view on this was not without a touch of humour. He felt that the demand for central negotiations was entirely unfounded. He held that the local trade unions in the district (*L*'s district) had dramatised the situation in a way that was not at all called for. Naturally he was not prepared to 'admit' that the decision had in any way been made in advance. Furthermore, he maintained that those who had taken care of the negotiations – that is, Abrahamsson and Kolinsky (and to a certain extent Perdfelt too) – had acted wrongly. He did not specify in what way, but he was convinced that the course of events would have developed differently, and the process would have demanded less time, had he managed the negotiations.

> I must say that it's really a pity that I haven't been able to participate in the negotiations myself in this case, since I've had so many other things to do. When we built *W* I conducted all of the negotiations, but I feel that it couldn't go on like that. My organization must learn to handle such matters. After all they're the ones who have to live with this organization. (M. Ziegler)

The situation was also such that he felt that it was Abrahamsson's task to implement the ideas and plans which affect a part of the *ES*-unit. After all, Abrahamsson was head of this unit.

I discussed the matter with Abrahamsson to find out how he regarded and experienced the situation. It was very difficult to come to any real clarity in this respect. His opinion was that the process was somewhat difficult to understand and that it had not followed the 'rules of rationality'. He said that the process had, in the main, been characterised by emotions, manoeuvres and even sabotage.

> I think that this process is beginning to take the long, thorny path. Everything's extremely exaggerated and all I can say is that we've abided by the conditions of the group, so to speak. We've sat at the negotiating table and discussed many aspects and attempted to subdue our feelings. As far as I can see we've been very involved in something which lies in the interest of the group (*L*'s employees). Yet still in spite of all this along came the MBL-central negotiations and the threat of damages. (L. Abrahamsson)

Moreover, Abrahamsson was convinced that there were some 'elements' in *L* who worked as agitators and who had encouraged the local representatives to 'get in the way'. He referred here, in the first instance, to an employee who had been in contact with the newspapers, and who had attempted to start up a general debate about the 'transfer tragedy'. Indeed, there were a few articles in a local newspaper, and in one evening paper, but not until two months later.

During the introductory phases of the process we have seen how Kolinsky gradually became involved and how, by means of various initiatives and actions, he was to relieve Abrahamsson of something he obviously experienced as troublesome. At that stage I thought that he would withdraw completely and allow Kolinsky to take care of the process. This seemed natural enough, bearing in mind the discussion of the subordination of L to the production department in W. But this is not how things were to turn out. Abrahamsson did not withdraw, but participated in the continuing debate. Kolinsky also participated, but more as a 'second hand'. All the same, at that stage I was not sure how it would all turn out. I therefore visited Kolinsky, who said that Abrahamsson strongly disliked the process and that he had felt the need to support his colleagues.

> This is to him [L. Abrahamsson] no doubt a very difficult experience. I still feel that he manages quite well in spite of the fact that he's often unsure of himself and, of course, this is due to his not knowing the rules of the MBL-game and the proper order of things. At the same time, I feel that this is a procedure that is filled to the brim with lessons, there are many of us who've learnt a great deal from it. (B. Kolinsky)

I noticed during my conversations with these gentlemen that on the one hand there were complaints about the unsatisfactory development of the course of events, and on the other they seemed to have resigned themselves to the situation. An atmosphere of revolt prevailed on all levels, and yet there was a fatalistic attitude towards the whole affair.

I decided to have a discussion with the local union representatives in (L's district) and took the opportunity to speak with L's employees and the local manager, R. Perdfelt. Judging by the statements made by L's employees, they were prepared to struggle with all the means available, at the same time as they were aware that these means were 'very weak and illusory'. They could still recall the information meeting with Ziegler in L on 6 March, which they experienced as a demonstration of power. They had no illusions whatsoever with regard to the MBL procedure, which they felt to be merely a formality which might possibly help them delay the process. Meanwhile, 'one can always hope that something will happen to change the trend'. Perdfelt agreed with the view of L's employees. He was more bitter than ever and began to side with L's employees: he began to approach in a more conscious way than previously the opinions and 'situational experiences' of the employees. To sum up his viewpoint, it could be said that he felt that: 'On the underdog's side there is some kind of a plaything called MBL which doesn't help a bit' (R. Perdfelt).

The letters from the local union representatives (Metall and SIF), were similarly composed. The heading read as follows: 'Concerning the broken down negotiations of the transfer at L'. It was notified in these letters, which were dated 19 April 1981, that central negotiations were to be demanded. The discussion which I had with them and the opinions which they put forward were in many ways a reflection of the description which I have given of the course of events since the time that they were connected to the case. They stated:

> We [Metall and SIF], the departments in [. . .] in the abovenamed company [L] have had local negotiations concerning the transfer of the business to the buildings of the parent firm in [. . .]. The parent firm is Goliat Inc. in [. . .].
>
> After local negotiations according to the minutes, the union [Metall and SIF] announced that the company [W] had, theoretically speaking, already made their decision, which is why we broke off the negotiations. We have made it clear to the representatives of the employers that we intend to demand negotiation in the matter with regard to damages for breach of MBL, and new negotiations on the point at issue.
>
> We apply, thus, for help with the central negotiations in the matter with respect to damages and the points at issue.
>
> On 6 March 1981 the managing director, M. Ziegler, informed the staff of L as to W's plans to move the firm to [. . .].
>
> On 27 March 1981 the organizations were summoned to MBL-negotiations with regard to the transfer of the business to [. . .].
>
> Since we had not previously received any information on the matter, we demanded all the documentation there was from the firm. Moreover, we received copies from the staff of their investigation which recommended Alternative IV implying continued activity in [. . .].
>
> On 31 March 1981 we received additional material on the matter which showed that the firm had conducted its own investigations.
>
> On 2 April 1981 SIF, Metall and representatives from the staff met in order to look through acquired material. All of the parties were in agreement that the firm had more or less taken its decision and that future negotiations would lead to no more than the transfer of the business. The union received an internal information pamphlet from the staff informing them that: 'L is moving to [. . .]'. On 14 April 1981 MBL-negotiations were taken up once again and were initiated with a discussion about the minutes of the previous meeting. We also received additional material on the subject. At the negotiations the union stated that they could assert, in view of the material which they had received, that the firm had already taken its decision which is why we broke off the negotiations. We made it clear that we shall demand negotiation for damages, and negotiation on the point at issue. The negotiations were brought to a close with a review of each point in the notes which the secretary had taken for the minutes, and all of the people present were in agreement as to the contents thereof.
>
> We later received proposals for minutes from the firm which do not reflect that which was taken up for consideration at the negotiation.
>
> Note well that no negotiation in the point at issue has ever taken place.
>
> We would also like to inform you that W's management will take a decision in the month of May. It sees our local negotiation as being

terminated, thus leaving the employer to make his decision.
(Summary of the reports from the local employees' representative – union representatives from SIF and Metall to their respective associations. The report is dated 21 April 1981)

Attached to the report were a number of appendices and copies of the documents which were referred to.

I was somewhat confounded when I left the representatives. A few days previously I had spoken to Ziegler but he had never mentioned anything about a decision which would be taken by the board in May. This was naturally an important factor in the context, and I decided to examine the matter. It was later to be seen that a board meeting had, indeed, taken place around the middle of May and that Ziegler, having reviewed the situation, was given the task of implementing the decision in accordance with the original intentions (the previous board meeting of 29 August 1980). This event had, for 'understandable' reasons, never been commented by anyone during this period. Perhaps there were two parallel processes going on at the same time: the one for the initiated (board meeting, internal decisions, etc.), and the other to satisfy, or to be in agreement with, the 'ought to' form of the process, so to speak – the ritual. That the latter ought to dictate the content of the former did not seem to bother anyone.

Towards the end of April notification was given to L by the Engineering Trade Union and the Industrial Salaried Employees' Association that they were in contact with the Metal Trades Employers' Association and requested central negotiations.

A day later, a letter came to L from the Metal Trade Employers' Association in which information was given as to the contacts just mentioned, and in which the firm was requested to make a statement on the presentation of the matter within a week.

I was present when these documents arrived at L. Perdfelt had no competence to reply to them and, furthermore, preferred to be no longer involved in the process. He felt that the only right thing to do would be to forward the matter to Abrahamsson. The latter was, as usual, troubled by virtually everything. He commented on the events which he called some kind of inexplicable plot, the work of evil powers whose primary wish was to damage the firm. After having had a short conversation with Ziegler he replied that: 'We agree to the initiation of central negotiations and ask you to see to the arrangements. We suggest that the negotiations take place in June.'

Central negotiations, thus, were to take place some time in June if all of the parties involved could be present at the same time. The letter was concluded as follows: 'Anyone wishing to gain additional details in the matter and the course of events is requested to apply to our B. Kolinsky.'

It was a desire clearly expressed by Abrahamsson to share the responsibility with, or look for support from, his colleagues. He later confirmed this when he said that: 'After all, it's B. Kolinsky who, in the future, will have direct authority over L, and thus he ought to be more involved in the development of the process.'

Waiting for . . .

The wait for central negotiations created an 'unreal' atmosphere in L. Even though it was quite clear to me that L's employees were more or less disillusioned, and that they did not expect very much from the outcome of the negotiations as a whole, I seemed to notice at least a touch of optimism. Was it possible to believe that the central negotiations would acknowledge that they were right? I discussed the matter with them and gained the impression that it was above all the time extension as such which gave occasion for optimism. 'After all, they can't just drive over us', said L's employees, including Perdfelt.

Even though they knew very well that it was merely a matter of formality, they were still glad: an apparent achievement. Most probably because in recent events it appeared that someone was paying attention to their interests. But was it like this? Could it not rather have been that each one of the parties involved (the local representatives in L's district, the Metal Trades Employers' Association, Metal Workers Union, and the Industrial Salaried Employers' Association) had to play their part and justify their existence by fulfilling their functions according to the regulations? I considered voicing my interpretation of the situation to L's employees to see how they would react. I abandoned this idea, however, for I had the feeling that to do so would destroy something: the 'constructed peace', if nothing else.

The central negotiations did not take place in June as was intended, but rather on 2 July 1981. On that day I went to the conference room in W and wondered what would happen. I could still recall the meeting of 14 April and all the other encounters to which I have referred earlier on in the text. I did not feel that this meeting would be characterised by the same aggressiveness as the others, but I was far from believing that it would take the form of some kind of 'mundane' meeting.

The meeting took place in the large elegant room with the heavy draperies in the windows, which I visited the first time, and which gave me occasion to describe it when I was relating the first board meeting at the beginning of this case study. The conversation moved around civil matters, and then Ziegler presented the case as merely a necessary rationalisation which was, *per se*, a part of the total reorganisation of W. He then presented an argument which I had not heard him assert before, namely that 'it's a better destiny for L to be integrated in W than to be closed down, for there are no other alternatives'. The gentlemen around the table seemed to agree, and the meeting was closed half an hour later with a total agreement that 'the whole transfer tragedy is actually merely a trifle, that no doubt L's employees will soon realise the advantages of being integrated in W, and that the whole affair isn't worth so much ado'.

After the meeting I stayed for a while with Ziegler, since I was curious about the argument which he had presented for the closing down of L. I asked whether this eventuality had really been considered or if it was merely an argument for the discussion. He explained that the idea had not been present from the beginning of the argument, but that it had begun to take shape in his mind against the background of the recent events. He went on to explain that, in spite of there being a distinctive need for L's products as a complement to W's assortment, he could consider a solution of closing down, to avoid having to split the organisation, and to regain the peace that was essential for the work of the firm. By this he meant that W's employees had felt somewhat troubled, considering what had happened with and in L, and that the eventuality of such a radical solution might calm them down. I was not prepared to agree with him on this, but he held to his conclusions.

When this took place it was the beginning of July. Bearing in mind the outcome of these negotiations, the decision about L's transfer would now be seen as taken. This implied that the remainder of the process could be seen as the officialisation of the transfer decision.

The way out

The employees were not particularly happy about the outcome of the central negotiations. They could not really understand what their respective associations had done. Neither did they dare to openly criticise them for what, to say the least, they experienced as strange conduct. The central negotiations had in a way 'sabotaged' the grounds for the demands for damages concerning breach of MBL § 11. This was due to the fact that, at these negotiations, it was merely stated that W could take its decision without taking into account whether or not the decision at issue 'seemed to have been taken earlier on', as had been held by the employees' representatives. What remained was breach of MBL § 19 which deals with the duty to provide information. The argument is such that the employer is obliged, before taking any decision, to negotiate as to the activities of the firm with regard to production, economy, etc., and to inform the trade unions and the staff thereof. Added to this was the fact that L had less than 50 employees, and could thus not have its own local union. There were instead two field representatives, one for SIF and for Metall. These field representatives could be given the task, by the local union representatives in the district, to serve as receivers of information. Otherwise the company would inform the local union representatives themselves. SIF's field representative in L was the receiver of information, and could formally be considered to have received the information, even if opinions were very split in this respect. Metall's field representative, on the other hand, was not a receiver of information, i.e. lacked orders from the local union, which meant that the Metall department in L's district ought to have been kept *à jour* with what happened in L. This had not taken place, and it was precisely in connection with this that the local union representatives demanded damages for breach of MBL § 19. The claim turned up in the letterbox soon after the 'collapse' of the central negotiations.

Abrahamsson, who received demands, declared that he could not understand why the local union was putting so much energy into insisting on 'getting us cornered'. 'Either it's pure persecution or else they have nothing else to do', he added. Ziegler was immediately informed, but he did not think that there was any cause for panic.

> We have not time for such things now. Write a kind letter to them and tell them that we'll come back to this later. If they want money they can wait. They need it for their training but we can't pay the whole affair. (M. Ziegler)

Abrahamsson then got in touch with the local union and explained to them that due to the holidays he had not been able to reach the persons concerned in order to make arrangements for negotiations, and he suggested coming back in the beginning of August with a proposition for a date.

July, unlike April, was rather uneventful as far as the advancement of the process was concerned. Most of the parties involved were on holiday, or they were otherwise not available. I used this time to finish off a new compilation of the gathered data and to make an attempt at a preliminary interpretation of the course of events which I intended to present to both W and L at the beginning of August.

At the beginning of August 1981 most people had returned to work. Activity seemed to be normal, with the exception of the short-time week in W's workshop which was to last until 18 September in accordance with the agreement, and the atmosphere among L's employees. A mixed feeling of optimism and insecurity still prevailed. The optimism was not exactly well-founded, events were to show, but as I have mentioned earlier, it was probably due to the fact that there had been a break. The threat of transfer was imminent, to be sure, but the actual physical transfer was far off in the future. This conception of the situation was not shared by *W*'s management who called a meeting on 4 August, at which it was decided 'now that there are no longer any formal obstacles, to accelerate the process so that the physical transfer may take place at the turn of the year'. Present at this meeting were, apart from myself, Ziegler, Abrahamsson and Kolinsky.

The first step that was taken in this direction was that Abrahamsson called for negotiations with regard to the claims for damages, with the condition that on the same occasion negotiations would be held about the transfer in accordance with MBL § 11. The summons went out to SIF and Metall as well as to the field representative in *L*. He had learnt from previous mistakes and wished to safeguard himself as much as possible by informing even those who were not directly concerned. The meeting was to take place on *L*'s premises on 1 September 1981.

On this day the employees refused to negotiate about damages. It was held that they preferred to postpone the question until later, and would rather concentrate on the development of the process. When I asked them what their purpose was when acting in this way, they answered that *W* would no doubt make other mistakes, and that it was more tactical for them not to take out the damages now. This could be interpreted in terms of them no longer having any interest in the process.

Thus the question of damages had been postponed whereas the transfer, as a decision actually taken, had become the object of officialisation.

PHASE VI – THE OFFICIALISATION

The officialisation of the process began on 6 August 1981. On that day I had a meeting with Ziegler and Abrahamsson. They discussed strategies that would be suitable for the carrying out of the transfer as smoothly as possible. I mentioned in passing the creation of small project groups with members from *L* and representatives from *W*. My idea was to attempt, in this way, to break the chilly attitude and the mutual suspicion which prevailed between the parties involved. Ziegler liked the idea, but Abrahamsson was more reserved. Once again he held that 'the less explicit one makes the process and the less one speaks of it, the better and easier the decision can be carried out'. Ziegler, who was of another opinion, and who obviously knew what Abrahamsson was thinking, simply gave instructions to start with the project groups and gave me the go-ahead to participate in their work.

Although I had been given a free hand by Ziegler to actively partake in the constitution and the work of the project groups, I found that it was meaningful for me to establish myself firmly once again with the coming group members and with Perdfelt. They were positive towards the idea since, as far as I could understand, they were more than willing to have someone to document what happened during the process. Most probably it was then that they began to experience me as some kind of an ally. Perhaps they acted so with the purpose of better being able to use me. It was unclear to me what, in my conduct towards them, had encouraged them to take up such a position. I was then confronted with what I considered (and still consider) to be typical scientific methodological problems. I questioned myself about what I was doing. How do I handle the problem of objectivity? The problem of unbiasedness? How about the matter of influencing the object of study? Can one 'refrain' from doing so? What are the arguments to perhaps render it legitimate? Which strategies are suitable for me if my role is in a process of transformation? How much of the reflections in connection with these questions ought to be accounted for? How much of the process of research must, in fact, be seen as a part of the studied process *per se*? I looked for texts in which these difficult questions were taken up for consideration; not in order to find some normative models which would dictate suitable strategies of action, but rather to increase my awareness with regard to the significance of these matters for the studies of social contexts.

The methodological studies which I was doing, moreover, would never have been quite as meaningful had I not been confronted, in practical reality, with the concretisation of the problems. Thus I was to find a complex theoretical world which offered, from numerous angles, arguments about several of the problems with which I was grappling. Psychologically schooled epistemologists seemed, to a far greater extent than sociologists, to have devoted attention to the ideas which are of relevance for descriptions of situations and courses of events in connection with empirical research. Such writers treat the problems and strategies related to the gathering of data rather than the problems related to the analysis of data. That was what I needed just then. The insight which I thus gained helped me to structure my methods of working in a more conscious way in the sense that I became more sure of that to which I ought to devote the most attention. What I mean is that the reading of this literature provided me with insight into the value of the perspectives related to the various approaches in processes of data-gathering and the relation this has to research with regard to what is seen or not seen, depending on the approach. We shall have occasion to return to the question of method later on.

The information in *L* actually started with a working session with Kolinsky in *W*. Apart from myself Abrahamsson was present. He wanted to decide more or less which of *L*'s employees could conceivably be included in the project groups. The reason was, according to him, that this would facilitate the discussion afterwards with those involved. We arrived at the conclusion that two project groups would be needed. One would take up problems of production integration, and the other would see that the integration was carried out as smoothly as possible from an organisational point of view. We met on 11 August in L. The employees had gathered in the lunch room where Kolinsky gave a talk providing information on the situation. He gave a brief review of what had happened at the central negotiations. He simply said that: 'Considering the outcome of the central negotiations, the firm [W] has the right to carry out a transfer.' The message was clear. In other words there was no point in carrying on the struggle. The race was run. The next point which he took up for discussion was how the transfer was to be effected. He then stated that the intention was to move physically at the turn of the year 1981/82. Production would be the last thing to be moved so that the period of transition would not need to imply any losses in orders. Deliveries would be planned three or four weeks later so that it would be possible to install the production establishment in the new premises. The third point to be discussed was that of the project groups – or, as I shall henceforth call them, the work groups. Kolinsky presented the idea of building two work groups. I was astonished by the indifference with which L's employees received this suggestion. Later they told me that this idea of work groups came as a surprise, and that they were actually suspicious towards W's staff. They were inclined to believe that perhaps there was, if not a trap, a tactic or a strategy which was difficult for them to grasp. I explained to them that the idea of groups as a way of working had come up by chance. I also explained that the intention, at least from my point of view, was to help them in so far as this was practicable to carry out the necessary transfer with the least possible loss, especially to L's employees. Furthermore, I felt that the process in the work groups could contribute to L's employees' learning about the rules of the game in general, as well as in W in particular.

Before this meeting was brought to a close, the parties involved more or less agreed on the composition of the groups. Group I, the production group, would be led by Kolinsky and would be constituted by four of L's employees. Group II, the organisation group, would be led by Abrahamsson and constituted by four other employees from L. Union representatives would be present in both groups. Perdfelt was appointed secretary in both groups. It was surprising that the groups were to be led by W's staff. The original purpose was to give L's employees a real opportunity to shape the final phases of the process themselves, and in a concrete manner to arrive at solutions to the problems which they experienced. Instead, the group leaders handed out tasks to the members of the groups who, understandably continued to 'make life difficult for the leaders'. This meant that the purpose of work groups was undermined in the sense that L's employees experienced it more as a 'new means of manipulation' from W than as a forum in which to channel their ideas.

Moves and counter-moves

Two days after the meeting in L, Ziegler wished to formalise the transfer with various authorities who might in one way or another feel affected. Thus notification was sent to the Employment Board in W's region, to the civil centre in L's municipality and to the local union representatives. In this notification Ziegler stated that:

> Now that we have executed local and central negotiations in accordance with the MBL-law, Goliat Inc. has decided to move the department L within W from [L's district] to [W's district]. The department employs twenty people. All have been offered work in W. The department has worked in its own modern buildings, which we now intend to sell [. . .]. (From M. Ziegler's notification)

I was not surprised to find these messages in my pigeonhole. The whole discussion had recently been directed towards the fact that the process had not been very well performed from the point of view of information. Ziegler no longer wanted to take the risk of once again being accused of having acted wrongly. Bearing this in mind, he sent copies to all involved, including L's employees. In other words, from W's side there was a wish to avoid giving the union representatives new occasion to delay the process. But this is not how it worked out. The union representatives found in these notifications occasion to assert new arguments. I was to learn of this when I visited them in connection with these messages. Their argument was that the decision by the firm (W) to move the activity entailed changes in the working conditions of the staff (in L). Thus, the union held,

> the employer is, in the first instance, obliged to negotiate in accordance with MBL § 11. This means that the union may take the initiative for negotiation, but that the firm must under any circumstances call for negotiations according to § 11. If this is not done, then the union may demand negotiations on the issue of fact in accordance with MBL § 12 and damages in accordance with § 10.

A few days later, i.e. about 20 August, Ziegler received these claims in two documents, one of them from SIF and the other from Metall. He became indignant over the conduct of the union, which he declared to be 'unfair'. This time he thought that 'the organization must take care of this'. Thus he forwarded the documents to Abrahamsson, who filed them in the '1 September file'. The reader might recall that the union was summoned by Abrahamsson on 1 September for a global negotiation about 'all' the subjects of contention. We also know that nothing special happened that day.

PHASE VII – THE IMPLEMENTATION

All of the people on W's side were more than ready to get started with the work groups as quickly as possible. Among the activities undertaken were comprehensive measures of which the purpose was to safeguard against the eventuality of any accusations for either of the union representatives. Kolinsky and Abrahamsson multiplied their efforts to provide information. Various meetings were organised with the union in W, with L's employees, and with the local representatives. A review of the minutes written during this meeting, plus various conversations of those involved, showed that the message was quite simply that 'everyone is in agreement that the transfer of L's business ought to be carried out'. The representatives of the local unions were to participate in the coming negotiations concerning the form for the implementation of the transfer and its consequences for the staff. Further, it was emphasised, 'before the transfer can take place, the negotiations about staff and organisational questions must have been concluded'. The expression 'everyone is in agreement' that was written in the minutes was by no means a reflection of the actual opinions held by the majority of the antagonists with regard to this matter. It was rather the opinions of the central persons in W.

Work groups

The task of appointing colleagues to work within the two groups was left to L's employees themselves: the production group or Group II and the organisational group or Group I. This took place towards the end of August.

Abrahamsson was thus notified of the composition of the groups, and in spite of the fact that everyone, at least in W, was eager for the work to start, L's employees declared that no meetings in the work groups would take place before the negotiations meeting of 1 September. The local union in L's district had demanded MBL-negotiations with regard to alterations in the working conditions of the staff. It was now to be seen, in retrospect, that this meeting gave no results in this respect. I asked L's employees if they had any special reasons for preferring to wait with the work groups until after the meeting of 1 September. Their comments did not provide me with any elucidation. From their point of view it was a strategical or tactical move, as many others had been. They knew with conviction that the negotiations would not change anything, or suddenly arrive at a miraculous solution. They had lost faith in the union's ability to resolve matters. The point was quite simply to make life a little bit harder for W's staff. As one of the employees said: 'Why should they always have the last say?'

To be sure, W's staff were very irritated over the delay caused by, as Ziegler said, 'the sulkiness of L's employees'. But it was a short period of time. The meeting would take place a week later. At the meeting the union declared that the negotiation of that day would merely concern the substantiation of the manning of the work groups, their constitution as well as forms for working. Furthermore, the parties came to an agreement that negotiations would be continued parallel to the work in the groups. These negotiations would be taken up two weeks later, starting on 15 September 1981. Besides this, all of the parties present at the meeting seemed to agree that 'this form of work group is a good model for the implementation of the decided changes in a quick, effective and human fashion'.

The assignments of the work groups

This source of irritation soon passed over. Abrahamsson and the others from W who were involved had now learnt to handle such negotiating positions. It no longer seemed troublesome to conduct two, or even three, negotiations parallel to each other. On 9 September, Abrahamsson summoned the work groups to the constitutional meeting. The production group was called first, and the organisational group some two hours later. The work in the groups lasted right until the end of November, when most of the questions had been treated or at least discussed. During this period the production group had five meetings, whereas the organisational group had contented itself with four. I was present at each of these meetings and, to a certain extent, also participated in the work within each group. At the first meeting, Abrahamsson and Kolinsky made it clear to all those who were present that henceforth I should partake in the meetings of the work groups as a 'participant observer'. All of those present knew who I was and what I did; I had taken the opportunity earlier, on several occasions, to speak to them in connection with various phases of my investigation.

My line of conduct, during this and the other meetings, was to attempt to understand as far as possible the logic of action of the actors from the perspective of the actors involved, and not so much from the perspective of an outsider or 'absent' observer. There are those who may wish to protest here, and who may assert that the process of data-gathering must be carried out in an objective way. They imply that the researcher should adopt an 'impersonal–colourless–detached attitude'. In other words, one is supposed to function independently of the reality that is met. Or, to put it differently, one must not allow oneself to be influenced, or to influence the social world with which one comes into contact. I shall attempt to discuss these questions and other similar questions in the chapter on method. The work groups and their activities became meaningful to me inasmuch as I could reach and have an understanding of the meaning which the whole situation had for the members of the groups. When this kind of understanding is one's goal then the argument is not that knowledge is something 'out there' which we can discover by 'being objective', but rather than knowledge must, with necessity, be grounded in our personal participation in the praxis.

The constitutory meetings took place in *W*'s premises. Kolinsky served as chairman in the production group while Abrahamsson took on the post of chairman in the organisational group. The process was, theoretically speaking, repeated twice from the one meeting to the next. After a brief introduction the chairman went over to the directives for work. The employees' representatives took on a chilly attitude while the representatives of the local unions from *W* were expectant and passive. Perdfelt, who was a member of both groups, tried to show a worthy bearing intended to emphasise that he was very well aware of the 'intrigues which could and would develop there'. The instructions and directives were not, as such, controversial, which allowed for the meetings to be held without any greater disturbances. The reason for my mentioning this is that earlier meetings – for example, the negotiations meeting to which I have referred earlier – had been stormy. This does not, however, imply that everyone now 'bathes in an elixir of consensus'. It merely implies, according to my conversations with those involved, that each one experienced these constitutory meetings as the introduction of a new phase in the process. Thus, it was a matter for each one, so to speak, to wait for the moves of the opposing party before deciding on a suitable strategy. The assignments of work were the same for both groups and read as follows:

— The forms of work are to be of the kind that as many decisions as possible may be taken within the work groups.
— Within these work groups, smaller groups will be appointed which can work with parts of the problems.
— Questions which cannot be solved in the work groups are to be taken up for negotiation.
— Minutes are to be held from the work meetings.
— Minutes are to be handed out to the employees' representatives in *L*'s district (Metall and SIF's departments).

– The point in time for the transfer is to be notified at the latest two months before the date of transfer.
(From the minutes of the meeting 820909)

As far as the directives were concerned, the production group was given the task of

– [...] arranging *L*'s production activity within the framework of the premises available in *W*.
– Striving for the greatest possible degree of integration with *W*'s resources of production with a retained or higher efficiency in *L*'s production.
– The planning of the transfer so that, if possible, it could take place at the turn of the year 1981/82.
(From the minutes of the meeting 820909).

The organisational group was given the task of

– Programming the integration of *L*'s organization in *W* and seeing to the maintenance of *L*'s identity externally.
– Adapting the time plans to Group I (Production group)
(From the minutes of the meeting 820909).

These not very concrete directives, particularly in the organisational group, were henceforth taken to imply a broad interpretation of the concept of integration.

The internal relations of the work groups

The work of the groups continued more or less in accordance with the above-mentioned assignments and was terminated towards the end of November. Already at the first meeting, i.e. the one which took place a few days after the constitutory meeting, a special pattern began to develop which came to characterise the working groups and the attitudes of the members *vis-à-vis* one another. What I am trying to say here is that the various interests represented by different individuals were reinforced within each work group, and the borderlines between the different blocks became sharply drawn. From the point of view of *W*'s representatives, it was more a question of giving orders and of handing out tasks than of letting the work groups discover problems and find the way to solutions. For *L*'s employees it became 'natural' to be against almost everything, and in general to find the opportunity to lay claims in connection with each proposition. Of interest in this context is that they never held the initiative during the entire process with the work groups. Kolinsky and

Abrahamsson were the ones who held it. They came to the meeting well prepared and when the opposition grew too strong in any particular question they could always use their authority to get themselves out of a difficult position. The union representatives from W oscillated between an expectant, passive attitude, and clearly shown irritation in the face of the demands made by L's employees. Once again Perdfelt, who was secretary in both of the groups, was in a difficult position. He had previously withdrawn from all of the negotiation activities; but even though this was not a matter of negotiating in any formal way, the debate often, or nearly always, ended up in a negotiation-like discussion. This meant that it became difficult for him to partake in the debate as the others did. As soon as he tried to do so he was immediately silenced by the chairman of the work groups. He was more or less neutralised, and his contributions to the debate were reduced to a few single careful formulations. L's representatives looked upon Perdfelt's 'neutrality' with suspicion. They did not hesitate to comment on his position to the others in the firm. This implied a further deterioration of the relations between the employees and Perdfelt. From L's side it was now openly declared that he was incompetent and should have nothing to do with the position of local manager.

Now that I have outlined the conditions prevalent in the work groups, it is important to depict the way in which the work was carried out in these groups and the arguments which were presented by the antagonists. I shall not reproduce each meeting *per se*; instead I shall give a cross-section of all of the meetings (they amounted to nine plus the work meetings within each group) with particular emphasis on how the group members have acted, the strategies they have attempted to further, and how they have interpreted each other's conduct. We shall thus begin with the production group.

The production group on the wrong track

It was truly an experience to partake in these meetings. I was convinced that the discussion would concern the working conditions of L's employees and the integration of L's production in W. Instead the debate developed around a number of unessential details such as, for example, if L's employees would have their own basin in the working premises or not. At each turn L's employees attempted to lead the discussion towards the real problems of the integration, such as the responsibility for purchase and planning, the utilisation of certain specific machines in another end of W's premises. In the same way, Kolinsky and Abrahamsson answered by leading the discussion to more diffuse areas, no doubt essential from a technical point of view, but which L's employees had no chance of evaluating and thus no possibility of taking a standpoint. This 'unreal' situation was then used by *W*'s staff so as to assert the need for additional investigations and they could then, through such means, hand out tasks to *L*'s employees.

The organisation group and identity conflict

The running point in this group was the identity of *L*, and *L*'s employees' new job descriptions, after the transfer. In the beginning *L*'s employees struggled to maintain *L*'s identity. They argued for the need to keep their forms, letters etc. with *L*'s name. The battle was fought with such tenacity that I wondered whether it was not rather a matter of *L*'s employees' own identity. After much ado and various lesser investigations, the group agreed that *L*'s name would remain on the order forms. This was agreed since otherwise *L*'s customers might think that *L* had been closed down and contact other suppliers. It was basically the same argument as the one conducted with regard to *L*'s telephone number. Here also a hard struggle was fought for the sake of *L*'s identity. The arguments put forward by *L*'s employees seemed to me to be logical enough. They argued that the customers were used to speaking to any employee in *L*, and that he or she would know exactly what the customer wanted and could deliver it to him or solve his problems quickly and effectively. If instead this were to go via *W*'s switchboard, it would take far too long to get an answer. The switchboard was overloaded. Secondly, the customer would then be referred to the order department where there was no-one who could speak to him in the same way as an employee from *L* would have done. Furthermore, the customer would be forced to give the number of the product instead of merely naming it as he would normally do. Briefly, the point of *L*'s employees' argument was to retain the same character of contact with the customer after the transfer. What astonished me most in this argument was that it was *L*'s employees who were the most troubled by the customer relations and *L*'s future, whereas *W*'s representatives did not seem to realise this. It is also possible that, bearing in mind the strained and opposed relations characterising the confrontation between the groups, even if Abrahamsson and Kolinsky could see the common sense of *L*'s employees' argument, it was still 'necessary' for them to adopt a contrary position. Nonetheless, in the end a compromise was reached. The existing switchboard of *L* would be converted into an extension of *W*'s switchboard. None of *L*'s employees were really satisfied with this decision but there was obviously nothing that they could do about it.

The question of the job descriptions was discussed during the last two meetings. I suggested that it might be interesting first to allow *L*'s employees to make an attempt to describe their actual job so that one could later expand on this and together produce new job descriptions. The attempt was unsuccessful for two reasons. The first was that L's employees proved to be incapable of describing their tasks. Their various fields intersected to such an extent that it was difficult to gain any clear picture as to what each one did with the exception of a few specific tasks. The second reason was that Abrahamsson had already completed the new job descriptions when the question was discussed for the first time. These were received with lively protests but were gradually accepted. The employees on the administrative side would be spread in W's different units, while Perdfelt's situation was to change drastically. From having been the local manager for the entire unit he would now be the planning manager: a very undefined position.

Common to both of these work groups was that neither of the antagonists really got what he/she wanted. Indeed, one did debate, but about what? Mostly details. Many times the discussions were held with an intensity that was out of proportion with what was being treated. At other times this involvement would be totally diminished for no special reason. L's employees told me that they were dissatisfied with what had taken place (and with the way in which it had all been managed) in the work groups. They held that they had participated in these groups for the sake of formality. 'To make use of the right of belonging to the group and to show that we weren't unaware of the game that was being played.' What may perhaps be said to have characterised the atmosphere was the strain in the air at the end of each meeting, especially the last two meetings, when Abrahamsson and Kolinsky recapitulated the points to which one had 'agreed'. People just sat where they were on the chairs around the table and embarrassedly looked at their shoes.

Fear: the bearers of knowledge abandon ship

During the previous three months four people from the workshop in L had resigned. There was also an incessant circulation of rumours that the remainder of the staff would move to W only if they could find no other employment. As the process gradually advanced and its outcome became clearer, L's employees began openly to declare their intentions. This was a source of great concern within W. 'Had it been worth the trouble of going through the whole process to integrate L's knowledge in W, if the bearers of knowledge were now quitting?', people in W wondered. When the discussions in the work groups were as good as ended, Abrahamsson sent a notice to all those concerned where he mentioned the wage settlement as well as the conditions for a possible commuting compensation. He also pointed out, once again, that the transfer could now begin on 1 January 1982, and then concluded the notification with a plea to the staff not to abandon ship:

As we all understand, the transfer will during a transitory period imply great strain for all of us, both as regards to work load and our private lives. All the same, we have arrived at a solution, mutual understanding, which will alleviate the problems. I hope that you will find the solutions attractive enough for you to make an attempt to come with to [*W*'s district].
(From L. Abrahamsson's notification, 811106)

PHASE VIII – THE STILLBORN REVOLT

We know that two blocks were formed in *L* and gradually drifted apart as the physical transfer became apparent. We also know that Perdfelt had been appointed scapegoat by several parties. From this point of view the situation was very explosive in November and even thereafter. Without exaggerating one could speak of intrigues, plots and tragedies in this context. On one occasion Perdfelt and I drove together to one of the last work meetings. He was in very low spirits and literally said that the situation had become untenable and that he would surely have a breakdown. He said that he felt that he had been appointed scapegoat and that virtually 'everyone was against him'. At the same time, he said, he had worked day in and day out but that time was too short. The firm had received many orders at the same time as *W*'s staff gave him extra work in connection with the transfer. Products must be codified and the prices re-calculated so that they would fit in with *W*'s computed system. Furthermore, he said, he had new problems, more personal ones, but which were directly related to the course of events at his place of work.

The attempted coup

I was not quite sure at that point in time (November–December 1981) as to why I was considered to be some kind of an ally. Those who came to me with their personal problems and let me know their views were not only people from *L*, but also leading persons in *W*. Naturally I was pleased with the situation, which gave me a good opportunity to gain a deeper understanding of the process at issue. At the same time it was rather uncomfortable since each one of my confidants was sure that what he or she said to me would remain between us. I was forced to act with diplomacy to retain my privileged position without causing anyone damage. I had no other solution to the problem. Furthermore, I was quite careful to avoid any double-sided games. I emphasised at times that my interest was (and is) primarily that of research, even though I expressed my sympathies for either the one or the other group or action. I believe that the actors involved in the process understood my position and my striving to retain my integrity from the point of view of research ethics.

In November a person from *L* got in touch with me. The person in question was in possession of valuable knowledge as regards the construction and production of *L*'s products. The person, P., phoned me in the evening and explained that this was the only time he could phone since during the day it was impossible as there were people who might overhear the conversation who ought not to do so. I was surprised at the secrecy and asked for an explanation. He explained that the 'loyal' group (excluding Perdfelt) had decided to take over the firm (*L*) or to start up their own firm! The group wished for some help with a number of concrete problems which they assumed would arise in connection with the takeover of the establishment. What were the possibilities? Where could one ask for economic support? Which strategies were most suited with regard to *W*? Is all lost or can one still hope for a change in the development of the course of events? P. raised a number of such questions. He also wanted to explore the possibilities of retaining or buying the name of *L* in the eventuality of the establishment of a new firm.

This was a situation which I had not expected. I made note of the questions and asked him to call again. I discussed this matter with my colleagues. It was less the questions *per se* that I wanted to discuss than the fact that they were posed just to me. Someone said: 'If you help them then you will lose the object of your research.' The matter of interest in this case was the very process between *W* and *L*. If *L* were to break away, then there was a risk that the area of tension which held them to *W* would cease to exist. On the other hand, I thought that the surprising change in the situation might be eventful and intensive in itself. Perhaps it would be a tension of another nature, but it would still be an extension of the process I was studying. Another colleague took up entirely different aspects: the ideological and research ethical aspect. What is my viewpoint in the context?, he asked. For example, did I consider the transfer decision to be without grounds, etc.? I found myself in an awkward situation and wanted to be careful. I was perhaps a little afraid of being compromised. I searched for a thousand reasons to justify my cautiousness and this did not feel too good. I knew that deep inside I felt sympathy for *L* and *L*'s employees. They ought to have been given the chance to develop in their way. I certainly would have liked to partake in the process even more actively and to influence its course of development. But the reality that presented itself was another. The decision had been taken and the transfer was now a fact. Moreover, for ethical reasons I did not wish to enter the process and act behind *W*'s back. At the same time I had the impression from P. that it was all a matter of vague ideas and that there was no real decision to take over *L*.

Nonetheless, I investigated the questions posed by P. and found that the opportunities were very limited. I told this to the 'loyal' group, which, for that matter, was in possession of virtually the total collected knowledge in L. If they were to establish their own company, W would be forced to close down the business, and in such a way the group would have the opportunity to keep the market. This on condition that they were allowed to keep the name L, which was not very likely, and that the salesman, Malisman, agreed to the coup, which was even less likely since he belonged to the other block. I took this opportunity to try and understand the release mechanism which had brought them to think along such lines. No doubt the process as such had forced them to reflect on their situation and to specify their thoughts. The experiences which they had endured during the various negotiating work meetings had stirred thoughts which had been latent and unarticulated. They realised, they said, 'how little actual opposition we put up'. They also gained insight into how little they knew of their business, of their competence, of their products as a complement to W's assortment, of the market, of the economy – in brief, of everything concerning their existence as a group within L.

During the following weeks the group got in touch with the bank, the local authorities, the secretary of trade; made calculations, and learnt about the business which was theirs. But the difficulties were great: the banks demanded substantial guarantees, the institutions wanted thick, well-worked-out reports and business descriptions. This was too much for the 'loyal' group who were, in fact, not particularly motivated, and who perhaps preferred the security which W, none the less, offered them. The revolt was stillborn.

Does L's problem exist in W's mind?

The answer to this question is, strangely enough, no. As someone has said, the existence of a problem is conditionally connected to a construction which exists for the purpose of realising that there is a problem somewhere. During and after the attempted coup I spent a lot of time in W to try and see the whole affair from a possibly broader perspective. I took another look at W's present organisation and realised then, clearer than before, that the structural arrangements were, in their effects, identical to those of the old S-division's construction. It was exactly this construction from which one had hoped to escape.

On 9 December I had lunch with W's managing director. He wanted to know what my impression as a whole had been and I, for my part, wanted to tell him how I had described and interpreted the process which I investigated. I explained that the problem of L began to seem more and more of a paradox to me. The argument which I held could be summarised as follows: I suggested that *L*'s transfer was a side-effect of the problematic organisational situation in *W*. The sales organisation with its status as independent juridical unit was a construction that had failed. The competitive capacity of the products on the market decreased considerably as a result of the various mark-ups which the sales organisation was forced to make so as, in its turn, to be able to show a profit to *W*. In connection with this, a general spirit of an indifference prevailed in *W*'s various units with regard to the customers and the service which they ought to have. The production, the stores department, the logistics totally lacked what I would call 'customer- or service-oriented culture'. I had already noticed this during the discussions in the organisation group. The staff on the logistics side were completely incapable of understanding the demands for customer proximity posed by *L*'s employees, and what this would mean in the form of quick deliveries, service, etc. For example, the juridical unit could be integrated within *W* as a sales department. In this way one could liberate the price differences and use them so as to cover other costs of relevance to the market. It was then that Ziegler stated that he had been thinking along similar lines. The problem, to him, is of a global nature, and embraces the organisational construction of *W*.

> I feel that something must be done with *W*'s structure as a whole. Indeed I do want to gather everything under one roof, but it's primarily a matter of the administrative and sales sections. The production unit can very well remain outside as long as they're profitable. The problem is that we've invested in a system for the handling of acquisition and the planning of production as well as stock-keeping. This makes it difficult to plan with our present construction. (M. Ziegler)

I then pointed out that this meant that all of the fuss over *L* had not been necessary. The unit could have continued on its path without any disturbance to *W*. More than one and a half years of investigations, meetings, negotiations and energy to no avail. The process once initiated had then been driven by a logic of its own. Ziegler also admitted this and added that 'the decision was right when it was taken. But now there are other preconditions to be considered.'

W's reorganisation – L falls into oblivion

Ziegler revealed on this occasion that a month earlier he had engaged a well-known international firm of consultants to try to do something about *W*'s troublesome situation. I had heard about this, but we had never spoken openly about it before. Ziegler felt that my diagnosis was quite close to the one posed by the firm of consultants, and thus he wanted me to take a closer look at their reports and to discuss them with him and with some members of W's board. From the beginning I was meant to function as a discussion partner to the management.

On 12 December, as agreed, I was back at W. I had read through the reports and was prepared for a detailed discussion. It was agreed that, apart from some kind of statement on the consultants' report, I would present a summary of my investigation and my interpretation of the situation. Present at this meeting were two board members and Ziegler. I began to outline roughly that which the reader has just read. My description was considered by those present as being correct and as coinciding with the 'actual' events. This was in spite of the fact that certain antagonists in the process were presented as somewhat unskilful. Some adjustments were made and I added them to the text at the moment of re-editing.

L was given very little place in the discussion that followed. Instead the interest was focused on W's overall problem. I tried to suggest the view that the problem of L could be seen as a symptom or an indicator of the mentality of action within W. I gained no hearing for this. The people present preferred to forget L and the embarrassing process that had been generated. Afterwards we discussed the reports of the consultants. I shall now summarise some of my contributions, yet without directly referring to the confidential contents of the reports.

In spite of the fact that the reports were very professionally presented, with great clarity and often of good consistency, they were weak with regard to depth of the statements and the recommendations were founded on quantitative data alone, which had sometimes been taken from quick telephone interviews. The consultants firm disregarded entirely the historical development of W. They considered the sales organisation as a pure sales department and thus overlooked the essence of the problem — namely, the internal discussion between the production and the sales units, which were dependent on the organisational construction of W. Furthermore, the market was regarded in the reports merely from a local point of view. This implied that the measures which were suggested were based on far too limited data. For example, it is suggested that W cut away some parts of the ES-activity since they were primarily relatively new products on the Swedish market and did not have any notable success. W, however, was active abroad, and could also hope for a share of the market there. Furthermore, these products were based on an advanced technology which from a long-range strategical viewpoint, was valuable to W. The reason that these products had not met with success was due more to the organisation of W than to the products themselves.

Finally the consulting firm suggests that W should assign the sales to the strongest organisation within Group A (the base unit, see Act I). This group sells base products on a contract basis. The consultants maintain, further, that approximately 50% of the sales corps of the firm visited the same customers as W, and beyond this they only sought something to chat about. The base products sell themselves. Of interest in this context is that the base unit is the largest within the Goliat Inc. corporation. The board members of W who were present at the meeting believed that what the consultants were arguing in the context was merely the desire of the corporate management to reinforce further the position of the largest firm. This might seem reasonable from a broad perspective, but for W it is not a good solution. W would merely become a supporting unit to the base firm which may be in the interest of the base firm, but not so much in the interest of W.

Those who were present agreed that W ought primarily to strive for its own strong sales organisation. Details were vehemently discussed for a few hours. None of us who were present were sure of the solutions provided by the firm of consultants. Gradually we began to discuss alternative propositions. I suggested the idea that one ought in W to strive, in the long run, to structure the organisation in a matrix form. I explained that this was a relatively long process (two to three years) which presupposed that all of the actors in the organisation gained an understanding of this way of organising and what this implied. What was needed in W was to build up a new mentality among its members: a kind of cultural revolution. The entire organisation had ossified and the radical change that was needed could only be carried through if everyone realised the need and the use of such a change and actively participated in it.

When the meeting was brought to a close we had come to an agreement that we would stick to the organisational idea at which we had arrived, and that I would attempt to present a plan for its accomplishment.

The base firm wins

We had a few additional meetings in January 1982. I had then managed to prepare a more precise report of the reorganisation. Ziegler's task would be to anchor the idea among the management of the corporation. Without going into detailed descriptions, the management of the corporation reasoned that 'it is the base firm which stands for 75% of Group A's total invoicing and approximately 40% of the total invoicing of the corporation. Therefore the base firm ought to be given priority and its sales organization ought to be reinforced'. W's third attempt at reorganisation, thus, once again brought the firm back to the old troublesome construction of the S-division.

THE ENDING OF THE CHRONICLE

On 1 March 1982 *L*'s physical transfer was implemented. This was planned for February, but *L* received a large order in January. The employees wished to complete this order before the transfer so as to avoid the eventuality of a delay. Kolinsky and Abrahamsson regarded this with suspicion: 'Were these not yet additional tactics so as to cling onto *L*?' After further conflicts the employees were given permission to complete their work and the transfer took place a month later than had been planned.

I had decided from the beginning to follow the case right until the physical transfer, or to any other outcome of the process. It was an eventful and complex case. I am convinced that the wealth of detail in the case contributes, to a great extent, to the understanding of intra-organisational processes with all that is implied by these with regard to the ideas, intentions, actions, tactics and strategies of the individuals concerned. In other words, with regard to power relationships.

I visited *L*, which is now in *W*, three times during the spring of 1982. The period of installation lasted the whole of March and production was delayed and reduced since a number of important customers had been lost. Furthermore, yet another skilful technician had resigned. More invest-ments were made on standard products, partly due to the fact that the skill needed for the special products was now lacking, and partly since it is easier from an integrational point of view to incorporate into *W*'s system the planning of acquisition, orders and production. The annual results from 1982 did not seem to be positive. *L*'s employees regretted this since, in spite of everything, they had produced positive results for the year 1981.

They had been promised the status, organisationally speaking, of a unit of a sub-department within the production department. Instead, as it had turned out, they now officially fell under a sub-department and thus have a manager who himself is subordinate to Kolinsky. This may seem to be a small point, but in *L*'s employees and Perdfelt's world it was none the less a significant matter. Perdfelt was himself subject for a transfer in May. He was no longer needed as local manager and the activity took on a development which implied that his competence became superfluous in the context. In July 1982 he was transferred to *W*'s drawing office. This is regarded as a step backwards. *L*'s workshop is now totally integrated in *W*'s *ES*-workshop. Neither does any noteworthy identity remain. The work of the organisation group was, in this regard, a waste of time. From the original staff there are now only about ten who remain, and two more resigned during the spring of 1983. They gave me this information themselves in January 1983, when I was busy re-editing this ending.

CHAPTER 3

Generating Knowledge and the Theory of Discourse

In this chapter I shall discuss the third and fourth dimensions of method used in this work and which I have mentioned in the Introduction. The first part of this chapter, *generating knowledge*, refers to the third dimension of the method. The second part, the *theory of discourse*, refers to the fourth dimension. The first and second dimensions of the method were treated in the Introduction and Chapter Two respectively.

GENERATING KNOWLEDGE

Introduction

A discussion of method can be conducted from a number of perspectives and articulated on different levels, all of which are relevant for the procedures of production of knowledge. Yet there seem to be two principal approaches often chosen by social scientists when expounding their methodological deliberations: there are those who embark on a more or less exhaustive epistemological discussion, account for the majority of the theories of science, and sometimes state their own scientific interest or ideals. There are also those who choose to reduce the problem of method to the mere description of a practical mode of procedure in the gathering of data and of the principles of data-processing. The first version demands a great deal from the author if it is to be fruitful. Apart from the fact that he must have a very good command of the subject, which in itself almost amounts to an impossibility, he must also be able to outline, in a relatively limited space, the various traditions and schools of thought and relate such to each other. It seems that there are very few who succeed with this task. The classics in this field usually take *one* epistemological tradition as their point of departure and then proceed to argue for or against other traditions (Habermas, Sartre, Foucault, Kuhn, Feyerabend, Cicourel are good examples of such classics). What the 'ordinary' social scientist usually manages to accomplish is, at the most, a superficial review of the

114

literature at second or third hand. The endeavour then takes on the appearance of a general presentation of the theories in the same style as a mediochre report on the subject that is separate from the object of study, or alternatively as some kind of an 'examination' aimed to show that the author has at least read something about the area in question.

Although the second version may be easier to write and to handle, it is problematic inasmuch as it reveals nothing about the actual method. A description of the procedures involved in the gathering of data is, naturally, an essential part of the method as a whole, but this essential aspect does not gain significance unless it is related to the epistemological context within the framework of which a particular approach becomes meaningful.

My choice of approach is here connected to the fact that this section on method, *generating knowledge*, is related to the empirical considerations. This implies that the epistemological discussion which I shall henceforth conduct is directly relevant to the problems with which I have been confronted during my empirical work. These discussions will help to place my view in relation to the epistemological debate at large. I have drawn attention to the problems to which I have just referred, as they have emerged in the case study, yet without treating them in a specific manner. The idea, then, is to consider in this section the epistemological and philosophical questions which these problems invite.

I shall not, thus, mention anything in this section about the second dimension of the method; *fieldwork*. In the case study I gave a running account of the various instances of this dimension as they gradually appeared to be significant for the understanding of my approach.

To my mind, matters concerning method have an ideological meaning. A philosophy of life, or an outlook on life, must come to light; a mode of conduct must be articulated. My relations to the world which I am trying to study must be articulated. It is no exaggeration to say that the personality of the author ought to be evident in the text, particularly in the section on method. I am not in agreement with the opinion that the author should adopt a neutral position in the text; that he/she should write as if it were *de facto* someone else that was writing; or that he/she should hide behind various annihilating grammatical constructions, the purpose of which is to clothe the text with an illusory objectivity which, in reality, depersonifies it and weakens the argumentation. The author is always present in his/her narration no matter what he/she may do to avoid this. Instead of striving to disappear from the text I choose rather to be consciously present in it. This seems to be the golden rule in other types of literature. In scientific contexts it is all the more important to show who one is in the sense of marking out one's clear position in the jungle of the epistemology of science.

During the introductory phases of my schooling in method I was to learn, as most students do, that culture, the social structure, norms, socialisation, values, etc., are important factors in the studying of social situations. I was to learn that there are important connections between, on the one hand, theories and statements in the social sciences and, on the other hand, the current methods deemed to be worthy of usage in empirical investigations. The general notion was that one ought to formulate hypotheses on the basis of a review of the literature on the subject concerned, that these hypotheses are thus theoretically legitimate and that they can then be tested empirically. The idea is then that the empirical content (regardless of the way in which the studies are carried out), reflects the reality 'out there' and that a good researcher is a value-free researcher.[1]

As I became increasingly involved in the question of method I was to realise that it was primarily a matter of the articulation of an outlook on life, of an ideology and of a fundamental philosophical view. It was gradually to become clearer to me that a method was not something which one could simply choose as one would choose, for example, a postcard, but rather that the choice of method involved a lengthy process of maturation. There are some ideas that cannot be communicated in, for example, a lecturing situation. They must be internalised through insight gained in repeated personal confrontations and the problems arising from them. Such is the case, for example, with the relation between the method which one chooses to work with and the overall philosophical reflections from which the method is derived. Another important relation is the one between the method and the problem of research. The problem which one chooses to tackle can be formulated in different ways depending on the researcher's philosophical awareness and fundamental orientation. The method which one applies, apart from being directly relevant to the researcher's approach, opens, or alternatively closes, certain aspects of the area of research.

In the study of power, for example, a certain method and a certain angle of approach may be superior to another in rendering possible the 'seeing' (as described in the work of Castaneda since 1974) and understanding of certain fundamental dimensions in the mechanisms of power. However, this is not something that can be discovered by going out and purchasing a handbook in method on the method market. Sartre writes in the introduction to his great work, *Critique de la raison dialectique*, that method is a philosophical question whereby research expresses itself. The way that the research result may be relevant is a matter 'determined' by the researcher's conscious assumption of a standpoint in relation to the philosophy which shapes the cultural environment at the time (Bourdieu, 1979; Foucault, 1966). The method plays a decisive role in determining whether one will be able to grasp meaningful dimensions of reality or whether one will merely reproduce one's own and the existing cultural prejudices.

There are those, for example Nicolaus (1966), who maintain that social scientists *de facto* know something about 'the occupied populace', and that this knowledge can be used against it in order to influence it, control it, etc. Indeed, knowledge can, without doubt, be used instrumentally in the service of power, and the relationship power–knowledge (Foucault, 1975) is deeply rooted in a long historical–political praxis. The problem is that one presupposes that social scientists possess a 'unique' knowledge of what is called 'the occupied populace', and that the relationship between the procedures of research and this knowledge is quite without problems. But it is precisely there that the problem lies. The production of 'unique', perhaps valuable, knowledge is if anything intimately associated with the researcher's insight into epistemological problems[2] (Mills, 1940a; Gouldner, 1971). It is this very insight that enables us to approach a problem, or an object of study, in such a way as then possibly to succeed in generating such knowledge (Feyerabend, 1978). The ways in which such authors as Sartre, Foucault, Popper, Lakatos, Toulmin and many others tackle different problems, and the theories and statements they present, are by no means value-free. Indeed it is more likely that the opposite is true. However, the reasoning is of a high standard and the values of the researchers are transformed into arguments. Actually, this lies in the nature of the matter: a researcher can hardly venture to claim that research is free from values. As soon as I hold a pen in my hand, and start to interpret my material (no matter which method of interpretation I may use), the moment will always arrive when it is I exclusively who choose to write one interpretation rather than the other. Indeed, I can argue for my choice, but the decisive factor, on a deeper level, is nonetheless the set of values which I hold and which form an integral part of my personality, no matter how much I may claim the contrary. As early as the 1940s a number of social scientists vehemently attacked the model of value-free research (Mills, 1940a). However, the criticism has also been directed towards the lack of empirical grounds for the theories, due largely to the fact that the researchers were seldom in the proximity of the object of their research. They could not observe the interactions which they *de facto* claimed to analyse (Cicourel, 1973).

Awareness of method is also a practical matter which must thus be concretised, partly in the course of empirical work. For example, all of us involved in social science know that the attitudes, actions, views, etc. of the individual are all influenced by the interpretations which he/she may give to situations of interaction. In spite of this there are few social scientists who seriously regard the procedure with empirical work as a form of interaction equivalent to that which one *de facto* wishes to study. Hyman (1949) was perhaps one of the first to pay any attention to this problem, and he accused social scientists of 'not being prepared to admit that the empirical work is, in fact, a social situation in itself'. What seems to happen is that the researchers, with excessive academic carefulness and pseudo-scientificity, transform these social chains of events into constructed sequences. The result is that one by-passes that which one ought to understand, and the knowledge that is generated is very slight or nonexistent. Recently a number of contributions have been made in this context. Authors such as Rosenthal (1966), Friedman (1967) and Nunnally (1967) have devoted much attention to the specific relation between the epistemological competence of the researcher, the procedures of data-collection and the 'quality' of the knowledge which can then possibly be generated. One of the more outstanding writers in this category is Cicourel (1964) who in his book, *Method and Measurement in Sociology*, shifts the focus from the analysis of data and problems of interpretation to strategies for the gathering of data and to the relations of these strategies to overall epistemological and philosophical problems.

Processes of data-gathering

By consciously reflecting on my journey through the case, and by trying to understand what exactly had happened to me and to others during the gathering of data, I was able, in a decisive manner, to extend my perception of, and increase my understanding for, the actual determining mechanisms behind that which I *de facto* was studying: the phenomenon of power. In the case study I have on a number of occasions rendered an account of these reflections and relations. My concern on each occasion has been, as Weber has said, to understand the *meaning* of people's actions.[3] Another concern was to find a way in which I could adequately communicate this understanding to others. I have attempted to solve the latter on three different levels:

(a) By choosing a narrative construction for the case description that does not reproduce the course of events in a chronological order, but rather in the order in which the events gained significance for the persons involved and for the development of the course of events. This enables the reader to acquaint himself/herself with the context, both as I myself have been confronted with it, and as those who were involved experienced the events as these gradually took on a specific meaning for them.

(b) By showing in the chapter on method (by means of reasoning and argumentation rather than proof) how my way of working during the process of data-gathering is directly related to a specific epistemological perspective. The understanding of this relationship allows the reader to internalise the approach which I have used in the empirical investigation. It also enables the reader to accompany me on the meandering path which I have taken, and within which I have formed an idea, and finally reached a certain understanding of the object of study. It is thus only by understanding my journey and my means of travel that the reader can understand the essence of the object of this study. In other words, the reader 'ought to' give the terms of this text a reasonable chance.

(c) Finally, and still with regard to the communication of an understanding, I shall attempt in the following chapters to emphasise clearly the dimensions of action and interaction in my interpretation of the course of events. Thus, in my interpretation I insist upon the action perspective, and the aim of the argumentation around the interpretation is to integrate precisely these three ideas.

Everyday situations and studies of social processes

The traditional literature on method has assumed as its principal mission the cautioning of researchers against the possible dangers with which he/she may be confronted during the empirical work (but also before and after), which could involve a distortion of the understanding of the object of research and thereby affect the credibility of the research result. Researchers are advised to sweep all traces of subjectivity away and to protect themselves from themselves in so far as they should differentiate between their own opinions and knowledge acquired through research (something which is easier said than done, and which cannot, under any circumstances, be logically proved). One is advised neither to influence, nor to allow oneself to be influenced by, that which one is studying; the ideal is to place oneself under a glass cover and, in addition to this, to be invisible to those whom one is studying. There remains a risk that one allows oneself to be influenced (perhaps unconsciously) by that which one sees. Thus, the ideal should then really be neither to see nor to be seen: to study the imaginary. But even the imaginary can influence. What remains is merely to pretend that one is objective, unbiased, uninfluencing and uninfluenced, etc., simply by asserting that such is the case. Naturally there are certain rules and criteria, but these are not free from paradoxes. The paradox lies in that the 'durability' of these rules and criteria rests upon principles of exclusion,[4] resulting in an agreement as to what during a given period may be regarded as good research praxis and not any absolute law.

Many of the factors (or sources of bias) against which one is cautioned are, in fact, those which give content to everyday life and which render possible interaction and communication among people: various characteristics, races, sexes, age, psychosocial criteria such as religion, faith or social status of people, their personalities, values, prejudices and very many other factors along with their ways of reacting in different social situations, of making interpretations, of acting thereafter, etc.; all this is as much part of a social process which is the object of research as it is a part of other everyday situations. Goffman, for example, conducts an extensive discussion as to the ways in which individuals act in different situations, depending upon the nature of the interaction and the meaning of the actions.

> When an individual enters the presence of others, they commonly seek to acquire information about him or to bring into play information about him already possessed. [. . .] Information about the individual helps to define the situation, enabling others to know in advance what he will expect of them and what they may expect of him. (Goffman, 1959: 1)

The above-mentioned may seem trite in this day and age but this 'triteness' is nonetheless ignored to a large extent in the social sciences. The idea of the interplay between the process of data-gathering and the research situation has been described by Riecken (1962: 25). The process of collecting data about human behaviour is itself a social process and shares features in common with other situations and events of human interaction.

This idea has been of guidance to me both during my empirical work and subsequently with the analysis of the acquired data. To put it differently, there will always in all social research be factors that are considered to be irrelevant (or disturbing) when seen from the traditional point of view of rules and criteria for scientific value such as, for example, in the positivist point of view. We must, however, bear in mind that these factors are highly relevant for the social context that we are studying. Cicourel, who has inspired both Glaser and Strauss (1968), and Berger and Luckmann (1966) and who, in addition to this, has headed the halting discussions in the 1960s about ethnomethodological and symbolic interactionalist methods, comments here on some of the implications which this argumentation may have in a simple interviewing situation.

> The respondents and interviewers' stock of knowledge and their definitions of the situation will determine their mutual reaction to the questions posed. The relevancies not related to the substance of the interview per se will also determine the amount of extrainterview bias or error which exists. This is a necessary consequence of not treating each other only as objects for rational consideration, their attractiveness or unattractiveness to one another, their bodily presence, the social, physical, and role distance, all produce bias and

error *naturally* because these are basic to the structure of everyday conduct. (Cicourel, 1964: 79–80)

The argumentation conducted so far has been of guidance (generally speaking) with regard to my attitude towards the empirical work, and coincides with my mode of working in the field and with the narrative construction within which I have chosen to report the data. The profusion of detail in the case study, the emphasis on specific contextual situations including the physical environment,[5] are some of the many factors upon which I consciously insist so as to transmit to the reader the structures of everyday conduct of the persons involved (at least as regards the structures concerning the transfer process). This is important since it is within these very structures that the mechanisms of power studied here are granted a meaning (both for the actors in the process and for the reader of the case) and come to the fore.

FUNDAMENTAL VIEW

There is a fundamental paradox in the study of social systems: what we know about social systems depends on the methods we use for studying these; our methods, on the other hand, depend on what we know about the social systems. If this is true it is some kind of vicious circle of which we must become aware, and which we must understand if our research is to be built on firmer ground and generate more relevant knowledge. The circular reasoning unfolds as follows: in order to be able to carry out research and find out more about social interactions in organisations, I need to have a better method. At the same time, however, in order to find this method, I need already at the point of departure to know a great deal about the social interactions which I intend to study.

Many schools of thought within the social sciences have neither adequate methods nor lucid theories as regards social behaviour and action. However, this lack does not prevent the researchers from formulating statements and theories about all sorts of social phenomena. This is due to the fact that the researcher must have as his point of departure some sort of view (more or less implicit) of human nature and modes of action. In spite of the fact that this view is seldom made explicit, the reader can usually trace it from the researcher's way of working, from the interpretation and theories that might be suggested. It is, thus, meaningful to my mind to clearly define my outlook and to express my opinions explicitly. I see this as a phase in the consciousness which I have discussed above, on the one hand, and, on the other, as a tentative way of personifying my research activity. Another advantage of explicitly defining my view is that it allows the reader to gain insight into the guiding principles which are decisive for the internal criteria of logics and consistency in the text. An unarticulated view may on the one hand be criticised for want of articulation, and on the other escape trial and criticism. An articulated view can, apart from possibly becoming an object of criticism and discussion, usually throw light onto the interpretation and the generation of theory. At the same time, however, I must point out here that even though I consciously attempt to elucidate my view, it could still remain unclear since a fundamental outlook can at times contain dimensions which are difficult to express, or, as Goffman (1963: 3) states: 'assumptions about human nature [. . .] are not easy to uncover because they can be as deeply taken for granted by the student as by those he studies'.

The personal interest

I am of the opinion that most people are self-centred (this does not necessarily mean in an evil sense), and that their actions are primarily governed by personal interests. These interests and individual orientations cause people to act in such a way as to maximise pleasant experiences and minimise unpleasant ones. I do not mean that people are evil and that they do not care for others, but rather that when they do so, it is because they themselves feel all the better for it. Sartre (1964: 23) describes his relationship with his grandfather (Charles Schweitzer) in his autobiographical literary work, *Les Mots*. After the death of his father at the age of 30, the young boy Sartre became, as indeed did the rest of the family, dependent upon his mother's father. The latter, writes Sartre, 'loved in me [the child Sartre] his own generosity'. Another writer, Lenski, with lesser literary pretensions, writes that:

> When men are confronted with important decisions, where they are obliged to choose between their own, or their group's interests and the interests of others, they nearly always choose the former – though often seeking to hide this fact from themselves and others. (Lenski, 1966: 30)

That which I am suggesting here, and which is expressed by those whom I have chosen to quote, must not be taken as an expression for some kind of pessimism as regards human nature, but rather for my belief in the immovable particularism of the individual no matter how much the social systematic regulations may 'attempt' to mould him/her into a homogeneous mass.

The individual's need for particularism

When people form organisations (or organise work which they must carry out together), then the organising is in itself a solution to a primary and fundamental problem: cooperation among individuals, and the coordination of various tasks. The organisation and the process of organising is not something self-evident in human nature. Rather, it is a necessity (a rational one) and thus a 'human artefact'.[6] This implies that in all categories of community and organisation the individual remains individual. The problem thus becomes that if I am to understand the mechanisms of interaction upon which all organised activity is based, I must first be able to understand what happens when people's personal interests and diverging orientations meet, and to understand what it is that is decisive for the way that people act in different situations (including in everyday situations). What is it, then, that people attempt to bring out, to keep, and strive to develop in their interactions with others? Relatively little has been written on this concept, at least as far as its existential meaning is concerned. A number of socio-psychological models of explanation of such a concept are to be found in the sociological literature (Asch, 1952; Israel, 1979), but among these there are seldom any attempts to grasp its deeper meaning – that is, related to the essence of the individual – for that is what it is basically all about. Instead one speaks of reference groups, values, and of social norms as general concepts to explain all sorts of phenomena. The argument that is presented, and which is presumed to legitimate these concepts, very seldom throws any light on the essential question of why people act in the ways they do. According to the existentialists, the principal motive behind the actions of an individual is the need to maintain undiminishable freedom, and of the striving to maintain a certain level of autonomy so as to be able to 'experience' his/her will, intentionality and responsibility. What would an individual be were it not for his/her capacity to negotiate with his/her will (explicitly or implicitly)? Perhaps a thing. Individuality ceases to exist when the grounds for autonomous action are administered away. On the other hand, in praxis, this individuality never ceases to exist despite the most advanced constructions intended to annihilate it: each individual is a specific case with his/her own particularism, a certain will, particular interests to accomplish, a wish for a certain degree of freedom to strive for or maintain (or even to expand), etc.

Freedom of choice and responsibility

Man is always free to choose between the alternatives which he can see and which are possible for him. I do not, however, mean this in any absolute terms; many are the situations in which we are 'forced' to choose between alternatives which are not totally desirable. Moreover, also under constrained conditions, for example, with insufficient information about the implications of the alternatives. In this sense a person is always responsible for his/her choice.[7] Not to choose is also a choice. To deny that man always has a possibility of choice (in the philosophical sense) is what Sartre calls 'La mauvaise foi' (bad faith). People are in 'bad faith' when they attribute to iron necessity what they themselves are choosing to do (Berger, 1963: 144).

It is precisely this argument, with inspiration from existentialism and phenomenology, which has been brought to light in the discussions, well-known among social scientists, around the idea that man is a social product. At the same time, society is a human product and the structures which are experienced as confining are merely human creations and are thus able to be influenced and are open to change.

Interaction and exchange

The majority of social situations in which people interact are characterised by a process of exchange. In order to reach their goals and to secure their interests, people (especially in organisations) are involved in processes in which various categories of values are exchanged in material (e.g. salaries) and non-material terms such as emotions, prestige, social recognition, moral support, and not least, space of action. From my perspective space of action is of prime importance. I see this as an expression of (and as that which is *de facto* exchanged in the end in an interaction) the individual striving for freedom, for autonomy and for personal interests.

Inner and outer harmony

As I see it, people are confronted (especially in organisations) with two kinds of problems: one is to reach and maintain an inner harmony; the other is to reach and maintain an outer harmony with the social environment. In the seventh letter Plato comments on the advice which he gave to Dionysios, the heir of Syracusa, when the latter was about to lose his position of power due to the (for the structure and ethnical composition of Syracusa) unsuitable form of government. The Prince, says Plato, must first of all be in consonance with himself; i.e. reach an inner harmony. It is thanks to this inner harmony that a good interaction between the Prince and his people may be established: inner harmony is a prerequisite for outer harmony.[8] In an organisational context an individual can find satisfaction in the one or the other activity, depending on his possibilities and his capacity. Alternatively the individual may find himself in what he experiences as harmony (inner or outer) and which he evaluates higher than the other. After Ziegler's manipulatory attempts in connection with the writing of the minutes, Perdfelt 'decided' to withdraw from the negotiations. He felt that the conditions of the negotiations, together with the demands that were made of him, had disastrous consequences for his principles and for his inner harmony. Rather keep this inner harmony at least somewhat intact and sacrifice the outer harmony with the management. Another possible interpretation is that Perdfelt legitimises his action (or lack of action) by referring to his principles.

Before proceeding to the next phase of the argument, I would like to point to a number of factors of importance with regard to the relationship between everyday situations and studies of social phenomena. This relationship primarily concerns that for which I have argued above, namely that similar social processes characterise both everyday social activities and the activities implied by the process of data-gathering. This is not really a new thought. As far back as in Weber's action theory, which was later combined with other contiguous European traditions, traces of it could already be found. Perhaps the first school to seriously consider these aspects was the school of symbolic interactionism (George Herbert Mead, 1863–1931). These thoughts were later to be developed by Blumer (1966), and also by Goffman (1969 in particular). Of tantamount importance for these ideas was the ethnomethodological perspective with Harold Garfinkel (1967) as 'originator'. The ideas which he develops derive their origins from Edmund Husserl's (1859–1938) phenomenology, via a more sociological formulation by Alfred Shutz (1899–1959). Berger and Luckmann (1966) have elaborated the same ideas, but they have also based their work on that of Karl Mannheim from the 1930s. Ideas about the application of action theory in a symbolic interactionist perspective were the most strongly expressed in Cicourel's (1964) work. He asserts, among other things, that the researcher, instead of aiming his investigations at a certain field of study – where he chooses a certain aspect of society or a certain social category or group as the subject of his investigation with the purpose of giving a sociological (or social scientific) version of the order within that field – should study the methods and processes whereby the members of the society (or the organisation including the researcher himself), produce an order and structure in their world. Cicourel holds that we, as researchers, ought to problematise that which we normally take for granted. The problematisation of the process of data-gathering as social interaction has significant implications for the subject (or problem area) about which the gathering of data is presumed to provide knowledge (Cicourel, 1964, 1973). It is time, then, to go on and to problematise my own method of data-gathering.

PARTICIPANT OBSERVATION AS A RESEARCH STRATEGY

Suppose we were to do a comparative study of eating habits in the United States and France. Say that we were to find the food better in France and of a higher quality and more refined taste than that of the United States. Our interpretation of such a result would naturally be influenced by our existing knowledge of the two countries. We have perhaps lived in, read about or visited them. We would most certainly use concepts such as those of culture, history, and tradition, as arguments for our results and interpretations. Concepts which in actual fact have nothing to do with the investigation, but which we all to a certain extent bear within us from our schoolbooks or any further literary schooling that we might have had. For example, we would speak for France's rich cultural tradition, the Frenchman's propensity for excellence, for the aesthetics, and, on the other hand, discredit America for her brash status of newcomer, and the Americans for their lifestyle which seldom allows for more sophisticated food than a super-quick hamburger. Whether right or wrong, this type of interpretation would be determined by our previous knowledge of France and the United States.

If this is the case, it seems that our interpretations of any empirical results, no matter which ones they may be, depend upon what we already know beforehand about the object of investigation or about similar objects. In other words, the researcher who is totally free from previous knowledge (in this sense one usually speaks of being unbiased and objective) does not exist.

As researchers we gain precognition of that which we study, be it people, groups, society, or specific phenomena, by means of direct and indirect experiences; by means of our acquaintance with literature, history, etc. Yet the most direct way of acquiring such knowledge is by participating in the world in which the object of one's studies is articulated and/or in which those whose actions one wishes to understand are in interaction. Many researchers have realised the value of participant observation as a research strategy for the purpose of reaching an understanding of the meanings shared by the individuals or groups in whom one is interested. The method has primarily been developed by anthropologists and sociologists in the so-called Chicago school.[9] As can be seen in the case study, I have used the method of participant observation to a large extent in the investigation for the gathering of data. Those researchers who have been interested in this method have insisted upon the significance of the subjective dimension of social interaction. The concept of subjective is an antonym to the concept of objective. The meaning which the concept of subjective has for me is very close to that expressed by Nathanson (1970), who was primarily directly inspired by both Husserl and Sartre: a subjective understanding, for example, is quite simply an understanding related to a person; a subject in the sense of an individual. However, the fact is that for most social scientists the questionnaire, and to a certain extent the interviewing method, are regarded as objective ways for data-gathering. Amongst these researchers it is primarily a question of an attitude *vis-à-vis* science and scientific value; an attitude which is a sign of their acceptance of the principles of behaviourism, empiricism and positivism. As a result of this they insist upon hard data and upon precision measuring of unquantifiable social phenomena. The apostles of this view claim that the world is totally objective and that there are objective facts to be found 'out there in reality'. However, reality is neither 'out there' nor 'in here', it is omnipresent; and the world and the actions of people in it are not 'totally objective'. Neither do social phenomena have an objective structure, least of all the phenomenon of power. To my mind, and as I argue throughout the book, power is not something concrete in itself, but is rather more like a quality of a relationship. It comes about in interaction and is expressed in action. In this sense I can study and understand the phenomenon of power 'only' by means of an action perspective (interactional and meaning perspective).

Interaction and meaning

Organisation research has to a large extent been focalised on the study of various forms of social interaction (trade, marketing, relation between the producer and the consumer, financial transactions; leadership, organisational changes, etc.). Actually, one could assert that organisation and administration as a subject may be looked at from an interactional perspective. From my perspective I see action as that 'behaviour' which is meaningful to the actor (Husserl, Sartre, Parsons, Schutz and Weber are among many who have stressed this view). My interest is thus directed towards interactions in which two or more individuals react upon one another's actions. Even those researchers who work with phenomena on a micro-level, such as particular dimensions of accounting or specific sequences in a decision process, can be said to be working with different patterns of interaction. As Wilson (1970) says, the interactional process is the logical focal point in the social sciences; whereas Weber goes a step further and claims that:

> In general, for sociology, such concepts as 'state', 'association', 'feudalism' and the like, designate categories of human interaction. (Weber, in Gerth and Mills, 1960: 55)

Yet although interaction is central in our research we often fall short of the mark in this regard since, for the most part, we use inadequate methods. We need data on social processes, and questionnaires do not provide such data. Who is to provide such data? Somebody who is out in the field observing what is going on, perhaps even a participant observer (Whyte, 1969a: 47).

It is not only interaction which we do not attain with our usual methods, however, it is also the dimension of meaning. This limitation ought, meanwhile, to be placed in a larger context. Kuhn says that in each discipline there is a paradigm that dictates the rules and criteria whereby one formulates the ways in which the science within this discipline ought to be carried out. In this sense the scientist is provided with a sort of a map of orientation, and also with directions as to how these maps are made.

> Paradigms provide scientists not only with a map but also with some of the directions essential for map-making. In learning a paradigm the scientist acquires theory, methods, and standards together, usually in an inextricable mixture. (Kuhn, 1962: 108)

The way in which researchers within the social sciences conceptualise social interactions is one of the factors contributing towards the building of the paradigm of this science. The dominant view seems to be that the actor is regarded as the holder of certain positions, and that certain rules and standards accompany these positions. The explanation of the interaction then becomes a question of the connection between the attitudes, personality, etc. of the actors, on the one hand, and the role-expectations associated with their positions, on the other. Blumer, one of George Herbert Mead's students, discusses this, which may be seen as an insufficient 'structural conception':

> The conception presumes that a human society is structured with regard to (a) the social positions occupied by the people in it and with regard to (b) the patterns of behavior in which they engage. It is presumed further that this interlinked structure of social positions and behavior patterns is the overall determinant of social action; this is evidenced, of course, in the practice of explaining conduct by such structural concepts as role requirements, status demands, state differences, cultural prescriptions, values and norms. (Blumer, 1966: 542–543)

The conceptualisation which is here rightfully criticised by Blumer is based upon the assumption that the members of a group share common symbols and give the same meaning to that which is taking place around them. Language and gestures are seen here as a means of communication in the interaction of the members. The reader will recognise Parsons' (1960,

1965) structural consensus perspective, which in this context means that a 'culturally established cognitive consensus' exists within all groups, and that one can speak of a group's 'shared cognitive culture' that can be taken for granted by researchers with an interest in the group concerned. This outlook may have implications for research basis; implications which are not always positive. The assumptions which, from the beginning, are so carefully and consciously adopted can later easily be taken as a matter of course. Expressing the matter differently, they may be transformed into unconscious prejudices. The researcher transfers his/her own structural conception onto the object of study and the empirical result is marked more by the researcher's own conceptions than by the reality of the study object itself.

There is, however, another way of conceptualising interaction; namely as an *interpretative process*. Blumer (1954, 1956, 1966), Garfinkel (1967), and Turner (1962), all use a phenomenological existential tradition as their basis, and regard as fundamental the ongoing development and change of meaning during the process of interaction. Compare this with the structuralist (structural–functionalist) outlook, which has as its point of departure a prevalent stable (static) consensus. It is actually a question here of a dynamic vicissitude of the meaning in relation to the actions and interactions. One could speak of a dialectical relationship between interaction and meaning, or as Blumer has expressed it, 'in the flow of group life there are innumerable points at which the participants are redefining each other's acts' (Blumer, 1966: 538). That is to say, the perceived purpose and meaning in the other's actions are always provisional and subject to revision in the light of subsequent events in the course of interaction.

For my part, the interpretative view has implied that I have focused upon action from the perspective of the actor. In his actions the actor proceeds from that which he apprehends, sees and interprets. As far as possible I have tried to see the situations in the same way as the actors see them, to conceive of various objects in the same way as they do, and to grasp the meaning which these have for them. I have also tried to see how the actors organise their actions, and which logic of action they have as their point of departure. In short, I have attempted to clothe myself with the role of the actor and so see his world from his point of view. Now I am very aware that this is virtually impossible, but the main thing is that I have had this approach as my point of departure and have consistently acted in accordance with it. It has been my logic of action in the context. It has also, among other things, implied that I have devoted much time to attempting to understand various situations and their backgrounds.

Knowledge and experience

Earlier on in the text I mentioned that this view of the interpretative process derives its origins from a phenomenological–existential tradition. According to this tradition, knowledge is produced through immediate and intuitive perception of the human experience. R. D. Laing has grasped the essence of this approach in an elegant formulation:

> The task of social phenomenology is to relate my experience of the other's behavior to the other's experience of my behavior. Its study is the relation between experience and experience: its true field is inter-experience. (Laing, 1967: 17)

For phenomenologists such as Schutz (1962, 1964) and Nathanson (1963), social reality consists of the meaning which actors give to their actions (and the actions of others), and the situations which they experience. This would imply that an essential factor that ought to be taken into account in a research situation (that is, if one considers this approach to be meaningful) is that the structure and order existing within a society or an organisation are produced by the social actors and not by the researcher. Those conceptions and assumptions of which he/she might possibly be the bearer must not, under any circumstances, overshadow those which actually exist and which take place in the investigated situation. There are those, for example, who feel that a consensus should prevail in organisations with regard to the question of the distribution of power. This implies that, no matter what the actual conditions may be in a given organisation, these researchers will either see the consensus of which they themselves are the bearers, or they will judge (measure) the state of consensus in the organisation according to an ideal state of consensus. One thus totally ignores the reality of the organisation and its members' experience. In order to be able to understand this reality produced by the social actors, the researcher must reach an understanding of the construction of meaning, i.e. what different things mean to the actors, how meaning is changed through time and what influence this meaning has on their actions. Awareness and meaning are key words in the phenomenological–existential tradition with regard to the interpretation of social action. The most appropriate methodology seen from this point of view is participant observation. Included in this should also be the methods of working which the ethnomethodologists and social inter-actionists stand for. Many writers have commented on participant observation as a research strategy. I content myself here with the presentation of a definition which, to my mind, sums up the essentials of this strategy:

For our purpose we define participant observation as a process in which the observer's presence in a social situation is maintained for the purpose of scientific investigation. The observer is in a face-to-face relationship with the observed, and, by participating with them in their natural life setting, he gathers data. Thus, the observer is part of the context. The role of participant observer may be either formal or informal, concealed or revealed; the observer may spend a good deal or very little time in the research situation; the participant observer may be an integral part of the social situation or largely peripheral to it. (Schwartz and Schwartz, 1955: 343)

OBJECTIVITY

In the light of the argumentation carried out so far, it is obvious that my interest lies, on a general level that is, in the understanding of the grounds of social action. On a specific level, that is to say during my empirical work with the transfer process, my interest has been to understand and to describe the logic of action of the involved. A logical consequence of this is that my intervention could not be made from a detached perspective, but rather from the 'position of the actors'. As the reader will no doubt have noticed while reading the case study, I have used a combination of approaches in order to attain this; participant observation in different situations (meetings, visits), interviews, studies of documents, etc. This has often implied that I have had to adopt a standpoint with regard to various questions. It has also implied that my role has been transformed as the process has been under way and that I have been involved, in various ways, in the process which I have studied. A problem which automatically presents itself is that of *objectivity*. Have I been objective? This word has, as we all know, a particular resonance in all kinds of scientific work, and is looked upon almost as a holy cow. There are those who maintain that objectivity is (and ought to be) the norm of science (Storer, 1966). But exactly what is implied by objectivity, no-one can say.

Most dictionary definitions of the concept of objectivity insist upon 'being without bias or prejudice; detached; impersonal'. The more general formulations to be found in the literature speak for the necessity for researchers not to allow their values, preferences, beliefs, etc. to interfere with the processes of data-gathering analysis and interpretation. There exist more or less forceful formulations on this matter, the sum of which is that the researcher should be totally independent of the reality with which he/she is confronted in his/her empirical work.

The data-collection is objective; once the investigation is under way, the investigator is bound to follow the data whatever way they may fall – for or against his hypothesis (however cherished) for or against his personal preferences as a man. Biased procedures in collecting data have no place in science, nor has biased perception of the result. (Berelson and Steiner, 1964: 16)

Another drastic formulation reads as follows:

Objectivity means that the conclusions arrived at as the result of inquiry and investigation are independent of the race, colour, creed, occupation, nationality, religion, moral preference, and political predispositions of the investigator. If his research is truly objective, it is independent of any subjective elements, any personal desires, that he may have. (Bierstedt, 1963: 17)

If one were to follow these 'instructions' the researcher would function exactly as a data-gathering machine, and any other 'research machine' would be able to attain identical results. One could then ask: How good are our machines? Not very good, I'm afraid, at least if one takes objectivity as a criterion. When one's goal is to reach an understanding, then one cannot regard knowledge as being something *out there* to be discovered by being objective. Knowledge is by necessity rooted in our personal involvement in the action-praxis. The essential aim is to reach an understanding of the meaning which a studied object 'has' for those who experience that phenomenon. Naturally, one can argue that there exists no scientific procedure by means of which one can attain such a goal. Perhaps this is so, but in that case the crucial point is that of questioning our conceptions of science rather than refraining from attempting to reach meaning and understanding.

However, the discussion of objectivity is not that simple. There is a paradox in it. The most devoted behaviourists, for example, claim that we are able to know only that which we observe, and that we should not admit that the people whom we are studying have any experiences of their own. At the same time, all our knowledge seems to be a result of both observations and inferences. No matter which method the researcher may use, he is always forced to base his research upon certain assumptions and to make inferences that stretch beyond the actual limits of data. As a matter of curiosity, we can take a look at Tolman's commentary as to how to go about predicting the behaviour of rats.

But, in any case, I in my future work, intend to go ahead imagining how, if I were a rat, I would behave as a result of such and such an appetite and such a degree of differentiation; and so on. (Tolman, in Bakan, 1967: 80)

Thus we have here psychologists who are studying rats and who are forced to make assumptions as to how it is (or how it feels) to be a rat; quite a difficult exercise for a human being. But we can never know how close to the truth the psychologists come. Luckily for them, rats can neither as yet talk into a tape-recorder, nor fill in a questionnaire. For a person studying human actions the problem is of a different nature. He/she *knows* what it is like to be human and therefore assumes that humans have certain fundamental characteristics in common. Both in the gathering of data and in the interpretation of the same, however, the person acts as if he/she 'owned' the necessary knowledge for making inferences based on what people have said and on how they have acted. This means that the interpretation of data is carried out on the basis of the researcher's *own experiences*; and there is no other way that it could be. My point is that even those who believe themselves to be carrying out research in accordance with the pure criteria of objectivity – not to mix one's own experiences into the interpretation of the phenomenon to be studied – are in fact not doing so. There is no way that we can escape from ourselves, not even as 'objective researchers'.

As R. D. Laing (1967: 25) says, as participants in a social situation we are influenced both by actions and by experiences:

> When two [or more] persons are in relation, the behavior of each towards the other is mediated by the experience of each of the other, and the experience of each is mediated by the behavior of each. [. . .] My experience of you is always mediated through your behavior.

The understanding which I have attempted to attain, and the knowledge which I have hoped to produce by my way of working in the described process, together with my interpretation of the acquired data, have been possible thanks to my having focused on the interaction and experiences of the actors, as well as the relation between the actors' experiences and their actions.

INVOLVEMENT

When speaking of objectivity in the social sciences the argumentation is inevitably conducted towards the question of the researcher's involvement in the object to be studied. It may concern involvement in so far as the thoughts and opinions of the researcher are concerned, or it may mean involvement in the sense of partiality for a particular group or person, or for a certain idea. The problem of involvement becomes especially significant against the background of the research strategy which I myself have chosen. I believe that involvement is (to varying degrees depending upon the situation) a necessity within the social sciences if we, as researchers, have the ambition to attain and to pass on knowledge about real and experienced phenomena.

No doubt there are as many types of involvement as there are those who are involved (in a situation or other field/subject/phenomenon that is the object of research). But a categorisation into principal types is naturally possible, and although it may not be exact, it still corresponds, to a large extent, to the experiences made by the observer. Gans (1968) writes that the researcher can, in one and the same process of research, conceive of his involvement in three different ways. The total participant, who is totally and emotionally involved in everything which happens around him and who, not until he has left the field, returns to his role of researcher and begins to write down that which he has experienced. The researcher participant, who partakes in the process which he is investigating, but who is not fully involved in it. Finally, the total researcher, who observes that which takes place without any involvement whatsoever.

For my own part I have functioned on different occasions during the empirical work in accordance with one or other of the categories drawn up by Gans. I was, for example, in the role of 'the total participant' during some of my conversations with R. Perdfelt in which he talked about his private life and the extent to which it had been influenced by the course of events. It was obvious that the situation caused him a great deal of suffering and I could not as a partner in the discussion – and many a time as confidant – refrain from becoming emotionally involved. This no doubt influenced my subsequent conduct in the process, at least to a certain extent. I naturally tried to think this over and to convince myself not to take definite sides with one or the other party. I was equally involved in connection with the constitution of the work groups, and later in their work with the integration of L in W.

I never really had the role of 'the total researcher', except perhaps in the very beginning when I came into contact with the process in connection with a meeting for negotiations. Indeed, I sat quietly and took notes, but even though I was not involved verbally, I was nonetheless involved simply by being there. Unlike that which Gans claims, I feel that even 'the total researcher' is involved in that which he observes and studies: participant observation is *per se* an involvement. Besides, intervention (or involvement in that which one is studying) should not be a problem for social sciences. Even in the natural sciences, in quantum physics for example, it has long since been recognised that the researcher's actions – when he is carrying out an experiment with a certain phenomenon which he intends to explain – become a part of that explanation at which he will eventually arrive.[10]

My way of working during the major part of the process of data-gathering, however, can best be described by the third variant, 'the researcher participant'. I was partially involved in the entire situation. This involvement increased somewhat towards the final stages of the process, perhaps due to my having been socialised to such an extent that it became natural, both from my own perspective and from that of the others, to take up a more definite stand. The value of a certain amount of involvement is, among other things, that one has the possibility, as a researcher, of registering kinds of reactions, patterns of behaviour and actions other than those which are solely expressed verbally.

It seems that there is widespread agreement that we, as researchers, must begin to question our traditional methods[11] if we really wish to gain knowledge from and about essential phenomena. When our interest is inclined towards process and interaction, meaning and social relations, then it is also self-evident that participation and even active involvement are appropriate strategies of research. Our understanding of society depends on our experiences in society; or, to put it differently, since the observer is a human being studying other human beings, he has access to the inner world of experience. This direct access is sympathetic understanding and intuition by means of which the observer can view cultural phenomena from within (Tiryakian, 1965: 678).

Naturally, I do not mean that the researcher should strive to identify himself with those whom he is studying or to experience their experiences: this is an impossibility. What I mean, however, is that we usually deem an opinion or a statement that is based upon experience as having a greater value than one that is not. As a participant observer I have a certain experience of the context I am studying, even if my experience of it is not identical to that of those who live with it and experience it. (In general, my experiences can never be identical to anyone else's.) In such a case, participant observation, as a knowledge-generating strategy of research, is to be preferred to other research strategies: the researcher experiences at least a part of the process or of the phenomenon being studied. This is precisely that upon which the phenomenologists and existentialists insist with regard to studies of phenomena in 'the terms of the phenomenon itself': the observer's immediate experiences. As Schutz says:

> To a certain extent, sufficient for many practical purposes, I understand their behavior, if I understand their motives, goals, choices, and plans originating in their biographically determined circumstances. Yet only in particular situations, and then only fragmentarily, can I experience the other's motives, goals etc briefly, the subjective meanings they bestow upon their actions, in their uniqueness. I can, however, experience them in their typicality. (Schutz, 1954: 267)

This is possible since people share, to a certain extent, the same intersubjective world. Last but not least, a few words as to the possibility which the researcher has of communicating the knowledge he has acquired and the experiences which he has had. There are a great number of problems attached to this task; not only epistemological, but also problems of a stylistic nature. One way of tackling such problems would be, at least in part, to give a documentary presentation in the empirical report of the path taken by the researcher as regards the acquirement of knowledge and the experiences which he/she has had in connection with the research. The description should be full of detail, both with regard to the approach and to the actual course of events. The reader should be able to reach an understanding as to how the researcher's newly acquired knowledge and experiences merge into the research situation. In this respect a recommendation by Douglas might provide an appropriate ending to this section on the *generating of knowledge*.

> The simple expedient of insisting on more publication of the *actual*, as opposed to idealized or reconstructed procedures followed would help a great deal. (Douglas, 1970: 222)

THE THEORY OF DISCOURSE

So far I have reasoned around the epistemological problems directly or indirectly related to the empirical work and to its presentation in the case. That is, the third dimension of the method or the generating of knowledge. In the following section I shall take up entirely different methodological aspects, namely those which have to do with my standpoint *vis-à-vis* the theories and statements about power which I shall go through in the following chapters. That is, the fourth dimension of the method or *the theory of discourse*. The principal message in the section on *the archaeological perspective* and *the genealogical method* is, thus, composed of ideas as to how a discourse emerges, is built up and develops. Later on in the text (Chapters Four to Six), I shall use these ideas to analyse the discourse of power.

THE ARCHAEOLOGICAL PERSPECTIVE

My intention here is to lead the argumentation on to a *discursive* level. By discursive level, I mean the level where the argumentation revolves around the *conditions* that render possible the articulation of a vision, of a mode of thought, and of a mentality which, in turn, provides the basis for the production of knowledge (theories and statements) about a certain phenomenon or object. It is a dimension which has served as a guideline with regard to the review which I make of some of the theories and statements about the phenomenon of power, i.e. the discourse of power. It is not a theoretical review in the usual sense, but rather an analysis, in a double sense, of the constituent content of the discourse, on the one hand, and on the other hand of the explanatory potential and value of the concepts. By the constitution of the discourse I do *not* exactly mean the components of the discourse (i.e. concepts, theories and statements), but rather that which has been presumed not to be of any value in its constitution. This argumentation is concretised in Part Two. In this chapter I shall, as I mentioned earlier, lead the argumentation on to a discursive level. In the reasoning about the theory of discourse I have proceeded from Foucault's archaeology and Nietzsche's genealogy. These two perspectives (or metamethods) overlap since the latter (Nietzsche) has influenced the former (Foucault); but for the sake of clarity I shall keep the two perspectives apart as much as possible.

When Foucault published the book *The Archaeology of Knowledge* (*L'archéologie du savoir*), AS (1969), three years after his great work, *The Order of Things* (*Les mots et les choses*), MC, his intention was to throw some light on a number of epistemological problems that had been stirred up by this work and which were the centre of a lively debate both in France and elsewhere. MC had been regarded as a great intellectual happening and many critics and commentators had declared that the book was an unequalled application and illustration of structuralism. It was also held that, as a result of this, structuralism could now be regarded as the strongest intellectual movement to be developed in France since existentialism. Foucault was thus thought by many as being the new apostle of the movement. Whether or not this was true was at the time unclear. One could even venture to say that it was partly due to this confusion that the book *Les mots et les choses* was so indubitably successful. Foucault should perhaps have contented himself with this, but, instead he published AS as an elucidatory work. The latter was felt by many to be dreary and dry. It had no great success as compared with MC. Apart from this, the book has many strong theoretical and methodological features of importance for the understanding of Foucault's standpoint, both in his previous works and in those which he was to publish at a later stage. Gilles Deleuze (1975) comments on Foucault's AS as being 'more like poetry about his previous work than a discourse on his method'. Where others have found a highly stringent, difficult text, Deleuze has appreciated the text as an expression of the fact that 'Foucault's work has reached the point where philosophy, by necessity is poetry.' Perhaps this is so. Nevertheless, the most important point is still to attempt to find out what kinds of clarification he makes. A review of Foucault's text will show us that the elucidations occur in two dimensions.

Man: the subject and the concept

The first dimension, the most fundamental for Foucault himself, takes up and discusses a number of problems, all revolving around a common denominator: what is the status and the role of the subject 'man' and the concept of man in human sciences?

The principal idea of Foucault's work is to 'rethink' (repenser) man (the concept of man) as a subject and to give him a different position to the one which he has held for the last 300 years – from Descartes to Sartre. It was not, however, a matter of expanding the usefulness of the concepts and the method which characterise the structural–linguistic outlook. The confusion that was to arise was also due to the structuralists, each in their own way having a particular idea of the concepts of language and structure. It is in this sense that readers of *MC* can have believed Foucault's work to be an expansion of the structuralist perspective. In many respects, however, Foucault's work stands, with regard to object and method, in direct opposition to this perspective. Instead of 'freezing' the historical chain of events into structures, he looks for explanations of the nature of historical change. Instead of seeing language as structure, he sees it as *action* and as *happening*. Unfortunately, however, he had used the concept of structure in previous works, long before the breakthrough of the structuralist 'movement', in order to identify the type of analysis with which he was working. It was, however, a tautological usage of the concept. He could just as well have spoken of analysis instead of structural analysis. On the other hand, however, he used the concepts of *sign* (signe), *signifier* (signifiant) and *signified* (signifié). These are structuralist concepts, but for him they were quite simply designations for the material he dealt with. These concepts are not Saussure's 'inventions', but are rather as old as the civilisation of the Western world. For example, they are of central importance in the 17th century grammar of Port Royal.

It appeared from the studies he made of the general grammar, Natural History (L'histoire naturelle), and the analysis of wealth, that the entire classical age (the 17th and 18th centuries) was structuralistic. Knowledge during this era was based upon representations and signs, as well as on the analysis of relations between various solid elements which excluded both history and man as concepts. The last two factors were not incorporated in the thinking until the 19th century. In other words, Foucault's work shows that some kind of a structuralist frame of reference existed in the classical age, but that it disappeared at the beginning of the 19th century with the emergence of modern thought. The structural elements thus belong to Foucault's object of research rather than his method.

The historical periodisations

The second dimension concerns a number of difficulties aroused by *MC* of which he became 'aware' only after the book in question had been published. They were things which he himself gradually realised, or which others pointed out to him and which demanded elucidation, and relate to the question of the historical periodisations. One point of departure is that history may be seen as a series of isolated events without any self-evident connections. The historian's task then becomes to discover patterns of relations between these events, perhaps even causal relations. Proceeding from these patterns the historian then attempts to divide these events into manageable periods. The opposite way of looking at history is as a continuous process whereby occurrences and events give rise to one another in a causal sequence. In this case the historian's task would be to find breaches and transformations in this continuity. An important point which Foucault stresses here is that of the change which the history of ideas and general history went through: they changed sides. The history of ideas which traditionally focused on continuities now seeks, in Foucault's version, to find discontinuities. General history, on the other hand, tends to find stable structures.

From total to general history

The historian has traditionally regarded discontinuities with which he was confronted as obstacles for his work, but, nonetheless, as part and parcel of the material he was dealing with. Recently, historians have begun to see the discontinuities as the actual work *per se* rather than as obstacles. These are no longer seen as external circumstances, but rather as analytical instruments, positive rather than negative. What Foucault means here is that the idea of a 'total history' has gradually been transformed into that of a 'general history'. In the 'total history' all events converged towards a unique centre, being those principles, meanings, world-views, forms, etc. which constitute a society or civilisation. It is a form of historicity which one can find in the economic, social, political and religious ideas and praxis. These are objects of the same kind of transformation. The temporal sequences of events and occurrences are divided into large periods each with its own principles of consistency. In 'general history', however, one speaks rather in terms of series, segmentation boundaries, differences in level, time shifts, anachronical remains and possible relations. In other words, one does not attempt to join together various historical or various economical, political and cultural sequences. Neither does one try to find analogies and coincidences between these sequences.

Subject and history

The epistemological change which history is going through is, as a phenomenon, neither finished nor is it new. Marx was first in questioning the idea of a total history with uninterrupted continuities; the Hegelian idea of history. He intended to show – with his analysis of the economic, social and political relations – that all human activity, including human belief, is determined by conditions external to the consciousness of the individual subject. Nietzsche is also one of those who have sharply criticised the idea that man as a concept has always held a central position. He did this in his 'Généalogie de la morale', in which he showed that the most fundamental and the most 'pure' ideas about the moral of man, in fact, derive their origins from the most 'naked' power struggles. Recently psychoanalysis, linguistics and ethnology have thrown new light on the relations between man as a subject and his relations to the rules governing his desires, to his language formations and to his belief and praxis. But, says Foucault, these radical attempts to undermine the central position of man as subject, have been countered by an external opposition, on the one hand, and by 'intra-disciplinary' trends that stand for the opposite opinions, on the other. In this way Marx has been interpreted as a 'historian of totality' and as an apostle of humanism, whereas Nietzsche was seen as the transcendental philosopher of origins. As for Freud, he was regarded as the pioneer who, within a context of social and moral conformism, opened the door to individual self-realisation.

The cry goes up that one is murdering history whenever, in a historical analysis – and especially if it is concerned with thought, ideas or knowledge – one is seen to be using in too obvious a way the categories of discontinuity and difference, the notions of threshold, rupture, and transformation, the description of series and limits. One will be denounced for attacking the inalienable rights of history and the very foundations of any possible historicity. But one must not be deceived; what is being bewailed with such vehemence is not the disappearance of history, but the eclipse of that form of history that was secretly, but entirely related to the synthetic activity of the subject ... that ideological use of history by which one tries to restore to man everything that has unceasingly eluded him for over a hundred years. All the treasure of bygone days was crammed into the old citadel of this history; it was thought to be secure; it was sacralized; it was made the last resting-place of anthropological thought; it was even thought that its most inveterate enemies could be captured and turned into vigilant guardians. (Foucault, 1972: 14)

The transformation of the history of ideas

Thus *AS* is a study of the problems posed as a result of the usage of such concepts as discontinuity, interruptions, boundaries, series and transformations of the history of ideas. The history of ideas and the history of thought lend themselves appropriately to Foucault's enterprise since these concepts suggest that there exists, beyond the statements themselves, beyond individuals' conscious and unconscious intentions, a latent discourse beneath the one that is manifest. In other words, Foucault undertakes to isolate the conditions which make the statements possible without necessarily sorting out large amounts of facts which cannot be related to one another.

> It is in order to be sure that this occurrence is not linked with synthesizing operations of a purely psychological kind (the intention of the author, the form of his mind, the rigour of his thought, the themes that obsess him, the project that traverses his existence, and gives it meaning) and to be able to grasp other forms of regularity, other types of relations. Relations between statements (even if the author is unaware of them; even if the statements do not have the same author; even if the authors were unaware of each other's existence); relations between groups of statements thus established (even if these groups do not concern the same, or even adjacent fields; even if they do not possess the same formal level; even if they are not the locus of assignable exchanges); relations between statements and groups of statements and events of a quite different kind (technical, economic, social, political). (Foucault, 1972: 28–29)

The formation of the discourse

Against the background of this theoretical argumentation, Foucault looks back on his earlier work. He finds that the seemingly concrete entity upon which such large groups of statements as medicine, economics and general grammar depend is, in fact, illusory. He argues that these statements are characterised more by unconnected sequences, by distances, by substitutions and by transformations. These statements are far too heterogeneous to form an entity and to simulate continuity from one period to another. After having confirmed this, he set out to describe the discontinuities themselves so as to seek in them some kind of a system, of a regularity or hierarchy; order in disorder or systematics in madness. That at which he aims is the *system of dispersion* (système de dispersion) of the statements. The system of dispersion of the statements gradually forms a theory, a discipline, or a science. According to Foucault, these terms are misleading and historically loaded. He suggests the expression *discursive formation* (formation discursive). Since a theory or a science is never fully developed, the noun 'formation' seems to be more appropriate. When a number of statements form, in one way or another, a 'unit', they can be moulded into a theory which will eventually assume a scientific status. This theory or science constitutes a discourse 'about' something. Discursive formation is, then, that process of development and construction which, out of dispersed statements, makes up a discourse. The conditions and circumstances to which this formation is subjected and which, at the same time, make it possible, are given the designation of *rules of formation* (règles de formation). So as to polish up his concepts, Foucault makes a new investigation of the areas which he has treated in his earlier works: medicine, economics and general grammar. The purpose is to achieve a clear formulation of the historical *theory of discourse*.

> Is there not a danger that everything that has so far protected the historian in his daily journey and accompanied him until nightfall (the destiny of rationality and the teleology of the sciences, the long, continuous labour of thought from period to period, the awakening and the progress of consciousness, its perpetual resumption of itself, the uncompleted, but uninterrupted movement of totalizations, the return to an ever-open source and finally the historico-transcendental thematic) may disappear, leaving for analysis a blank, indifferent space, lacking in both interiority and promise? (Foucault, 1972: 39)

The rules of the discursive formation

Foucault goes on specifying the concepts in taking up for consideration a particular discursive formation, e.g. psychopathology. The question he asks is: How is such an object of discourse formed and what are its rules of formation? He could then distinguish three types of rules. The first type, *surfaces of emergence* (surfaces d'émergence), describes the special social and cultural areas within which a certain discursive formation appears. For 19th-century psychopathology these areas consisted of the family, the social group, the work situation and the religious congregation. All these had their own specific boundaries of acceptance beyond which one ran the risk of being classified as mad. These areas were not new to the 19th century, but they were organised in a more sophisticated way than previously. Moreover, they were combined with new surfaces of emergence, namely sexuality and the organisation of punishment. Sexual deviance from established norms became for the first time the object of medical observation and analysis. Within punishment, criminal behaviour (which now was distinguished from madness) was looked upon as a form of deviance, more or less related to madness. The second rule is *authorities of delimitation* (instances de délimitation). In cases of madness these authorities were represented by the medical profession whose knowledge and authority were recognised both by the administration and by public opinion. Other authorities of significance in such a case were the legislators who were able to decide who should carry the responsibility, and the church which was the qualified authority with the warrant to distinguish between the mystical and the pathological. The third rule is what Foucault calls *grids of specification* (grilles de spécification). These rules describe the systems used by the psychiatric discourse to specify different types of madness and relate them to one another. These systems were composed of the soul, which was looked upon as a group of hierarchical properties, the body, and the life and history of the individuals.

The discourse and its object

The three rules of formation which I have outlined above should not be understood in such a way that they are assumed to produce finished objects which can then be labelled and classified. An object of discourse, and the discourse *per se*, appear and develop together in one and the same process. In the same way the three rules do not exist independently of one another, but interact in a complex pattern so as to constitute the conditions that make a discourse possible. This means that the relations which could conceivably be found between the institutions, economy, the social processes, belief and praxis etc., do not belong to the object *per se*: it is not constituted by them. An object of discourse should not be confused with what the linguists call 'le référé' (the referent or the signified), i.e. that to which an oral or written sign refers. The discourse is not about an object; rather, it produces its own object.

> We are not trying to find out who was mad at a particular period, or in what his madness consisted, or whether his disorders were identical with those known to us today ... whether witches were unrecognized and persecuted madmen and madwomen or whether, at a different period, a mystical or aesthetic experience was not unduly medicalized. (Foucault, 1972: 47)

From statements to discourse

A significant question in this context is: what are the mechanisms that join the different statements together to form a discourse? In one chapter of *AS*, 'The formation of enunciative modalities' (La formation des modalités énonciatives), Foucault shifts the focus from *statement* (énoncé) to *enunciation* (énonciation). Enunciation does not refer to words that are conveyed by writing or speech. The concept describes rather the speaking or writing in itself as action – it describes the context within which the words are articulated and the position or status of the writer or speaker. *Enunciative modalities* (modalités énonciatives) refer to the laws which are decisive for the development of the discourse. These are the *status* of the speaker or the writer, the *organisations and institutions* from which the statements are uttered and dispersed, along with the *position* which the subject of the discourse has in relation to the contents of the discourse: status – since a medical statement, for example, cannot be made by anyone whosoever. The value of such a statement is inseparable from the person whose status in the field gives him/her the 'right' of expression. Organisations and institutions, since such a statement can only come from recognised and established authorities that have the confidence of the public; position, since the person making a statement always makes it in relation to a certain level in the field that is embraced by the discourse.

In this sense a statement is an integral part of the discursive formation. The former is defined by the latter:

> The subject of the statement should not be regarded as identical with the author of the formulation – either in substance or in function. It is not in fact the cause, origin or starting-point of the phenomenon of the written or spoken articulation of a sentence; nor is that meaningful intention which, silently anticipating words, orders them like the visible body of its intuition. . . . It is a particular, vacant place that may in fact be filled by different individuals, but, instead of being defined once and for all and maintaining itself as such throughout a text, a book or an *oeuvre*, this place varies – or rather it is variable enough to be able either to persevere, unchanging, through several sentences, or to alter with each one. . . . To describe a formulation *qua* statement does not consist in analysing the relations between the author and what he says (or wanted to say, or said without wanting to); but in determining what position can and must be occupied by any individual if he is to be the subject of it. (Foucault, 1972: 95–96)

Before going further in this argument, it could be meaningful to summarise that which I have said up to now with regard to the construction of the discourse, rules of formation, its object, as well as the statements and the discourse. It is a matter of a number of ideas and concepts that are related to each other in a specific manner so that they constitute what I refer to as the *theory of discourse*, or at least the fundamental principles of such a theory. This is thus a theory which gives us the instruments and concepts necessary to analyse a certain discourse. It also states the logic to be followed in order to be able to investigate the construction of a certain discourse.

Systems of dispersion is a concept on a general level. It refers to the system, the hierarchy and/or the order which governs the dispersion of the statements in a discourse.

Discursive formation. The dispersion of the statements in a certain order forms a 'theory', i.e. a discursive formation. This refers to the process which, from disparate statements and concepts, forms a discourse; but this process in itself obeys a number of laws and is governed by a number of rules. This leads us to the next step.

Rules of formation. Here it is a matter of the rules, laws and circumstances which constitute the conditions making a discursive formation possible. There are three main rules:

1 *Surfaces of emergence.* These indicate the social, political, economic and cultural spheres in which a discursive formation appears.
2 *Authorities of delimitation.* These authorities are represented by experts who are 'formally' competent to express their opinions in a certain field; but it is also the field of knowledge which is 'established' and 'recognised', and which automatically bestows a legitimate authority upon the 'possessor of knowledge'. In some cases these authorities may also be represented by the church, the state and the legislator.
3 *Grids of specification.* Within one and the same discourse there may be reason to differentiate between different types of objects that are treated by the discourse. Grids of specification refers to the classification system used for correlating or differentiating various objects in relation to one another.

Some observations

(a) These rules of formation do not produce ready-made objects that the discourse only has to label.
(b) The relationship of discourse to object is not causal: it is not the case of an object being the cause of the emergence of a discourse. Both object and discourse emerge in one and the same indissoluble process.
(c) Thus, the discourse should not be seen in terms of a theory about an object which in turn governs the formation and development of the theory. The discourse *produces* its object.
(d) The three rules of formation constitute the conditions which render possible the emergence of a discourse, its development, and its capacity to gradually begin to produce its own object.
(e) These rules of formation contain the discursive formation which, in turn, contains the formation of enunciative modalities, which is the next phase in the argument. This means that without conditions of possibility (rules of formation), we have no discursive formation; but when such does begin to develop, it states its own criteria of development: what belongs to the discourse and what remains outside; criteria and codes for the production of the discourse; procedures of exclusion and various types of prohibition.

The formation of enunciative modalities. As has just been said, this refers to the rules and criteria which govern (from within) the production and development of the discourse.

It is at this very level that it is necessary to distinguish between statement (*énoncé*) and enunciation (*énonciation*) – speaking and/or writing as action. The questions can always be asked: how are the statements combined to form a discourse? Which system of rules is fundamental to its formation etc? These are fertile questions in this context. Of greater interest, however, is the consideration of these modalities in terms of enunciation. This concept has greater chance of saying something about the 'internal' systems of rules which govern the production of the discourse since it refers to:

(a) speech and writing as action and not to the statements *per se*;
(b) the contexts within which the statements are articulated;
(c) the status of the speaker and/or writer.

This implies that statement is an integral part of the discursive formation while enunciation is an action that is an essential ingredient in this formation. What then, against this background, are these 'enunciative modalities'? They refer to:

(a) the status of he/she who has 'acted' orally or in writing (i.e. '*L'énonciateur*' = he/she who has made an enunciation);
(b) from which institution and/or authority the enunciation at issue originates;
(c) the position of 'l'énonciateur' in relation to the discourse within which the enunciation at issue is intended to be integrated.

These concepts, and the specific way in which they relate to each other, thus constitute the fundamental ideas in the theory or the set of instruments which, like Foucault's approach, can be used to analyse a particular discourse. This is not in order to prove its scientific value or to establish whether it is true or false, nor to analyse a discourse from the outside and make an assessment of its stringency or consistency. It is rather to illuminate the legitimacy of the discourse in relation to the area with which the discourse is concerned. An important element in this is that these instruments make it possible for the analyst to understand the special conditions that have allowed for the construction and development of a discourse. Later in the text I shall elaborate on the idea that the construction of a discourse is, in most cases, based upon principles of exclusion: the rules of formation of a discourse are more prone to state what ought not to belong to the discourse than what does belong to it.

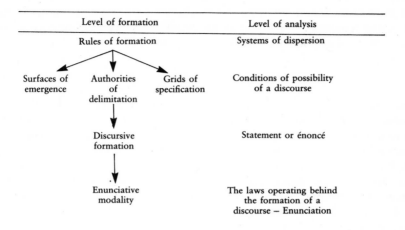

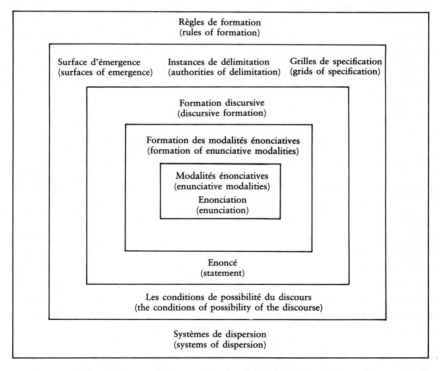

FIGURE 3.1 The theory of discourse. Analytical instrument and concept for analysing a discursive formation and its legitimacy.

This is also the case with the discourse of power. Naturally, this is on a relatively high level of abstraction, and I have no illusions of being fully comprehensive. In my analysis of the discourse of power I implicitly use the above theory as a whole, though emphasising its rules of formation, and its related principles of exclusion.

Discourse and power

The definitions of the concepts of *statement* (énoncé) and *enunciation* (speaking and writing as action), which I have outlined above, lead us to the following observation: an analysis of the discourse of power poses two essential questions. The first is that the discursive formation of the theory which has as its object the phenomenon of power, is possible thanks to the particular system and the particular conditions within which the statements can be articulated. Bearing in mind the rules of formation of the discourse, this means that the analysis of its formation ought not to be based upon its own statement, but rather upon that which is excluded in order for the articulation of the statements to be possible. I refer here to the principles and mechanisms of exclusion which make the formation and formulation of theories at all possible. Later in the text I shall deal with the implications which this argumentation has for my criticism of the discourse of power. The second question poses, in a general manner, the problem of power in the centre of the analysis of the discourse. Even if in this case it is a matter of an analysis of the specific discourse which makes a statement about power; all types of discourses pose a problem of power as fundamental for their formation. As I have mentioned earlier, a discourse should not be understood as something which is about an object. The discourse produces its own object. This means that when we speak of *the discourse of power* to denote the discourse which articulates statements, builds theories and assumes the shape of a discourse of power, we refer in the same train of thought to *the power of the discourse*, i.e. the power produced by the discourse in the form of rules, criteria, and disciplinary patterns as to what belongs to its territory and what remains outside. We also speak of the prestige, the status and the authority which such a discourse receives or acquires as a result of its being accepted by others as *de facto* saying something 'objectively true about an object'. The analysis of the discursive formation of power will thus not be a matter of assessing the validity or lack of validity of such and such a statement; rather it will concern its conditions of possibility.

From the history of ideas to archaeology

The archaeological perspective, as I have attempted to describe it in general terms, should not be confused with the history of ideas in the traditional sense and the principles in accordance with which one works in that tradition. As Foucault himself says, the history of ideas describes the transition between loosely formulated concepts, on the one hand, and philosophy, science and literature, on the other. Three principal themes are dominant in this discipline: genesis, continuity and totalisation. Archaeology is diametrically opposed to the history of ideas whose postulates and procedures it repudiates. The history of ideas operates in two ways: on the one hand it seeks continuity and unity in separate and marginal events, and on the other it tries to bridge different disciplines and to re-interpret from them the outside. Archaeology recounts the by-ways and margins of history; not the history of the sciences, but that of imperfect, ill-based knowledge, which could never in the whole of its long, persistent life attain the form of scientificity (the history of alchemy rather than chemistry; of animal spirits, of phrenology rather than physiology; the history of atomistic themes rather than physics). The history of those shady philosophies that haunt literature, art, the sciences, law, ethics and even man's daily life; the history of those age-old themes that are never crystallised in a rigorous and individual system, but which have formed the spontaneous philosophy of those who did not philosophise. The analysis of opinions rather than of knowledge, of errors rather than of truth, of types of mentality rather than of forms of thought (Foucault, 1972: 136–137).

The methodological principle of archaeology

The methodological principles of archaeology could be said to take heed of innovations, analyse oppositions, draw up comparative descriptions and explain patterns of transformation as they are, with their discontinuities and their oppositions. In the archaeological analysis the oppositions in a discursive formation are not merely surface effects to be linked together; rather they are objects *per se*, to be described and understood. Comparisons can be drawn between different discursive praxis (e.g. two theories, their formation and their scope, their implications and implicit assumptions, etc.). But comparisons can also be drawn between a discursive praxis and a non-discursive praxis. The latter denotes the institutions, political events, economic and social processes which build up the infrastructure in which a discursive praxis appears and where its development is rendered possible.

The idea of comparisons between discursive praxis and non-discursive praxis has a specific meaning in the archaeological analysis and deserves some specification. Such a comparison does not have as its purpose the uncovering of significant cultural continuities or the causal mechanisms of an era. In *AS*, Foucault exemplifies this with the formation of the medical discourse, its development as discursive praxis and its relation to non-discursive praxis. This reasoning is fundamental in Foucault's contribution to the theory of discourse: it is a matter of discovering the articulation systems which exist between discursive and non-discursive praxis. At the same time one must avoid two traps: on the one hand the hardly creative search for, and quoting of, homologies and coincidences. On the other hand the reproduction of a Marxist-inspired analysis in which the discursive formation is conceived of as *caused* by the non-discursive praxis. The first is merely an expression of the second. Foucault, after having studied under the supervision of Louis Althusser for a certain period, is well aware of the latter's attempt to 'save' the theory of determinism by the substitution of the 'base–superstructure' model with other units of analysis and semi-autonomous authorities with causal relationships. However, this reasoning is of a far too reductionistic nature for Foucault. In confrontation with the historical changes which came to pass in medical discourse in the 19th century, a causal analysis would endeavour to find connections, mechanistic explanations, and preferably continuities.

> To discover to what extent political changes or economic processes could determine the consciousness of scientists – the horizon and direction of their interest, their system of values, their way of perceiving things, the style of their rationality; thus, at a period in which industrial capitalism was beginning to recalculate its manpower requirements, disease took on a social dimension; the maintenance of health, cure, public assistance for the poor and sick, the search for pathological causes and sites, became a collective responsibility that must be assumed by the state. Hence the value placed upon the body as a work tool, the care to rationalize medicine on the basis of the other sciences, the efforts to maintain the levels of health of a population, the attention paid to therapy, after-care and the recording of long-term phenomena. (Foucault, 1972: 163)

Instead of treating the problem in such a manner, the archaeological analysis would consider it in the light of an entirely different mode of thought. How, for example, would medical discourse (a discursive praxis) be related to the infrastructure around it (a non-discursive praxis)? If archaeology brings medical discourse closer to a number of practices, it is in order to discover far more direct relations than those of a causality communicated through the consciousness of the speaking subjects. It wishes to show not how political practice has determined the meaning and form of medical discourse, but how and in what form it takes part in its conditions of emergence, insertion and functioning. This relation may be assigned to several levels. First, to that of the division and delimitation of the medical object: not, of course, that it was political practice that from the early 19th century imposed on medicine such a new object as tissue lesions or the anatomo-physiological correlations, but it opened up new fields for the mapping of medical objects. (These fields are constituted by the mass of the population administratively compartmented and supervised, gauged according to certain norms of life and health, and analysed according to documentary and statistical forms of registration. They are also constituted by the great conscript armies of the Revolutionary and Napoleonic period, with their specific form of medical control; and also by the institutions of hospital assistance that were defined at the end of the 18th and the beginning of the 19th centuries, in relation to the economic needs of the time and to the reciprocal position of the social classes.) One can also see the appearance of this relation of political practice to medical discourse in the status accorded to the doctor, who becomes not only the privileged, but also virtually the exclusive, enunciator of this discourse, in the form of institutional relation that the doctor may have with the hospitalised patient or with his private practice, in the modalities of teaching and diffusion that are prescribed or authorised for this knowledge. Lastly, one can grasp this relation in the function that is attributed to medical discourse, or in the role that is required of it, when it is a question of judging individuals, making administrative decisions, or laying down the norms of a society. It is not a question, then, of showing how the political practice of a given society constituted or modified the medical concepts and theoretical structure of pathology; but how medical discourse as a practice concerned with a particular field of objects, finding itself in the hands of a certain number of statutorily designated individuals and having certain functions to exercise in society, is articulated on practices that are external to it and which are not themselves of a discursive order. If in this analysis archaeology suspends a causal analysis, if it wishes to avoid the necessary connection through the speaking subject, it is not in order to guarantee the sovereign, sole independence of discourse; it is in order to discover the domain of existence and functioning of a discursive practice. In other words the archaeological description of discourses is deployed in the dimension of a general history; it seeks to discover that whole domain of institutions, economic processes and social relations on which a discursive formation can be articulated; it tries to show how the autonomy of discourse and its specificity nevertheless do not give it the status of pure ideality and total historical independence; what it wishes to uncover is the particular level in which history can give place to definite types of discourse, which have their own type of historicity and which are related to a whole set of various historicities (Foucault, 1972).

To sum up, it could be said that the archaeological description of a certain discourse, in this case the discourse of power, seeks to discover those areas which form the basis for the discursive formations: authorities and institutions, economic processes and social conditions. The description focuses on the ways in which the discursive formation of power is articulated in these areas. When, later in the text, I discuss and analyse some fragments of the discourse of power, I shall try to bring to light some of the particular connections that may be found between the meaning of the discourse and the thought patterns preceding and dictating it. This does not imply, however, that I 'find' (or create) causal connections; rather that I try to show how the thought processes which precede the discourse are, in fact, a part of the conditions which make it appear. By means of such an analysis, the apparent specificity of a certain discourse comes forth as merely contingent to the conditions of possibility of the discourse. Thus, I do not see the discourse of power as being totally independent, nor as being an ideal discourse. Rather I focus on its arbitrariness and on the procedures of exclusion which direct its emergence.

FOUCAULT AND NIETZSCHE: THE GENEALOGY

It is necessary, when speaking of the archaeological perspective in Foucault's work, to relate it to Nietzsche's work as a whole, on a general level, and to his genealogy in particular.

After May 1968 the French government decided to split up the concentration of the Parisian university in Le Quartier Latin. This was done by the creation of a number of autonomous units in the periphery of Paris. Foucault was invited to head the department of philosophy at one of these units, Vincennes. The government hoped in this way to gather the 'gauchists' of all shades in some sort of a ghetto in which they could give vent to their debates without too much damage to the establishment. Vincennes was soon to become a battlefield in which different forces were grouped together to form two principal wings: Leftist-intellectuals without any concrete ideological affiliation and communists. These vehemently attacked each other with the aid of theories, interpretations, analyses, social ideals, etc.[12] Foucault looked on from the outside even though he was in the middle of the battlefield. Indeed, he too attacked, but when he did so it was with other aims in mind than those of the antagonists in the field. For example, he never entered the debate which had various interpretations of Marxism as its object. Instead, he questioned the usefulness of 'historical materialism' in the analysis of today's social, economic and political conditions, yet he did so with points of departure other than those given by the 'historical materialism'.

In Vincennes everyone was free to say whatever he/she wished, at least in theory. In reality everyone spoke about the same thing, and what one person said was not very different from what another had to say. In the midst of the confusion Foucault spoke of Nietzsche. Not only that, but he spoke well of him. He even devoted a number of lectures to his philosophy; but it was not until the middle of the 1970s (five to six years later), that what he was trying to say was rediscovered by the 'new philosophers'.[13] To talk about Nietzsche in Vincennes was strange in itself; but to find support in Nietzsche's ideas when trying to discover or reveal the mechanisms of power in society was even stranger. For Nietzsche was still, for many, associated with fascism, antisemitism (and sometimes even nazism). Now everyone knows that this was a false picture which his family,[14] through diverse intrigues, had given of him. I do not mean to say that Nietzsche's rehabilitation was due to Foucault's lectures; rather that his 'reactivation' in our contemporary thought, both in France and elsewhere, is due to a large extent to the role which he played in the formation of Foucault's ideas. In this sense I would say that Foucault contributed to the reintroduction of Nietzsche and to the throwing of new light on some essential and until then ignored sides of his work.

The lectures at Vincennes culminated in a collective publication, led by Foucault: *Nietzsche, la généalogie, l'histoire* in *Hommage à Jean Hyppolite* (1971). This is the only occasion when Foucault explicitly discusses Nietzsche's genealogy as a method, as well as its implications and applications. In the rest of Foucault's work Nietzsche is quoted sparingly, often merely as a sign, in arguments demanding his presence rather than his voice. This presence is dominant in *AS*; he is hardly quoted at all, yet he is very much present. It is as if all direct reference to Nietzsche would be completely superfluous since the whole of the theory which Foucault produces as his working method, the archaeology, rests on Nietzsche's ideas. Foucault's descriptions of the Nietzschean genealogy in *Nietzsche, la généalogie, l'histoire*, are indeed applicable to Foucault's own archaeology.

Power as a theme

The majority of the readers of Foucault are inclined to believe that it is he who has introduced the theme of power to the analysis of discourse. In a personal discussion with him he said that this was not the case and that, on the contrary, he was surprised at the difficulties which he had in formulating the theme. He meant that in *L'histoire de la folie* what he was actually talking about was nothing but power in relation to the discursive formation of the psychiatric discourse; yet without then being able to articulate this. He also admitted that the question of power in the analysis of discourse ought to have been made more explicit in *AS*, since, after all, it is a work about the theory of discourse. On the other hand the theme of power seems to be less absent in, for example, *L'histoire de la folie* (which is an earlier work) since the discourse of madness is described in relation to the institutions from which it emanates and to the rules of formation constituting its conditions of possibility. The theme of power is implicitly there even if it is not explicitly taken up for consideration. Foucault became conscious of this, according to what he himself has said, after having written *AS*. Naturally, Nietzsche played an important part in this consciousness. This then resulted in Foucault renaming his archaeology to the Nietzschean concept of genealogy. The theme in Foucault's later works thus became: *The genealogy of power through the archaeology of discourse.* He asserts that it was Nietzsche who was the first to specify the relations of power as being fundamental for the philosophical discourse. For him Nietzsche is the philosopher of power. Furthermore, he managed to think in terms of power without confining himself within a political theory.

The theme of power in relation to the rules of formation of the discourse comes to the fore in Nietzsche's work primarily in his striving to reach the *origin* of things.[15] With this procedure he attempts to grasp the exact essence of things and their well-protected identities. This procedure presupposes the existence of phenomena hidden behind the external façades; the invisible behind the visible, and it is precisely this procedure which was to become Foucault's approach throughout his work. The totality of history is repudiated and the ideal essence which things are *a priori*, by and large, assumed to have prove to be artificial fabrications. A scrutiny of the history of reason, for example, shows that it was begotten by a combination of coincidental circumstances rather than by something absolute and by God given. The search for truth and the precision of the scientific methods derived their origins from the passions of the academicians, their mutual persecutions, their fanatical and endless discussions and their competitive mentality; it is these personal conflicts which *peu à peu* have shaped the weapon of reason (Foucault, 1971a).

In *Le gai savoir* (1882–1950) Nietzsche writes about man's illusions and his 'collective lie'. He demonstrates that our highest values (as moral principles) rest upon a history that is far from decent. In this history both body and soul are objects of 'indoctrination' and 'normalisation': the body is bent and shaped by the rhythm of work as well as poisoned by food and values. Foucault, in addition to doing work on the same theme, examined the meaning of punishment in this context, i.e. as a means of indoctrination and normalisation (*Surveiller et Punir*, 1975). The relations between the works of Nietzsche and Foucault are so numerous, both implicit and explicit, that it should not be an exaggeration to say that the latter's research is nothing but a continuation or an application of the ideas and methods of the former. The idea of the existence of a will with particular motives and strategies behind all aspiration for truth, knowledge and cognisance is a very Nietzschean notion, but it also permeates Foucault's work. On several occasions Nietzsche reasons about that which he calls *the will to knowledge* (La passion de la connaissance) and 'the decisive role that it plays in the enabling of man to raise himself out of the nihilism into which he has allowed himself to sink'.[16] It is no coincidence that one of Foucault's works (1976a), has as its title: *The will to knowledge* (La volonté de savoir).

The genealogical approach

'The visible world reveals itself to our eyes through our own values. It is ordered and chosen because of these', Nietzsche says in *Volonté de puissance* (1948). Nietzsche draws our attention to the fact that knowledge and cognition (theories and discourses) are permeated by values. He thus paves the way for a new line of action in research: the genealogical approach. My review of some fragments of the discourse of power follows the main lines of thought in this approach. It constitutes a critical examination of the discourse's *a priori* points of departure that are based on values (and the value of these) of various kinds. The method implies that I attempt to discuss what lies behind the normative actions given in the discourse. The analysis is thus aimed towards that interpretation of reality that lies behind them and which, in turn, is based on original values.

Nietzsche proceeds from the concrete existence in which values are normally grouped together so as to form what he calls value structures or 'tables de valeurs' (*Zarathoustra*, 1885–1968). This value structure constitutes that which he has defined in other texts as 'moral' in the same category – conceptually and methodologically – as the concept of 'ideology' amongst Marxists. The difference is that for Nietzsche the themes of the values and existence are essential, whereas the Marxist analysis is based on the conception that man's praxis is determined as social production.[17]

The genealogical approach implies that I describe the discourse of power so as then to critically analyse its value and discuss the ways in which it influences our understanding of the phenomenon of power in organisations. In order to be able to do this I must first evaluate the point of departure of the discourse, since I consider the discourse at issue to be a set of symptoms which emanate from a certain mentality. I also discuss the way in which the discourse produces its own object, i.e. the phenomenon of power, and then proceeds to shape it into a specific form which will then be decisive for the way in which the phenomenon in question is interpreted and understood. In this way the argument will pose two ideals against each other: the primitive conception of power in the prevailing discourse of power (primitive in the sense that it is limiting and does not allow for an understanding which reaches beyond that which is given), and a conception of power which has its basis in the origin of the manifestations of power, i.e. the individual's conditions of existence. I shall later discuss these conditions with the help of concepts taken from the teachings of the existentialists.

The above-mentioned makes special demands on the criticism. For criticism to be convincing it must usually have as its ambition to discuss and perhaps to reject, with the aid of logic, an argument or a theory. However, this criticism is aimed primarily at the evidence, without changing anything which might be at the bottom of any inaccuracies. A criticism which has as its ambition to discuss the origin of the inaccuracies does not see these as merely being weaknesses in the logic or in the logics and the evidence of the discourse of power, which are of interest to me, but the mentality from which it derives and the norms which it produces. On this point the archaeological perspective and the genealogical approaches meet. The norms produced by the discourse of power specify partly what power is, on the one hand, and on the other hand, how it should be understood and studied. These norms thus both specify and are specified by the rules of formation of the discourse.

PART TWO
The Discursive Formation

CHAPTER 4

Power, Politics and Action in Organisations

Most people have an intuitive understanding of what the concept of 'power' stands for: one tends to associate it with strength, leadership, authority, control, influence. One also associates it with different roles: tyrant, dictator, king, leader, ruler, general, subject, slave. One may see it in a more global context: the ruling class, the elitists, the state, the party, etc. However, there appears to be no unequivocal definition of the concept. At the same time there is no doubt that power, whatever it may be, is to be found in organisations, and that, recently, renewed interest has been shown in this phenomenon. This, to a great extent, is due to the political nature of organisations, and to the general debate as seen from a macro-sociological perspective in which questions concerning the distribution of power constitute a part. The question as to why power exists in organisations and in social interactions on the whole, has been answered in a variety of ways. Berle (1967: 7), for example, maintains that: 'given a choice between chaos and order, organization members have opted for order and stability, which relies to a great extent on power'; whereas Zaleznik (1971: 17) simply states that: 'organizations operate by distributing authority and setting a stage for the exercise of power'.

There are many differing opinions which, as I argued in the Introduction, may be assigned either to those writers who support the traditional theory of management, having as its point of departure the view that organisations are rational and harmonious entities, or to those writers with an inclination towards apocalyptic presentations of organisational class struggles.

Beyond the theoretical discussions, which in themselves are significant for the development of knowledge, the empirical experiences which I have reported indicate that the organisations can advantageously be regarded as political negotiable entities. This opinion has also been expressed, amongst others, by Clegg (1975) and Burns and Buckley (1974). This implies that we can assume that the actors, in their daily interactions in the organisations, are constantly involved in implicit and explicit negotiations.

159

In an almost continuous manner they are shaping and reshaping groups and coalitions, and their actions are of a tactical and strategical character. The totally passive and apolitical actor, as presented in the literature for 'industrial psychology' and the 'sociology of organizations', is very rare, if not non-existent.[1]

As has been illustrated (in the case), survival in the organisation has often taken the form of political action. By political action I mean those actions which bear implicitly an element of tactics and strategy with the purpose of either attaining a certain end, or of protecting oneself against others, the consequences of their actions, or both. Other immediate examples where politics is an everyday act are the universities.[2] The political nature of the organisations and the strategical moves taken by the actors are fundamental characteristics forming the basis for the forthcoming discussion. The theoretical discussions which I will present, and the notions and statements which will be generated for the analysis and the interpretation of the case, are to be seen as a reflection of the empirical reality. It should perhaps be observed, at this stage, that I refrain from making any moral issue when I describe the processes involved in organisations as political actions; this description has, as far as this context is concerned, potential empirical relevance.[3] Bacharach and Lawler (1980), in their discussion of the Watergate affair, are surprised by the fact that the available theories and concepts, whether in political science, organisations theory or elsewhere, have such a mediocre explanatory potential.

> What we saw on television screen during the Watergate hearings, for better or worse, told us more about organizational reality than all the theses and academic articles that have been published since 1972. The innermost workings of one of the largest and most complex bureaucracies in the world was exposed daily for our scrutiny. Machinations of this type – although not necessarily corrupt ones, like those – were, and are, a basic reality of organizational life. (Bacharach and Lawler, 1980: 2)

Myth and reality

The question as to why organisation studies of the last 15–20 years have been marked, for the most part, by an apolitical perspective, is worth discussing. Prominent examples of these studies are Blau and Schoenherr (1971), Hage and Aiken (1970), Pugh et al. (1968), to mention but a few. There are those (Clegg, 1979a) who maintain that this strange attitude could be due to a misinterpretation of Weber's (1947) contribution to organisation theory. Different groups of social scientists, particularly 'sociologists', have, with the use of different methods, devoted far too much time and energy confirming or rejecting the empirical relevance of

Weber's ideal bureaucratic construction. Crozier points out, not without a touch of irony, that Weber is the most quoted 'organization theorist'; but if one takes a closer look at the manner in which he is quoted, one notices that it is practically always in connection with the few pages in which he presents his ideal type of organisation.[4]

Many organisation theorists seem to have overlooked the fact that the Weberian perspective primarily implies that the attention should be focused on the *actions* of the individuals and the groups. The concept of action is central in this study and will be discussed in detail later in the text. Weber, in specifying the primary organisational structures, also regarded these as a product of conscious political decisions taken by the groups. Organisations, according to Weber, are by no means rational, simple, determined systems of interdependent structures. Precisely this kind of simplification is often to be found in the literature and serves to maintain the myth of the apolitical and oversocialised organisational member; but in empirical reality it appears that, beyond rationality and simple determined systems, people act through continuously renewed premises (Silverman, 1970) which cannot be confined to any single model. What we have observed is that within the relationship W–L, political tensions were born and renewed time and time again between the antagonists. Weber (1947) saw the organisations as *imperatively* co-ordinated systems. However, the subsequent organisation researchers tended to focus their attention on the theme of coordination with little, if any, emphasis on the imperative dimension. In other words they have concerned themselves with the formal mechanisms of coordination and neglected the implicit and explicit political negotiations as well as the power relationships. Blau and Schoenherr (1971), who represent this one-sided perspective, find justification in Weber's work for the exclusive study of the formally interrelated attributes of organisations. There are, however, some authors who are dissatisfied with this interpretation. Collin comments that:

> Weber's examination of organizations transcends this important, but nonetheless circumscribed, concern with formal coordination. The Weberian perspective also includes an emphasis on interest groups, tactics and compliance. (Collin, 1975: 75)

It would not be true, however, to claim that the imperative dimension has been paid no attention whatsoever. Etzioni (1961a), for example, examined power relations among groups and among individuals in organisations. Another Weberian author, Blau (1964), asserted that it is through the studying of power in social relations that we can hope to reach an understanding of the ways in which social structures emerge.

Apart from the 'misinterpretation' of the Weberian theory by certain researchers, there seem to be other explanations as to why the development of a power-political theory of intra-organisational dynamics has been inhibited. These reasons are perhaps connected with, and are a consequence of, the concentration on merely one of Weber's perspectives. There is a tendency to define organisations as if they were normatively integrated systems, thus ignoring the political conflicts and other tensions which are made manifest in power relationships. One tends also to regard organisations as holistic entities. This conceptualisation overlooks, or perhaps renders impossible to identify, the diverging interests and orientations of the actors, the formation of coalitions and all the other intra-organisational actions upon which the development of a political perspective is based. In other words the conceptualisation of organisations as apolitical can never be more than merely a theoretical frame of reference with no correspondence in reality.

The studied process clearly demonstrates that the professed normative integration is hardly reflected by the course of events. The direction in which the course of events developed could rather be seen as a reflection of the actions taken by the actors – the strategies from which these emanated and the power relations in which they were manifested. The way in which the process developed was a product of the meaning and interpretation given by the actors to their actions and their experiences of the situation (Schutz, 1953, 1954; Nathanson, 1963). This point of view was stressed by Weber, although it has to a certain extent been overlooked. He defined the social sciences as a field of knowledge which

> attempts the interpretative understanding of social action in order thereby to arrive at a causal explanation of its course and events. In 'action' is included all human behavior when and in so far as the acting individual attaches a subjective meaning to it. Action in this sense may be either overt or purely inward or subjective; it may consist of positive intervention or acquiescing in the situation. Action is social in so far as, by virtue of the subjective meaning attached to it by the acting individual (or individuals), it takes account of the behavior of others and is thereby oriented in course. (Weber, 1947: 88)

A concept of central importance in Weber's discourse is *verstehen*, the essence of which is the understanding of the meaning given by the actors to their actions. In spite of Weber's prime interest being in generalisations – i.e. in the external, visible conditions – he was nonetheless concerned with the meaning of the actions. In *The Protestant Ethic and the Spirit of Capitalism* (Weber, 1930), he concentrated on demonstrating the connection between the religious affiliation and the accumulation of capital, on the one hand, and on the religious motives deriving their origins from the ethical dimension of ascetic protestantism, on the other. According to

Weber, human behaviour cannot be understood without reference to the motives of the actors and to the meaning which they give to their own actions and to those of others.

It is perhaps necessary to point out that my concern here is not to state anything about Weber's theory *per se*. The point is rather that the many organisation theorists who claim to be Weberians, tend, for some obscure reason, to disregard the important side of Weber's contribution, namely that which emphasises the political character of organisations, the meaning of the actors' actions and their interpretations of situations.

There are, however, a number of authors who have recently argued for the necessity to study the phenomenon of power in organisations. From a political point of view there are some who have presented statements of interest for the meaning of political power in organisations. Crozier (1964, 1976) and Selznick (1949) emphasise the centrality of this theme for the understanding of intra-organisational behaviour. Crozier, for example, asserts in this context that studies of power have not made much progress since Machiavelli and Marx. Even if I am inclined to agree with him on this matter, the fact remains that researchers such as Weber, Michels, Lipset, Dahl and many others have devoted much attention to this subject.[5]

Allison (1971), Baldridge (1971), and Pettigrew (1973), like Crozier, focus their attention on intra-organisational behaviour. The attained results, however, do not seem to provide a good explanatory potential with regard to the political character of organisations. Interesting attempts have been made elsewhere to develop a macro-institutional theory for the analysis of organisations in the light of the political economic theory (Aldrich, 1979; Karpik, 1972a,b, 1977; Zald, 1970). Recently the political perspective has secured a more prominent position in the search for knowledge regarding the nature of organisations, but there is still much to be done in this direction. The knowledge required is precisely that which would illuminate intra-organisational power and political processes. Pettigrew (1973: 23) regrets the lack of such knowledge when he holds that only political scientists appear to have collected extensive data with the concept of power in mind.

However, political scientists are not the only ones who have devoted attention to power in a specific sense. The phenomenon of power has, to quite a large extent, been studied by both sociologists and social psychologists (Tedeschi, 1970; Tedeschi et al., 1973), even if the chosen perspective has ignored the actions of the actors and the organisational political processes. The 'Community power debate' illustrates the political scientists' approach to the study of power. This debate will be taken up for consideration later.

On the other hand, organisational and industrial psychologists have devoted attention, from their initial Hawthorne study (Roethlisberger and Dickson, 1939) until now, to cooperation, control over workers, motivation, leadership, etc., but have ignored the political character of organisations. It has been shown in this case that control and leadership are actual problems in the process, but it also seemed that these problems are manifestations of fundamental antagonisms of a political nature.

The contributions which depoliticise the analyses of organisations seem to constitute a certain tendency within the field of organisation theory. Many theorists have uncritically adopted the assumption of the totally controlled and oversocialised individual, with the result that the subsequently presented studies are often one-sided. The question is whether the 'organisation man' has ever existed – he or she who is highly willing to cooperate, who strives exclusively for social recognition and who does his/her best in order not to disturb the generally prevailing spirit of consensus (Whyte, 1956). In Wrong's (1961) classical text a possible explanation of this one-sidedness is to be found. Wrong argues that in having the oversocialised idea as their point of departure, both psychologists and organisation sociologists make the same basic assumptions about human behaviour and action in social situations. The psychologists maintain that what motivates people is the desire to obtain the normative recognition of others, whereas the sociologists regard the social situations as being governed by the idea of consensus. The contributions dealing with leadership, motivation, work satisfaction, etc. are often based on this sort of assumption; that is to say, behaviour is both motivated and controlled almost exclusively by the normative striving for reward and social recognition. Parallel to this, sociologists are concerned with the mechanisms of coordination and structures, assuming that people are doing their work quietly and without disturbance of organisations in which a spirit of consensus and cooptation predominates. When these two research traditions meet they tend to result in organisational perspectives free from power, politics and conflicts power. Examples of such results appear in the contributions dealing with the structuring and design of organisations (Bennis, 1975; Burke, 1976; Friedlander and Brown, 1974; Nord, 1975; to mention but a few). One exception in this context is Pfeffer (1978).

These assumptions have no empirical relevance, and this lack is substantiated by a number of interesting empirical and theoretical studies (Crozier, 1964; Crozier and Friedberg, 1977; Child, 1972b, 1973; Silverman, 1970). These studies, among others, have in recent years revealed the complex and manifold character of intra-organisational processes. As shown in the case studied, traces of an operationalised consensus mentality have not been easy to find. The actors in the W–L process seemed to interpret situations differently and to base these interpretations on their own personal interests. They acted as antagonists rather than oversocialised cooperative parties driven by a common motivation. Relations among them amounted to the creation of situations in which the space of action of one of the parties was expanded at the expense of that of the other. Beyond the simple model of an endeavour for normative recognition, the antagonists seemed rather to strive for *autonomy* and for *freedom* to realise their *intentions*. Even though the final outcome has not been as expected, the process has nonetheless been marked by struggles in which the actors have strived to attain their personal goals. As an extension of this, the antagonists developed various *strategies* with the intention of counteracting the strategies and actions of the opposing parties, and as reaction against the organisational rules and regulations which were felt to be inhibiting and constraining. In other words, it could be said that the case did not show passively approving organisational members who adjust their behaviour to rationally designed systems of rules and regulations, but rather *individuals* whose *particularism* dictates the appropriate course of action to be taken.

It could be said that the theory of organisations seems to be confronted with an epistemological dilemma. There is far too much emphasis on the way in which things *should* be, while the way in which they actually *are* is ignored. This often occurs as a result of the researcher's basic assumption, the chosen perspective and the way in which the study is methodologically carried out. One possible solution to this dilemma is to place the concept of action centrally within the framework of organisational analysis. I am not arguing for the substitution of the concept of power by that of action. Rather, I mean that the *action perspective*, seen from the methodological point of view, is central in the understanding of the mechanisms which constitute and are constituted in power relationships. The action perspective implies that the researcher attempts to understand and explain the way in which individuals act in a given context. We need not start out with any assumptions about a hypothetical state of 'harmony–consensus' in the organisation. What seems more justifiable is the examination of the network of relations among the actors, the interpretations which they make of their situations, and the actions which they subsequently take. The action perspective, in this sense, should enable the researcher to study the ways in which the actors interpret situations where power is manifested and also to study their strategic and tactical actions with the purpose of realising the desired outcome. This approach acknowledges the political character of organisations and the strategical character of the individuals' actions. It is also against this background that the power relations and the meaning of the collective actions may be understood and gain significance within the framework of intra-organisational processes.

UNIT OF ANALYSIS

Given the conceptualisation of organisations as political arenas we are confronted with the task of specifying the unit of analysis in the study of political actions. Hirschman (1972) has maintained that organisational members are often confronted with a dilemma when they are forced to choose between two alternatives; 'exit' and 'voice'. This implies that dissatisfied members can express their dissatisfaction by voicing and then act accordingly, or they can leave the organisation (exit). The practical relevance of this assertion has been shown by the case studied. Some of *L*'s employees (the most highly skilled) have, due to the development of the unsatisfactory situation, applied for and received work in other organisations. Others have stayed behind and continued to express their dissatisfaction in one way or another. However, the concepts of 'exit' and 'voicing' cannot give an ample description of what has actually taken place. In the beginning of the process an employee left *L* without having expressed any opinion whatsoever concerning the development of the course of events. Others have left the company but continued to protest against *W*'s behaviour. There were also those who chose to stay yet without expressing any dissatisfaction (some members of the 'disloyal' group). Finally, there are those who stayed to continue the struggle.

Hirschman's 'exit' and 'voicing' can be considered as a manifestation of the intra-organisational political processes, but it is probably a simplified version. When Hirschman wrote his text in 1972 it was perhaps easier to leave one job and hope for another. 'Exit' was then a relatively realistic alternative. Today the situation on the labour market is somewhat more problematic, which accounts for the members of *L* being forced to remain in the company, and thus accepting the situation which they experienced as being unsatisfactory. This, in turn, led to the reinforcement of the experienced conflict and strengthened the need for tactical and strategical action. Barry (1974) and Aldrich (1979), for example, who have contributed with some developments of Hirschman's theory, have maintained that an individual can 'exit' without protesting; he can 'exit' and raise a protest; he can stay behind without raising a protest, or he can stay behind and protest (voicing). These variations seem to broaden the explanatory potential, but there are still other aspects which should be considered at this point. Individuals who are highly skilled and specialised and who have, moreover, worked in an organisation for a longer period of time (for example the engineers at *L* who had been in the company since its foundation), are interested in remaining in the company and expressing their opinions at the same time as taking political actions. They feel that they have invested in the organisation, that their opinions are important and should be taken into consideration. Furthermore, since their competence/worth – or prestige – is at stake they also feel that they are personally involved. At the same time they may find it difficult to resist openly that which they perceive as a centralised power exercise aiming to control and to dominate. They feel vulnerable as individuals and are thus more inclined when taking political actions to do so in groups. The two blocks, the 'loyal' and the 'disloyal', which were constituted in *L*, can be regarded as political groups within which individuals could develop their own strategies, and through which they could channel 'voicing'. Needless to say, the discussion here exclusively concerns the explanation of the political dimension. This means that if we are to consider the formation of blocks *per se*, then they must be seen against the background of the specific relationships in their contexts. A suitable unit of analysis of the political actions of the individuals could be to place these in the context of groups: work groups, interest groups, and coalitions. Dahrendorf (1959) has developed ideas along similar lines.

Work groups (figure 4.1) can represent different departments, they can

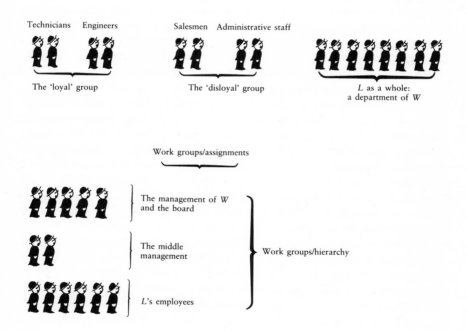

FIGURE 4.1 Work groups differentiation with respect to departments, assignments and hierarchical levels.

have special assignments which differentiate them from others, or they can belong to a particular hierarchical level. The loyal group in L was constituted by technicians and engineers, unlike the disloyal group which was constituted by administrative personnel, mainly salesmen. It could even be alleged that L as a whole, i.e. a department of W, could be regarded as a work group. At the hierarchical level we can consider the management of W; middle management (L. Abrahamsson and B. Kolinsky) and L's employees. Each level constitutes a political group with its own particular interests and subsequent strategies and actions. R. Perdfelt's position in this context is hard to define. He had been excluded from all the groups. His ambivalence and 'dividedness' (something of which he was accused, but which he himself did not necessarily experience) contributed to this exclusion.

Interest groups (figure 4.2) can represent groups of actors who share common motivations in the broader sense of the term. With this I do not mean the common goals which can be connected to certain assignments. I refer rather to political interests as, for example, those which were the basis for the actions of the different groups: the interest of the 'loyal' group for the continuity of L in unaltered conditions. They would rather that W would invest in L than in the stake which was now being made in connection with this transfer. The members of the 'disloyal' group had no particular personal interests in the move. As salesmen they had their respective home districts as bases. They saw in the conflict the opportunity of ingratiating themselves with the management and 'middle management' by aligning their own interests with those of the managers. Furthermore, they had long since been in a conflict with both R. Perdfelt and the 'loyal' group, and this allowed them to take revenge by adopting an opposing standpoint in the matter concerned. The management in W (M. Ziegler and the board of directors) had seemingly economical and organisational reasons, at least in the beginning of the process. Later, other aspects were to come into the picture. The chief concern of the middle management was to obey the orders given by the senior manager, for better or for worse, and to implement the decisions taken by the latter. The local union representatives in L's district had other reasons: to play the part of spokesmen for L's employees, on the one hand, and on the other, as the development of the course of events was gradually to demonstrate that the whole affair was hopeless, to confirm their position or their power as parties in the case and thus, so to speak, to legitimate their own existence. The concern of W's union representatives was to guarantee employment for union members, all the more since W had introduced the short-time week. They were more than willing to take over the work done by L's employees, but not so the employees themselves.

The complexity and diversity of interests and orientations amongst these

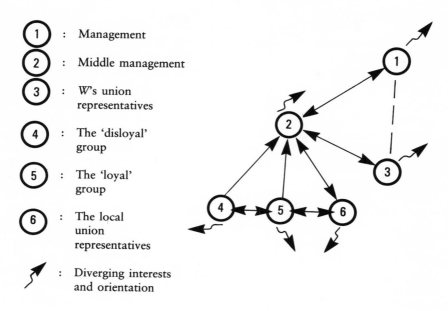

FIGURE 4.2   Interest groups.

groups resulted in the politicisation of the process and sometimes an accentuation of positions. It is of relevance in this context to analyse those actions intended to lead to a desired result or to satisfy a certain interest. The analysis should thus be focused on the actions of the groups (as a representative of a particular interest), and on the actions of the individuals within the group (the individual may orientate the concerns of the group as a whole). The analysis must naturally also focus on the group's interactions with other groups and on the strategies and actions which then become significant from the point of view of one group or another.

Finally, *coalitions*[6] (figure 4.3) can be said to be combinations of at least two interest groups who wish to accomplish something together which will further their specific interests. This definition of a coalition is not that of a combination of one or more groups becoming homogeneous and having a common incentive. Rather, it must be regarded as follows: groups having fairly diverging interests can, in interaction with or against others, for tactical–strategical–political reasons, act as though forming a front; this in spite of the fact that there may exist conflicts within the coalition, i.e. between the two groups forming the front. An interesting question from the point of view of power relationships is: 'Under which conditions are

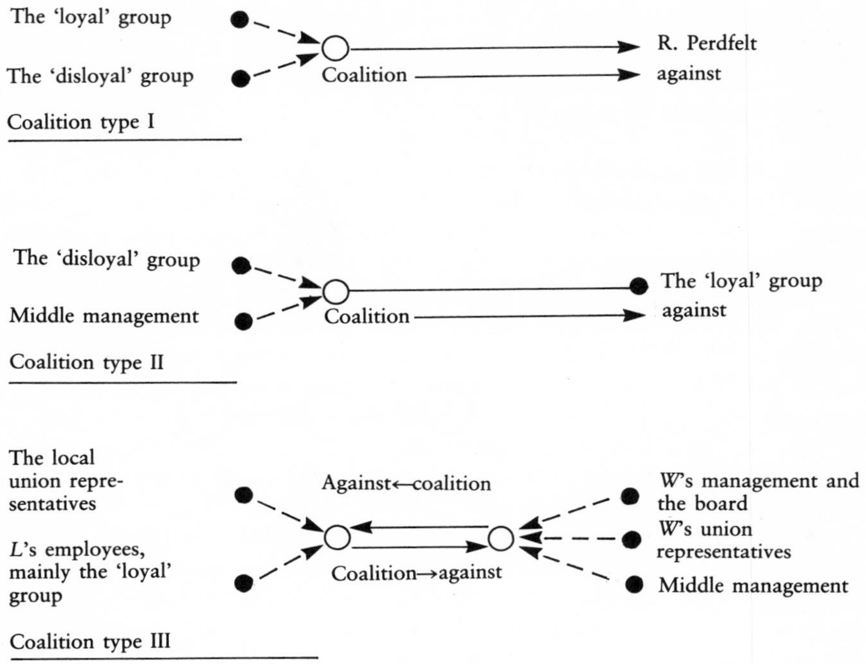

The 'loyal' group

The 'disloyal' group

Coalition

R. Perdfelt
against

Coalition type I

The 'disloyal' group

Middle management

Coalition

The 'loyal' group
against

Coalition type II

The local
union repre-
sentatives

L's employees,
mainly the 'loyal'
group

Against←coalition

Coalition→against

W's management and
the board

W's union
representatives

Middle management

Coalition type III

FIGURE 4.3 Coalitions.

coalitions of pressure groups formed, and how are the actions of the individuals related to the political games of the coalition?'

Examples of such coalitions can be found in the process studied here. The loyal and the disloyal groups, for example, have diverging orientations, but when it was a matter of making R. Perdfelt a scapegoat, they formed a coalition since they both wanted to project the failure on to him. This was despite the fact that there was much antagonism between the two groups concerning other matters. Another coalition was that of the disloyal group and the middle management against the rest of L's employees and their struggle. This was in spite of the individual convictions – L. Abrahamsson for example – of whether the transfer was motivated or not. A third coalition is illustrated by the local union representatives of L's district, on the one hand, and L's employees (mostly the loyal group), on the other. In the beginning these two groups had the same overall interests: namely that the activities of L should be able to continue as before. Later, interests were moved to another sphere. The union representatives must now assert themselves, justify their function and fight for some kind of recognition from the other parties. The interests of *L*'s employees were also to change with time: from having hoped for a turn in the course of events they continued their struggle for the sake of principle, and finally made a last desperate effort with their attempted coup. On the opposite side, there was another coalition which consisted of *W*'s management, the middle management and *W*'s union representatives. These three groups had completely different ideas on the process and represented totally different interests, yet they were to form a coalition against the other coalition. We know that Abrahamsson would much rather that *L* had continued as before, but he was forced to obey the management's orders if he wished to retain his position. Kolinsky seemed to have an indifferent attitude. He was new in the organisation and had no historical involvement to consider. He had every reason to believe that the transfer was a well-thought-out decision. The union in *W* felt that they could not afford to cause problems for the management. Times were hard, they had problems of their own (the short-time week), and the brotherly concern which they should actually have shown towards *L* had to be set aside.

The significance of emphasising *work groups, interest groups,* and *coalitions* as important units of analysis, has to be seen in the context of the dynamics of the organisations. Far too many organisation researchers regard behaviour and action as predetermined and apolitical, thereby implying a static view of organisations. This is often due to the fact that these researchers assume that, apart from the organisation's elite, the rest of the members are totally indifferent as to what happens and as to the ways in which the resources are distributed. In the process studied the individuals and groups seemed, indeed, to show signs of resignation, but they never become totally indifferent. On the contrary, when for *L*'s employees all seemed to be lost, they went back to the attack in attempting to carry out a coup. This was perhaps an extreme example of their non-resignation, but there is more to be found in the description of the process. As I have mentioned earlier, individuals will often try to implement their political actions and to channel them through groups. They do this primarily in situations in which the sanctions against such actions may be difficult for the individual to bear. The groups thus provide protection against such sanctions and become a source of courage and strength. As Marx, Weber and Durkheim claimed in their different ways, individuals become political in groups, and groups are capable of effecting, and often do effect, structures.

This implies that an understanding of the political character of organisations is of special importance for that which is fundamental in this context, i.e. power relations. In other words, we introduce interacting political actors who form groups and coalitions which in their turn interact – all within the framework of a political process. The question which I will henceforth attempt to answer is: when, where and how do the individuals and the groups mobilise power within this process of interaction, and how is this mobilisation made manifest?

CONCLUSION

In this chapter I have primarily focused on the political dimensions of organisations and on the significance which these dimensions have for the understanding of intra-organisational processes; i.e. power relationships among interacting individuals and groups. In this sense I suggested the action perspective which from a methodological point of view seems to be central in the identification and the understanding of the mechanisms which constitute and are constituted in power relationships. The action of the political actor, unlike the behaviour of the oversocialised member, must be seen in the light of the actor's 'particularism'. In their interaction with others, individuals act strategically in the pursuit of their intentions. They strive for a greater space of action, greater autonomy, and a broader margin of freedom. However, apart from the political actors, analysis should be directed towards the groups and coalitions through which they channel their political actions.

CHAPTER 5

The Discourse of Power and Organisation

Power as a concept, a phenomenon or an empirical reality has pervaded the discourses of political scientists, sociologists, psychologists, and economists through all time. The debate has been multi-faceted, rich, and, above all, long-lasting. To discern in this flora that which is specific for the theory of organisations is by no means a simple task. There are those (Clegg and Dunkerley, 1980) who claim that organisation theorists began to take an interest in the phenomenon of power in connection with the identification of informal relationships (Roethlisberger and Dickson, 1939). Before the Hawthorne study the attention of the theorists had been devoted to the formal dimension of organisations, and power was thereby related to the legitimate authority. This was against the background of the classic theory of bureaucracy which stressed the indispensability of rational action within organisations if they are to be effective (Weber, 1947).

Power and organisations

As I have discussed in the previous chapter, the attention has been focused on one side of organisational reality: coordination. This has led to power being defined, in these contexts, in static terms with emphasis on the legitimate, formal authority at the expense of that which was then to be understood as forbidden power. Thompson (1956) has held, in this context, that classics of bureaucracy theory, such as for instance Weber, have contributed towards the phenomenon of power being neglected in organisation studies. Thompson's accusation seems rather paradoxical, as has also been remarked upon by Clegg and Dunkerley (1980), considering that Weber, one of the greatest classics of the theory of bureaucracy, is commonly looked upon as being the author of the renewed interest in the 20th century for the phenomenon of power. No clarification as to this paradoxical situation is provided by the literature; but there are some writers (e.g. Gouldner, 1954, 1971; Clegg, 1975, 1977; Hearn, 1978) who maintain that the root of the paradox is to be found in the context of the translation of Weber's work, *The Theory of Social and Economic Organizations* (1947) by Parsons and Henderson.

> In a much remarked upon footnote by Parsons (Weber, 1947: 152), the concept of *Herrschaft* is translated as 'authority', thus preserving what Gouldner (1971) has called Parsons' 'superordinate' view of power, as if it were Weber's. (Clegg and Dunkerley, 1980: 433–434)

This superordinate view of power has led to the conceptualisation by Parsons of power and authority in two ways. Gouldner, who has studied this question, writes that Parsons' view is

> either as two different stages in development, in which, for instance, power is viewed as the degenerated or the immature form of authority; or as two alternative ways in which one person or group can structure the behaviour of others. In both cases they are viewed as mutually exclusive, as if, when one exists, the other does not . . . if it had been looked at from the standpoint of *subordination* in the social world, power and authority would more likely be viewed as dual structures, both *simultaneously* present, in subtle and continual interaction. Power, in short, exists not simply when authority breaks down, or before authority has had a chance to mature. It exists as a factor in the lives of subordinates, shaping their behaviour and beliefs, at every moment of their relations with those above them. . . . Legitimacy and 'authority' never eliminate power; they merely defocalize it, make it latent. (Gouldner, 1971: 294)

Power and authority are thus not two phenomena that exclude each other. Rather they presuppose and produce each other. According to Gouldner, authority, even the legitimate authority, never eliminates power. It is there, immanent in relations. The problem is that this was said by Gouldner in 1971; and since the translation of Weber's work into English a number of contributions about power relationships in organisations have been produced by organisation researchers. Thus, Parsons' followers have analysed power on the basis of his view of power as a superordinate concept, as something separate from authority, as something which emerges informally rather than formally. The discourse of power in organisation theory was woven around this theme. The principal definition which emerged in nearly all organisation theory (Votaw, 1966; Tedeschi, 1974; Clegg, 1979a) is based upon the duality of the formal–informal dimension. Authority is seen as a potentiality to influence. This potentiality is, in turn, seen as being based upon the hierarchical position which a person may have. Power is seen as the actual capacity to influence.[1] The conceptualisation of power in this way implies that the unit of analysis, or its focal point, is that of deviations from the formal structure. This means that the formal structure appears in the analysis as the depiction of a perfect, well-oiled and over-rationalised state in relation to which the deviations of power are to be measured.

A technocratic dream

Even if this formal structure does exist in reality, and not only in model-thinking, what is it that we are to measure? In the first place we must assume that the existence of an ideal state is given and not only desired. Second, we must assume the existence of a resource which gives power, and which is owned by those who have it. Third, we must establish causal relationships between these elements. None of these conditions, however, seem to have any empirical relevance, nor any anchorage in reality. The formal structure with all its perfection, as far as balance and consensus are concerned, is, and continues to be, a technocratic and totalitarian dream. In order to be able to measure any deviations from such a structure in the studied case, it would be necessary to begin by first constructing such a structure. I am not suggesting that there is no structure in W–L; rather than the existent structure is one which differs vastly from those upon which the analyses of, for instance, Mechanic (1962) and Hickson et al. (1971), as well as many others, are based. Moreover, the conceptualisation of power or its resources as property, is a way of handling the problem that is far too simple, the purpose of which is to force the analysis into a causal scheme. Neither property, with regard to power, nor even causality itself, in social relation, is self-evident.

It could be said that among the essential tendencies in power studies within organisation theory are those which define it as the exercise of 'something' which, in turn, rests upon a base. Weber (1947) maintains that it is the will that is exercised, Mechanic (1962) holds that it is strength, while Thompson (1956) lays emphasis on the right to make decisions. What is problematical here is that these bases are related from the point of view of measurability to people as their property. When they have not been looked upon as a person's property, then they have been regarded as resources that are controlled by certain individuals, and which render possible the exercise of power. French and Raven (1959) have drawn up an *a priori* formulation of what would be counted as the resources of power; but the idea of these resources can never become universal. A resource that is valid in one instance might very well become invalid in another. Moreover, this would imply that the 'exerciser of power' would have to possess a comprehensive knowledge of the resources which he/she has, and of the value of these in a particular situation. This is, under normal conditions, an impossibility. Situations change through time, and people act on many premises other than merely those resources which they are assumed to have.

The relevance of resources has, in the case studied and in the sense outlined above, been very slight. M. Ziegler, for instance, 'has' this resource that rests on the base of hierarchy/authority in his role of managing director. But what have the implications of this resource been for the exercise of power in the context of the process? According to 'mainstream' theory it would be a matter here of adjustments within the framework of a balanced formal structure. Alternatively it may be possible to measure the deviations from this structure, and perhaps redistribute the resources so as to restore the perfect balance. In fact, that which Ziegler gains from his 'resource' is a certain space of action; but the size of this space of action is directly and indirectly dependent upon the actions taken by the other actors, and the actions of the subordinates as much as of anyone else. The inverse relation is also true. If, however, we confine ourselves to the notion of resources, we run the risk of conceptualising power as property, as a privilege, which can only be had by those who have access to resources. The step from this to the power definition based on the duality: dominant–dominated, determining–determined is very short. Power is not, to my mind, a property, but rather a *relation*. It appears and is immanent in relationships. It is exercised, not only by the dominant, but also *by and through the dominated*.

The 'equilibrium' fixation

One of the greatest problems in the discourse of power in organisation theory seems to me to be that of the implicit assumption of balance and consensus. The question of the redistribution of resources becomes then something given which is related to the structure and to the given positions. Power becomes, in this context, a simple study of deviations from a structure which is assumed to be entirely unproblematical. This view was to characterise most of the contribution from the 1950s and 1960s. The mechanistic models of Dahl (1957) often served as a guideline. It was the bases of power that were of most interest. Crozier (1964), inspired by Cyert and March (1963), introduced the concept of 'uncertainty control' as a base for the exercise of power. It might be said that the idea of uncertainty control is a metaphorical adaptation from the cybernetic and systems theoretical endeavours of the time which sought to find a perfect analogous model for organisations. Other writers, such as Thompson (1956, 1967) have also toyed with the concept of uncertainty control.

Hickson et al. (1971) have suggested what might be called a recipe as to how one can assess and predict the power which one unit might have over another unit. The 'contingency theory' has been criticised to quite a large extent for the way in which data are interpreted within this theory for the determining of relations between the structure of an organisation and its contextual characteristics (Child, 1972a,b). Another criticism which has been launched against this theory is directed towards the total lack of serious attempts to understand the phenomenon of power (Child, 1972a; Zey-Ferrell, 1981). Although Hickson et al. (1971) may be regarded as an exception, the central assumption of the determining role of the environment which is the principal idea of the 'contingency theory', is nonetheless present in their 'analyses' of power. The theory which they present is a blend, the major ingredients of which are Blau's (1964) 'exchange theory', Crozier's (1964) 'uncertainty control', as well as Dahl's (1957) somewhat modified 'mechanistic model'. This blend is mixed against the background of a structural–functionalist perspective. Hickson et al. (1971), who may be said to represent that branch of 'contingency theory' to have taken up the problem of power in its studies, claim to provide explanations of the phenomenon of power in organisations. The value of these explanations has been strongly challenged (Child, 1972a,b; Clegg and Dunkerley, 1980; Zey-Ferrell, 1981, etc).

> In the 'strategic' variant the concept of contingency is explicitly used to predict the power of a 'sub-unit' in a theoretical schema, rather than being an extrapolation from a data analysis. A sub-unit, A, is seen as being more or less contingent on the other sub-unit in the organizational system. The less contingent, or dependent, a sub-unit is on these other sub-units, then, ceteris paribus, the theory predicts that it will be more powerful. The components of the ceteris paribus clause in this instance are that the sub-unit should also be highly unsubstitutable by any other sub-unit, that it should also be central to the organizational system, for which it must manage a high degree of uncertainty; these, in conjunction with contingency, predict power. (Clegg and Dunkerley, 1980: 437)

In this conceptualisation of power we have on the one hand the condition that power be localised with someone or with an elite (for example a department), and on the other hand the ability of 'units' to adapt themselves to change in the environment and their ensuing superiority as compared with other 'units'.

> Organizations deal with environmentally derived uncertainties in the sources and composition of inputs, with uncertainties in the processing of throughputs, and again with environmental uncertainties in the disposal of outputs. They must have means to deal with these uncertainties for adequate task performance. (Hickson et al., 1971: 219)

Thus power is considered in terms of adaptation and is measured in the degree of the ability to adapt oneself. This can, no doubt, be done; but does it mean that one understands power? The political dimension of interaction, evident in the studied case, and for which I have argued in the previous chapter, is overlooked. Let us picture the application of this theory of adaptation to the case. Assume that a change of environment for L and W has 'caused' the transfer decision, and that W's management and L's employees represent two 'competing' units. Who can then be said to be the most skilful at adapting themselves, and thus to have power? Let us first consider the question of adaptation here. W's decision or L's revolt or something else? Second, what would the adaptation imply? A consensus, a solution of compromise, that L complies with W's decision and stops acting, or that W refrains from pushing the process? None of this has occurred, and it can be asked whether such oversimplified situations as the ones that are apparently presupposed by this theory do in fact ever occur.

It was not a matter, in this case, of adaptation in the simple sense of the word, but rather a matter of strategic action for the bringing about of a reduction of the control which the opposing party had over one's own space of action. It was a matter of an incessant struggle for freedom, autonomy and the possibility of being able to retain a position about which to negotiate implicitly or explicitly. It is precisely these dimensions, rather than skilfulness at adaptation, that are the manifestations of power and that are immanent in all power relations.

Harmony and balance or individual interests

The problem already referred to, concerning the strivings of the models for and their basic assumptions of balance and consensus in organisations, is, to be sure, a theoretical obstacle which renders difficult the understanding of power. Thus power, and the problems ordinarily related to it, is conceived of as a dysfunction and an anomaly which disturbs the harmony of the system and threatens its state of balance. But which harmony and which balance is it that is at issue here? It is that of the models and ideals, not of the reality of organisations. For in this reality there is neither artificial harmony nor a balance to be had on request. The people in the studied case had personal interests, individual and even, to a certain extent, collective interests. They acted on the basis of these in spite of the possibility of their actions 'disturbing any eventual prevailing harmony'. Both Machiavelli and Hobbes laid emphasis on the significance of the notion of interest from the perspective of the individual and in political life. These two dimensions coincide, to my mind, in organisational contexts. The individual, so as not to lose his/her particularism in organisations, undertakes a number of political actions. According to

Hobbes,[2] the purpose of these actions is to liberate some of the potential anarchism and egoism to be found within each one of us. Interest is, according to Hobbes (1928, 1958), the expression of the subjectivity of the Cartesian ego. Interest is not constant, but rather changeable, as it does not accept the rule of anyone over itself other than itself. In order to avoid incessant conflicts and clashes of ego, people implicitly agree to maintain at least a certain measure of cooperation.

According to Hobbes, the cooperation which develops between people is no 'natural state' or 'precivilised state' that could be seen as an innate quality, but 'the state of nature'. This state of nature is a hypothetical state implying that people would 'allow their egos to totally decide their actions, were it not for their fear of the eventuality of social sanctions'.[3] Perhaps this is why we, on the one hand, act intentionally to attain a certain personal interest, and, on the other hand to a certain extent respect the rules of the game. At times our interest may lie in being unpredictable, especially when we are confronted with a situation where the primary purpose of the systematic mechanisms is that of making us predictable. This is clearly illustrated by the antagonists in the studied case. They withheld essential information from each other, and often took each other by surprise. Each of the actors involved strived to reduce his/her own predictability, partly by setting him/herself up against the 'established' system and acting in an unexpected fashion, and partly by disguising data and information through keeping it secret. At the same time, all the antagonists knew where to draw the limit. In the chaos created, a certain order was to be found: everyone knew that in order to carry on playing the game the rules must be respected,[4] even if these were often experienced as severe. Whenever there were signals from *W*'s management and middle management indicating that they intended to reduce the unpredictability of *L*'s employees, this always resulted in a reaction aimed to counteract the confining constructions within which these signals were articulated.

Honour and space of action

'Why don't you sabotage the entire works?', I asked Perdfelt once. The reason for my asking this was that I was struck by the contradiction in the situation which meant that whereas *L*'s employees were extremely dissatisfied with the process and its development, their work was nevertheless very well done. Naturally, it may be pointed out that they had no choice. They were forced to perform well in order to keep their jobs. It might also be conceivable that they wished to show, by means of good performance, that they were worth backing (in *L*'s district). Perdfelt thought that the extensive effort put into good performance was due to the belief held, right up the end, that something would happen to alter the course of events. In such a case they wished to have the opportunity and the satisfaction of saying that it was thanks to their own efforts that management withdrew its decision.

Hobbes wrote in *Leviathan* that power, or the energy that moves it, has its basis in people's striving for *honour*. That which distinguishes us from animals, he said, is our 'voluntary motion'; our ability to speak, to move and to move parts of our body according to what we wish to happen. These 'voluntary motions' are actions which are called 'desire' (endeavour) when they are directed towards something which 'causes' them. The desires of animals are unconscious, whereas those of man are consciously formulated so that he can attain the interest which is related to his 'desire'. The means is power, 'The power of man is his present means to obtain some future apparent good' (Hobbes, *Leviathan*, 1958: 78).

The concept of honour is of interest in the context, but ought only to be seen as a complement to another concept, namely that of space of action. In this case *L*'s employees knew that their space of action was dependent upon a large number of factors, such as, for example, their own ability to show a good result. They believed this on the basis of the assumption that the logic of action of the management was, as had been maintained, a logic of performance. I think that it is now also possible to see the strivings of *L* to expand their space of action and thus to improve their negotiation position as a way of improving their competence and ensuring themselves of a certain measure of honour. According to Hobbes, the concept of honour is related to power, but it also has an ethical, moral and religious dimension (*Leviathan*, 1958: 80–86).

> Power as a mean to an end can become an end itself, and, as such, an object of appetite or desire in, and for, itself, which will be signified by the honour in which a man is held. (Hobbes, *Leviathan*, 1958: 79)

A concept contiguous to honour is that of *prestige*; the prestige for *L*'s employees to show that they are capable of improving the company's position on the market, but also prestige in relation to themselves. They hope to prove to themselves that they were able to cope with the difficult situation. From the opposite perspective it could be said that, for *W*'s management, the outcome of the process became a question of prestige as the situation gradually deteriorated. The process which had initially been a consciously initiated action took on towards the end a certain logic of its own. It was as if the development of the course of events continued on its path quite regardless of the actual intentions of those involved. The original intentions of *W*'s management, based on an economic logic, had gradually been replaced by something as difficult to define as prestige where the decision must be put into effect no matter what the costs may be. Alternatively, the documents and preparations that were intended to lead to the transfer were so far advanced that it became impossible to change the course even if this had been wanted.[5]

A PRIMITIVE CONCEPTUALISATION OF POWER

As has been indicated in the beginning of this chapter, there exists a long-standing and polemical debate about power. One could say that there are as many definitions as there are authors. Unfortunately, however, these contributions constitute neither complementary parts and views of the same problem nor diverging starting points. It seems rather that all of the available contributions are, each for itself, isolated occurrences, irreconcilable with each other. This confusion seems, to my mind, to stem from what I would like to call a *primitive* conceptualisation of power. I look upon power as an abstraction, or an abstract phenomenon as, for instance, love, friendship, morals. Everyone knows what it means at the same time as no-one knows. To attempt to force physical precisions upon these concepts is to make oneself guilty of an intellectual violence which 'inevitably' results in primitive conceptualisations.

Is it at all appropriate to ask what power is, or ought we rather to pose another question if we wish to understand the phenomenon? An idea becomes apparent in Foucault's work which implies that the history and identity of a society can only be understood if one looks at the 'opposition' picture of society; that which is excluded and debarred by society, and at the principles of these mechanisms of exclusion. This implies that the analyst can never get closer to his/her object by looking at its dialogical core, but rather by scanning its borders. The cage is more important than the bird, perhaps provides a suitable analogy. The point is that madness, folly and the violation of accepted norms say far more about that which is permitted than does that which is established itself. This is due to the most important cultural line of division always running between the normal and the pathological. The question that we should rather pose concerns the 'borders of power', where its opposite is made manifest, its outer territory which is revealing for its identity. The borders and the outer territory of power are only identifiable in actions taken by the individuals involved in power relations. These actions would, in analogy with what has already been said, be the pathological in relation to the normal, the outer in relation to the inner and to the identity. Is the normal in organisations equivalent to conduct in accordance with the approved norms? Is the pathological to refuse to part with one's particularism, to refuse to be transformed to a passive cog? Is the pathological to persist in striving for a certain autonomy, a certain margin of freedom and to attempt to expand one's space of action so as not to be suffocated by 'lack of action'?

The question is not what is power, but rather what is it that can sensitise us about its identity. Where are the borders of power or, so to speak, the limits of its territory? What is the 'outer' definition of power that may provide insight as to its 'inner' nature? These questions do not imply that our discourse should cease to address itself towards power. They only imply that we must adopt, in our analysis, a different conceptual view and a new conceptual orientation.

Before going further in the discussion, it might be appropriate to take a closer look at the primitive conceptualisation, so as to place it in contrast with the view outlined above.

Conceptual and empirical orientations

One way in which to approach the primitive conceptualisation of the concept of power might be to distinguish between the two principal orientations to be found in this debate: the conceptual, with a comprehensive supply of theories, statements and specifications; and the empirical, with emphasis on measuring instruments and the measurement of power in concrete situations. However, none of these measuring instruments and methods of measuring seem to have any tenable connection with the 'concrete' phenomenon. The views of writers such as Clegg (1975), Clegg and Dunkerley (1980), Lukes (1974), Abell (1975), and Gustafsson (1979), who have devoted much attention to the formation of the existing knowledge about power, all coincide in that the theories in this field are chaotic, unsystematic and even, to a certain extent, irrelevant to the phenomenon about which they are making statements.

In order to gain insight into the debate within the discourse of power in organisation theory, I suggest an investigation into the fundamental epistemological assumptions of the conceptualisation of power and its rules of formation. Furthermore, a distinction must be made between the attitude towards the phenomenon held by the theoreticians – who stand for the conceptual orientation – and that held by empiricists.

The empiricists ordinarily work inductively: the statements on power are derived from what are considered to be its empirical manifestations. Power, as a concept, is thus seen as the designation of an empirical phenomenon, while its essence seems to be totally ignored. This leads to most empiricists apparently asking themselves what power looks like in concrete situations, yet without being able to give a satisfactory explanation for the nature, and perhaps the identity, of the phenomenon.

Symptomatic of this simplistic approach is the research carried out concerning various social and organisational contexts. The empiricists proceed, in most instances in this type of research, from one major question which they ask people: 'Do you partake in the decisions in your organization?' The answer to this question – and other contiguous questions – determines which definition is to be given to the phenomenon of power. This implies a focus on measuring at the expense of the epistemological and theoretical problems. The latter dimension, with a few exceptions (Clegg, 1979; Lukes, 1974; etc.), is lacking in the literature on power. Yet from entirely different points of departure it is this very dimension which, for thinkers like Foucault, is the most important.

There is a debate in progress (primarily during the 1950s to 1960s and 1970s) within the empiricist wing which led to an all but unequivocal view as to what power actually is. The battle reaches its heights when the researchers interpret, or rather reinterpret, and discuss each other's data and the interpretation thereof. In most cases the interpretations made by others are rejected with the motivation that they are merely distortions of the empirical reality. The simple explanation that the differences might depend on the fundamental views of the researchers and on the different approaches is thus overlooked. An example of this is the well-known battle between elitists and pluralists. One can see in the argumentation of these two groups that they implicitly proceed from an identical conceptualisation of power, and that they differ only in their respective interpretations of the empirical data. In reality it might be said that they have two different points of departure; and it is these that seem to result in differing interpretations. The point of departure of the one group is quite evidently a conceptualisation of power resulting in a pluralist interpretation of the political situation. The point of departure of the other group results in an elitist interpretation. Thus the empiricists seem to think, in most cases, that agreement prevails between themselves and other researchers with regard to the view of power.

The theorists, on the other hand, seem to be aware of their differing points of departure, yet still do not succeed, in any systematic way, to integrate each other's insights. As illustrations hereof one might mention Dahl (1957); Bierstedt (1950); Etzioni (1969); Emerson (1962); Thibault and Kelley (1959); and Blau (1964), but there are many others. This may give the feeling that different theorists argue for different conceptualisations of power which are in conflict with each other rather than being complementary.

Yet perhaps there is one common element in the theorists group. Everyone seems to be in agreement as to Weber's very general definition that 'Power might be seen as the probability which an individual has of implementing his will in spite of opposition.' However, beyond this definition there are as many perspectives as writers engaged in the subject. According to Bierstedt (1950), for instance, power is a potential strength which can, when necessary, be used for sanctional purposes. Bierstedt also distinguishes between influence and authority. He sees authority as coercive, which implicates involuntary submission, whereas he sees influence as persuasive, implicating voluntary submission.

Another theorist in this context, Dahl (1957), proceeds from Weber and expands his analysis in such a way as to differentiate it from that of Bierstedt. He combines the potential and the actual 'use' of power into one and the same dimension. Furthermore, to him power and influence are the same thing. Dahl's conceptualisation of power is causal.[6] His view of power is quite simply that we can speak of the exercise of power each time someone causes a change in the behaviour of someone else. Strength, potential and influence (Bierstedt, 1950) are blended in one and the same 'unequivocal' concept. According to Dahl an unused potential is not power, since power presupposes successful use of the potential.

Whereas Dahl erases all distinctions, Wrong (1968) makes three distinctions: 'potential power', 'actual power' and 'the potential for power'. Wrong holds that there is a distinct difference between 'potential power', the potential ability to mobilise power and the use of power. The latter is, according to Wrong, 'actual power'. An interesting aspect of Wrong's thought is that power need neither implicate the use of the potential, nor could this use be successful, since the potential *per se* may be sufficient to influence the behaviour of others. According to Wrong, an actor can 'have' power without using it. Other people's subjective expectations that the potential can be put to use if necessary is reason enough for them to behave in the 'right way'. The existence of the potential makes its use unnecessary. There is an idea implicit in this argumentation which might be likened to that of the balance between superpowers. Perhaps the idea is plausible in high political contexts: the awareness which one country may have of the neighbouring country's access to a significant potential military strength, may induce it to refrain from declaring war upon its neighbour or from behaving in such a way that might motivate the neighbouring country to use its military potential. The situation in organisations seems to be another. For example, the managing director (who, in Wrong's presentation would be the one to have this potential at his disposal) is not spared from the many norms and regulations governing people's actions in various contexts. He has to stay within a certain framework and to respect (to a certain extent) the rules of the game such as the legislation. If we look at the relationship between L's employees and Ziegler in the light of Wrong's argumentation, then L's employees would have proceeded from the following idea: 'M. Ziegler is managing director and we are the grassroots. He has "potential power", "actual power" and "the potential for power". We ought therefore to resign ourselves to the decisions taken, act in accordance with them, or we will provide motivation for Ziegler to mobilize and use his "potential power".' The studied process shows another picture: Ziegler's power is, in fact (in Wrong's terms), a question of Ziegler's space of action. Of crucial importance for this space, are, on the one hand, the contextual rules of the game, i.e. the structural arrangements and system of rules as well as the legislative context, and, on the other hand, the actors involved in the process with regard to the way in which they interpret Ziegler's actions and how they themselves act. This implies that what we may see in the studied process is a group that develops its proficiency in controlling particular resources of power, and that acquires, in the specific relation, 'the potential for power'. In order to avoid the epistemological trap, however, and thereby avoid conceptualising power as an attribute, we ought to focus our attention on the specific relations in which this power is manifested and the mechanisms through which it is articulated. The relationship of Ziegler to L's employees may be seen as a process of exchange; but it is neither strength nor terror that is exchanged, but *space of action*.

It seems to me that this space for action is the border of power *per se*, which is given and formed by power as its opposite picture. This space of action, which is constituted as the outer territory of power, reveals more about the identity of power than does the primitive notion of it. The interpretations which the actors make of other's actions and actions of the actors themselves, their strivings for autonomy, unpredictability and margin of freedom, are all oppositions to power which converge in that which is exchanged in a relationship of interdependency: the space of action. This space varies in size and intensity; in *expansion* and *contraction*. Through interaction the space is exchanged. These relationships, and the exchange within these, are omnipresent, whereas the expansion and contraction of the space have a contextual basis.

Before going further in this argument, it might be of interest to note here that what is characteristic for the primitive discourse is that its advocates, apart from their particular approaches, often strive to capture the phenomenon of power in definitions. Power researchers (Blau, 1964; Etzioni, 1961; French and Raven, 1959; Mechanic, 1962; Kaplan, 1964) are, as has been mentioned earlier, numerous, and their fragmentary contributions create more complexity than elucidation. The following are a few examples of some definitions by those authors who have traditionally been considered to have contributed with knowledge within this field:[7]

(a) Weber (1947): 'Power is the probability that one actor within a social relationship will be in a position to carry out his own will, despite resistance, and regardless of the basis on which this probability rests.'
(b) Blau (1964): 'Power is the ability of persons as groups to impose their

will on others despite resistance through deterrence either in the form of withholding regularly supplied rewards or in the form of punishment inasmuch as the former, as well as the latter, constitutes in effect negative sanction.'

(c) Mechanic (1962): 'Power is defined as a force that results in behavior that would not have occurred if the forces had not been present.'

(d) Dahl (1957): 'A has power over B to the extent that he can get B to do something that he would not otherwise do.'

(e) Kaplan (1964): '[Power is] the ability of one person or group of persons to influence the behavior of others, that is, to change the probabilities that others will respond in certain ways to specified stimuli.'

(f) Bierstedt (1950): 'Power is latent force. [. . .] Power itself is the prior capacity which makes the application of force possible.'

Implicit in these definitions is that power is placed within an interaction. The authors also seem to imply that the actors show consideration for each other; but still the analysis is aimed towards power *per se*, it is attributed to an actor as if it were a property, and the ambition is the measurability of the phenomenon.

I suggest that, instead of stopping at the definitions, thereby annihilating the possibility of understanding the abstract dimension, the evasive essence and the identity of power, we carry the discussion further to the premises that might conceivably be related to the phenomenon of power as an abstract idea as well as to the manifestation of the phenomenon. These premises, which have been discussed and will be developed henceforth, are: action perspective; political perspective; autonomy/freedom; predictability/unpredictability; will; space of action and, in addition to this, the dimensions within/through which these are constituted: form and content.

FORM AND CONTENT

The dimensions of *form* and *content* which, as I see it, play a part in all social relations, facilitate the understanding of the phenomenon of power.

I use the concept of form to denote the fundamental configuration within which actions and interactions take place. I refer to the generic characterisation of the phenomenon which tends to be present in all concrete and empirical situations. Examples of these characterisations are the relationships and interdependencies which are typical for all power relations. Another example is that all power relations in one way or another seem to implicate a certain type of sanction. The difference in this case lies in how one conceptualises this sanction. In my opinion it is that which is expressed in the actions of the interacting actors: that which is of a strategical and political nature, that which, apart from striving to expand the autonomy and margin of freedom of the actor as well as his/her space of action, also aims to reduce the corresponding spheres of interest of the opposing party. The intensity of the form may vary from one situation to another, but it is nonetheless present in all empirical manifestations of power.

There are numerous examples of such interdependencies in the studied case. Some of these are the interdependencies between the union representatives in *L*'s district and *W*'s management, between middle management and *L*'s employees as well as between *W*'s management and *L*'s employees. On another level an interdependency between *W*'s management and middle management is discernible. On yet another level one can see interdependency between actors regardless of which hierarchical position they may belong to. As examples of such relationships one might mention those which developed between Perdfelt and Abrahamsson, and between the latter and Ziegler, as well as among the actors within *L*, both within the same group and across the confines of the groups.

I use the concept of *content* to denote such dimensions that are not omnipresent, but which are rather contextually related and situationally specific. Content is a 'fluctuating' concept. The dimensions which it describes vary both in intensity and in 'presence'. Influence is an example of content.[8] It may be seen as a specific content where power is manifested within the framework of a relationship without implicating a necessity: all types of power are not always a matter of influence, and all power relationships are not always relations of influence. The presence of influence in a power relationship depends upon the context and on the specific situation. At one stage of the development of the course of events in the case studied, Ziegler felt the need to intervene in the specific relation which he then had with the union representatives in *L*'s district so as to frame a protocol and thereby to *influence* the further development of the course of events. The attempt failed. Influence was not manifested in this particular context. The form in this context was the interdependency between Ziegler and the union: dependencies and interdependencies may always be found between people in social contexts. Content – in this instance influence which may be seen as Ziegler's attempt to expand his space of action in this specific case – is not always manifested. Influence (content) was not present in this interdependency (form).

After having presented the concepts of form and content, I shall now discuss what they stand for in detail from the perspective of this study. The discussion will be portrayed in relation to the primitive discourse of power and will be illustrated with situations from the studied case.

Form: relationship and interdependency

Tendencies have emerged in recent years in the traditional discourse of power which have given priority to the relational dimension of power (Hinings et al., 1974; Pfeffer, 1978; Crozier and Friedberg, 1977; Giddens, 1976, 1979). This does not imply, however, that the preceding authors, for instance, Parsons (1939, 1951), totally disregarded this dimension in their power studies. The problem is that this point of departure never remains for long in the argument, but is transformed to another implying that power is seen as a structural phenomenon. Blau (1964) and Blau and Schoenherr (1971), for example, advocate from the start an interactional approach, but end up by conceptualising power as one of the structural attributes of the organisation. The definitions which I have presented earlier are a reflection of this tendency. Let us, in the following section, reason around the most essential dimensions of the phenomenon of power as regards *form*: the relational and interdependent dimensions.

The relational dimension of power

This dimension is, to my mind, crucial for the understanding of the phenomenon of power and its manifestations that are always immanent in relations. Without such relations, the premises and conditions for the possible manifestations of power cease to exist. What is most important in the studies of the phenomenon of power in organisations, regardless of our unit of analysis (individual, group, coalition or organisation), is to pay special attention to the interactional dynamics of power relationships. This in combination with the logic of action of the actors. What has traditionally been seen as the power of one organisation *vis à vis* another, might rather, in this sense, be seen against the background of the logic of action and mechanisms governing the interaction of the actors and groups involved. If we look upon W and L as being two separate organisations, then it is not enough to be content with the assertion that the 'biggest' and 'strongest' of these, i.e. the one that has access to most resources, is the most powerful. This assertion, even if it were true, does not help us to advance in our understanding of power. If, on the other hand, we identify the individuals, groups and coalitions in both organisations, study their processes of interaction and attempt to understand the immanent mechanisms in these relations (various logics of action), then perhaps we might see, beyond the given resources and the visible structures, that power is exercised as much by and through the dominant as by and through the dominated. What I mean here is that when study is directed towards the relationships, then the analyst has the opportunity of seeing the possibilities which the one or the other has of mobilising various types of resources, and of seeing how the seemingly subordinate might bring about, by means of strategic actions, a contraction of the space of action of superiors.

Traditionally, one speaks also of the power of the organisation *vis à vis* its members (Hinings et al., 1974; Pfeffer, 1978). This way of looking at the matter is typical of the widespread understanding of power as a primitive concept. It is not here a matter of a relation, but merely of one-sidedness: power is seen exclusively in terms of dominance, exploitation and repression where 'The grassroots in an organization are trampled upon by the ruthless elite.' Such a way of approaching power puts an end to its further examination. All is said. If we ask what then is power? They answer that it is a product of the structure.[9] However, the case studied points to another reality. Had we proceeded from the idea that the matter was one of the organisation's elite (Ziegler and middle management), exercising 'its' power over the members (the grassroots in *L*) – then we would, with 'necessity', have focused on the structural properties of the organisations, and related our analysis of power to the thus-given authority. In this way we could perhaps have discussed the relation between the structural hierarchy of the organisation and authority, as well as the role of the authority in the decision process. We would, no doubt, have overlooked the mechanisms of power. I do not ask: 'What is the power of the elite over the grassroots in the organisation?' I ask instead: 'How do the individuals, groups or coalitions interact with each other against the background of the organisational and contextual situation?' 'What do the relations among these look like (and how do they develop), against the background of the logics which govern the actions of the involved?' A different picture is thus revealed. The difference must already be evident at the stage of data-gathering: attention must primarily be devoted to the relational and interactional dimensions as well as to the action perspective. The formal structural arrangements, and the hierarchy and authority associated with them, have proven to be of lesser importance with regard to the understanding of the mechanisms of power. There are far too many weaknesses in the discourse of power which point to this. It is apparent, on the level of analysis, that what has been decisive in the studied process is not the one-dimensional exercise of power of the elite upon the grassroots, but rather the interaction between these two: *L*'s employees have never been totally passive and 'powerless' nor has *W*'s management ever been able to implement an action in total accordance with the intention. The parties acted as if they were involved in a game (Crozier and Friedberg, 1977). Many times *L*'s employees managed to reverse the situation, delay the process, expand their space of action in a particular situation and thus, for a period of the process, be transformed into 'the elite' in a specific context. This implies that if one is to understand the fundamental mechanisms of power one must refrain from thinking in static terms. The elite, the grassroots, A or B, is not a linear, constant and unalterable state. It is a state which is contextual and dynamic. The relational dimension of power is, to my mind, that form within which the varying states appears as constituent for the content.

In the previous chapter I argued that the unit of analysis can be an individual, a group, a coalition or an organisation. It may sometimes be necessary, even if an individual is the unit of analysis, to analyse the individual actions which are channelled through a group or a coalition. Such actions are often of a political nature. If, for example, we take Perdfelt's actions as a unit of analysis then we must place them within the framework of a *form*. This is constituted by the *relational* and *interdependent* dimensions within which Perdfelt's actions are motivated, take place and gain significance. Perdfelt's relations to L's employees must first be seen from several perspectives: relations to each individual; relations to the group as a whole and relations to the 'loyal' block and 'disloyal' block respectively. He is also related to Abrahamsson in one particular way, and to Kolinsky in another. He is related to W's management and to the union, both in L and W. The relationships are constant in the sense that they are always present and valid throughout the process. Moreover, they are present in all social contacts. Let there be no mistaking that it is the relationships as such which are of interest here and not the relations from the perspective of R. Perdfelt (R.P.). He serves here as a point of reference with regard to other parties in the relationships. The actions themselves which will be taken up in the argumentation must, indeed, be related to him, yet with the specification that they are possible only within the relational dimension and the particular conditions constituted by/within the same.

The interdependent dimension of power

The second aspect which follows the form and which is significant for the analysis of power is that of *interdependency*. This dimension has been the object of commentary in more ways than one. Blau (1964), Emerson (1962, 1972b), Thibault and Kelley (1959), and Homans (1974) are some of those who have incorporated the concept in their analyses of social exchange. Seen from my perspective, power is of central importance in the analysis of social relations with regard to exchange, at the same time as the dimension of interdependency is of central importance for the analysis of power. I have argued earlier in the text that what is exchanged in a power relation is space of action. This implies that interdependency is that which gives the exchange a constituent dimension as a power relation. Without interdependency there is no reason why any exchange should take place. The parties can strive to attain their interests in total isolation; but this is not the case. Interdependency is an omnipresent dimension in social life, and exchange is immanent in all social relations. An actor's space of action is dependent partly on the actor's own actions, and partly on the actions of other actors; those actions which they can execute simultaneously and those which come about as a consequence of the actions of the first actor. The dimension of interdependency implies that power, in order to be understood, must be seen against the background of the interactions and interrelated actions of the actors, groups, coalitions or organisations. Thibault and Kelley (1959), who argue on the basis of 'The social exchange' theory, emphasise the significance of dependency and inter-dependency in social life:

> In this sense, there are few human experiences that do not occur in the context of dependence relations. One might even argue that the hermit living in the mountains, by choosing to ignore the outside world, is minimally dependent on it. The main point is that social exchange, however rudimentary or infrequent, is ultimately grounded in dependence. (Thibault and Kelley, 1959)

Naturally enough, interdependency is not constant, even though it is always to be found in social relations. It may vary from case to case depending on the circumstances and on the context. The dimension of interdependency in the studied process may be seen as an integral phenomenon that is characteristic for all relations. The variations in these interdependent relations, however, are situationally based. This may be illustrated by the relationships between L's employees and the workers in L's district. At the beginning of the process the space of action of L's employees was notably dependent on that with which the union hoped to succeed; namely to change the situation. It was later to be seen that this hope was in vain. Thus L's employees lost confidence in the union. Their dependency on the union was weakened and their space of action was thus threatened. It soon became necessary to develop new logics of action and to relate the actions to other dependent relationships that they had with W's management; with the 'disloyal' group, with R. Perdfelt etc.[10] Let us illustrate this with R.P.

Interdependencies must naturally be seen from the perspectives of at least two parties, but the starting point is always that of the dependency of one actor or group on another. What I mean is that the analyst must begin his analysis from one perspective and relate it to the next, and so on. The interdependencies may in this way show that R.P. is, in the first instance, dependent upon W's management. But Ziegler is also, to a certain extent, dependent upon R.P. as he is responsible for one of *W*'s units. This dependency was reinforced in the context of the process due to R.P.'s closeness to *L*'s employees, and also due to the reliance of *W*'s management on R.P.'s support in his role of employer's spokesman. This same interdependency relates R.P. to middle management, and then, above all to L. Abrahamsson. The two of them had previously shared the same place of work and it was Abrahamsson who, once he was employed by *W*, had called R.P. to function as the local manager in *L*. The relationship between them was to deteriorate markedly when they 'discovered' each other in new situations with altered conditions and perhaps even personalities, R.P.'s dependency on Kolinsky was, in the first phases of the process, rather weak. Kolinsky was new in *W*'s older history, and he saw in R.P. a sort of ally who might possibly help him in the struggle against the 'rebels' in *L*. Gradually, as the process advanced, R.P. grew to be more and more dependent on Kolinsky. The latter had become conscious of the internal game which was going on among the actors involved and he too began to take part in it. Furthermore, it was now clear that *L* would be subordinated to 'his' production department after the transfer.

There are also other types of interdependencies to be seen between R.P. and *L*'s employees, on the one hand, and between R.P. and the union, on the other. *L*'s employees might be regarded, as I have suggested in the previous chapter, either as one group (interest group), or as two interest groups (the 'loyal' and the 'disloyal' block), or even as a coalition of two groups, depending on the political situation in the organisation and on the contextual interests felt to be acute. There are naturally also such interdependencies as those relating R.P. to various individuals among *L*'s employees. All these dimensions of interdependency were considerably transformed during the unfolding of the process.

L's employees, as a group, experienced themselves in the beginning, as being rather dependent on R.P. He was, after all, head of the department, and even though it had begun to be suspected that he was perhaps no 'genius' as far as negotiations were concerned, there was still a certain degree of belief in him and in his capacity. As for R.P., he seems to be an open person. He gave account to *L*'s employees in the introductory phases of the process of the discussions in which he took part together with *W*'s staff. Neither was he afraid of copiously commenting on the situations, people, actions as well as strategico-political moves which he considered to be decisive for the process. *L*'s employees had invested their hopes in him, and thus they felt dependent on that which R.P. could accomplish. As for R.P., he began to identify himself with the group in *L* rather than with *W*'s people, or at least began to feel the need to do so. Emotionally, he became more dependent on the acceptance and approval of *L*'s employees than of W's staff. During the remainder of the process, and against the background of the development of its course of events, R.P.'s relation to W's staff deteriorated, implying that he was in need, more than ever, of the support of L's employees, thus becoming very dependent on them. As for L's employees, they had ceased to count on him at the same time as they were formally dependent on him in his role as representative for L against W. Indirectly, but also directly, they reproached him for this situation as if he were the only one to have created it. Finally, and in spite of the conflict with L's employees, R.P. began to struggle against the transfer exactly as the others did, perhaps even more forcefully, simply to prove to them and to himself that he was one of them. The more he did so, the more dependent he became on their acknowledgement of his work as being of value. The situation which he experienced might be illustrated by what Crozier and Friedberg (1977), *à propos* the prisoner's dilemma, have called 'the internal logic'. W's people had disqualified him as the employer's spokesman at the same time as L's employees had also disqualified him, but as the workers' spokesman. When he chose to take a stand on the part of the employees he had already been passed as unsatisfactory by them, since for them (1) he is head of the department, (2) he had acted in an unsatisfactory manner and (3) he had withdrawn from the negotiations. He was caught between two extremes: heavily dependent on W's people and heavily dependent on L's employees.

L's employees are divided into two interest groups (two blocks) with diverging interests and orientations, and with different opinions with regard to the transfer. R.P.'s dependency on the group follows this same division. He feels more sympathy for the 'loyal' block, which means that when he strives to identify himself with L's employees as a group, it is, in fact only with one part of this; the 'loyal' block. The interdependency between R.P. and L's employees, as it is described above, must be related to this block, since it is they who experience the process most vividly and who consider themselves to be the most affected by the transfer. R.P.'s interdependency with the 'disloyal' block is marked by a greater degree of ambiguity. On the one hand he is more dependent on them as a part of L's employees, while he feels, on the other hand, less sympathy for them. They do not like him and even consider him to be incompetent as local manager. It is this predicament, added to the fact that this block acts as ally to middle management, that makes R.P. extremely dependent on them. The opinions which they have of him, and which they express, and the actions which they take during the process, notably affect his situation. They, on the other hand, are less dependent on him, since they interpret the process in different ways; they are 'on good terms' with W's staff and are not particularly affected by the transfer.

R.P. finds, in certain specific situations, that he is dependent on both blocks at the same time as these from a coalition on a specific dimension where they suddenly find a common interest in nominating him as scapegoat. Similar situations with coalitions arise when the 'disloyal' block joins forces with middle management. In situations such as these, R.P. is heavily dependent on these coalitions, on what they think and say and on what they do and do not do.

So much for the *form*, relationships and interdependencies. I now suggest that we proceed to the *content* and discuss its constituent elements.

Content: space of action

The form of power is denoted by the relational and interdependent dimensions of power. These dimensions are to be found in all power relationships. The *content*, on the other hand, varies from one relation to the next. It is contextual. In other words power relationships differ with regard to content, but are 'identical' with regard to form.

Content is usually discussed, in the traditional discourse of power in organisation theory, in terms of authority and influence, as varying dimensions in connection with power. As has been mentioned earlier, great confusion prevails as far as the distinction between the concepts of power, authority and influence are concerned (Peabody, 1964). Simon (1953), who bases his assumptions on Barnard, defines authority as 'the right to make decisions that affect the activities of others in the organisation'. This would imply that the superiors think up a decision, make it, and put it into practice without any resistance from the subordinates, and regardless of the nature of the decision. The right of the superiors to make decisions in this context is legitimated by the rules and structural arrangements of the organisation. The subordinates, by accepting the right of the superiors to make any decision they wish, must simply submit. The implications of Simon's argument would seem to refer to an unreal situation where people are no longer thinking individuals with a certain will and a certain amount of dignity, but merely shadows. I presume that what Simon had in mind must be an ideal state, a utopian model as to what an organisation should look like. Bacharach and Lawler justifiably wonder:

> Accepting the right of the superior to make such decisions, subordinates feel obliged to comply with the decisions. The unique aspect of authority is that subordinates acquiesce without question and are willing to (1) suspend any intellectual or moral judgements about the appropriateness of the superior's directives, or (2) act as if they subscribed to the judgement of the superior even if, in fact, they personally find the directive distasteful, irrational, or morally suspect. (Bacharach and Lawler, 1980: 28–29)

Naturally the subordinates in the studied process did not behave in this way; they acted. As we have seen, looking upon authority as if it were the content of a power relationship has not proven to be elucidatory from an analytical point of view, since – as Bierstedt (1950) comments – 'authority implies involuntary submission'. *Space of action*, on the other hand, implies that we are dealing with conscious and acting individuals. They interpret their situations, their actions and those of others. They have personal interests which they wish to fulfil. They strive for a greater degree of autonomy and a greater margin of freedom. They strive to render their actions as unpredictable for others as possible. They act strategically in their interactions with others. These interactions are constituted within/ through the interdependencies and converge in the object of implicit exchange in these relations: space of action. As far as I can see, it is precisely the contraction or expansion of space of action which constitutes the very expression of power in a specific relation. Tannenbaum and Massarik (1950), and Gamson (1968), have conceptualised the concept of authority in ways similar to that of Simon. All see authority as an uncritical acceptance on the part of the subordinates. Only few authors argue the idea that 'in all power relations the subordinate has some degree of power' (Simmel, 1950). Crozier and Friedberg (1977), however, are among the few who advocate this view. Authority, in this sense, can therefore not be merged with the concept of space of action as the content and object of exchange in a power relationship. Influence, on the other hand, might, to a certain extent, be of interest in this context, since the concept implicates a dynamic and tactical element.[11]

At another end of the discourse of power, perhaps in its most traditional part, the concept of influence is usually associated with that of power, and even considered to be identical to it. Influence is seen here as a relation between individuals, groups, organisations, etc. It is defined in the following way: A influences B to the extent that A gets B to do something which B would otherwise not do. That which one wishes to confirm is the existence and direction of influence: who influences whom? One would also confirm the relative influence of different individuals, and, for the sake of comparability, the extent of A's influence over B. It is quite impossible, Dahl (1963) writes, to discuss political life (even political life in an organisation) without comparing the influence of various actors. The principal idea in Dahl's reasoning is: the greater the change caused, in any sense, of B's inner or outer behaviour, the greater the influence of A over B. Let us not forget that this is a mechanistic way of looking upon influence. It is said in mechanics that object A exerts a force on object B if A brings about a change in the velocity of B.

Other researchers who concentrate on influence and relate it to power are Lasswell and Kaplan. They argue that the possession of various resources imbues the individual with power:

> By influence is meant the value position and potential of a person or group. Values may be grouped under 'welfare' and 'deference' and positions described in regard to each value (or set of values). (Lasswell and Kaplan, 1950: 55)

The concepts, or rather their values, are of importance here from the Lasswell and Kaplan's 'welfare' and 'deference'. An implication of attribute is evident in the specification below, which involves the conceptualisation of power in relational and interdependent contexts, and which gives an intimation of the causal mode of thought as in Dahl's 'A- and B-replique'.

> By welfare values we mean those whose possession to a certain degree is a necessary condition for the maintenance of the physical activity of the person. Among welfare values we are especially concerned with well-being, wealth, skill and enlightenment. [...] Deference values are those that consist in being taken into consideration (in the act of others than the self). Most important of the deference values, for political science, is power. Other important deference values are respect, rectitude, and affection. (Lasswell and Kaplan, 1950: 55)

Power and influence merge together in this argument with its lack of specification as to level, degree, intensity, form and content. Thus, it came to be regarded quite simply as the ability to partake in the making of decisions. G has power over H with respect to the values K if G participates in the making of decisions affecting the K-policies of H (Lasswell and Kaplan, 1950: 75).

This would seem an argument which is otherwise merely a reproduction of that of Dahl, who also places power on a par with influence when discussing power in its political gestalt. Yet what we have here is also a highly simplified view of power, its value and its meaning; a simplification which seems to permeate the primitive conceptualisation of the concept of power, which formulates on the basis of simplistic questions and assumptions heavily axiomatised and often unrealistic definitions of power. The *content* of a power relationship seems to be constituted, as far as I can see, by a number of elements which designate various aspirations, all converging towards the 'ultimate' aspiration, i.e. *the expansion of space of action.*

MYTHS AND REALITY OF POWER

Our simple conceptions of the nature of power seem to have their basis in the myth of 'a technocratic dream come true'; a myth where reality is squeezed into models, the central ingredient of which is our own fixation on 'equilibrium', on balance and on harmony. The way that the primitive discourse conceptualises the phenomenon of power in axioms seems to be in accordance with the Western ideology of controlling 'the reality out there'. Skolimowski writes that

> Within the framework of Western secular ideology religion became identified with stagnation and backwardness. As a result, the inward perfectability that religion advocates and the inner powers that it wants to develop, were seen as antiquated things of the past. For this reason alone, forms of power that pertain to the spiritual realm of man became viewed as quaint and passé. Furthermore, secular eschatology preaching fulfilment here on earth and using the vehicle of material progress as the instruments of the physical transformation of the world became openly contemptuous of non-material aspirations of man. This is the background which has led to the elevation of the myth of power. (Skolimowski, 1983: 26)

Beyond the myth upon which the primitive conceptualisation rests, there is the dimension of the reality of power which can neither be waved aside nor ignored. Power is not only important for the understanding of organisations and for the intra-organisational processes, it is also, in a broad sense, omnipresent. It is produced at each moment, everywhere and in all relations. Bertrand Russell says, when commenting on the significance of power in social contexts, that the fundamental concept in the social sciences is that of power in the same way as energy is the fundamental concept within physics. As soon as one begins to examine, in organisational studies, the factors involved in the formation, development and survival of organisations as also the decisive (and revealing) factors in the intra-organisational processes, the discovery is made that power (including the political dimension) is of central importance.

Nonetheless, in spite of the acknowledgement by many writers of this importance, great confusion still prevails, as we have seen, as to how to define power and what role it actually plays in organisations.[12] As was mentioned in the previous chapter, everyone has an intuitive understanding as to what power is, since 'it [power] as a phenomenon, is simple and universal, it is everywhere, whereas as a concept on the other hand, it is multifaceted and evasive' (Crozier and Friedberg, 1977: 55). Other authors, apart from attributing power to a specific person or persons, seem to fall in with Bertrand Russell's idea: 'The formation of an organization can be seen as the direct result of a person's desire for power or the things that power can provide' (Hicks and Gullet, 1975: 261).

A contiguous idea is that expressed by Crozier and Friedberg (1977) when they say that the organisation must be attractive to potential members (recruits) since their loyalty is necessary for the operationality of the organisation. We have, in both these cases, an intimation that power functions, to paraphrase Russell (1939), as some kind of 'social energy', which, so to speak, gets the wheels of the organisation rolling, as the organisation provides various alternatives for the satisfaction of the needs of the individuals in a broad sense. Power, in this sense, 'transforms diverse individual desires into cooperative activities for mutual benefits' (Crozier and Friedberg, 1977: 55). It is perhaps precisely this way of conceptualising power that is able to provide some indication, beyond axioms and models, as to the reality of power. It is indicated here that power seems to be 'necessary' for the initiation of cooperation, for the guaranteed continuity of this cooperation, and for its reinforcement. The continual readjustment of this cooperation is also necessary, and it is power, seen here as a central mechanism of regulation, which answers for its maintenance.

The idea of power as a central mechanism of regulation in organisations may seem somewhat precipitate at this stage of the argument. I shall further specify this idea later in the presentation. The idea as such, however, is consistent with the concepts and instruments that have been presented in the text thus far. By way of proceeding from the view of power as a central mechanism of regulation, I hope to shift the attention from the attribute and property perspective to the relational and interdependent dimensions which I have presented. Thus I do not, in the analysis, focus on power *per se*, but rather on its opposition, its outer territory; i.e. that which emerges and is implicated by the existence of power as a phenomenon. I see power, in this sense, merely as an abstraction. It is not measurable, but its identity seems to be apprehensible only if the analysis is directed towards the actions related to 'the idea of power'. I refer here to the concepts and instruments which I have suggested in contrast to the primitive conceptualisation of power.

The essence of my argument is therefore that the analysis of the phenomenon of power must go via other premises than those dictated by the primitive discourse of power. The focus of the analysis on the opposition of power, can, I believe, provide us with more information as to the identity of power than can the coercive idea of it. It can perhaps pave the way for a new understanding and a new conceptualisation of this phenomenon. As with Foucault's and Nietzsche's methodological attempts, I suggest that we, metaphorically speaking, go over to the *other side of the mirror*[13] in our studies of power. In his analysis of the history of madness, Foucault wonders how one can 'justify' the process that madness has gone through? That which was at stake was highly significant for the Western world: by banning its demons it was a matter for the Western world of discovering its own face; excluding and confining its madmen, insane, fools, so as to delimit its territory; creating outer ghettos so as to structure its inner. The classic era (l'âge classique) needed its opposite image in order to be able to define itself. Similar to Foucault's analysis of the identity of the Western world through the history of reason and to Nietzsche's study of morals via the origins of values, I suggest an analysis of power which goes via that which appears against the background of its mere existence: aspiration towards *space of action*. Space of action is seen as a constituent element of content. It is not stable but rather contextual and changeable. It is dependent, at every moment, on the aspirations of others and on the actions which they take in order to fulfil these aspirations. It is not to be seen in isolation, but should be placed in a context, i.e. the form; within the framework of the relational and interdependent relations. Furthermore, the unit of analysis may nevertheless be a group, a coalition or an organisation. The notion of aspiration is a comprehensive designation for everything serving as a propelling force, or motive, for that series of interrelated actions purposing to satisfy or realise a personal interest, to reach a greater degree of autonomy and to experience a greater margin of freedom, as well as to feel that one is in control of one's own will. These aspirations are neither mechanistic, nor are they causal or separated in time. Rather, they might be said to form an aggregate which is constituent for the action, and, to converge, all of them, towards the ultimate finality: the expansion of space of action.

This means that the common denominator here is the concept of action. The philosophers who had devoted attention to this concept emphasise the relationship which exists between *action, freedom* and *will*. Additional concepts which are essential in this context are *interest* and *autonomy*. I associate the first with will and the second with freedom. I shall return to this. I now suggest that we reason, step by step, around the concepts of action, freedom, and will, along with the relations between them.

ACTION[14]

'La condition première de l'action c'est la liberté' says Sartre (1943: 487). The first condition of action is freedom. Our first task in this section will be to elucidate this relation. It is strange, says Sartre, that one has argued back and forth about determinism and about freedom without having attempted in any serious way to render explicit the structures contained within the idea of action. This concept 'contains', in fact, a number of interrelated notions.

Agir, c'est modifier la *figure* du monde, c'est disposer des moyens en vue

> d'une fin, c'est produire un complexe instrumental et organisé tel que, par une série d'enchaînements et de liaisons, la modification apportée à l'un des chaînons amène des modifications dans toute la série et, pour finir, produise un résultat prévu. (Sartre, 1943: 487)

> to act is to modify the *shape* of the world; it is to arrange means in view of an end; it is to produce an organized instrumental complex such that by a series of concatenations and connections the modification effected on one of the links causes modifications throughout the whole series and finally produces an anticipated result. (1977: 433)

Our initial point of departure should be that action is *intentional*[15] (action intentionelle, Sartre, 1943). If I, out of carelessness, were to leave a lit cigarette in the ashtray causing my manuscript to burn up, then one could not say that I had acted. It might be said, on the other hand, that Ziegler, when taking up the tug-of-war with Faiblén in connection with the acquisition of *L*, did act, in the sense that he intentionally realised a conscious project. He knew what he wanted and he knew what he was doing. This does not imply, however, that it is possible to foresee the consequences of all of one's actions. Ziegler did not foresee, when he won the tug-of-war and incorporated *L* in *W* (as a department), that he would create a situation which could later lead to the destruction of precisely that which was genuine and attractive in *L*. Yet he did still act in so far as he realised his project by winning the tug-of-war and leading *L*'s competence to *W*. The relation between intention and result does not suffice for us to speak of action. Sartre suggests that we go further.

> Nous constatons que l'action implique nécessairement comme sa condition la reconnaissance d'un 'desideratum', c'est-à-dire d'un manque objectif ou encore d'une *négatité*. (Sartre, 1943: 488)

> we establish that the action necessarily implies as its condition the recognition of a 'desideratum'; that is, of an objective lack or again of a *négatité*. (1977: 433)

The intention to incorporate *L* in *W* could not have occurred to Ziegler without his having identified, in advance, something which was objectively lacking in *W*. There were notable tendencies to be seen on the market which indicated the advantages of mechanised and robotised products in the branch. It would be good for *W* if one were to succeed in acquiring the very competence that was lacking. The action of incorporating *L* in *W* can only be understood as action if it is preceded by a mental conceptualisation of the advantageous situation which would result from the incorporation.[16] But this conceptualisation is by no means a simple representation of the advantageous situation as *possible*.

Elle le saisit dans sa caractéristique essentielle qui est d'être un possible désirable et non réalisé (Sartre, 1943: 488).

It apprehends [it] in its essential characteristics, which is to be a desirable and not yet realized possible (1977: 434).

This means that when we conceptualise an action, our consciousness goes over from the actual world, of which it is 'conscious', i.e. that which exists, *being*, to that which does not yet exist: non-being or *nothingness*. Since that which exists is in our consciousness, how then does our consciousness find 'good' motives for going towards that which is not? At the board meeting on 29 August 1980 the situation in L was relatively good; L had 'raised itself up' and the result was better than before. How did Ziegler conceptualise the action (and the formulated intention) in connection with the then desired transfer?

> The outcome of the unit has improved markedly, but a depression could drastically change the situation. The goal will thus be to strive to minimize the risk of losses in the future at the same time as retaining the know-how and the unique products. A transfer of the unit [. . .] in combination with the purchase of heavy processing and assemblage is the likely solution. Also deemed to be of considerable value would be a combination of L's and ES's sales departments. The sale of the premises in [. . .] would also imply a liberation of capital. (From the protocol of the board meeting 29 August 1980)

The depression and the possibility of a drastic change taking place; the minimisation of the perceived risk and the desire to retain know-how; the possibility of delegated production and the combination of sales functions; the possibility of sale of premises and the desired liberation of capital. It might be said that these elements constituted the projected idea, and together a *négatité*, i.e. that they refer to that which is not, not to that which is. To say that 'a depression can drastically alter the situation' is to look at the situation that *is* through another 'absolute goal-situation' that is *not*. In other contexts, Ziegler speaks of capacity utilisation in L and advantages of integration with W. To look upon the situation in such a way implies that one sees it as being inadequate as if the situation suffered the lack of something: *nothingness*. It appears as such only if, beyond this, one has in mind another *a priori* ultimate-situation that functions as a value (or as an absolute criterion). Ziegler pictured an 'ultimate situation' with full capacity in W, and even more that L's problem of capacity utilisation would be solved when L was integrated in W. But the reader and I know that in the 'then situation', there was nothing to indicate that this 'ultimate situation' would come about. More likely the opposite was true. We know that it was W who had problems of capacity utilisation and that a short-time week had even been introduced. This 'ultimate situation' can, therefore, not be conceptualised by Ziegler only from the angle of the 'is-situation':

> la plus belle fille du monde ne peut donner que ce qu'elle a et, de même, la situation la plus misérable ne peut, d'elle-même, que se désigner comme elle *est*, sans aucune référence à un néant idéal. (Sartre, 1943: 489)

> for the most beautiful girl in the world can offer only what she has, and in the same way the most miserable situation can by itself be designated only as it *is* without any reference to an ideal nothingness. (1977: 434).

Sartre suggests that we invert the generally accepted notion which holds that it is the difficulty in a situation that brings us to conceptualise another state of affairs in which everything would improve to the benefit of all. On the contrary, says Sartre, it is when we can conceptualise another situation that a new light is suddenly thrown on the difficulties in our 'is-situation'. Then we see the 'is-situation' through the contemplated 'ultimate-situation'. We see nothingness in being. But is this possible when our consciousness constitutes, and is constituted by, that which is, exclusively? Do we evaluate, do we plan, or perhaps merely imagine by using *nothingness* as an ideal? Why do our ideal models never work? Why are our plans never carried through and realised as we have first imagined them? Goliat Inc. bought L for the sake of its competence. Ziegler struggled to incorporate it in its entirety since it could contribute a good complement to the existing assortment. Thereafter followed the creation of W, which was to become the object of constant restructuring, rationalisation, and reorganisation. One 'ultimate-situation' followed another. In one of these ultimate-situations, which referred to a contemplated global ideal state for the whole of W including L, Ziegler suddenly began to see what was lacking in L, and even what would be lacking in the future: he began to see nothingness in L's being. Out of this nothingness he created a new nothingness.

The reaction of L's employees to the transfer procedure may be understood against the background of the fact that they could imagine, with relative facility, that their 'is-situation' was nonetheless 'more advantageous' than the 'ultimate-situation' that was now being offered to them in connection with the transfer. They would vanish in the crowd, lose their identity; their margin of freedom and their space of action would be contracted. This interpretation would be reinforced if we were to add to it the effect which the transfer could conceivably have on their private lives. In each family one partner would have to find other employment, the children would have to change schools and the families owning a house would have to sell, buy something new and move. For them it was not difficult to imagine the 'ultimate-situation' as being worse than the 'is-situation'. If, for instance, one decides to lower the wages then it is easy enough for a worker to perceive that his present standard of living is still not lower than that which one is trying to force on to him. Before the transfer process had started *L*'s employees saw no reason to act (to revolt). They did not see their situation as being precarious (something which Ziegler, on the other hand, seemed to see), not because they resigned themselves, but due to the simple reason that they 'lacked' the necessary culture and mode of thought which would have 'enabled' them to see another, 'better', situation. Ziegler, however, could picture this, on their behalf, so to speak. Sartre describes this as a paradox. A paradox which leads to action. In the case of *L*'s employees, this led to an action of revolt.

The conclusion of this argument might be that the 'is-situation' can never, *per se*, be a *motive* for action. It is not until a possible change has been projected and a new situation created – in the borderland between two situations where the 'old' peaceful 'is-situation' has been snatched away and an ultimate-situation appears on the horizon that the former is experienced, against the background of that which has been projected, as untenable. Two essential observations:

> (1) aucun état de fait, quel qu'il soit (structure politique, économique de la société, 'état' psychologique, etc), n'est susceptible de motiver par lui-même un acte quelconque. Car un acte est une projection du pour-soi vers ce qui n'est pas et ce qui est ne peut aucunement déterminer par lui-même ce qui n'est pas. (2) Aucun état de fait ne peut déterminer la conscience à le saisir comme négatité ou comme manque. (Sartre, 1943: 490)

> (1) No factual state whatever it may be (the political and economic structure of society, the psychological 'state', etc.) is capable by itself of motivating any act whatsoever. For an act is a projection of the for-itself toward what is not, and what is can in no way determine by itself what is not. (2) No factual state can determine consciousness to apprehend it as a négatité or as a lack. (1977: 435–436)

In order perhaps to clarify the above even further: no 'is-state' (or 'is-situation') can determine consciousness to define it. Every action has as its condition the 'discovery' of a state as 'lack of . . .' (Sartre, 1943: 490). This implies that one perceives a 'négatité' in that which is. The phenomenon which is object of the consciousness is that which is, i.e. for-itself (pour-soi). This implies that an 'is-state' of affairs – with which I am satisfied or dissatisfied – is only through the possibilities of the 'negation' of 'for-itself'.

This means that the *motive* for the action of revolt taken by *L*'s employees must be sought in the permanent possibility of the consciousness to regard the 'old' peaceful is-situation that was snatched away in a new light; it is no longer. Thus this situation took on a particular significance for them against the background of the new situation which was projected and which meant, for them, a nothingness in two senses: in itself and in relation to the first situation. From the beginning they had been satisfied with what they had, without pondering over it. When the transfer procedure was initiated they all of a sudden found themselves in a border situation where the old situation and the contemplated, projected situation had significance. Their motive for action was constituted in this significance. Against the background of the point of departure used in this analysis it is possible to associate the idea of motive with that of the personal interests of the actors. However, for the sake of simplicity, I shall henceforth only use the concept of motive.

We may speak of the same process, from the perspective of W, e.g. Ziegler. It is the knowledge of a desired and possible, though not yet realised, 'improvement' of L's 'is-situation', i.e. a projection towards an 'ultimate-situation', that was to throw new light on L's 'is-situation' (the 'old', and to them, peaceful situation). It is thus against this background that Ziegler began to see the 'is-situation' in L as 'suffering from the lack of something'. It was in this negation (*négatité*) that the argument for the 'need' to change was constituted. It was here that Ziegler's motives for the transfer were constituted.

We face a problem here. I suggested earlier on in the text that when we conceptualise an action our consciousness goes over from the actual world of which we are conscious, i.e. from that which is, *being*, to that which is not yet: *nothingness*. I emphasised, at the same time, that that which is, is in our consciousness. Thus the question then becomes: how does our consciousness find, in that which is, *motives* for projecting towards that which is not? This implies that we assign to consciousness the possibility of negation *vis-à-vis* the world and *vis-à-vis* itself. What then, are the conditions of this possibility?

> Il faut reconnaître que la condition indispensable et fondamentale de toute action c'est la liberté de l'être agissant. (Sartre, 1953: 490)

> We must recognize that the indispensable and fundamental condition of all action is the freedom of the acting being. (1977: 436)

Freedom will be the object of discussion in the next section. Before then, I suggest that we reconnect these arguments to that towards which the analysis of power should, in fact, be directed: *space of action*. I suggested that the expansion of this space of action is the 'ultimate finality' and that action is the common denominator. Thus I shall henceforth reconstruct the relations *action-freedom* and *will* as processes converging towards an expansion of the space of action. This does not imply, however, that it is a matter of separate sequences which are causally related. They might rather be said to constitute one and the same project.

Freedom

A discussion of the concept of freedom must proceed via a discussion of the relationships between and within the series: *motive–intention–action–finality*. There are those (the determinists) who maintain that there exists no action without motives and that even the most trivial gesture (scratching your head, or lifting your arm) has its motives which give it significance. Despite the absurdity of this argument we cannot but agree that since all action is *intentional*, every action therefore has a finality which in turn refers to a motive. Contrary to that which is claimed by the determinists, however, it is by no means a matter here of causality. The decisive question must be posed beyond the series motive–intention–action–finality: how is the motive constituted? Once again when I say that there is no action without a motive, it is not in the sense that there is no phenomenon without a cause. A motive, in order to be a motive, must be experienced as such (Sartre, 1943: 491). This does not mean that it needs to be verbalised or made explicit. It is sufficient that it is an object of the consciousness for-itself for it to gain its value as a motive. It might be said that the motive, in this sense, can only be understood via the finality. Thus, the motive is, in itself, a negation (*négatité*). The reaction of *L*'s employees towards the transfer project may be seen as a fear. This fear is the motive; but it is a fear of losing the 'old' peaceful 'is-situation', as well as being a fear of vanishing in the process of integration within the framework of the projected 'ultimate-situation'. This implies that the fear of *L*'s employees can only be understood within the finality of which it is the fear. In other words, the motive might be said to be constituted by that which is not; by an ideal state or by something in the future.

Bearing in mind what has been said so far in connection with the argument about action, we may presume that the insight into the action of revolt as a possibility gives to the situation of *L*'s employees (in the borderland between two situations) its value of motive. The conclusion thus becomes that: it is by escaping from one situation towards our possibility to change it that we organise the situation in various motives (Sartre, 1943: 497). This escape, and the various attempts to modify a border situation, in this case the transfer situation, may well be illustrated by *L*'s employees' struggle during the process of transfer. The transfer situation itself had, with its various phases and procedures (negotiations, schisms, coalition formations, manipulations, etc.), been organised in various motives. To see motives in a situation for the projection of its modification, and to project the modification of a situation by seeing motives for it in this, are *one* and the same. This means that if there cannot be an action without a motive, it does not imply that the motive is the cause of the action: the motive is included in the action. The project/striving of *L*'s employees to change the transfer situation is inseparable from their action. Motive, action and finality are constituted as one. The significance of each of these 'structures' is constituted by the other two. Together they are constituted as one (pure) phenomenon (être-en-soi; Sartre, 1943) and become *one* with *freedom*. Thus action is an expression of freedom.

But precisely as Sartre (and even Heidegger) argue, we cannot content ourselves with simplistic considerations as far as the concept of freedom is concerned. A specification of the concept is necessary since freedom constitutes the fundamental condition of action. Here we are immediately confronted with a difficult problem. By description we usually mean an explanatory activity aimed towards the essence of a particular structure. But freedom has no essence. It does not comply with a logical necessity. It is held by Heidegger that existence in itself ('dasein' in general and freedom in particular) precedes and governs the essence, and Sartre adds, that:

> La liberté se fait acte et nous l'atteignons ordinairement à travers l'acte qu'elle organise avec les motifs, les mobiles et les fins qu'il implique. Mais précisément parce que cet acte a une essence, il nous apparait comme constitué: si nous voulons remonter à la puissance constitutive, il faut abandonner tout espoir de lui trouver une essence. Celle-ci, en effet, exigerait une nouvelle puissance constitutive et ainsi, de suite à l'infini. Comment donc décrire une existence qui se fait perpétuellement et qui refuse d'être enfermée dans une définition? La dénomination même de 'liberté' est dangereuse si l'on doit sous-entendre que le mot renvoie à un concept, comme les mots font à l'ordinaire. Indéfinissable et innommable, la liberté ne serait-elle pas indescriptible? (Sartre, 1943: 492)

> Freedom makes itself an act, and we ordinarily attain it across the act which it organizes with the causes, motives, and ends which the act implies. But precisely because this act has an essence, it appears to us as constituted; if we wish to reach the constitutive power, we must abandon any hope of finding it an essence. That would in fact demand a new constitutive power and so on to infinity. How then are we to describe an existence which perpetually makes itself and which refuses to be confined in a definition? The very use of the term 'freedom' is dangerous if it is to imply that the word refers to a concept as words ordinarily do. Indefinable and unnamable, is freedom also indescribable? (1977: 438).

Yet there is one way of speaking of freedom, of describing it – by directing the description towards the 'existing' itself, in its singularity, and not towards the essence. The philosophers of freedom, the existentialists, maintain that as an individual I cannot possibly describe a freedom that would be common to myself and to the other (autrui). I have, in other words, no possibility of conceiving of the essence of freedom. It might rather be said that freedom is the base of all essences.

C'est en dépassant le monde vers ses possibilités propres que l'homme dévoile les essences intramondaines. (Sartre, 1943: 493)

since man reveals intra-mundane essences by surpassing the world towards his own possibilities. (1977: 438)

It is by focusing (consciously) on my possibilities of completing this manuscript in time that I reveal the essences in my world. These essences have as their base my freedom which I must bear and which must be expressed in the action of completing the manuscript. When I, when one, and when we speak or write of freedom, we can, one can, I can only speak and write of *my* freedom. Freedom is an extremely individual matter. My *cogito* determines my *freedom* as a purely factual necessity, as existing, and as such I cannot refrain from experiencing it. I, since I exist, learn about my freedom through my actions. But this freedom is not a quality or a property of my nature. It is one with my being. *L*'s employees learn about their freedom by acting in the project to change the transfer situation. Ziegler learns about his freedom by acting in the project towards a finality; an 'ultimate-situation', desired but not yet realised. To be free does not signify 'getting what I want', but rather 'consciously deciding that *I want* (in the sense of choosing)'. Successes, in other words, provide no measure of freedom. The general conception of the notion of freedom produces associations with the moral, political and historical contexts which imply that freedom is 'the ability to attain a chosen finality'. The philosophical meaning, however, which is at issue here, is that of 'the autonomy of choice' (Sartre, 1943: 540). Beyond systemic regulations, beyond laws, norms, morals and conventions, man is free, and his freedom has its expression in his actions. But why then did *L*'s employees not act much more than they did? Why did R. Perdfelt not act more, or differently? In an extreme formulation, Sartre asserts that: Je suis condamné à être libre; I am *doomed to be free*. This implies that it is neither the regulations nor the laws, norms, morals or conventions that confine my freedom but my freedom itself. In other words, *I am not free to cease being free*. It is due to this, the existentialists say, that we experience anguish in the face of our irreducible freedom. We attempt to disguise it, we refuse to recognise it: It is difficult to bear. *L*'s employees say: 'We can't do anything, we're powerless, "they" decide everything'. In the same way, when they projected the coup which was supposed to lead to an 'ultimate-situation' with an increased sense of freedom, then this anguish came over them. The anguish of suddenly not having any limits other than one's own freedom. Between the two possibilities of choosing either recognising and experiencing their freedom and acting in the project to change their situation or of disguising their freedom and resigning themselves to the idea of the world as determined, they chose the latter. They chose, but convinced themselves of not having any choice.

This may, to my mind, be seen as part of the effects which the primitive conception of power has on the way in which man conceptualises his possibilities of action. In organisations the superiors and the subordinates alike seem to be bearers of that ideology which sees power as a means of dominance and manipulation. The superiors exercise power coercively and seek to transform the interdependencies to dependencies. The subordinates answer on the basis of the same ideology with various mechanisms of protection so as to reduce the opposing parties' control, and so as to expand their own margin of freedom and space of action. Yet they do so without the possibility of being able to get out of this ideology, and of taking the step towards recognising and bearing their irreducible freedom and acting accordingly. The studied process illustrates how this leads to vicious circles with devastating effects on organisations. It also illustrates that power is not only exercised by the superiors but also *by and through the subordinates*. This, in turn, brings up a methodological approach which I suggest here. Beyond the models of the primitive discourse of power and their low explanatory value, an understanding of the mechanisms of power may be facilitated, and perhaps attained, if we focus the analysis on the opposition of power *on the other side of the mirror*. This implies that the analysis must be directed towards the concepts and phenomena which designate – and appear within – people's interactions and which, for reasons of determinism and convenience, have been excluded from the discourse of power.

Will

A discussion of will in this context can have one purpose only: to bring to us a better understanding of the meaning of *freedom* and to throw some light on the relation which this has to the *will*. A common conception is that of assimilating free actions with actions of the will and reserving determinist explanations for those actions whose driving force is considered to be the emotions or 'passion' (Sartre, 1939, 1943). According to Descartes, for instance, 'the will is free but the soul is filled with passions'. Man would, according to this conception, be both free and determined. The problem would, in this sense, be that of the relation between this unconditional freedom and the determined processes of the psyche. How then could one dominate one's passions so as to use them in one's own interest? The stoics advise us to learn to handle our passions so as better to be able to dominate them. They advise us to behave in the world in the same way as one behaves *vis-à-vis* nature; one obeys it so as to be able to control it better. The sailor obeys the laws of the winds so as better to be able to use them for his sailing. The reality of man appears, in this sense, as 'a freedom surrounded by a set of determining processes'. Thus a line of distinction is drawn between completely free actions, determined processes which can be governed by free will, and processes which in no way can be governed by human will.

The existentialists reject this conception. A human being, who is after all *one* (whole), cannot be constituted by a series of determining elements on the one hand, and on the other by a spontaneity which only determines itself. Should this mean that there exists a link between the free will and the determined passions? Impossible, the existentialists answer (Sartre, 1943; but even phenomenologists such as Ricoeur, 1969, 1977 and Merleau-Ponty, 1953, 1971). Neither is it possible to conceive of the passions ruling over the will: a determined process cannot influence spontaneity in the same way as an object cannot influence consciousness. Spontaneity is precisely as a negation of the passions (i.e. they are constituted on the outside) as that which spontaneity is *not*. Spontaneity is, in this sense, both will and consciousness. Against this background Sartre (1943) sees two possible solutions:

> Ou bien l'homme est entièrement déterminé (ce qui est inadmissible, en particulier parce qu'une conscience déterminée, c'est-à-dire motivée en extériorité, devient pure extériorité elle-même et cesse d'être conscience) ou bien l'homme est entiérement libre. (Sartre, 1943: 497)

> Either man is wholly determined (which is inadmissible, especially because a determined consciousness – i.e., a consciousness externally motivated – becomes itself pure exteriority and ceases to be consciousness) or else man is wholly free. (1977: 442)

According to the existentialists my freedom exists 'through' my will. Passion belongs to the same 'category' as the will. Both are primarily projections towards a finality (an ultimate-situation) which throws light on the nothingness (that which is lacking) of the 'is-situation'. Both have finalities which are identified as non-existent. '*Néantisation*' (to realise the nothingness in the being; that which is lacking in that which is) is, in effect, the basis of freedom (*l'être de la liberté*). This implies that the will, which is an expression of freedom, presupposes an irreducible freedom for it to be constituted as will. This irreducible freedom is inseparable from man. We strive for it, in various projects, beyond determinism and beyond the structures of the world. Will, in this sense, is a conscious decision in relation to certain finalities. It does not create these finalities, but rather places itself in relation to them: as something for which to strive.

In the tug-of-war against Faiblén, Ziegler expressed his will in the project to incorporate *L* in *W*. The finality was the incorporation of *L*'s competence and thereby the supplementation of that which was lacking in *W* as an enterprise. Even though the tug-of-war was perhaps not carried out in the most fair-play fashion, it was the finality that was of most importance. This finality may, in turn, from Ziegler's perspective, be seen as a vision of a stronger position, a more advantageous situation, but also as an increased manoeuvring ability, an expansion of space of action, and, at the root of the matter, as an expression of Ziegler's irreducible freedom and as a striving to increase the experience of this very freedom. Among many other situations in the process studied, we might mention the time when he chose (consciously) to disregard acceptable and less acceptable means of attaining the finality of the transfer when he attempted to 'rewrite' the text of the protocol. At this stage the process had reached such proportions that it was no longer a matter of economical rational motives, but only of whose finality was to win; *L*'s employees' or M. Ziegler's. If here we focus on the action as such, setting moral considerations aside, then it is quite easy to see that freedom is in this case assimilated with the existence of the actor, and that it constitutes the basis of the finalities which they try to realise through the will (or even through passionate and emotional efforts).

> La liberté n'est rien d'autre que l'existence de notre volonté ou de nos passions, en tant que cette existence est néantisation de la facticité, c'est-à-dire celle d'un être qui est son être sur le mode d'avoir à l'être. (Sarte, 1943: 499)

> Freedom is nothing but the existence of our will or of our passions in so far this existence is the nihilation of facticity; that is, the existence of being which is its being in the mode of having to be it. (1977: 444)

The will is constituted within the framework of the motives and finalities which I place in relation to a project and its possibilities. How else could we understand the weighing up of different ways in which to attain a particular finality? If a finality is already there, for example, that *L*'s employees are opposed to the transfer or that Ziegler wishes to activate them, then what remains to be done is to choose a mode of action *vis-à-vis* this finality. Well, who is it that determines this mode of action if not

Ziegler himself or *L*'s employees themselves? Who decided that Ziegler would attempt to 'rewrite' the text of the protocol? Who decided that the bearers of knowledge in *L* would abandon ship? Who was it that decided that the 'loyal' block would attempt to carry out a coup, etc? If we accept the idea that it is circumstances that entirely determine our actions, then we are implying in the same breath, that there exists no freedom at all (Sartre, 1943). An anti-argument might be that there are those who wish to be governed, thereby becoming free from responsibility; those who prefer the security of not having to choose and who submit to being taken care of. To this the existentialists answer that the attitude of *not choosing* is also *a choice*. An action of the will does not only imply that I want to: I must also want to want (Sartre, 1943: 499). In another context Sartre (1939) explains that if I, for instance, faint out of fear in the face of an external threat, then this fainting serves to annihilate the threat by annihilating my awareness of the threat. Thus, there is, even here, an *intention* to faint with the purpose of escaping from an uncomfortable world which is looming up towards me through my consciousness which is involved in it.

Although this example may appear to be somewhat extreme it does, nonetheless, illustrate an essential idea in this context: Man is *responsible*, he *is* only if he *chooses*. Perdfelt chose to be divided, he chose not to choose which foot to stand on: as spokesman for the employers or as advocate for *L*'s employees. He is afraid of losing his job when he chose dividedness. His fear is free and is a manifestation of his freedom. He invested all his freedom in his fear and chose himself to be divided. In the same way the individuals in the 'loyal' block invested all their freedom in courage when they chose to attempt to carry out a coup. Ziegler acted in the same way when he chose to attempt to 'rewrite' the text of the protocol.

Freedom is, as we have seen, fundamental for the understanding of *action*, *will* as well as the *motive* and *finality* of action. Yet there remains more to be said in this context about freedom and responsibility. A discussion from this perspective naturally has moral implications, but it also leads to the question of how man bears this irreducible freedom and how it is expressed in action. One may speak, in this context, of at least two kinds of responsibility: a responsibility of duty related to the nature and function of the work (for example the managing director is responsible for the company's results), and a moral responsibility which directs the question beyond the duty responsibility, towards the action *per se*, and seeks to respond to the actor's relation to himself, to the world and to others. It is the latter alternative which will be considered here and which I deem to be of significance for the understanding of the mechanisms of power.

Freedom and responsibility

Let us recall the most essential points taken up for consideration in the argument on the preceding pages: 'Man is doomed to be free, he bears the weight of the world on his shoulders, he is responsible for the world and for himself' (Sartre, 1943: 612). The *responsibility* is, in this sense, quite simply that one is the incontestable subject (author) of an event or an object. In this sense the responsibility might be said to be difficult to bear inasmuch as that which exists, *exists* through the actions of the subject. The existentialists say that I must bear the consciousness of being responsible for my actions, no matter what the situation, nor however difficult it may be. At the moment of writing the author experiences a strong feeling of loneliness. Perhaps this might be due to there not being any external determining circumstances between my pen and the paper excepting for my thoughts and my awareness of what I am writing. Yet my responsibility for my manuscript is nonetheless easier to recognise and to bear than is Ziegler's responsibility in the process. That which was so desirable and genuine in *L* was shattered without anyone actually wanting that to happen. The moment of writing perhaps does not vastly differ from the decision process: we experience in both cases the feelings of loneliness and anguish due to the responsibility. In the decision process, however, it is easier to call on the external circumstances for help. Ziegler disguised his responsibility by hanging on to a problem of capacity utilisation, in itself non-existent, and on to certain conceivable and desirable advantages of integration, etc. As for *L*'s employees, they considered the whole affair to be entirely independent of themselves, out of reach of anything they could do. However, responsibility cannot be reduced to the acceptance of an outer world, it is simply a logical consequence of our irreducible freedom. Do not put the blame on outer circumstances, the existentialists say, nothing like that decides what You feel, what You experience and what You are. That which happened to *W* and *L* happened through Ziegler and *L*'s employees themselves. It is not, as the primitive discourse of power has taught us to think, a matter of who has power, who decides, and who exercises what over whom. It might rather be said, if at all we are to speak of power, that it is a matter of power being exercised by and through the 'dominated' and the 'dominant' alike. A shared responsibility, or rather that each one is responsible for his/her share. The simplistic model would have us believe that A has power over B if A can cause a change in B's behaviour, as if B were a billiard ball without initiative, without will, without freedom, but also without finality, without intention and without motive or interest. But man *is* all of this and we shall never demystify the primitive discourse of power unless we proceed from that which man is. Man *is* his actions; and his actions are an expression of his irreducible freedom.

It is towards these actions, towards people's interactions and their strivings (whether they may be strong or weak) to expand their space of action and experience their irreducible freedom, that the analysis should be directed. The reason why the analysis should be conducted in such terms is that it is precisely this which has been excluded from the mechanistic and simplistic discourse of power. In order for it to be constituted as a mechanistic and causal discourse with simple connections, this discourse brushes everything aside that does not *a priori* fit into the preconceived model 'as being dysfunctions which disturb the system'. As I have attempted to show previously, the primitive discourse of power is constituted by a set of concepts which in order to be viable are based on principles of exclusion. Yet that which is placed outside the discourse, which is defined as its outer territory is, in part, more revealing as to the way in which the primitive conceptualisation of power is constituted, and also more informative as to the phenomenon of power *per se*.

I have used the concept of *opposition* earlier in the text to denote that towards which the analysis is directed in relation to power. A clarification of opposition would, I feel, be appropriate at this stage. The concept should be understood in this context as a denotation of that which is considered, from the perspective of the discourse, to not be acceptable as a part of the conceptual framework of the discourse since it is assumed to disturb its harmony. Thus it is placed outside; but this is not always done explicitly. It is through a genealogical study of the discourse at hand, bearing in mind the object of the discourse, that one may discover that the *sine qua non* conditions of the object have been excluded *pour raison de pensée*. The *sine qua non* conditions of power are people's actions and the structures related to the action which we have just gone through. These conditions are not measurable, however, and are difficult to handle. Furthermore, they provide insight into a way of understanding power which differs from the view of it as a means of dominance, control and manipulation. They do not fit in *la pensée*. But is this way of constructing a discourse, i.e. on the basis of principles of exclusion, an isolated occurrence confined to the discourse of power? This does not seem to be the case. This mode of thinking seems to permeate Western thought as a whole. The genealogical study by both Nietzsche and Foucault of the discursive knowledge of man has shown that every culture has its borders, its methods of defining what belongs to it and what is to remain on the outside, what it accepts and what it rejects: the great, monotonous, all-embracing line of division runs in our culture between the normal and the pathological. Each culture has its own particular acts, forms, gestures, in order to reject and exclude, to control and to keep in place; its own way of shutting its eyes to that which it does not wish to see, and of declaring null and void that which it does not wish to hear; the liberating, the challenging knowledge of ourselves does not come through our knowledge but through what we do not wish to know.

It is perhaps so that the liberating, the challenging knowledge of the phenomenon of power in people's existence, does not come through our knowledge; i.e. via that which the primitive discourse of power allows us to *see*, but through that which the discourse does *not want to know*, that which it places outside and defines as belonging to its outer territory. Schumacher (1977) tells of the time when he visited Leningrad (August 1968). He had in his hand a map from which to take his bearings. It was not as easy as that, however. He could see immense churches in front of him, but none of them were put out on the map. An interpreter came by and 'helped him to understand'. He said 'We do not show any churches on our maps'. Schumacher protested and pointed to one that was clearly indicated on the map. 'That's not a church', the interpreter said, 'That's a museum, not what we call a living church.' 'We don't show living churches on our maps.' What seems to be the most important is not what is indicated on the map, but rather what is *not* indicated and *why* it is not:

> It then occurred to me that this was not the first time I had been given a map that failed to show many of the things I could see right in front of my eyes. All through school and university I had been given maps of life and knowledge on which there was hardly a trace of many of the things that I most cared about and that seemed to me to be of the greatest possible importance for the conduct of my life. I remembered that for many years my perplexity was complete; and no interpreter came along to help me. It remained complete until I ceased to suspect the sanity of my perceptions and began, instead, to suspect the soundness of the maps. (Schumacher, 1977: 9)

The fundamental principle of those who draw the map seems to be 'leave it out if it is dubious'; dubious in the sense that it disturbs the harmony of the pseudo-knowledge. Within the primitive discourse of power the reality of man is doubted. Beyond the obvious paradox that power, with all said and done, emanates in the reality of man, it is the philosophical principle of the artificial map that determines what is to belong to it and what is to be left outside. It is as if reality must coincide with maps, and not the opposite.

The concepts, the form and the content

The relational and interdependent dimensions of power denote the form of power. In all manifestations of power two dimensions are to be found. The content is varying and contextual: the striving of the individuals for the ultimate finality; i.e. the expansion of space of action can be expressed with more or less intensity depending on how the individuals experience and interpret their situation, and what may be called the nothingness of their situation (that which is lacking). Thus, the striving for space of action, expansion, is always immanent in a form: i.e. the content is identifiable and analysable within the relationships and interdependencies.

The relation of the concepts to the unit of analysis

The concepts thus outlined may, in turn, be placed in the perspective of the unit of analysis. I argued, in the previous chapter, for the possibility of conducting the analysis of power (of its opposition) from the perspective of an individual, a group, a coalition or an organisation, depending upon which motives and interests are the strongest at the time, and on what the actor experiences as being the most important.

SUMMARY

I have discussed in this chapter the primitive discourse of power as it is portrayed in the theory of organisation and attempted to show how its rules of formation are constituted around them. Power is seen as something which develops with, or alongside, the legitimate authority and is seen (or analysed) as a dysfunction which disturbs the assumed balance and harmony of a given system. Power is thus seen from a one-sided perspective. It proceeds from the view that it is exercised exclusively by the dominant, and seeks to satisfy the criterion of measurability. Researchers of power are 'forced' to conceptualise power as if it were a property which can be related to the individuals, or as if it were a resource which certain people may have. The result is then that the actual mechanisms that are fundamental for all manifestations of power are ignored; i.e. the political dimensions of the organisations; the particularism and personal interests and motives of the individuals, as well as their strivings to expand their space of action no matter what their hierarchical position might be.

I have also argued for the need to demystify the primitive view of power and its conceptualisation as a means of dominance, control and manipulation. I have then suggested a number of concepts and modes of thought which may be significant for studies of the phenomenon of power. Form and content are important features in this context. *Form* is present in all empirical manifestations and is constituted by the *relational* and *interdependent* dimension. Content, with regard to its intensity is, on the other hand, contextual and therefore varying. It is constituted by implicit and explicit *exchanges* of *space of action* and by the strivings to expand this space. The common denominator of this striving is *action*; but action in itself is an expression of freedom which, in turn, must be related to the *will*. This is constituted within the framework of man's motives and interests. Man's *responsibility* for his action thus becomes a logical consequence of his irreducible freedom.

The above mentioned concepts and the relationships between them constitute what I call, from a methodological perspective, the *opposition* of power and which is the object of this analysis. This implies that we, instead of aiming directly at the analysis of power *per se*, go over to *the other side of the mirror*. There, metaphorically, we direct the analysis towards the outer territory of power; i.e. towards that which the primitive discourse of power, so as to be constituted, has excluded and placed outside. That which has been presumed to be irreconcilable with the conceptual framework of the discourse and which has been presumed to be *pathological* and thereby perceived as a disturbance for the models' assumptions of harmony and balance.

CHAPTER 6

The Genealogy of Power in Organisations

INTRODUCTION

I have conducted an argument in the two previous chapters in which I have concentrated upon the generating of concepts and dimensions of explanation based on a review of the discourse of power in organisations. I have attempted to place this discourse, or rather fragments of it, in relation to the empirical experiences reported. This I have done against the background of the argumentation developed in Chapter Three which I have called the *theory of discourse*. It has been my intention to *deconstruct*[1] the rules of formation of this discourse so as to elucidate those conditions which render it possible. By this I mean those principles, which are for that matter often implicit, that are decisive for its construction, production and dissemination. We might note already at this stage, however, that the discourse of power in organisations is in many respects based upon principles of exclusion. That mentality, that world-view or that philosophy which governs its formation, serves as a model for what ought to, or ought not to, belong to it. In this way a number of essential dimensions in people's actions and interactions have thus been excluded from the discourse at issue. On the other hand we have seen that in the study of the phenomenon of power in people's activities, it is precisely these dimensions, ignored by the discourse, that are decisive for the manifestations of the phenomenon concerned. These dimensions are therefore of great importance for the understanding of the phenomenon of power in organisations.

We could perhaps, as an extension of this understanding, sensitise our thinking with regard to the demystification of the primitive conceptualisation of power which seems, to my mind, to produce an attitude towards the phenomenon which greatly limits our understanding of it. This is, however, easier said than done. The prevailing conceptualisation of the phenomenon of power seems to be deeply rooted in the culture of the Western world. Power is seen rather as an attribute than as a *quality of a*

217

relation. It is exclusively associated with the given hierarchies of the social structure. It is 'used' coercively as a means of dominance and repression. This attitude is not only found on the level of discourse. It seems to be widespread among us, even if only implicitly, and is made manifest in our actions. The superiors and the subordinates in organisations act in their interactions on the basis of this attitude. This is clearly illustrated in the case studied. Each one of the actors involved attempted to protect him/herself from coercion and arbitrariness. As is shown by this case, the parties concerned ended up in destructive vicious circles. Everyone was suspicious of everyone else, and, finally, it all came to a crash. The desired competence of L disappeared and the advantages of integration never saw the light of day. Everyone was involved in the pushing of the process in the direction opposite to the one that was actually desired. L has been transferred, to be sure, but it was not the transfer *per se* that was the intention. The intention was rather the integration of L's competence in W and the straightening-out of problems of capacity utilisation along with the integration of L in W's organisation. It was but a disabled L that was finally to be transferred to W. The case should really be called: 'the art of destroying oneself without actually wanting to do so'. It was as if the course of events had been activated by a logic of its own, almost independently of the intentions of those involved. This destructive logic seems, to my mind, to derive its origins from our view of the phenomenon of power, and from the way in which we conceptualise its manifestations.

Even if we were to succeed, however, hypothetically, in changing this view, people would not cease to consciously strive for the satisfaction of personal interests and orientations in addition to attempting to expand their space of action in their interactions with others. Action is *one* with the essence of man. What might happen is that the striving for space of action could assume another character, as it would, of 'necessity', be interpreted in a different way by the actors. If the actor is no longer subjected to a coercive exercise of power he might then no longer need to develop strategies so as to protect himself against arbitrariness, nor will he need to define himself by means of counter-coercive activities. As a result we might perhaps have organisations in which people channel their energy (or at least a part of it) into productive tasks rather than into the construction of mechanisms of protection. This sounds like a utopian scheme, as no doubt it is; but my point is that the phenomenon of power, no matter how it may be conceptualised, is omnipresent. It does not help to persuade oneself to ignore it; it does not let itself be ignored. Power is manifested in people's actions which come about and are further developed within organisations; but it is the understanding which people have of power, and the attitudes towards it, that seem to be crucial for the nature of actions. In other words the strivings of people for space of action bear intrinsically (and are a reflection of) a particular conceptualisation of power. This striving could, as is shown in the case study, develop *negative dynamics* and lead to destruction processes in a number of various forms.

It is tempting to speculate here on what sort of dynamics a different conceptualisation might lead that is not based upon the primitive discourse of power. Perhaps not *positive dynamics*, which would imply a life in the organisation free from disturbances – discussion always runs a risk of landing up in utopian models with the myth of harmony and consensus as a main ingredient – but, hopefully, at least less negative dynamics. I am inclined to believe that the course of events would have taken a different route had the actors in W and L possessed access to the language and the dimensions of understanding developed in this book. Insight into the essence of the problem and into what was actually at stake might perhaps have been gained at an earlier stage. Above all, one could have avoided *destroying*, with much energy, diligence and even precision, just that which it was hoped to *save*. If the primitive conceptualisation of power, as a discourse, produces its own object in the sense that it dictates the way in which power should be understood and studied, one might also say that it produces a mentality and an attitude as to what power is and how it is interpreted by people in organisations. If, in turn, the way in which people act, and the striving for space of action, is based upon this interpretation, it might also be said that intra-organisational processes have their origins in our attitudes towards and our interpretation of the phenomenon of power. As extension of this argument, we might add that power, no matter how it may be conceptualised, is the central mechanism of regulation in organisations.

The generated knowledge

I intend, in this section, to sum up the knowledge generated in this book and to elucidate the relationships to be found between the concepts and dimensions of understanding developed from the empirical case and from its confrontation with the primitive conceptualisation of power. A summary in the usual sense of the word often involves the repetition of that which has already been said. It is not a very rewarding task and entails the risk that the text becomes laborious, if it is not already so, or that such laboriousness is amplified. But neither am I sure as to my ability to avoid a certain lack of elegance in the text due to 'unavoidable' repetitions and unclear formulations. One solution would perhaps be to suggest a 'new' argument as regards that which has already been said, and to illuminate the generated knowledge against the background of this argument.

The existence of power in organisations

There is no doubt as to the existence of power as a phenomenon in our lives. The phenomenon of power has been the object of numerous studies in various categories and from different perspectives. The extent of these studies ranges over long periods – from before the Christian era up until today. It is no longer a matter of questioning the existence of power in people's interactions (Crozier and Friedberg, 1977; Hicks and Gullet, 1975; the total works of Foucault; and many others) and in their organised actions. Rather it is a matter of the way in which power is to be understood. Is power something which is concrete, which can be grasped and understood as an observable, empirical reality, or is it an *abstract idea* which demands a special approach in order for it to be analysed and understood? Foucault says in *La volonté de savoir* (1976: 122–123) that 'power is neither an institution, a structure, nor a strength, for some people to own'. This is not, however, the case in the primitive discourse of power in organisations. Although the existence of the phenomenon of power in organisations is accepted as a fact, the phenomenon is treated as if it were a dysfunction disturbing the balance and harmony of the system or, as a 'for-want-of-something-better concept' which is taken up for consideration in the last instance, perhaps an attempt to explain one or another peripheral effect. Such attempts are numerous, but that which is common to them all is that they conceptualise power as an attribute and/or as a possession; they aim their analysis at power *per se* (that is, they are forced to see it as a concrete reality which is thus observable and measurable). Moreover, as a consequence of this conceptualisation upon which they base their assumptions, they draw the analysis of power out of its context. As has become apparent in the case study, a complex reality exists beyond these models, a reality which can hardly be explained away as being a dysfunction or an exception. What we have seen is a complex network of human interaction with potential strategical and tactical features. There seem to be no empirical grounds for the myth of harmony and balance and totally regulated social systems, bearing in mind the course of development taken by the process. Instead, what we have been able to see, is individuals and actors who refuse to be reduced to abstract functions and who act strategically on the basis of their interpretations of that which they have experienced and of the situations which have arisen. Survival has, during the entire course of events, assumed the guise of political action.

The *first step* of the knowledge generated in this study is the acceptance of the existence of power in organisations. This question might, indeed, not be an open subject of controversy since most people recognise this fact, but there are nonetheless those who recommend that it should be ignored.

The reason for this may be that the concept of power is regarded as being troublesome and difficult to deal with, or that the negative impressions associated with it stave off researchers of organisations who prefer to direct their attention elsewhere.[2] This acceptance should lie on a level of understanding, i.e. that which we bear within us intellectually, as an idea, when we approach the study of power. On the same level, neither must we neglect the *political character of organisations*. It is not a matter of merely considering the question peripherally in the argument; it might rather be said that the whole idea of the existence of power in organisations only becomes meaningful when we acknowledge the political character that marks people's interactions in organisations. How then can this political dimension be understood if not via the actors' strategical actions and strivings for personal and diverging interests and orientations? There are perhaps other ways, but it seems to me, bearing in mind that which has come to light in the process studied, that the strategical character of people's actions is essential if not even decisive. The strategic actions within the framework of the parties' diverging orientations seem to constitute the very pith of politics, whether it be a matter of relationships between super powers, activities between or within political parties or deliberations concerning wage contracts, etc.

The strategic action

The traditional discourse of the design and structuring of organisations, which is based upon ideal modes and rational[3] systems, has impressed upon many of us a 'false' idea of organised action. We overestimate the rationality of the organisation and are over-confident in the excellence of the design. The effectivity of the system thus becomes a self-evident and expected result. We paint a metaphorical picture in our minds of well-directed mechanistic organisations. This clockwork often looks fine as an ideal model, but as soon as we are confronted with the reality of the organisation we discover the complexity of the world of people and the ambiguity of the processes. A number of interesting studies have, nonetheless, been carried out concerning the 'real life' of organisations (i.e. the way they actually are, not how they ought to be) and one is struck, repeatedly by the complexity which is characteristic of people's actions and which accounts for the fact that these actions can never be imprisoned in simple, deterministic models.

It could be said that this large gap between the theory formation in the traditional discourse of organisations and the actual, everyday reality which is manifested in the same, is due to the fact that the individuals always retain, no matter how strong and confining the systemic rules may be, a certain degree of freedom. This freedom is then necessarily expressed in actions whose primary purpose becomes that of the safeguarding of the actors against the arbitrariness and coercion of the system. Thus the strategic character of the actions then becomes a question of the striving after personal interests and individual orientations. The reactions of *L*'s employees, and the actions taken by them in the presence of an impending threat of transfer, might be seen during various phases of the process as strategic attempts to alter the direction of the course of events. The splitting up of *L*'s employees into two blocks – that is, the loyal and the disloyal – might be considered as a manifestation of diverging interests and orientations. Other strategic actions were carried out in various contexts, by, for example, Ziegler in connection with the attempt to rewrite the minutes or to accelerate the process and so pull the wool over the eyes of *L*'s employees. Abrahamsson's manoeuvring in connection with the report and his weak conviction as to the necessity of the transfer, which stood in opposition to the orientations of Ziegler, might also be seen as a set of strategic actions. The appointment of work groups and the way in which the work was carried out in them could also be included in this category, as also the dividedness of Perdfelt when he was split between serving different orientations as employer's spokesman or as *L*'s employees' ally. Finally, the attempted coup was no more than a last desperate attempt at action, which could be seen as a reaction against a system that was experienced as coercive and as a possible strategy which would possibly have favoured the personal interests of *L*'s employees (the loyal block). Seen from this perspective, nearly every action in the described process was of a strategical nature.

It seems to my mind that it is justifiable to maintain that it is not possible to understand the real grounds for the intra-organisational processes if one does not take into account the individual's irreducible freedom and his/her possibilities of action. These dimensions may, from a deterministic perspective, appear to be insignificant, but this does not mean that they would not play a decisive part in the organisational modes of function. It goes without saying that human actions cannot be reduced to a mechanistic product presumed to correspond to the formal structural arrangements of the organisation. These structures, which I have already discussed, are nothing but a product of the conscious political actions of individuals and groups. Instead of regarding action within organisations as by-products or dysfunctions, it might be more fruitful to regard such actions as a point of departure if our ambition is to understand general intra-organisational processes and the phenomenon of power.

The *second step* in the knowledge generated in this study is thus that the *strategic actions* of the actors are decisive for the formation of intra-organisational processes and for their further development. This is not merely based upon empirical studies, but also upon an extensive range of literature on the subject which draws attention to the need to consider the strategical character of action. It could be said that the acceptance of the existence of power in organisations as an abstract idea, that is, as a quality of a relation, is thus connected to the recognition of the political dimension of organisations. This demands, from an analytical point of view, that we as researchers shift our perspective from that of the systemic regulations to that of the actions of people. The idea of the totally passive, apathetic and apolitical actor stems from the myth of the rationally designed and totally regulated system.

Objections might be raised as to the generality and absoluteness of the conclusions which I draw from a limited empirical experience and a fragmentary review of theory, but I feel justified to claim, on this level, that the actions taken by actors in all sorts of organisations are, in one way or another, of a strategical nature. Beyond the empirical case used here there is also the everyday reality in which we live. The examples are innumerable, whether it be a matter of world political events or a tiny individual situation, in which it is indicated that actors act strategically within the framework of a political game. Our strivings for personal interests and our diverging orientations seem to provide no other alternatives. The Solidarity movement in Poland, the struggle for succession in large companies or the interests of capital in the amalgamation of firms (Johannisson, 1980), are merely a few of these examples.

The strategic actions which took place during the W–L process of transfer cannot either be explained by the traditional view (Chapters Four and Five) which either ignores the existence of power in organisations or else conceptualises it as a quantifiable and measurable attribute. This view disregards the strategical character of the actions, and thus cannot provide satisfactory explanations as to the development of the course of events. We are aware of the extent to which W's management (and Goliat Inc.) was interested in the competence of L as a complement and as means of increasing the competitiveness of W's assortment. We also know, however, that in spite of this interest and these orientations, actions were nonetheless taken in the opposite direction, and this finally led to the crash as we have seen. One possible interpretation might be to examine the decision process in connection with the transfer. One could then speak of socio-political decision processes (Robinson and Majak, 1967; Cyert and March, 1963) in which the point of departure is a certain set of values of how things ought to be. In this context the effort is directed towards the conciliation of the opposing values and interests of different individuals and groups in the organisation. This often leads to negotiations and coalition formations. Thus it might be said that what the process amounts to is the formulation and reformulation of organisational goals. Examples of such processes have been observed and documented in connection with the democratic planning and governing of organisations (Allison, 1971; Baldridge, 1971; Pettigrew, 1973), as well as in connection with the setting of wages and the distribution of resources (Pfeffer and Salancik, 1974) and with changes and innovation (Normann, 1975 and others). Yet in the case studied the process did not *de facto* amount to the conciliation of opposing values and interests, and to the reformulation of organisational goals. Even if one seemingly attempted to reach a common standpoint so far as the necessity of a transfer was concerned, these attempts had completely different effects. If it was the intention and interest of W's management to integrate, and, above all, to retain the competence of L, why then did they act as they did, in direct opposition to these interests?

One interpretation which seems to have an acceptable explanatory potential for this phenomenon might be that the primitive discourse of power produces a mentality and a view of the phenomenon of power that has no correspondence in empirical reality. Both the superiors in W and the subordinates in L were bearers of such a view and such a mentality. The former saw power as related to their hierarchical status, whereas the latter saw the actions of the former as the exercise of a coercive dominant and repressive power. The subordinates, in attempting to protect themselves against the arbitrariness of the superiors, developed various strategies and tactics which in turn led to various repressive counter-measures on the part of the superiors. One landed up in vicious circles with locked positions, coercive and counter-coercive actions and with resultant losses for all the parties involved. It is therefore via the understanding of the phenomenon of power, its conceptualisation and its mechanisms, that we might be able to grasp the intra-organisational processes and modes of function.

TOWARDS A NEW CONCEPTUALISATION OF POWER

If the argument conducted so far seems meaningful, and if the need to understand the mechanisms of the phenomenon of power feels acute, how then can we proceed? Which questions could it be relevant to pose: 'what is power'?, or 'in what way can it "best" be conceptualised and understood'? We have learnt, from the primitive discourse of power, to define it in static terms with emphasis on the legitimate, formal structure and authority. Power is seen, in this discourse, as the actual capacity to influence, and its conceptualisation aims at the direct analysis of power *per se*. It is measured either as an actual, acquired effect or as a deviation from the formal structure. The fundamental definition of power in this discourse is that A has power over B if A manages to bring about a change in B's behaviour[4] or, as Hickson et al. (1971) say: 'Power is the potential determination of behavior of one social unit by another.' Implicit in this definition, and which has wide applicability in theory formation concerning the discourse of power, is that the phenomenon of power is considered in terms of attributes and property. Indeed a number of attempts have been made to modify this definition, but everything points to the dwelling of these attempts on the surface rather than the changing of anything fundamental in the definition (Tedeschi, 1974; Gustafsson, 1979). It has long been discussed, for example, which unit of analysis would be the most appropriate: the power of the individual or the power of the group. Berle (1967: 36), for example, maintains that 'despite the fact that intra-organisational power relationships may be between groups, power is ultimately a personal phenomenon'. As for Perrow, he clearly expresses the property aspect when maintaining that:

> Power can be thought of as a property of groups but that particular caution must be taken in attempting to generalize from individual characteristics of power relationships to relationships of groups. (Perrow, in Zald, 1970: 80)

The questions that are raised in the primitive discourse of power are primarily *what* is power, *who* has power and *how* does one measure it. This approach is hardly fruitful: it says no more about the phenomenon than that with which people, in general, imbue the concept in everyday speech. What is even more serious is that it is this way of thinking (in terms of power) that produces and spreads the very mentality and view that we have seen exemplified in the case. The property and attribute perspective is not merely a set of analytical concepts to be found on the level of discourse; these concepts also constitute the fundamentals of the discursive formation of the primitive conceptualisation of power. They are thus the object of the discourse (to the extent that the analysis is aimed at them), at the same time as their dissemination contributes towards the reproduction of the discourse. This means that such vicious circles with regards to the conceptualisation of power are even to be found on the discursive level. It is perhaps not so surprising that power has been discussed for thousands of years, since long before the Christian Era and up until today, without our necessarily being capable of knowing with any certainty what the phenomenon is about.

The other side of the mirror

The *third step* in the generated knowledge has to do with the intellectual conceptualisation and analytical approach which might be 'best' suited for the understanding of the phenomenon of power. The answer from the perspective of this study is simple: If we wish to study and understand power, then it is *not* power *per se* that we should search for, nor should we attempt to aim our analysis (and our analytical concepts) directly at the phenomenon itself. Power does not exist, as I have argued earlier, as a concrete reality, but merely as an *abstract idea* (or as an abstraction). This abstract idea, however, does not exist in a vacuum; we bear it within us, it is deeply rooted in our culture, not only as a pure idea, but loaded with subjective judgement. The history of our knowledge and its archaeology bears witness to the significance which the idea of power as a means of dominance has had for our present conception of it. I shall return to this argument. The question which I pose, thus, has as its object the *identity* of power as a phenomenon. Since power does not exist as a concrete reality *per se*, but is rather manifested as a reflection of our *conceptions* of it, the essential question must therefore be aimed at these conceptions. At the same time our conceptions of power are produced by our discourses of it. I stated earlier that a discourse is not about an object (as if the object were 'out there' as an entity to be dealt with). Instead, the discourse *produces its own object*, which in turn contributes towards the further development of the discourse and its reproduction. This means that the discourse and the object are produced and develop in one and the same indivisible process. If this is so, are we capable of discussing our conceptions of power without reproducing them: are we capable of leaving the vicious circle and seeing through the *conceptions of our conceptions*? The thought here is similar to Foucault's analyses of the cultural identity of the Western world via its opposite, and to Nietzsche's study of our morals via the values upon which they rest and the *value of these values*.

My suggestion is that we examine our conceptions of power via the value which these have in relation to the manifestations of the phenomenon. But how can this be done? One possible way is via the examination of the discursive *rules of formation* (règles de formation). In the works of both Nietzsche and Foucault a methodological approach, which illuminates our ideas about knowledge and truth from new angles, comes to light. The construction of the rules of formation of the discourse rests upon an arbitrary process in the sense that the conditions of possibility of the discourse are procedures of exclusion. The discourse, in order to come about, operates by first stating and defining its borders, deciding what belongs to it, and finding acceptable procedures of gathering for that which is included in it. It might thus be said that the identity of a discourse is determined more by that which is external to it than by that of which it is constituted. The identity of the discourse is thus to be understood in the context as the conditions of possibility of the discourse and the value of the knowledge and conceptions thus produced. In other words, the outer territory of a discourse tells us more about its value than do the statements of the discourse itself. It is here, I think, that my suggestion could be significant: I suggest that we, conceptually and analytically, go over to the *other side of the mirror*, metaphorically speaking, so as to see, beyond the given, that which the primitive discourse of power has placed outside and excluded from itself, together with the procedures which have regulated this exclusion. The *theory of discourse* is a useful guideline in this context.

1. Three types of prohibition. The most commonplace procedures of exclusion governing the formation of a discourse (which are a part of the discursive rules of formation and are produced by/within the discourse) are, in the first instance, three types of prohibition: (a) the object as a taboo, (b) the contextual rituals, and (c) the speaker's (or writer's = l'énonciateur) privileged or exclusive right to express himself (Foucault, 1971a: 11). These three types of prohibition reinforce and compensate one another as well as never ceasing to be transformed and readjusted. Power, as an object of knowledge, has been treated sparingly in the traditional theory of organisations and in the contiguous subjects from which organisation researchers have drawn inspiration. Argument on this can be found in the two previous chapters. The main reason that this is so is that the concept of power is associated with something negative. It is seen as some sort of pathology with which the harmony, equilibrium and balance of the organisation is afflicted. The making of statements on the subject of power as a central phenomenon thus became an *object of taboo*. At the same time, one nonetheless came to the realisation that power, whatever it may be, actually does play a part in organisations and in people's lives in general. One was to 'realise' that the lack of success experienced with the use of rationally designed systems could perhaps be due to 'disturbances' which were 'caused' by certain obscure variables and unpredictable events. The *ritual* which has prevailed since the development of the doctrine of organisations up until today has been 'to invent the organisational clockwork'. Power was then treated as the dysfunctioning of this clockwork and/or it was related to the formal structural arrangements and hierarchical authority of the organisation; all this in accordance with the secularised primitive conceptualisation of power as the coercive means of dominance and repression. One began to speak in terms of power bases, power resources, functions of power and effects of power; i.e. that which throws the clockwork out of balance, but which at the same time can be used as a sanctioning measure in the re-establishment of this very balance. However, one might ask who are the authors (les énonciateurs) of these statements? They are pluralists, functionalists, conflict theorists, contingency theorists, etc.,[5] all basing their statements on different ideologies, yet having one common denominator: who *possesses* power, how is it distributed and which are the methods of measurement most suitable for the fathoming of its 'size'? The concept of power seems to be conceptualised, generally speaking, in two ways in these statements. Those who speak of power as a relative concept, for example, the pluralists, who base their argument on an implicit ideal as to what power *ought to be*; a matter of equality and an absolute balance of power. Statements of power will therefore be aimed at deviations from an ideal; the perfect equilibrium. If we were to begin to examine the arguments closely, however, it would soon become apparent that these ideals themselves are formulated within the primitive conceptualisation of power. Power is thought of here as a means of coercion and repression which certain people *possess* at the expense of others, which if only it were distributed evenly would result in the negative effects of its abuse being reduced or disappearing. It is as though we would run less risk of murdering each other if we were each to receive a pistol. The other way, which is widely spread among the majority of power researchers, implies that one speaks of power in terms of an 'amount' or a 'sum'. The primary purpose is then that of measuring[6] at the expense of the further insight into and knowledge about the phenomenon of power. Paradoxically enough, 'statements about power' in the primitive discourse reveal very little about the phenomenon itself (Gustafsson, 1979). Meanwhile, those who make statements have formed schools thereby legitimising the production of this primitive discourse. The 'statements' could not lead, with given criteria as to which is the 'right' or 'wrong' ideology, along with rules for the production of knowledge (positivist and reductionist modes of thought), to anything but the reproduction of the bases of the primitive discourse.

2. *Division and rejection.* Apart from the types of prohibition considered above, there is another principle of exclusion that is also crucial for the construction of the discourse and for its rules of formation, namely that of division and rejection (Foucault, 1971a). This principle is decisive in the determining of what is to be included in the discourse, in terms of knowledge, and what is to be rejected. The approach of the researchers in the primitive discourse of power, as well as in the traditional discourse of organisations, is to a large extent reductionist, and subsequently the experiences and situational interpretations of the actors are far too sparingly considered. This might be due to the fact that researchers proceed, in most cases, from a given rationality, and from given assumptions as to how people *ought* to behave in organisations. The situational experiences and conscious actions of the actors are looked

upon as deviations from an ideal rather than as essential factors to be taken into consideration for the understanding of a particular context. Those criteria according to which the work is carried out dictate an approach implying the *freezing*, analytically speaking, of events and experienced situations and their reduction to bare facts. This is due to it being assumed that all the facts will fit into models.

When for example, Dahl (1957) discusses 'the amount of power' as one of the variables with which to work in a general model of power, he means that this 'amount' may be stated with a value of probability. This means that if B obeys A in nine out of ten cases, and obeys C in one out of ten, then A holds a greater power over B than C does.[7] The actual outcome, reduced to a number, becomes that which is taken into consideration at the expense of the dynamic situation in which the fact itself has a meaning. Meaning, interpretation, situational experience, and subsequently action, are then dimensions that are of no interest whatsoever for the model, as they are neither directly observable, quantifiable, measurable or axiomatisable. *Rejection* often takes place already in connection with the procedure of data-gathering. Neither contingency theorists, elitists, or pluralists assign any scientific value to the methods of knowledge production which attach significance to the individuals' interpretations of their situations and experiences. Instead, neutral questions are posed, often in the form of questionnaires, where the answer is predictable. Examples of such questions might be: 'How often do you take part in decisions of the type x_1?'; if A has taken part in that decision seven times (or in the process leading up to it) and B only twice, then we are told that A has more power than B. Questions such as what power actually is, how it is manifested, why has A taken part in the decision-making process to a greater extent than B has, why B has taken part to a lesser extent than A, how this is experienced by A and B, etc., remain unanswered.

The particular principle of exclusion concerning division and rejection seems to be based upon a *discrediting* of those from (and about) whom the knowledge is to be generated. Surely we must proceed, when studying the phenomenon of power in a particular social context, from the people who live in (and experience) the studied context (and the phenomenon of power). It is after all, that very power that is manifested among them which we wish to study and understand. If this is so, why then do we not listen to what they have to say about the phenomenon? Why do we neglect their discourse? I am not suggesting that we pose direct questions to them as to what they think of power. What I mean rather is that we should carry out more thorough studies of the actions of those involved, instead of asking how often they partake in a particular decision and other questions of a similar nature. By asking such questions, we are not going beyond ourselves, our own way of looking at things, the view that is dictated to us by our models, and the preconceived conceptualisation as to what power is. It is as though the situational experiences and the interpretations of the actors had nothing to do with it all. It is as though we, as researchers, arbitrarily believed more in our own reason than in the reason and logic of action of the actors. The fact that it is the actors who experience the phenomenon that we are studying, and not ourselves, is more or less overlooked: 'If the reality of the phenomenon does not coincide with our idea of it, then too bad for the phenomenon and for the reality of the actors'.

This principle seems, to my mind, to be deeply rooted in Western thought. An interesting and illuminating analogy is to be found in Foucault's (1961) work, *Histoire de la folie à l'âge classique* (*Madness and Civilization*, 1965). The same principle has been decisive in the oppositions between *reason* and *madness*. Since the Middle Ages the discourse of the madman has not been able to circulate to the same extent as that of the reasonable. Those who were considered to be mad had no right to speak. Their speech was worthless. They could neither witness in court, sign contracts, nor partake in a Church High Mass under the same pretexts as others could. Paradoxically enough, however, strange qualities were at times ascribed to the madman: all of a sudden he could make statements about the future and see 'truths' that no-one else could see. For centuries in Europe, the discourse of the madman was either not heard or, if it was heard, it was imputed with some form of mystical truth. Whatever the situation, however, the discourse of the madman did not exist, for either it was excluded and silenced, or else it was regarded as an item of curiosity. The primary effect of this was the confirmation of the madness of the madman: the sane perhaps reasoned that he who makes statements about the future could not be anything but mad. But who was it that assigned the mad such qualities? Not the madman himself, but the reasonable. Strangest of all is that the very discourse produced by the reasonable about the madman was used to identify the latter. Never, according to Foucault (1971a), had the thought occurred to any doctor up until the end of the 18th century, to seriously conduct a dialogue with the madman and to document his discourse. When one did begin to listen to him it was done merely symbolically; as in the theatre where the madman is a part played by the reasonable. In the same way, I wonder whether the researchers of the primitive discourse of power do not also have their madmen? The methods which they use to study the phenomenon, and the *a priori* conceptualisations which they make of it, imply that they attach no value whatsoever to the experiences of the actors involved in the phenomenon. The interpretations and situational experiences of the actors are alienated in the researcher's conceptions, in the same way as the madmen of the Middle Ages were alienated in the discourse of the reasonable about/by him. What we have here, then, is a stage play which cannot, by any means, be acted by the original actors. This is partly because the play no longer has to do with the reality of the actors and partly because it is not, in fact, intended to be acted by anyone but the researchers themselves. In the primitive discourse of power, the researcher of power, 'the reasonable', makes a division between scientific knowledge and non-scientific knowledge about the actor, the madman, who experiences the phenomenon. The entire discourse of the madman is rejected and a new one is produced in its place: one which is deduced from the reality of the madman and which is adapted to the discourse of the reasonable and its rules of formation.

3. The opposition true and false. The third principle is perhaps the most fine-meshed and the least visible, particularly if, from a logical perspective, the discourse is regarded from within. The opposition between true and false, seen from this perspective, seems to be neither arbitrary, institutional nor modifiable. If one regards the primitive discourse of power from within and examines it on the basis of its own terms, then the question of true or false as a principle of exclusion is not even debatable. What might possibly be discussed is whether or not power is a causal relationship between individuals and whether causality can, for example, be bound to an axis of time (Simon, 1957). One might discuss and assign different values to the likelihood of A being able to cause a change in B's behaviour (Dahl, 1957; Harsanyi, 1962a,b, etc.). Also debatable is which variable is the most suitable measure (if one wishes to measure power), which are the resources giving power, the changes of behaviour or more obvious effects such as how many times one has taken part in a decision or how often A does that which B wants him to do. Discussions of this kind are abundant in the primitive discourse of power, where advocates for various views correct each other's variables, add new ones, bring about slight adjustments; all done on the premises and stated rules of the discourse itself. That which is true or false is, on this level, stated by the discourse itself as well as by the criteria according to which it functions. It is regarded as self-evident that that which is observable and measurable is true, irrespective of its value for the studied phenomenon. That which is false, in the sense of being dubious from the scientific point of view, are those dimensions that are neither quantifiable nor axiomatisable (e.g. Harsanyi, 1962a,b).

A different picture presents itself, however, if the question is aimed, from a genealogical perspective, at the opposition *per se*, and at the base upon which it rests. Whence does the desire to produce true knowledge arise, and in what way does it govern the knowledge which is *de facto* produced by means of our discourses? From this perspective it is no longer a matter concerning the logic and the scientific value of the discourse, but rather the *arbitrariness* upon which the opposition *true* and *false* is based (Foucault, 1971a: 16–17). The opposition itself seems to be constituted historically, and its premises have been modified depending upon the social, political, economic and cultural spheres in which the discourse has been manifested (*surfaces of emergence* – surfaces d'émergence). The truth of a discourse among the ancient Greeks (600 BC) did *not* have so much to do with *what* was said, but rather with *who* said it and *how* it was said. The discourses that were regarded as bearers of truth were those which were said by the one(s) who held the legitimate right to say something, and who did so in accordance with the prevailing rituals.

> True discourse, that which inspired respect and terror, that to which all had to submit because it held sway over all, was the discourse spoken by men as of right and in accordance with the required ritual; it was the discourse that meted justice, that, prophesying the future, not only foretold what would come to pass, but participated in its coming, bringing to it men's acquiescence and thus weaving itself into the fabric of fate. (Foucault, 1971a: 71)

A century later, in the period of transition between Hesiodes and Plato (Foucault, 1971a), the truth came to be associated with what the discourse *said* and no longer with what it was and what it did. The truth had thus been shifted from the ritual action (*enunciation* – l'énonciation) to the *statements* themselves (l'énoncé). The focus was now upon the meaning, the form and the object of the statements, along with their relations to the phenomena that were the objects of study. This historical division has to a great extent, according to Foucault, influenced our view of knowledge and truth; at the same time as the premises of the opposition continue.

The major scientific mutations (e.g. paradigmal shifts) might be interpreted against the background of new inventions and new insights (Kuhn, 1962), but they may also be interpreted as the reflection of new attitudes towards the truth and new forms for our will to attain it. The truth of the discourse seems, at present, to have to do with its scientific value, which in turn has to do with the system of standards: the latter determines the scientificity of the discourse and thereby also its truth. The journey of the historical opposition (the opposition between true and false) seems to have brought us back to the time when the *truth* of the discourse was intimately related with *enunciation* (l'énonciation' as a ritual action, rather than to the statement (l'énoncé); yet with a slight variation, since enunciation today has more to do with *how* than with *who*. It would be wrong to claim that anyone, no matter whom, could make a statement as long as he/she dared to do so in the 'right' way. It could be said, however, that *how*, the ritual action, the enunciation determines the boundaries of the discursive territory in such a way that it is not possible for just anyone to make a statement. This implies that when someone makes a statement, *who*, he does so as spokesman for the system of norms: *how*.

The system of norms of the primitive discourse of power seems to derive its origins from the English empiricism[8] introduced by Bacon in the 17th century and later formulated with precision by Locke. This particular philosophical tradition experienced its era of greatness around the middle of the 19th century and its influence is still significant, even though it has been challenged in recent times by other traditions. True knowledge, in empiricism, must be based upon actual and simple observations. There must be an object which can be observed, measured and classified. There must be, as in the primitive discourse of power, an A and a B, a measurable resource or base of power which can be weighed against other bases and resources, and a classifiable (and even axiomatisable) size of power. Dimensions such as *action*, *will*, and *freedom*, are without meaning in this conception of reality. Statements that include these concepts are not real statements, and people assigning them significance need to be liberated from this misunderstanding. The empiricists would have it that reality is nothing but the order which is accomplished by science (according to the empiricists' system of norms) and it would be a meaningless insinuation to claim that anything can exist outside of this order. The primitive discourse of power and its system of norms dictates a mode of conduct, as far as research is concerned, which implies that the researcher adopts a special position *vis à vis* the object of research and that he fulfils a particular function as regards the same. He/she must observe rather than *read*, verify rather than *comment* (Foucault, 1971a: 19). The words read, and comment, signify here the understanding of people's actions and of the mechanisms which are their moving force.

The primitive discourse of power produces, within the framework of this opposition between true and false, a special knowledge of power as if it were true. Above all, however, it produces a mentality and a view of power that reflects the system of norms of the discourse and consolidates the idea of power as a concrete reality, as an attribute and as a means of repression. In the section, 'The genealogical perspective', I stressed the particular relationship between the discourse and its object. I discussed the way the discourse produces its own object, develops parallel to it and spreads a certain view of, and attitude towards, it via its own rules of formation. One essential rule of formation is that of the *authorities of delimitation* (instances de délimitation). The opposition, as a principle of exclusion, gains support from and furthers itself via those authorities constituting the institutional field that legitimises the discourse: for example, scholars and researchers whose authority is legitimated by the educational system and by research institutions. It is via these authorities, amongst others, that the primitive discourse of power and its 'truth' concerning the phenomenon is confirmed. In addition to this it is also spread and confirmed by the pedagogical system and its methods, by the activities of consultants in enterprises and organisations, and last but not least in a vulgarised version by the mass media.

The identity of the primitive discourse of power

I have suggested that in order to bring out and elucidate the *third step* in the generated knowledge we might orientate our view, metaphorically speaking, at the *other side of the mirror*. This implies an examination of the rules of formation of the primitive discourse with respect to its principles and procedures of exclusion. I have therefore attempted to lead the reader into the backyards and outer territorium of the discourse so as to render perceptible the conditions of its formation. Using Foucault's *theory of discourse* as a guideline we have considered the three most important procedures of exclusion: (1) the three types of prohibition, (2) division and rejection, and (3) the opposition between true and false. I have shown that these principles are neither isolated occurrences, nor are they successive sequences which come about independently of one another. Instead, they are an integrated part of the rules of formation of the discourse and are thus difficult to discern, even though I have attempted to discuss them separately for the sake of the argument. My intention is, on the one hand, to elucidate and draw attention to the dimensions of human interaction that are excluded from the primitive discourse, and on the other hand, to provide an explanation of the background to these principles.

The purpose of this approach is the 'demystification' of the discourse and the substantiation of its low explanatory potential. It is of no help to us to read, in every study of power, what an evasive phenomenon it is, and that the only way to deal with it is to reduce it to blunt facts which do not, when all is said and done, reveal more about power than that which we knew right from the start. Power is, after all, a part of people's everyday lives, even if only as an abstraction, and it seems quite logical that we should be able to discuss and understand it in a more satisfactory way than that which has been achieved so far by the primitive discourse. An essential question is of relevance in this context: what are the grounds for the fact that our discourse of power, and, above all, the way in which we study the phenomenon, has not changed to any noteworthy extent despite the very slight successes of the studies? One possible answer might be that we take our knowledge and particularly our conceptions of things as being far too self-evident, as if it were a matter of unshakeable truths. It is not, to my mind, so obvious that the phenomenon of power can only be understood from a reductionist perspective.[9] This opinion has, however, been confirmed to a large extent by practically all researchers of power, who after having worked with different variables, come to the conclusion that these are not operationalisable in the phenomenon of power and that we therefore still do not know anything about it (Crozier and Friedberg, 1977; Schelling, 1960; Lenski, 1966; Dahrendorf, 1959; Mills, 1956 and a number of others whom I have discussed in this text). One possible explanation for this situation might be that the indoctrination of the primitive discourse of power is so strong that it becomes difficult for us to leave the notion and the conceptualisation of power that it produces. In addition to this there is the predisposition of power researchers towards the ideal of the natural sciences with regard to the production of knowledge. This sort of approach is no doubt applicable in other fields, but is unfortunately not suited to a phenomenon so undefinable, evasive and imprecise as that of power.

What I mean by suggesting a transition to *the other side of the mirror* is that our analysis should not, to begin with, be aimed at power *per se* if we really wish to understand the phenomenon. Power is considered here to be an idea which is manifested in our actions in accordance with our interpretation of it. We cannot reasonably aim our analysis at something which does not exist; we can, on the other hand, analyse people's actions. Secondly, this way of working might be regarded as an attempt towards the demystification of the primitive discourse of power and this can, to my mind, be equated with the disclosure of the *identity* of the discourse. Earlier in the text I argued that the identity of a discourse is determined more by that which is defined by the discourse as belonging to its outer territory than by the inner terms of the discourse itself. By examining the principles of exclusion of the discourse I have attempted to show that the dimensions that are defined by the primitive discourse of power as not belonging to it are the very dimensions which are of significance for the people experiencing it. It seems to me that knowledge of power is a knowledge which must emanate from those who experience it: their discourse, their situational interpretations, their experiences, their strategies, their intentions, their fight to maintain a certain degree of freedom and their actions are the very dimensions which are constituent for the phenomenon of power. Paradoxically enough, it is these dimensions that are excluded due to the principles which I have discussed previously. The identity of the primitive discourse of power thus not only shows that theory formation in this discourse does not have a satisfactory explanatory value – all power researchers are in agreement with this – but also what this fact is due to. At the same time we may see which dimensions are in fact significant as regards the study of power.

The empirical manifestation of power

The fourth step in the knowledge generated in this study is a logical consequence of, on the one hand, our excursion into the outer territory on 'the other side of the mirror', and, on the other hand, the discussion which I conducted concerning the identity of the primitive discourse of power. This argument shows that those dimensions which have been excluded from the discourse in order for it to come about are the very dimensions which have proven to be decisive for the direction taken by the course of events in the studied process. It might be said, on the basis of the case study and the theoretical argument carried out so far, that the actual empirical manifestation of power is constituted (in) and constitutes people's actions. By this I do not mean that power is action, but rather that it is manifested in one and the same process as action. The reader should see (or read) this statement, not in isolation, but in the contextual argument as a whole as well as in the light of the many illustrations which appear in the case studied. Is this statement, and the mechanisms which it describes, confined to the specific studied case, or is it generalisable to other organisational contexts? It is general in the sense that action is an integrated phenomenon in human existence and all sorts of contexts and situations. That which is debatable, of course, is the conceptual approach which I suggest, which implies the transition of perspective from power *per se* to its manifestations in action. I have considered these manifestations and their constituent mechanisms. I shall here only give a brief account of this knowledge as it is needed for the forthcoming argument. It is needed partly so as to be able to discuss the effects which the primitive conceptualisation of power has in organisations, and partly to raise the question as to how a demystification of this concept might be conceivable.

People strive, within the framework of a certain context, and on the basis of their understanding and interpretations of it, to maintain and/or increase their space of action (extension). At the same time they strive to contract the space of action (contraction) of the opposing party if this is in their own interest, i.e. if the expansion of their own space of action depends upon the contraction of the space of action of the other party. The reader no doubt recalls from previous discussions that the striving for the expansion of space of action is the finality of the action, at the same time as the action *per se* may be regarded as the common denominator of this finality. The factors of crucial importance for this striving and this finality are the personal interests and motives of individuals (or groups, coalitions etc), their diverging orientations, the politically profiled situations within which they are involved, and, last of all, the way in which they interpret the strivings, finalities and actions of others. But is it now the actual striving for an expansion of space of action, or the actions *per se* which we, as power researchers, are able to see? Judging from what I have learnt so far, I would say that it is the strategies of the actors that need to be in focus. Not on the basis of an abstract model or on an *a priori* rationality, but rather against the background of the context in which the actors interact, the possibilities and limitations characterising this context, along with the logic of action and individual rationalities of those involved. Every context and every situation has its own characteristics that are interpreted differently by different actors depending on the positions which they hold in the given context. This, in turn, influences the relationships and interdependencies that develop among the actors. The striving of the actors (or groups, coalitions etc.) for an expansion of their space of action is identifiable within precisely this framework of relationships and interdependencies.

From a conceptual perspective, and in order to facilitate the identification of this striving, I suggested two notions: form and content. Power is always manifested in a *form* which is constituted by two dimensions: relationships and interdependencies. Manifestations of power are always immanent in these relationships and interdependencies without which the premises and conditions of possibility for these very manifestations would cease to exist. It seems to my mind that when studying the phenomenon of power in organisations, it would be meaningful to devote attention to the two dimensions of form which implicate the acknowledgement of actual and empirical processes of exchange. This, in turn, implicates the fact that the phenomenon of power is not to be regarded as a concrete object which can be conceptualised as an attribute or as property, and can therefore not, *per se*, be an object of analysis. The analysis, I would argue, should rather be directed towards the *opposition* of power, i.e. that which comes to light against the background of the mere existence of power as an idea and the interpretation which the actors make of it. At this point the second notion is of interest: *the content*. Contrary to the form, whose two dimensions may be found in all categories of organisational contexts – after all, the bases of all organisations are constituted by the relationships and interdependencies which are established and which develop among members – the content (of the form) is contextual and varied. It consists of a number of elements and aspirations which all converge towards the ultimate finality: the expansion of the actor's space of action. It is precisely the space of action that is the object of exchange within the framework of relationships and interdependencies. It is also within this framework that the striving for an expanded space of action is manifested and may be identified. This brings us back to the strategic action of the actor, which can be identified against the background of the organisational context and the motives, interests, desires, rationalities and logics of action of the actors. The analysis of these actions might, as I have suggested, be conducted from the perspectives of different entities: the individual, the group, the interest group or the coalition.

The arguments which I have put forward concerning empirical manifestations of power have, as their common denominator, an existential philosophical standpoint as regards the concept of action. Of most importance in this context, beyond the methodological and conceptual approach inspired from the work of Foucault and Nietzsche, are the philosophical meditations which have something significant to say, each in their own way, as to what it is like 'to be a thinking and acting person'. Action concepts have been the objects of intense philosophical deliberations for the last 200 years. It is not my intention to map out the philosophy of action here; rather merely to elucidate my own standpoint, if for any reason this has not come forth clearly earlier in the text. At the same time I think that it is nearly impossible to explain human interaction without relating it to the philosophical traditions wherein a great deal of time and much thought has been devoted to this very problem. One of the main reasons for the low explanatory value of the primitive discourse of power seems to be due, paradoxically enough, to precisely this lack of anchorage of the discourse in the philosophical traditions with relevance for the studied phenomenon. We have seen how the discourse has cut itself off, by means of various procedures of exclusion, from the premises of the very phenomenon about which this discourse claims to make a statement. We are not philosophers, it is vehemently maintained in this discourse. We aim to produce practical knowledge about concrete things. The phenomenon of power is not concrete, however, nor is the knowledge produced about it practical or operationalisable. Simon (1957: 4) writes: 'indeed, until it is solved, political science defined as the study of power, cannot be said to exist.' After a very thorough review of the theories about power, and after brave attempts at systematising that which in it, is 'practically operationalizable', Gustafsson (1979: 352) arrives at a paradox: 'How can we know if our measurement of power is correct, as long as we *a priori* do not know what power is?' Such statements are no exception (Bachrach and Baratz, 1962, 1963; Blau, 1964; Cartwright, 1959; Clegg, 1975, 1979a; Dahl, 1957; Emerson, 1970; Polsby, 1963; Nagel, 1968; Crozier, 1964; Crozier et al., 1974; Crozier and Friedberg, 1977; Grémion, 1976; Lourau, 1969; Touraine, 1978, and many others). That which I have found most surprising, since I began to be interested in the phenomenon of power in organisations and other social contexts, is that in spite of the fact that all power researchers are in agreement as to the significance which the phenomenon has for the behaviour and actions of people, and in spite of their agreed opinion that we are still not able to make any noteworthy statements about the phenomenon, there are extremely few attempts to question or to redefine our fundamental notions, conceptualisations and methods of dealing with this phenomenon. It is as though the *main stream* power researchers cling to their pseudo-scientific procedures of precision more for the sake of conventions than out of conviction as to suitability of the procedures.

The way out of this dilemma should, to my mind, go via an investigation of the basis upon which our notions rest. These bases are often a matter of fundamental philosophical views. The fact that we ignore philosophy is by no means a guarantee that philosophy will ignore us. I am not suggesting here that we should proclaim ourselves philosophers. What I mean, rather, is that when we notice, time and time again, that our notions and procedures are sterile, then we ought perhaps to rethink the *myth of the given* upon which our research is based, at least as far as research on power is concerned. The myth of the given might be said to derive its origins from the rationalism of Descartes, and also to a certain extent from English empiricism, although many modern thinkers, from the middle of the 19th century onwards, have revolted against this conception of the world. Miss Anscombe, who belongs to the analytic tradition of the philosophy of action, sharply criticises the idea of 'facts as the only source of knowledge'. This criticism is identical to that of the phenomenologists and existentialists as far as knowledge is concerned, in spite of the differences that otherwise exist between these traditions.[10]

> Certainly in modern philosophy we have an incorrigibly contemplative conception of knowledge. Knowledge must be something that is judged as such by being in accordance with the facts. The facts, reality, are prior, and dictate what is to be said, if it is knowledge. And this is the explanation of the utter darkness in which we found ourselves. (Anscombe, 1958: 57)

It seems that our understanding of the phenomenon of power can never become 'complete' as long as we ignore the fact that our inherited conceptualisation of man is, philosophically speaking, distorted. These distortions originate in a mysterious and paradoxical situation which imply that man has become both *subject* and *object* of the knowledge he produces about himself, at the same time as knowledge *per se* has come to be regarded and defined as something external to man (Foucault, 1966). Consequently the primitive discourse of power develops in (and around) a normative 'ought-to system' (de Monthoux, 1981) which has no correspondence in the empirical manifestations of power in people's everyday interactions. It is these distortions that also make it possible for the discourse to reproduce itself without interruption, and to directly and indirectly dictate what we, as researchers, managing directors or grassroots, are to think of power. In organisations we act in accordance with this mentality, unaware of the significance of our distorted conception of power and its devastating effects on the intra-organisational processes. In order to 'rectify' this distortion we need to have a better understanding of man, as a concept and as an actor involved in various types of praxis (Bernstein, 1971). We have a great deal to learn in this context from the philosophers of action in general, as well as from genealogists of knowledge such as Foucault and Nietzsche. The latter advise us to search for (and to examine) the premises of our knowledge beyond that which is given, immediate and ostensibly self-evident. The former urge us to regard man as he *is*: a free, responsible and acting being, even when he is prisoner of his own discourses about himself. I am aware, however, that this mode of thought is not exactly commonplace amongst power researchers (whether they may be organisations theorists or researchers from other disciplines: sociology, psychology and political science). The idea of exploring the philosophical basis of one's subject, the rules of formation of one's discourse and one's own view of man, is usually waved aside with the motivation that it is a futile occupation, typical of mad intellectuals with a predisposition for metaphysical fantasies. Indeed one is entitled to make such a claim, but then one must also be able to argue for it. Or, as Bernstein says:

> The skeptic ultimately may be right in his judgement about philosophy, although I do not think he is. But it is clear that the evaluation of what he claims can come only after careful and patient study, not as an a priori bias based on ignorance. (Bernstein, 1971: 7)

I began this section with the suggestion that the actual empirical manifestations of power are constituted (in) and constitute people's actions. In the previous chapter I showed how this action is, in turn, constituted as one with the *being* of man in the sense that it is an expression of his *freedom*, *will*, and *responsibility*. I consider power to be an abstract idea and a quality of a relation. I regard people's actions in relations of power, being dependent upon the way in which they interpret it. Their interpretation does not arise from an empty nothingness; rather it is a reflection of the notion of power which the primitive conceptualisation produces. They then act on the basis of this dictated notion by the exercising of coercive and repressive activities, while others develop counter-coercive activities. In this sense it might be said that 'power is exercised' by both the dominated and the dominant, which implies that the responsibility for the action lies with all those actors who are involved in power relationships. It is therefore not a question of who is determining whom or what. It is a question of a complex strategy in which each participates and contributes in her/his own way.

The concept of action has proven to be fruitful as regards the explanation of the empirical manifestations of power in the case studied. As I have shown, it manages to bring together the most essential dimensions of the phenomenon of power in a meaningful way: those dimensions which are, from the perspective of the actor, of particular significance for his/her choice of action. Awareness, motive, finality, choice, will, responsibility and, last but not least, freedom, converge in the concept of action (Sartre, 1943). According to Sartre, a person is never entirely identical with what he has been or with what he is striving to be. He/she is always at a distance from him/herself, no matter whether our attention is devoted to the past, present, or future. Man shapes himself through his choices and his awareness. To be aware means to choose at every moment. By choosing to act in a specific way, man chooses what he is to become. 'We must choose in order to be aware, and we must be aware in order to choose', says Sartre (1943: 517). The choice and awareness are *one* and the same. Awareness is expressed through action. Sartre argues against the idea of unconscious decisions: this is to him an absurdity. We always choose even when we *choose not to choose*, and consequently we always act. By acting, we modify the structures within which we live, and by choosing we 'consume' our freedom. There are no limitations to our freedom in the sense that that which determines what we are to become is our own choice. That we are doomed to be free means that we are not free to cease being free, that we are not free to not experience our freedom: we *are* freedom.[11] The principal message of this maybe drastic formulation is the assignment of the ultimate responsibility to the acting individual, beyond all determinism. Moreover, our choices always start from that which we conceive of as nothingness in our present situation. This means that our existence is always to be found beyond our essence. Our essence is that which we are or have been, and our existence is involved with the constant projection towards that which is not.

> This implies for consciousness the permanent possibility of effecting a rupture with its own past, of wrenching itself away from its past so as to be able to consider it in the light of a non-being and so as to be able to confer on it the meaning which *it has* in terms of the project of a meaning which *it does not have.* (Sartre, 1977: 436)

But what is the basis of man's reality, whether considering his involvement in power relationships or anything else? To be, according to the existentialists, is to choose that which one is. We are abandoned to the inevitable necessity, which is hard to bear, of making ourselves into that which are are (Sartre, 1943: 494). This inevitable but hard necessity only means that we are totally free, free to choose and free to act. The difficulty of bearing this total freedom fills us with anxiety. Our desperate attempts to escape constitute what the existentialists call '*mauvaise foi*' (Sartre, 1943). We put the blame on outer circumstances, on determining factors, we claim that there are objective structures external to ourselves which dictate the ways in which we are to act and what we are to choose. We say that 'they have power' and we are dominated, or else we say that 'we have the right to exercise power' and 'they' must simply accept their obligation to obey. Although we may not explicitly say who has power, we are still acting upon it as if it were a concrete reality to which we attempt to assign the responsibility of our choices and actions.

The management of W could always justify what they did by saying that they carried out an objective evaluation of the situation, and that they considered the transfer to be necessary. It was their task, moreover, to carry it through. L's employees, on the other hand, could say that everything was decided beforehand, and that they had no say in the matter. This was, however, not the case. W's evaluation of the situation might be said to have been contradictory and inconsistent rather than objective. The attitude of L's employees was not as passive as they would have us believe. The interpretation which I have suggested is that the actors involved in the process had *de facto chosen to act* in a certain way, and that they have developed various strategies at various times. When they had chosen to act, they did so beyond the 'objective' situational evaluation and any possible 'determining' factors in this evaluation. It seems to me as if the actors chose to act in relation to their own 'being' and their own freedom. What other explanation could be provided for the fact that neither was the desired competence of L retained, nor did anything come of the integration in W?

The effect of the primitive conceptualisation of power

A discourse not only produces knowledge of a certain object, it produces and reproduces the object itself, and, above all, it produces and spreads (perhaps forces upon us) a certain conception of the object. In this case it might be said that the primitive discourse of power produces and spreads an idea of power which is then gradually taken for granted, as if it were a universal truth. This idea is then at the root of further discursive activities, being on the one hand the reproduction of the discourse and its promotion among the researchers, and on the other hand the development of the course of events in all non-discursive praxis-institutions and organisations.

This notion of power 'dictates a particular conceptualisation and particular ideas about power. I have also argued for the idea that the choices that people make and their strategies and actions – within an organisational context and against the background of a specific organisational reality – reflect the interpretations which they make of the idea of power as well as their particular view of it. What then are the effects of all this on intra-organisational processes?

The *fifth step* in the knowledge generated in this study is that of pointing to the negative effects which the primitive conceptualisation may have on organisations. I say 'may' since the conclusions which I present here are based upon only one case and can, therefore, not automatically be generalised to encompass all organisations. At the same time there are enough indications to be found in the present debate in organisations about funds and profit-sharing, about succession and joint-venture, and about influence in decisions, about changes and rationalisations, etc.; which point to the fact that the studied case is neither an isolated occurrence nor a problem that is unique. For example, Johannisson (1980) believes that joint-venture does not always reflect conscious decisions taken by the management. Structural problems and a number of random factors seem to play a crucial part. He illuminates the difficulties that might be encountered with such processes along with the particular demands which they lay on both the management and the employees.

The transfer process of *L* to *W* reveals similar tendencies, since the decisions taken and the actions embarked upon were not always consistent. They led to an outcome that differed from the one originally intended. Originally, *W* and *L* could be said to have shared a common goal: *W* needed the 'artists in *L*' that had special abilities and functioned well as a group. *L* was in need of various forms of support (financial, administrative, etc.). It might have been the 'perfect' combination, exactly the way all the parties involved wanted it. I am not speaking here of some kind of harmony or consensus model. All I am saying is that which happened need not have happened. For a period of some 23 months about 50 people were mobilised in various types of activity such as investigations and negotiations which they experienced as meaningless. In spite of great losses of energy, no-one was to attain their goals (at any rate, not the original goals). The 'artists' (the bearers of knowledge) abandoned the ship and *W* was obliged to content itself with a disabled *L* that was of no use whatsoever.

It might be maintained that in the case studied both the superiors and the subordinates acted on the basis of the primitive conceptualisation of power; i.e. related to the formal structure of authority (Thompson, 1956; Mechanic, 1962; Hickson et al., 1971), to the control over resources (French and Raven, 1959; Crozier, 1964), over 'strategic communication' (Thompson, 1967) and over sources of uncertainty (Hickson et al., 1971; Cyert and March, 1963; Crozier and Friedberg, 1977) to name but a few. Through their actions the superiors showed that they ignored (or attempted to ignore) the relationships and interdependencies linking them to the subordinates. They were dependent upon the subordinates in the same way (not necessarily to the same extent) as the subordinates were dependent upon them.[12] Thus, against this background, the superiors conceptualise power as *theirs* and exercise it in a coercive manner, that is, forcingly and repressively. The subordinates must then, in answer to this coercive exercise of power, develop strategies and tactics for their protection. In other words they develop counter-coercive actions against that which they conceive of and experience as the misuse of power. In so doing, it might be said that they 'substantiate', so to speak, the distrust of the superiors towards them. Thus, coercive and counter-coercive actions trigger off one another in a series of vicious circles where the *energy* is channelled into the building of mechanisms of protection against anxiety and the development of strategies. Both the superiors and the subordinates strive, in this way, to expand their space of action yet without having access to the kind of language which might possibly have provided them with a certain measure of insight into 'the identity of power'. The result of this, in the process studied, was that both parties drove each other to increasingly desperate actions. The situation has been marked by *low trust* and *negative dynamics*. Negative dynamics refers here to the strange phenomenon to be found in such processes whereby actors act in opposition to their own interests at the same time as they strive for these interests.[13] In this case it may have been due to the misinterpretation of the nature of power with subsequent consequences upon the mode of action.

Man, in organisations, as well as in other contexts, will always act and strive for an expansion of his space of action no matter what interpretation he may make of the idea of power. As far as I can see, the problem lies in that whenever an individual is subjected to a coercive action (or to something which he/she conceives of as a coercive action) this seems to trigger off an intensely strong need for mechanisms of protection and for the defence of his/her personal interests. Indeed, we all have these needs in various degrees depending upon our particular situation. The difference lies in that the nature of the coercive exercise of power is such that those involved in the relationship attempt to change the inter-dependent relationships into one-sided dependencies. Each regards the other (or acts as if he/she regarded the other) as a mere instrument and object to govern and control. It is as if one were blinded or insensitive to the interdependencies which always exist between people in organisations. These sort of relations do not disappear, no matter how one may act, but one acts as if they were not there. The fact that individuals are actors who act consciously, who always have a certain degree of freedom at their disposal, and who are never reducible to totally controlled objects is thus ignored. Power cannot be regarded as property, and the coercive exercise of it can never be forced on to others. Power remains an abstract idea and a quality of a relation. As soon as anyone in the process studied attempted to 'use' the 'idea of power' as an instrumental means by which to dominate and control, the automatic result was manipulative activities, low trust, negative dynamics and losses of energy.

It is thus that which is genuinely human (i.e. the action of man as *one* with his being and the relationships and interdependencies which exist between people in organisations) that is ignored, not only by the primitive discourse of power, but also by the discourse of organisation.[14] What seems to me to be a most serious problem is that people in organisations are evidently the bearers of this mentality and this conceptualisation. This tends to result in 'the art of destroying oneself without wanting to'. Another conclusion which seems to be justifiable is that the greater the attempt to *organise power*, as one might organise structures, the greater the obstruction of the intra-organisational processes. On the other hand, since power seems to be omnipresent as an immanent phenomenon in human interaction, we might speak rather of the *power of organisations*. Thus it is not a question of taming power, laying hold of, measuring and axiomatising it so as to redistribute via legislation or via rules. The question is rather one of learning to see its identity and of understanding how it is manifested in action.

CONCLUSION

I have strived in this chapter to present the knowledge generated in this study against the background of the value which it may conceivably have. This I have attempted to do by presenting the argument in a way which relates the generated knowledge to the empirical phenomena which I have tried to describe and relate to already existing theories. This knowledge grew out of a direct interplay between theory and practice as I confronted the already existing theory with the manifestations of the studied phenomenon. In addition to this, out of this confrontation, a number of ideas, dimensions of understanding and concepts emerged. These have proven to have a satisfactory explanatory potential. I have then attempted to bring these together so as to form a coherent frame of reference and mode of thought (and approach) which might possibly allow for the opening up of new perspectives with regard to the study, conceptualisation and interpretation of the phenomenon of power in organisations.

THE FRUITFULNESS OF THE GENERATED KNOWLEDGE

I intend in this section to discuss any possible potential which the knowledge generated in this study might conceivably have. The discussion

TABLE 6.1 The generated knowledge

Dimensions of understanding	Metaphor	Archaeology	Genealogy	Empirical manifestation
The political character of organisations				
The power of organisations				
Action perspective				
The strategical character of the actor's action				
Unit of analysis: Individual group coalition organisation				
The theory of discourse	The other side of the mirror	The discur- sive rules of forma- tion	Procedures of exclusion	Manifestations of power in action
Relationships and inter- dependencies	Form	Process of exchange	Freedom, intention, choice, will, responsibility	Strategies, tactics
Concept of action	Content	Space of action		Actions and counter-actions

may be held on two levels: specifically considering every step in the generated knowledge, and generally considering the knowledge as a theory or a frame of reference, focusing on its fruitfulness as a whole. Might the theory be seen as a *process* and, if so, to which possibilities for the development of other processes does it give rise and which new perspectives does it generate? Has the theory contributed with knowledge as regards the studied phenomenon, and, above all, is it likely to stimulate new studies, thus indirectly contributing to further exploration (Cicourel, 1964, 1973). Within the social sciences it is not a matter of absolute truths; neither is it a matter of setting up a number of criteria to judge what is true and what is false in a theory. It is rather a matter of taking up for consideration the characteristics of the theory and, in so doing, to discuss its generative qualities. Such characteristics have been summed up by Thomas S. Kuhn where he takes up for consideration that which might be said to characterise a good scientific theory.

> Among a number of quite usual answers I select five, not because they are exhaustive, but because they are individually important and collectively sufficiently varied to indicate what is at stake. First, a theory should be accurate: within its domain, that is, consequences deducible from a theory should be in demonstrated agreement with the results of existing experiments and observations. Second, a theory should be consistent, not only internally or with itself, but also with other currently accepted theories applicable to related aspects of nature. Third, it should have broad scope: in particular, a theory's consequences should extend far beyond the particular observations, laws, or subtheories it was initially designed to explain. Fourth, and closely related, it should be simple, bringing order to phenomena that in its absence would be individually isolated and, as a set, confused. Fifth, a somewhat less standard item, but one of special importance to actual scientific decisions, a theory should, that is, disclose new phenomena or previously unnoted relationships among those already known.[15] (Kuhn, 1977: 321–322)

Kuhn refers here to five characteristics which a theory should have if it is to be regarded as a good one. He does not mean that these characteristics are decisive for the scientific value of a theory; he refers rather to its qualitative dimension, i.e. that which gives the theory a good chance of becoming a success. For example, that it be subsequently adopted by other researchers.

The *first* characteristic is for the theory to be in touch with reality in the sense that it describes real and experienced events and/or that the statements derived from it are of use in the explanation of empirical phenomena: *accuracy.* Kuhn uses the concept of theory in a very broad sense, whereas I would rather refer to a set of statements and concepts or to a conceptual framework which might possibly open new perspectives. What is most important, therefore, is not whether or not the knowledge generated here can be regarded as a theory, but rather which criteria we might use so as to evaluate its relevance, either as a theory, as a set of statements and concepts, or as a conceptual framework. The conceptual framework which I have chosen has had a satisfactory explanatory value for the empirical events in the studied process. It explains why the course of events developed in the way it did. It also elucidates some of the reasons for the low explanatory potential of the models of the primitive discourse of power. As an extension of this, the approach which I have suggested could easily be used by other researchers for studies of the phenomenon of power in organisations: neither the phenomenon of power as such nor the approach which I have suggested are specific (or specifically adapted) to the studied case. The generated knowledge has been described in such detail that it could serve, without difficulties, as a guideline or as a source of inspiration for the understanding of intra-organisational processes and the part played by the phenomenon of power in these processes.

The *second* characteristic is that the theory be consistent, both internally and in relation to other theories which describe and explain contiguous phenomena: *consistency*. I have attempted to give an indication of the internal consistency in the generated knowledge by showing how its various levels are connected to and presuppose each other. My attention was already devoted, at the stage of the data-gathering, to the action perspective and to the actors' logic of action. This perspective has then been of guidance as regards the conceptualisation of the political character of the organisation and the actors' strategic actions. This, in turn, has proven to be decisive in connection with the empirical manifestations of power, as has been shown through the discursive analysis and the identification of that which has been excluded. I have then, on the basis of precisely these excluded yet empirically highly relevant dimensions, developed an alternative approach to the phenomenon of power. The five steps in the generated knowledge are stringently built and directly dependent on each other so as to form an integrated approach or conceptual framework. The criteria for consistency with other theories are to my mind fulfilled taking into consideration that the conceptual framework which I have developed is based upon a number of well-established theories and statements that are relevant for the subject at hand: the philosophy of action, the by now well-established archaeological and genealogical perspective, the exchange theory, and the statements concerning politics in organisations. Last but not least, the integration of these dimensions of understanding, of these concepts and statements, into the field of organisation theory.

The *third* characteristic is that the theory be broad, in the sense that it extends beyond the object for which it was initially designed or from which it has developed: *scope*. My interest with this study lies in the studying and understanding of the phenomenon of power in organisations and in the development of an alternative way of regarding and conceptualising this phenomenon. One case study, the transfer process of W–L, has been used to illustrate the argument; but does this mean that I have studied the phenomenon of power in connection with transfers, or merely in the specific process of W–L? Such is not the case. I have used the process W–L as an illustration of the way in which people act against the background of their interpretations of the idea of power in order to draw attention to the effects which these actions might have on intra-organisational processes. After a thorough review of this specific process I need no longer speak in terms of, for example, 'the relationship between M. Ziegler and R. Perdfelt', rather I can speak in terms of 'relations between superiors and subordinates'. The conceptual framework which I have thus developed stretches beyond a specific case and turns rather towards the manifestations of power in general (Cicourel, 1964). Moreover, since the manifestations of power are specific neither for certain types of organisations nor for a certain type of process, this conceptual framework could provide insight into the way in which various processes might be facilitated. As examples of such processes one might mention investment and de-investment, joint-ventures and fusions, cooperation between entities within or between organisations. Another example which is derived from the knowledge generated here is that of the intra-organisational processes with regard to cooperation between members, and particularly between superiors and subordinates.

The *fourth* characteristic is that the theory be simple or simplifying in the sense that it contributes towards the clarification of an otherwise diffuse and non-systematised phenomenon: *simplicity*.[16] I have on various occasions in this study shown how the theoretical contribution of the phenomenon of power in organisations is fragmentary and non-systematic. The aim of the conceptual framework which I have suggested is the illumination of the phenomenon from entirely different perspectives, and also the construction of an integrated view and instrument of analysis to be used in the study and understanding of this phenomenon. Furthermore, the insight derived from this conceptual framework might be elucidatory for the organisational dimensions which have until now been treated sparingly or in a fragmentary or peripheral fashion.

The *fifth* characteristic is that the theory be fruitful in the sense that it opens up new perspectives and gives rise to new research approaches and results: *fruitfulness*. The integration of the action perspective into the study of the phenomenon of power seems, to my mind, to be a new perspective *per se*. Moreover, this perspective allows us to continue towards an understanding of new aspects of the phenomenon of power which was not possible with the primitive conceptualisation with all its limitations. The conceptual and analytical (archaeology and genealogy) approaches which I have suggested, might also be fruitful in other fields. The theory of discourse is, theoretically, applicable to any discourse whatsoever, and the identification of an object against the background of its opposite is also applicable in other areas. It seems to me, then, that these 'methods' are fruitful no matter what the object of study may be: every object of knowledge is related to a discursive praxis and every discursive praxis has its rules of formation. On a higher level these rules of formation are, to a large extent, common to all discourses. The fruitfulness of a theory or a conceptual framework is, perhaps, according to Kuhn

(1977: 322 ff.), its most important characteristic. Depth and originality are important ingredients since these often implicate the exploration by the theory of new angles of approach, theoretically and methodologically speaking, which could give rise to new impulses for other researchers. The latter may then consider certain aspects of the approach or results to be relevant to their respective fields, or else they may derive new approaches and ideas from the contributions of this theory which they would otherwise not have thought of. It seems to me that the conceptual framework and knowledge with which I have contributed would primarily be of concern to power researchers, particularly organisations theorists, but perhaps even to others whose areas of research touch upon organisational processes (such as for example decision processes and structures, interaction and cooperation between groups, etc.). At the same time, and although I do not give any directly normative recommendations to practicians, I nonetheless feel that the knowledge generated here might be of use in concrete situations. As Plato has said: 'The art of governing others is learnt via the art of governing oneself.'[17]

THE BEGINNING OF THE ENDING

The book could be drawn to a conclusion here, but there are still some questions to be discussed. We have seen that the primitive discourse of power produces a mentality and a notion of power that is found both among those producing the discourse – *authorities of delimitation* (instances de délimitation) – and among those whose 'behaviour' and actions are supposedly explained by the discourse. In spite of the fact that the 'producers' of the discourse seem to have the same conceptualisation of power as people acting in organisations, the explanatory models of the former do not seem able to provide satisfactory explanations for the actions of the latter: a rather paradoxical situation, one might say. Both of these conceptualise power (implicitly or explicitly) as a coercive means of dominance, control and repression. Whereas the former isolate their models, however, and 'purge' them from all that is human, the latter act as people and as individuals, for that is the only way that they can act. Thus there remain two essential questions to be answered: (1) How can this paradox 'be explained', or in what terms might it be discussed? (2) What is the origin of the primitive conceptualisation of power? I intend to discuss both the first and the second question in terms of *demystification*. It is perhaps justifiable here to put forward a special safeguard with regard to the concept of demystification. No doubt many people might protest that the concept is hackneyed and lacks content, that everyone these days is trying to demystify something. Besides, what is it that is to be demystified, whose purposes does the demystification serve? I do not claim to have the answers to all of these questions, but I think that we cannot be content with the mere confirmation of the primitiveness of our current conceptualisation of power and of the negative effects which this conceptualisation has on organisations, as well as of the difficulties encountered in the understanding and study of power. This confirmation may in itself be understood as demystification since it reveals hidden areas in our mode of thought. I believe that we need to go one step further: how come we think of power in the way we do? Are we at all capable of stepping out of this mode of thought so as to be able to see it and discuss it? I am not saying that this is possible. What I am saying, however, is that it is perhaps the task of the researcher to come up with precisely this type of intellectual contribution. The privilege of the intellectual researcher is perhaps that like of the artist, of being able to see what 'others cannot see', and, by drawing attention to this increasing insight into the phenomenon being studied.

THE YOUNG MAN IN THE GALLERY

Our understanding of the phenomenon of power is limited and disabled by our way of conceptualising it. We see power as a coercive instrument for dominance, control and repression in the same way as we wish to rule over the world around us. To be masters over things and people, who in the process are reduced to things, is part and parcel of our cultural ideology in the Western world.

> We are a tough and rational civilization with the individual firmly entrenched as the beginning and the end of it all. Yet the transcendental yearning to go beyond one's own boundary persists in each of us. Craving for external power over things is our peculiar transcendental trip (Skolimowski, 1983: 26).

Skolimowski argues to show that we have 'chosen' to think of power as a brutal force to be owned, and by means of which we can handle the world and the people in it, since our whole cultural heritage is based upon the ideology of ownership and ruling. He writes that:

> The elevation of the myth of power to its present and dangerous position (in Western civilization) has happened because man has given up one form of salvation and has embarked (in the post-Renaissance times) on another form. The idea of salvation was removed from heaven and placed squarely on earth. In time this salvation came to signify gratification in the earthly terms alone (Skolimowski, 1983: 26).

This then means the conquering and exploitation of the world; which, in turn, implies having power over the world, things and people. The primitive conceptualisation of power must be seen against the background of the mode of thought, the ideology, and the moral conceptions of the Western world together with the battle between various cultural forces. Myths have during the course of history succeeded each other, struggled against each other and replaced each other; but those myths which form the basis of our conception of the world gradually become self-evident and turn into a part of the 'objective' reality. *The myths you act upon become the reality you live in.* Our ideas as to what power is have developed as a consequence of more or less random events and historical 'accidents' (see Foucault and Nietzsche). There is no necessity in our history (if it is analysed as a series of discontinuities; Foucault, 1969, see also Chapter Three) which implies that we must conceptualise power as we do.

> Yet (strange is the human mind) we behave as if this one-sided concept of power was all there is to the meaning of power and, indeed, to the reality of power. (Skolimowski, 1983: 33)

The ideal in the Western world, of the idea of power, seems to be based upon a lengthy cultural process from which some significant events may be distinguished for the sake of illustration. The alchemist Philippus Auredus Theophrastus Bombast von Hohenheim, known as *Paracelsus* (1493–1541) is an archetype of the striving of the Western world to rule over the external nature of things. The search for 'the philosopher's stone' ended in the search for the *naked* power; *Faust*. But there is also the side to the coin in the myth of Prometheus, the *Samaritan* who 'defies power and sacrifices himself for the good purpose'. Then came the idea of the *Prince*, with Machiavelli, whereby power was legitimised, no matter how manipulative or dominant it might be. Bacon thought of *knowledge* in terms of power, Marx pictured a social ideal in terms of antagonism and *power struggle*, while Lenin dealt with questions concerning the distribution of power in terms of a strict *pyramidal* organisation.

> The Paracelsian drive for physical transformations was combined with the Machiavellian idea of ruthless manipulation, which has further combined with Bacon's idea of knowledge as power, which was further compounded by Faustian quest for domination at whatever price, which was given a further twist by the Marxian conception of society as based on antagonism and class warfare; to which Lenin added the importance of organization, which was to some degree the product of Taylorism. We can finally identify the conceptual components of the present Western ideal of power: it is the Paracelsian–Machiavellian–Baconian–Marxist–Leninist–Taylorian concep-

tion of power which we cherish and which holds us in its embrace. (Skolimowski, 1983: 33)

If then, the situation is such that it is our cultural heritage and our ideology that make us think of 'power' in the terms that we do, how can we ever speak from another perspective as of pointing to the paradoxical nature of our knowledge and of that which we, out of habit, take for granted. The artist Escher[18] portrays what I feel to be the dilemma of knowledge in his lithograph, 'Print gallery' (1956) – see figure 6.1.

What we see in this picture is a gallery where a young man is standing and looking at a picture of a boat in the harbour of a small town. Judging by the architecture it might be a small town in Greece or on Malta, with

FIGURE 6.1 'Print gallery', M.C. Escher (lithograph, 1956, Collection Haags Gemeentmusem – The Hague. © Eschers Heirs 1983 c/o Beeldrecht Amsterdam).

arches and flat roofs. On one of the flat roofs a boy is sitting, while two storeys below a woman, perhaps the boy's mother, is looking out of the window of her flat which is directly above the gallery where the young man is standing and looking at a picture of a boat in the harbour of a small town. Judging by the architecture . . . Suddenly I, who am looking at the picture from the outside, realise that there is no way that the young man in the gallery can see that the picture he is looking at forms, in fact, the structure (the gallery) within which he is standing: *He is a part of the picture he is looking at.* The gallery is a part of the picture he is looking at. He is within the gallery. Will he ever be able to come out? The young man thinks that he is looking at a picture; but in actual fact he is imprisoned within it, for the picture constitutes the whole structure within which he finds himself. Escher's paradoxical 'Print gallery' may also be discussed graphically[19] as shown in figure 6.2.

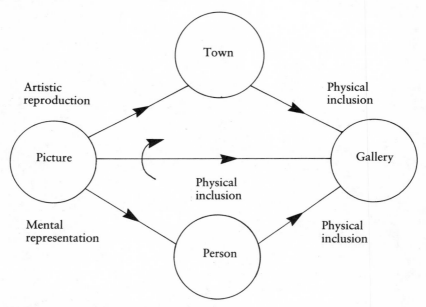

FIGURE 6.2 The gallery is physically included within the town (inclusion). The town is artistically reproduced within the picture (reproduction). The picture is mentally within the person (representation).

We have three levels above, but the number is entirely arbitrary. We could reduce the number to two, as in figure 6.3. The schematisation may be even further accentuated if we reduce the number of levels to one, yet still from the 'point of view of the picture', so to speak (see figure 6.4).

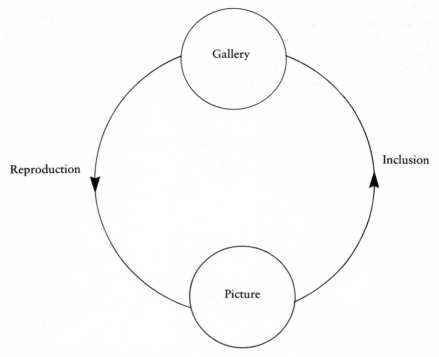

FIGURE 6.3 The gallery is artistically reproduced within the picture (reproduction). The picture is physically included within the gallery (inclusion).

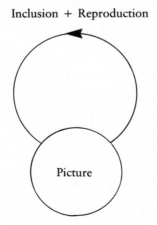

FIGURE 6.4 The picture both includes and reproduces itself.

But what happens if we reduce the number of levels, this time from the point of view of the person (figure 6.5)? It looks as though 'the young man in the gallery' is within himself, whereas we, who are looking at him, have the possibility of *seeing* that which he *does not see*. But can we tell him? Could it be that each one of us is sitting in his/her gallery? Perhaps we are, to a greater or lesser extent. Still, is it possible to 'go out' of one's own gallery so as to be able to point to the mysterious paradoxical nature of our thinking and our conceptions?

Inclusion + Reproduction + Representation

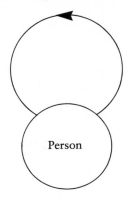

Person

FIGURE 6.5   From the 'point of view of the person' the three within steps are integrated together.

Looking back on the process that I have gone through, and the way in which my idea of the concept and the phenomenon of power has changed, it is thinkable that I myself was 'a part of a picture', so to speak, when I began this book. I, too, probably thought in the terms dictated by the primitive discourse of power, and what I have attempted to do is 'to go out of the picture or of the gallery'. However, as I have stressed earlier in various contexts, this illustrates the very dilemma of knowledge along with the impossibility of certain problems. We may make a statement about a particular ideology, criticise it, and even believe that we are doing so on the basis of an entirely different ideology, but of this we may never be certain. In this sense I wonder whether I have succeeded in getting out of the primitive conceptualisation so as to be able to consider it from the outside and to voice opinions about it? If this is the case, have I not landed up in another gallery where I have become a part of a picture without being aware of it? The problem seems impossible, and, on the whole, difficult to discuss. There is no want of philosophically impossible (unsolvable) problems in the existence of man. This does not mean, however, that we refrain from attempting to see more clearly into these problems; not by suggesting solutions, but by carrying the debate and discussion further: by producing discourses about discourses.

It seems to my mind that the producers of the primitive discourse of power and the organisational members might also, metaphorically speaking, be likened to 'the young man in the gallery'. Captured as they are, by a cultural heritage and an ideology which 'dictates' which notions they are to have of power, they produce their discourses and carry out their actions as if there were no other way of doing this. Nonetheless, even though both the producers of the discourse and the people acting in organisations seem to proceed from similar starting points as regards the conceptualisation of power, the models of the former do not seem capable of explaining the actions of the latter: The models annihilate and *exclude* that which is genuinely human, whereas actions are carried out according to these very exclusions. It is sufficient to say that conceptions of power as means of dominance, control and repression are the same. But whence do these conceptions arise?

CHAPTER 7

The Discourse of Power or the Power of Discourse[1]

The argument in this chapter stretches beyond the primitive discourse of power and its implications for organisation studies. I concentrate here on a discursive level and shall attempt to throw some light on the particular mechanism whereby a discourse that makes a statement about an object in fact produces it, feeds on it and gains 'authority' through it. By way of a discussion of the discourse of power, in particular, I shall analyse the mechanisms by means of which the power of discourse is produced. The analysis is nonetheless directed towards discourse as a whole.

Let us begin by once again referring to 'the young man in the gallery' whose situation might be said to symbolise the totalising effect of the discourse both on the producers and receivers of the discourse. Both parties seem to be mastered by the discourse, as well as by that ideology and that culture in which it has its roots. It seems, as I have attempted to show in the discussion about the conditions of possibility for the emergence of a discourse, that these rest more upon principles of exclusion and arbitrariness than upon 'legitimate' grounds. This is so since, as Foucault (1961) has pointed out, every culture has its borders, its methods of defining what belongs to it and what must remain on the outside, what it accepts and what it rejects. In our Western culture the great, monotonous, all-embracing line of division runs between the normal and the pathological. Every culture has its own particular acts, forms and gestures by which to reject and exclude, to regulate and to keep in place, its own way of shutting its eyes to that which it does not wish to see and of declaring null and void that which it does not wish to hear. Perhaps it is so that the liberating, the challenging, knowledge of ourselves does not come through that which we know, but through that which we do not want to know.

Skolimowski (1983) argues that the ideology of the Western world 'masters itself' and is marked by short-sightedness and even blindness: myths are transformed to reality and placed in the centre of our way of understanding the world, of our mentality, our moral and our ideology.

The primitive discourse of power may be seen as merely being a reflection of this 'pathology' and a reproduction of this short-sightedness. The conceptualisation of power as a coercive and brutal force for dominance, control and repression seems to constitute the fundamental assumption or base in the general discourse of power. A discourse which 'masters' itself would, in this context, mean a discourse that reproduces itself. It produces its object and feeds on it. It is constituted in a certain ideology at the same time as it constitutes it. A demystification of the discourse of power consequently seems, to my mind, to imply, in the first instance, that one extract the conceptualisation of the phenomenon of power, mentally and intellectually, from *the power of discourse*. This, I feel, also implies that one should conceptualise the phenomenon of power in a 'new' way, free from the myths in which the primitive discourse of power has its roots. This must be extremely difficult to attain, however, if indeed the situation is such that the discourse masters our thought, and it is this very mastered thought which must be abandoned if we are to produce alternative conceptualisations that are not dictated and shaped by the power of discourse. 'The young man in the gallery' would be confronted with the same difficulties should it 'enter his mind to free himself' from the picture of which he is a part.

Perhaps, in this case, one might say that the overcoming of difficulties – the dilemma of knowledge and that which is seemingly unsolvable in the problem – is when all is said and done merely a question of becoming aware of the nature of the problem: man's (the subject man) relation to himself (the object man). In other words, it is perhaps a matter of becoming aware that the *subject* and the *object* of the discourse are one and the same: man himself. Metaphorically speaking, one could say that he is embraced by the very discourse which he produces about himself, in the same way as 'the young man' is embraced by the picture which embraces the gallery. A graphic representation hereof might be as shown in figure 7.1. It may be seen in this figure, in analogy with the graphic representation of 'the young man in the gallery', that man as *subject* and *object* of the discourse (the producer and the receiver) is embraced by it (representation and inclusion). This would mean that awareness of the nature of the problem is by no means a guarantee for a liberation from *the power of discourse*. Therefore one might wonder whether it would be enough to declare one's good intentions of wanting to free oneself? How to evade the trap of producing new myths and new discourses which, in turn, produce their objects and embrace their subjects? As far as I can see there do not seem to be any absolute or best answers to these questions. Let us not imagine that the world shows us a readable face, which we merely need to decipher (Foucault, 1971a). The world does not comply with our knowledge and there exists no pre-scientific providence which

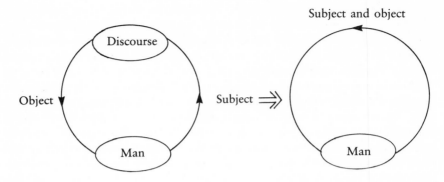

FIGURE 7.1 Man's relation to the discourse.

tunes it to our advantage. The face of the world is unreadable. What may perhaps render possible the legibility of the face is its 'opposition image'. The invisible is more important than the visible for the latter is constituted in the former.

As regards the primitive discourse of power, I have attempted to conduct a discussion around its essence and its rules of formation by *genealogically* analysing the discourse in its 'dialectical movement', separating it from its stated function and identifying the gap between the discursive praxis and the meaning of the discourse. Reason and rationalism, as these concepts are conceptualised within Western ideology, do not seem to rest upon a self-evident and legitimate base. It has been 'shown', in the works of both Nietzsche and Foucault, that our way of conceptualising reason has its basis in relation to the exterior of reason: to that which is defined by reason as the opposite. Our ideology and our discourses, along with the fundamental elements in them, have 'proven to be' based upon that which is excluded: the margins. On a discursive level, what is today intellectually and ideologically regarded as our territorium, in the broad sense of the word, seems rather to resemble a border behind which we debar all that we do not wish to know about ourselves and about our discourses.

'The linguistic structure masters man's total reality,' Skolimowski (1983) has argued in unison with many other thinkers such as Lacan, Barthes, Eco, and Kristeva. The discourse, in general, masters our thought; in the same way as the primitive discourse of power, in particular, masters our conceptualisation of the phenomenon of power. 'Man thinks but is not', writes Foucault (1966). Instead of *cogito, ergo sum*, one ought perhaps to say *cogito, sed non sum*. Why exactly this is so is a question to which an unequivocal answer cannot be given. Foucault (1966) argues that man as a concept, i.e. as subject and object of knowledge and discourses, is relatively new. The concept of man, as we know it today, emerged and developed as a consequence of the 19th-century changes in our conception of the world; but this change was not the first and our world-view, our knowledge and our discourses thus do not rest upon any stable, unshakeable, and self-evident base (Foucault, 1966). New changes in the world-view could well entail new bases for knowledge and for discourses where there might be no room for the concept of man. We are so blinded by the position of man in our mode for thought that we cannot even remember the not so distant past when the world, its order and the people in it, existed, but not man as a concept. It is held by Foucault that one can understand the immense impact that Nietzsche's thought has had, and still has, on us when he preached the imminent event – promise/threat – that man will disappear and be replaced by superman. In a philosophical sense this would imply that man had long since disappeared and continues to disappear, embraced by discourses about himself, and that our current conception of what the concept of man is, our pains over it, our humanism, sleeps calmly in his non-existence.

THE POWER OF DISCOURSE

The discourse is, as are also many other phenomena in our society, the object of a power struggle. It may be seen as a reflection of political contention and, at the same time, to constitute the stakes of desire and power. But is the discourse associated with any truth, and in that case which truth? It seems that the truth of the discourse must be sought in its position, in speaking as action, and in the strategy of the speaker (enunciation – l'énonciation – see Chapter Three). *What is said* is unimportant. The essential questions to pose are: *who says?*; *why* does he/she say what he/she says?; *who* makes the discourse into his/her *property* and for *which purpose* does he/she do this?

The discourse has been enclosed within a fortress of prudence and disciplinary measures (Foucault, 1971a). A terrible amount of prohibitions, taboos and barriers have been accumulated. The purpose is to control and censor the production and dissemination of the discourse. The rules of formation of the discourse and their stringency seem to serve as 'police' against any eventual crime of the discourse. The fortress, the rules of formation, the principles of exclusion, seem to symbolise some sort of logophobia which in turn seems to be a reflection of the fear which exists *vis à vis the power of discourse*. This means that the production of discourse, in all societies, is controlled, selected, organised and distributed through numerous procedures (see Chapter Three), the role of which is to prevent the discourse from 'falling into undesirable hands'.

At the same time it is not always evident that a certain knowledge produced within the discourse would not be 'true'. A discourse that states criteria for what is 'true' and what is not 'true' gives the impression of not being the object of the mechanisms of control just mentioned. A number of thinkers (Kristeva, 1969; Derrida, 1974, etc.) have, in this respect, attempted to perform an analysis of what it is that makes a discourse seem unproblematical, and the knowledge produced within it seem to depict an indisputable, given reality. These thinkers, like Foucault, have devoted their attention to the conditions governing the production and articulation of a particular discourse, as well as to the meaning which these conditions have with regard to the knowledge produced and its *legitimacy* (or its 'truth'). Kristeva holds that it is the common ideology of the producer and the receiver of the discourse which serves to disguise the ambiguity of the discourse and provides it with an illusory legitimacy. Kristeva suggests a 'translinguistic' analysis of the mechanisms forming the base of the message of the discourse (content) and of the discourse *per se* (form). Her discursive analysis, *semanalysis*, strives to go beyond the given to that which precedes the formation, production and articulation of the discourse. Put in the terms of this study, her results show that the discourse 'gets its power' from the totalising ideology within which it is constituted, but to the constitution of which, at the same time, it also contributes. Separated from the ideology the discourse shows another 'face', where arbitrariness and ambiguity, rather than truth, are the main features.

Semanalysis may, to a certain extent, be seen in extension of Derrida's *déconstruction*. Derrida's version of the 'deconstructional' analysis aims to uncover those notions and concepts considered to constitute the rules of formation of a discourse. The analysis is directed towards the notions and concepts that are marked by ambiguity and opposition and that indicate discursive paradoxes (unsolvable problems). Examples hereof might be the oppositional relationships between individual and collectivity or else, as is the case here, between the *subject* of the discourse and the *object* of the discourse. The deconstruction is thus directed towards the rules of the discourse so as to identify, by means of these, the conditions which render possible the articulation of the discourse. The analysis shows that these conditions are not given but 'created' by the rules which might thereby be said to 'exercise' a power, the purpose of which is to govern the production of knowledge.

Both semanalysis and deconstruction are aimed at the mechanisms that disguise the problematic relation between the subject and the object of the discourse and make the message (content) of the discourse look as if it were 'true'. Kristeva and Derrida see these mechanisms as suppressor(s) (supprimant); which implies that they prevent us from *seeing* the *origin* of the discourse. The production and articulation of knowledge within a particular discourse remain 'incomplete' since the discourse is *suppressed* (supprimé). It produces and reproduces just the type of knowledge that is conducive to its self-suppression (auto-suppression). Consequently it becomes further and further removed from its origin. The power of discourse in this context is based upon the mechanistics that prevent us from seeing 'the truth' about the discourse, not the discourse's 'truth'.

Behind the criteria of the discourse of 'true' and 'untrue' there is a *will* (Foucault, 1971a): a will to reach 'the truth'; but this will is neither self-evident nor unproblematical. The will to attain 'the truth' is upheld in the institutions and is distributed institutionally. It is constituted as pressure and functions as limiting power. Has one ever questioned why people want 'the truth', Foucault wonders? Which are the principles that determine the division of knowledge into 'true' and 'untrue'? The will to attain 'the truth' is not innocent. It constitutes an important instrument in the discipline of knowledge. It also serves as a mechanism of regulation for the directing of the articulation, production and dissemination of the discourse.

THE DISCOURSE OF POWER

Against the background of this argument it seems justifiable to maintain that a discussion on *the discourse of power* 'ought' to be opened by (or conducted on a parallel with) a deconstruction of *the power of discourse*, which has, as its chief purpose, the withdrawal of our conceptualisation of power from the totalising mechanisms of the discourse. We can no longer speak in this sense of power as property, as a privilege of the dominant class, exercised by them on passive and dominated classes. Neither is it a question of 'exercise' in the conventional sense of the word, but rather a process where power, which primitively we regard as a primary phenomenon, is merely a reflection – a secondary phenomenon – of the process; i.e. the way that people interpret different situations and the way in which they act. But the totalising mechanisms and mastering traits of the discourse dictate a mode of conduct with regard to power which, for the interactors, again becomes a primary phenomenon *per se*. For them it is 'actual' and it influences their actions. This means that it is not particularly fruitful to think of power in terms of classes. It is not unitary and its 'exercise' is not binary. On the other hand we might say that it is 'exercised' by and through the dominated, if we at all are to use such a language. In modern societies it is not the centrally 'exercised' power that has the most serious consequences for people. That which has disturbing implications for our societies, for people, which incapacitates, shapes and reshapes, adapts and normalises individuals down to the most individual and intimate details, is the power that 'is exercised' in small portions through endless functions in the society.

Micro-powers

These micro-powers are universally disseminated and organised in matrices and homogeneous networks. They correspond to functions which find their support in a certain knowledge that 'legitimates' the power which is thereby 'exercised' and which might be said to be produced within the pair power–knowledge. In this sense it may be said that power is 'exercised' via the accumulation of knowledge about those towards whom 'the exercise' is directed. The judges of normality (Foucault, 1976) are to be found everywhere. Power is spread in the whole social body. Each society is governed by various practitioners and reproducers of norms: teachers, doctors, educators, social workers and all kinds of experts 'who tell people how to behave at the breakfast table'. The universal reign of the normative is based on these and is 'exercised' on the behaviour, attitudes, gestures, bodies, and maybe even souls of the individuals. In days of old it was the lives of nobles and sovereigns that were documented, but nowadays individual cases are created of ordinary people. Knowledge of the former was for the sake of honour; knowledge of the latter serves as an instrument of supervision. 'The exercise of power' has its support in knowledge, and those towards whom this is directed are markedly individualised. The principle of the computer register is the same as that of Bentham's 'Panopticon', except that it is no longer made of cast iron and stone, it is no longer as visible; each individual is to be constantly within reach, *seen* without *seeing*, the object of information, not the subject in communication; the sorting instrument, once coarse and spatial, becomes more and more fine-meshed, more and more invisible (Foucault, 1966, 1976a). Power, in this sense, cannot be described merely in negative terms; it excludes, it oppresses, it censors, it hides. Power also *produces* and intensifies various objects and rituals which become 'reality'.

The paradox of freedom

The articulation of *the discourse of power* seems to go hand in hand with the production of *the power of discourse*. We have inherited a myth from the 'philosophers of the Enlightenment': Kant, and later Hegel, saw freedom in the moral dimension of their philosophy as a necessity. Paradoxically enough, however, this freedom rests on a disciplinary field: people are urged to submit to the higher authorities who know what is best for them. Out of its ideological context the *paradox* is revealed and suddenly appears as basic for the society of norms and discipline. Glucksmann (1977) writes that one says one wants to free the people, once and for all, finally and definitely, if only they could let go of their will and put 'it' at the disposal of the purpose. But in whom can one entrust one's will? Who shall take care of the liberation of the people? A higher governmental institution is Hegel's answer: individuals must sacrifice their particularism and individualism for the sake of society and, in so doing, they will find their freedom in a mutual and voluntary submission to a higher governmental power. Today it is perhaps not a matter of this higher governmental power in Hegel's sense, but the paradox remains. Disguised by the mechanisms of the discourse the paradox lives, by means of the institutions, organised in endless matrices across the entire social body. The discourse speaks demagogically of a problem-free, warded welfare person, while power is exercised in *micro-forms* and deprives man of his responsibility and will and reduces him to 'a tasteless, scentless and colourless object'.

POWER/KNOWLEDGE

When one examines *the discourse of power* against the background of the knowledge of power produced within the discourse, along with the 'dictated' conception as to what power is, how it 'ought' to be conceptualised and understood – i.e. *the power of discourse* – then the question of the relationship between *power* and *knowledge* is drawn to its peak. Is knowledge the prerequisite of the 'exercise of power'? Is knowledge with 'necessity' produced within the framework of a power structure? Or could it be that power produces and supports itself on knowledge in the same way as knowledge produces and supports itself on power?

These questions are ordinarily answered in the following way: (1) knowledge functions as a means used by 'those who are in power' to attain their own goals; (2) those who master a certain knowledge form a class for themselves and 'exercise' power over others. In the first case this would mean that a ruling class produces the ideology that is best suited to serve the interests of the class in question. In the second case it would mean that a new field of knowledge gives rise to an ideology which, in turn, creates a 'niche' for a particular class. However, evidently this simple dichotomy does not provide us with any satisfactory answers. The analysis, and the questions, must be directed towards the borderline between power and knowledge. One might also question whether there is 'anyone' who possesses knowledge, anyone who 'owns' power? In answer to this one might say that of course there are people who *know*, as well as individuals (or organisations and institutions) who *govern*. Of course authority is repressive at times, and knowledge and power have certainly been formed since the 1800s according to models best suited to the interests of the bourgeoisie, while a similar pattern may be seen today in the Eastern bloc. However, this does not imply that the ruling class knows exactly what to do and that they act according to some sort of recipe. The other party – and their actions – in a power relation are a necessity: the governed, the oppressed, the subordinates, the bureaucrats, etc., voluntarily or involuntarily, consciously or unconsciously, each do their own share so that the *borderline* between power and knowledge comes about.

The relation power/knowledge seems, to my mind, to be easier to fathom from the bottom upwards: on the small local levels of 'power struggle' where participants do not necessarily know what they are doing. The power that 'is exercised' on these levels is immanent; it is produced at each moment and is upheld by the knowledge which, in its turn, has produced it. Perhaps it is so that power and knowledge implicate one another; that there exists no power relation without a certain field for knowledge; perhaps also, that there exists no knowledge which does not pressupose and at the same time constitute power relations. Apart from the works of Foucault, no comprehensive studies have been made of these mechanisms of power. Power in its general and specific strategies, in its mechanisms, the relation between power and knowledge, the effects of the one upon the other, are aspects which have been ignored by the primitive discourse of power. The humanists assume by tradition that knowledge ceases as soon as one touches on power: power makes people mad; those who govern are blind. Only those who are far away from power, those who are not involved in its tyranny, well protected in their rooms, in their meditations, can discover 'the truth' (Foucault, 1975). Modern humanism is mistaken when it makes a distinction between knowledge and power. It is not enough to say that power needs a certain measure of invention, a certain form of knowledge. To exercise power means to *create* objects of knowledge, to let them come to the fore, to accumulate information and then to use it. The articulation of the relation power/knowledge may seem vague, but in fact it is well-rooted and actively integrated in the social body.

Really, one could say that power, as such, does not exist. The concept seems to be used to denote the 'existing' mechanisms in society. Power may be seen as an immanent phenomenon in social relations between groups and individuals. It is not unequivocal and cannot be conceptualised as property: every social relation may be said to be characterised by a certain 'form of power'. One could even say that every individual, every group is subject/object for a certain 'form of power'. As far as knowledge is concerned, it seems to be constituted more within relations between the fields of power and knowledge than in either of these fields *per se*. This means that knowledge is not a reflection of a certain power relation: rather it is immanent in it. In this sense power and knowledge may be said to implicate one another. Subsequently one could say that knowledge is neither 'objective' nor neutral: knowledge is political, not because it has political consequences or because it can be used politically, but because it 'is possible' within power relations. The conditions which make knowledge possible are thus to be sought in relations of power: 'the exercise of power', the production of knowledge and knowledge *per se* are constituted from the same base; the *archaeology* of knowledge goes via the *genealogy* of power and vice versa. A discursive analysis reveals that which is problematic (but seemingly unproblematic) in the formation, production and dissemination of the discourse. Thus, the illusory objectivity and 'truth' of the discourse may be seen against the background of the conditions which render it possible; for the crucial point is not whether a discourse is 'true' or 'untrue', but whether it is (or appears to be) legitimate or illegitimate in relation to specific relations of power.

Notes

INTRODUCTION

1. The concept of *discourse* denotes a set of statements, concepts, theses and theories in speech and in writing, which together form an articulated conception of something in particular. When using the concept of discourse in the context of this text I shall refer to the set of articulated conceptions as to the phenomenon of power, but I would also like to show, on a general level, that all forms of connected and interrelated statements 'voice an opinion', descriptively and normatively about something.

2. I devoted some time and interest during the period 1977–80 to the study of organisations theory. My primary concern was not, however, the discernment of the way in which power as a phenomenon, and as a concept, was conceptualised in this theory. My interest lay rather in such notions as rationality (Simon, 1947), situational descriptions and levels of aspiration of organisational members (Braybrooke and Lindblom, 1963; Lindblom, 1959; March and Simon, 1958; Simon, 1957, 1969; Vickers, 1965, etc.) and decision processes (with respect to the activities in connection with a particular decision) (Cyert et al., 1956; Snyder and Paige, 1958, etc.). Nonetheless, gradually it became apparent to me how the concept of power was treated within the modern tendencies of organisation theory, i.e. those tendencies which were a result of a critique against the schools of classical formalism (Taylor, 1911; Mooney, 1930; Fayol, 1949, etc.) and the neo-classical rationalist and systems theoretical approaches (Simon, 1947; Parsons, 1956; Boulding, 1956; Etzioni, 1961; Kats and Kahn, 1966; Ramström, 1963; Rhenman and Stymne, 1965, etc.). Although the concept was incorporated in the debate and, at times, even as an important element, it was seldom treated as central. This situation was not to change until the organisations theorists began to devote their attention to the processes taking place between people in organisations rather than to formal structures and the like. This is what Perrow (1973), not without a touch of irony, has called the battle between 'the forces of darkness and the forces of light'. My own interest with the concept of power was further kindled to the extent that I was to make new discoveries within the field of organisation theory. I shall leave out

the theories of 'contingency' and 'neo-contingency' and the theories of organisational development (OD), etc. The organisation theories which have had the strongest effect on me as far as my interest for the concept of power is concerned are those which emanate from the concept of *action*. These are represented by, amongst others, Silverman (1970), Cohen (1968); Filmer et al. (1972); Karpik (1972a,b,c, 1977, 1978); March and Olsen (1976); Weick (1976); Crozier and Friedberg (1977), etc. I have, in addition to this, no doubt been influenced by that which I have learnt from the European philosophy of *action* (Sartre, Heidegger, Ricouer).

3. For Taylor (1911), Mooney (1930) and Fayol (1949), these principles entail (1) extensive specialisation (Smith 1904/1776), division of labour between different groups; (2) each employee must have only one superior to whom he has to report and from whom he has to take orders – unity command; (3) each superior may have only a certain number of subordinates, i.e. a limited span of control; (4) communication and the exchange of information within the organisation must follow the formal structure. Gullick and Urwick (1937) suggested another example of these principles of management: POSDCORB (Planning, Organising, Staffing, Directing, Coordinating, Reporting, Budgeting). The argument in this context is principally concerned with the delegation of authority and responsibility, which is, to my mind, a way of implicitly treating the question of the distribution of power in organisations, Davis (1957: 20) writes in this context:

> Too much or insufficient delegation may render an executive incapable of action, the failure to delegate authority and responsibility equally may result in frustration for the delegates. Overlapping of authorities often causes clashes in personality. Gaps in authority cause failures in getting jobs done, with one party blaming the other for shortcomings in performance.

4. I have chosen to take a classic such as Selznick to illustrate the argument that the strategical character of the actions of the participants constitutes an essential dimension of the organisation. Selznick (1949) demonstrates, in his study of the 'Tennessee Valley Authority' (TVA) how top managers (administrators) use special strategies for defensive purposes. Similar patterns of action have been described by Burns and Stalker (1961). Whereas Selznick's administrators defended themselves against the unfavourable responses they had received for their initiation of changes, Burns and Stalker's managers reacted by opposing and by defending themselves against those changes which were initiated outside the organisation. However, there are many more studies which demonstrate the way in which organisational members, no matter which hierarchical level they may belong to, develop strategies and act thereafter in their pursuit of personal interest. One illustration of this statement is provided by Mechanic (1962), who has shown how subordinates can often, due to their access to the lower spheres of the organisation (important everyday processes, often inaccessible to the superiors), exercise what could be called 'implicit blackmail' on their superiors and thereby try to

secure their own personal interests. Gouldner (1954) has drawn attention to similar phenomena, but in this case in connection with a change of manager, whereby the successor knows less about some of the working conditions in the organisation than do his subordinates and these do not hesitate to take advantage of the situation. Gouldner, but also Crozier (1964), has also shown how subordinates may make strategical use of organisational rules. Crozier illustrates this with the case of the 'auditing bureau' where the top manager, in order to make decisions, first needs special information as to specific situations. The top manager is then dependent on the middle managers for this information. Their position in the system of communication permits them, in this context, to exercise a relative power over the top manager and thus to influence the decision to be taken. They manipulate the information so as to align the decision with their own interests. This action is systematically performed by the middle managers since their position in the context of the organisation implies that they are in competition with one another. This manipulation seems to be the only way in which they can affect the decision to be made, the contents of which could be of crucial importance for their space of action in their respective departments. They avoid going too far, however, knowing that information which is falsified beyond belief could result in the top manager making a closer investigation of the matter. This would be fatal for the source of power of the middle managers.

To argue against this assertion and to maintain that it could not possibly apply to all subordinates in all organisations would be a simple matter. It would be far more difficult to claim that the information always travels along an ordered, rational path, defined by the structural and rational rules of the organisation.

Gouldner (1954) suggested, while discussing the function of the bureaucratic rules, that their rationalising effect is neither self-evident nor one-sided. Indeed, the rules do restrict the freedom of the subordinates, but they also set the limit for the margin of manoeuvre of the superiors. For example, it is not possible for the superiors to exercise their 'sanctioning powers' except under certain specific circumstances. The subordinates are thus able to seek protection under the cover of these rules from the potential arbitrary actions of their superiors. If the subordinate manages to apply these rules 'in the right way', the 'power' which the 'superior has' over him will be reduced. It is commonly known that good results are seldom obtained by strictly following the rules. Those must often be at least partially reinterpreted and adapted to specific situations. In view of this it could be said that the superior is, in fact, often in the weaker position since he cannot, even if he wants to, force the subordinate to do more than what is set down by the rules. An appropriate example of this is that of air traffic controllers. Their work is governed by extremely precise rules and rationally designed systems instructing them how to act in every conceivable situation. Paradoxically enough, however, in order for there to be any air traffic whatsoever, it is necessary that the air traffic controllers quite simply ignore these rules and the system in which they are comprised. When they wish to lay certain claims, however, for example an increase in salary, they merely go slow, i.e. they follow the rules: this leads to chaos. (The two examples mentioned above can be found in Daudi, 1980).

Other studies of relevance to the theme at hand are Blau (1955), Dalton (1959) and Goffman (1967). That with which we are dealing here is the development of defensive strategies by the subordinates (Blau), the development of coalitions (clique – in this case 'management clique') with aggressive and defensive purposes (Dalton), or the use of the organisation for the reinforcement of one's identity (Goffman). Finally, it might be of interest to emphasise at this point that the theme of the actors' strategical actions is one which has been observed, documented and discussed as an essential dimension in the functioning of organisations, even if it has not previously been studied in a specific manner. Even the classical 'Hawthorne'-study (Roethlisberger and Dickson, 1939) could be seen as a case of the development and use of strategies on the part of the subordinates.

5. Let me mention here some game-theorists that are perhaps the most essential or who have directly or indirectly influenced this study: Gamson (1964); Harsanyi (1959, 1962a,b,c); Luce and Raiffa (1957); von Neumann and Morgenstern (1944); Shapley and Shubic (1954); Shapley (1953, in Kuhn and Tucker, eds); Peaucelle (1969). Schelling (1960) might be considered among the most relevant for this study. In his outstanding work, *The Strategy of Conflict*, he conducts a stimulating and even entertaining discussion whereby he relates the game theory argument non-zero sum games (conflict/negotiation). He then shows that it is not necessarily the one who manages to make his planned action in a given situation of conflict unpredictable and, in so doing, to extend his margin of manoeuvre, that always wins. It is even conceivable that he who reduces his marginal to nought (zero) and who thus renders his actions totally predictable, may win just because of this. Schelling illustrates this with the case of the railway workers on strike who fasten themselves to the rails in order to force a train, whose driver has broken the strike, to stop. This is, no doubt, a rather extreme example, but it does, nonetheless, illustrate the fact that there always remains a last way out even for he who is in an entirely disadvantageous position. In this case the 'games structure' is significant, since the action of fastening oneself to the railway lines is a strategic action, the meaning of which is related to the very existence of a structure; the railway lines which drastically limit (contract) the space of action of the train driver. He has only two alternatives: capitulation or massacre.

6. I will consider these schools of thought later on in the text with reference to the discourse of power which they produce. I would like to emphasise, however, that this classification is by no means self-evident, nor is it exhaustive. Political economists and anthropologists, for example, could be added to these groups. One could also speak of the historians who describe the 'actual' distribution of power in the past or the history of sovereignties and their conquest, possession and exercise of power. There are also writers within stratification theory who, for ethical and ideological reasons, consider power against the background of a set of criteria for its desirable and just distribution.

7. Thermodynamic, organic, biological, linguistic, cybernetic and many other

models and analogies are favourite subjects among writers in the traditional organisation literature. The extensive use of such models, however, does not always prove to be a success. Naturally such loans and transplantations of concepts and discoveries from the one discipline to the other may lead to new and interesting aspects, but only if carefully used and to a limited extent. Unfortunately, however, the use of such concepts often transcends the metaphor. The models then tend to become counter-productive as they cannot incorporate one of the most fundamental dimensions in organisations, i.e. that of people's actions. It seems to me that cybernetic and thermodynamic metaphors in organisational studies amount to no more than an unusually rigid form of functionalism. A functionalism which merely reproduces an attitude emanating from an elementary version of positivist rationalism and mechanical reasoning.

8. The discussion in this introduction is confined to a relatively general level. It could, however, be mentioned that the concept of action has been treated over quite a long period by various thinkers (this tradition can be traced as far back as Aristotle and perhaps even further). In modern times (19th and 20th centuries) the concept has been extensively discussed by existentialists, phenomenologists, analytical philosophers along with pragmatists and many more. Further, there seems to exist a stronger tradition in Europe than in the Anglo-Saxon world as regards the concept of action and its uses in the context of organisational analyses. Many studies based on this concept have, for example, been carried out in France: Bourricaud (1961); Kergoat (1970); Sainsaulieu (1965); Karpik (1972a,b,c); Touraine (1966, 1978); Kuty (1973); Rosanvallon (1976), to mention a few. While these authors have carried out and documented their studies with the concept of action as an essential and self-evident aspect, they have not discussed the actual concept *per se*. Silverman (1970), on the other hand, has specifically treated the concept and it could be said that it is here that his important contribution lies.

9. It is naturally extremely difficult to list in their entirety all those who have expressed an opinion about power in this way. There are many others who have done so but perhaps in a less direct and explicit manner. Those whom I have quoted here, Giddens (1976), and Crozier and Friedberg (1977) in particular, have explicitly discussed the mechanisms of power as seen against the background of the actions of the actors. Other interesting contributions to the study of power are those issuing from a Marxist perspective such as, for example, Clegg (1975, 1979a); Clegg and Dunkerley (1977, 1980); and Salaman (1979); or those who have attempted to show the complexity of the phenomenon of power and the consequences which this complexity has on its study: Bachrach and Baratz (1971); Crozier (1973); Lukes (1974); Bradshaw (1976).

10. Crozier and Friedberg (1977: 16–17) (also in Warner, 1977: 81–82).

> As will be recalled, this refers to the dilemma of two prisoners who have been arrested for the same crime, but against whom the police do not have any valid proof. In that situation each prisoner has the choice between two strategies only: either to confess, or to deny the charges. If both deny, the

police will be unable to have them convicted, and they will therefore go to prison for only one year on some minor charges. If one accepts to cooperate with the police by becoming a crown-witness, and the other does not talk he will go free and the other will be convicted to twenty years of prison. If both talk, both will be convicted and go to prison for ten years. Knowing these consequences, each of the prisoners knows that the success of his own strategy depends on the one chosen by the other. However, being unable to communicate, they have no way of agreeing on a common course of action.

The logic of the problem, which, in this illustration is conceptualised as a game, is that if each of the parties were to act *rationally* both would suffer the worst possible outcome of the game. This is so, since each player (prisoner) would try to win; in other words, would prefer to pursue his own interests rather than to give priority to those of his opponent. This example, although it may appear to be rather drastic and, at the same time, highly simplified, provides an excellent illustration of the idea that the strategical actions and strivings of the actors for their own personal interests are of central importance for the understanding of the intra-organisational processes as well as of the structuring and development of organisations.

11. In the review of the concept of power which I wrote from a historical perspective (Daudi, 1980: 19–45), I divided into groups, depending upon the ideological standpoints of the writers, the various statements that have been made on power. Due to considerations of space I shall name only the most important ones here. Among the radicals, those whom I found to be of most interest are: the Hebrew prophet Micah; Faleas de Chalkedon and Plato, *La République* (in *Oeuvres Complètes*): Winstanley, a Christian radical who lived in the 17th century, *Selections from his Work* (1944). A notable move in the radical direction was taken in the 17th and 18th centuries but this time with a greater acuteness of perception: Locke, *Two Treatises of Government* and *An Essay Concerning Human Understanding* (1689–90); but also Rousseau, *Discours sur l'Origine de l'Inégalité des Hommes*; Emile, *Du Contrat Social* (in *Oeuvres Complètes*, 1964). Between the 19th and 20th centuries the most important representatives of the egalitarian and radical movements began to devote their attention to the economical aspects of the distribution of power: the writings of Marx and Engels, and particularly *The Communist Manifesto* (in *Oeuvres Complètes*, 1934). The debate has, in modern times, seen a removal to the socio-political spheres with the emergence of conflict theorists and pluralists.

In the conservative block I found, among others: *The Law of Manus* (in *Sacred books of the East*, 1836), compiled by Hindu priests approximately 200 BC, in which they argue for the thesis that the unequal distribution of power in society is a God-given institution designed to further the well-being of the world. In *Politiques* Aristotle not only defended the institution of private ownership, but also that of slavery. One of the most striking illustrations of the conservative thesis was that which was rendered by John of Salisbury, a 12th-century English bishop, in his work *Polycraticus* (in *The*

Stateman's Book, 1927) also quoted in *Livres de Sentences* by Saint Thomas d'Aquino (1225–74) (see for example Chenu, 'Introduction à l'étude de saint Thomas d'Aquin', 1950). What the social philosophy of John of Salisbury amounted to was that society can be likened to a human body. The Prince is then the head, while the eyes, ears and tongue are the judges and the provincial governors – the senator is the heart, whereas the sides are the followers of the Prince. The hands are soldiers and officials, while the stomach and bowels are the tax-collectors and those who handle finances. Simple people are the feet, while the priesthood is the soul. The Prince, according to John of Salisbury, is subordinate only to God and to his representatives on earth, i.e. the priesthood. All others must obey and serve the Prince, especially the simple people since they are the feet of society.

Another illustration of the conservative thesis was the view of the Social Darwinists in the 20th century, a view that was expressed by, among others, William Graham Sumner in his book *Folkways* (quoted by Bottomore, 'Equality or Elites', 1966). Sumner saw the different classes in society as being an indication of people's social values which is ultimately an indication of people's innate capacities. Gaetano Mosca has expressed thoughts along similar lines in his book *Elementi di Scienza Politica* (The Ruling Class, 1939) wherein he attacked Marxist theory as being hopeless and utopic in its vision of a classless society.

The modern debate on the distribution of power from the point of view of the conservative thesis is represented to a certain extent by the Functionalists and the Elitists, whom, like the Conflict Theorists and the Pluralists, will be considered later in the text.

12. It might be suitable here to draw attention to one of the most difficult problems associated with the study of power, namely that of *causality*. There is a widespread tendency in the literature on power to reduce relations of power to causal relations. The problem is far too extensive to be discussed in detail here, but I nonetheless feel that a few important indications could be of relevance at this point. Take for example Dahl, whose statement: 'A has power over B to the extent that he can get B to do something that B would not otherwise do', has the support of many other researchers of power. At the heart of the problem lies the fact that when the concern is primarily that of the measurement of the concrete, empirically provable power, the attention is, in fact, focused upon the already endorsed influence and one thus tends to overlook not only the dynamics of power, but also the actual processes connected with power relations. The quest in so doing is the prediction of the individuals' behaviour, basing this upon a number of known variables. If a new variable is introduced (axiomatically), and a certain change in behaviour is obtained, it is then assumed that the behaviour has been influenced by this variable. March, for example, seems to bring some arbitrariness into the argumentation when he says:

> It is in harmony with the more frequent uses of the term 'influence' and with the present sense of that term, to say that if the individual deviates from the predicted path of behavior, influence has occurred and,

specifically, that it is influence which had induced the change (March, 1955: 92).

The arbitrariness is such that if A attempts to change the behaviour of B, and if in fact a change in B's behaviour does take place, then it is assumed that A exerts power over B. However, if A does not attempt to influence B, could it be maintained that A has no power over B? No, is the subsequent answer, there exists a real and a potential power – but for the sake of simplicity it is said that a change in A's behaviour causes a change in B's behaviour: in other words a causal relation.

As we all know, however, the concept of causality is a matter of much controversy in the theory of science. It has been discussed with a number of penetratingly acute argumentations by David Hume in his two important works *Treatise of Human Nature* from 1739 to 1740 (1938) and *Inquiries Concerning the Human Understanding and Concerning the Principles of Morals* from about 1748 (1951). Hume's criticism of the causal concept can be seen as a part of his argument against the rationalist ideal of absolute knowledge (Brunet, 1965). Hume is doubtful as to the existence of causal relationships and maintains that what we are actually observing is a certain correlation between various phenomena. 'Every relation is extern to its term' (Hume in Weinberg, *Ockham, Descartes and Hume*, 1977). The notion of causality is not, according to Hume, an idea that is innate. Then, from whence does it arise? Hume investigates the possibility of applying the observational and experimental methods to mental phenomena, i.e. the same methods as those applied to physical phenomenon by 'the incomparable Mr Newton'.

> It is confessed, that the utmost effort of human reason is to reduce the principles, productive of natural phenomena, to a greater simplicity, and to resolve the many particular effects into a few general causes, by means of reasonings from analogy experience and observations (Hume, 1748 (1951), sec. 4, pt. 1, par. 12).

A general law of causality, says Hume, which could be applied to impressions and feelings, does not exist for these have their own unknown 'reason'. For example I believe, due to certain signs in a book, that Caesar has actually lived. I see the sun rise and I say that it will likewise rise tomorrow. But words such as tomorrow, always and with necessity express something which is not granted by experience. Tomorrow is not granted until it becomes today. Hume maintains, in other words, that causality is a relation which implies that I transcend the boundaries of that which is given – I mention more than what there is, I add together, I anticipate, I expect, etc. Other illustrations of this notion are, for example, that I may observe an event: the sun is shining on the stone. I may then observe another event: the stone becomes warm. I have by no means been able to observe that the second event was caused by the first. I cannot observe any causal relation. The idea of causality does not derive from the *senses*, nor is it realised by *reason* as the rationalists would have it. A causal context cannot, according to Hume, be *revealed* by common-sense arguments. The idea is quite simply a result of *habit*. I observe repeated and similar cases in which A is followed by B; I see the sun shining on a stone and I then also perceive that the stone becomes warm. Therefore I *assume* that these two events will be consecutive the next time too. But what is it that creates habit? The answer is *association*. I associate A with B in my imagination yet, intellectually, I am still able to separate them. The capacity of the consciousness to fuse the events in my imagination constitutes habit, while the capacity of the intellect to make distinctions, implicates my belief in the probability of the existence of a causal relation between the events observed. The principle of habit (the fusion of similar cases in my imagination) and the principle of experience (the intellectual observation of distinct cases) combine to form a relation and what I believe to be true about this relation. Hume goes on to add that it is in this way that we imagine that causality comes into existence.

This is by no means an exhaustive discussion of Hume's criticism of the concept of causality. The reader who wishes to find out more can, apart from studying the writings of Hume himself, also find detailed indications in Aaron, 'Hume's "Theory of Universals" ' (1942); Aiken, *Hume's Moral and Political Philosophy* (1948); Brunschvigg, *L'expérience Humaine et la causalité Physique* (1949); Brunet, *Philosophie et Esthétique chez David Hume* (1965); and, in Nietzsche, *Le Gai Savoir* (1950). Now it must be clear that Hume's criticism of causality is by no means passé, nor is it merely philosophical cogitation. Popper proceeded from Hume's critique in his own discussions of the deductive method through causal explanation. He even hesitated to use the concepts of *cause* and *effect* in the arguments conducted in his book *The Logic of Scientific Discovery* ('both these terms I shall avoid', Popper, 1972: 60). He finds these terms restrictive when considered against the background of the meaning which these concepts have in the explanation of physical phenomena.

> Thus I shall not assert any principle of causality (or principle of universal causation). The 'principle of causality' is the assertion that any event whatsoever can be causally explained – that it can be deductively predicted. According to the way in which one interprets the word 'can' in this assertion, it will be either tautological (analytic), or else an assertion about reality (synthetic). For if 'can' means that it is always logically possible to construct a causal explanation, then the assertion is tautological, since for any prediction whatsoever we can always find universal statements and initial conditions from which the prediction is derivable. (Whether these universal statements have been tested and corroborated in other cases is of course quite a different question.) If, however, 'can' is meant to signify that the world is governed by strict laws, that it is so constructed that every specific event is an instance of a universal regularity or law, then the assertion is admittedly synthetic. But in this case it is not falsifiable, as will be seen later, in section 78. I shall, therefore, neither adopt nor reject the 'principle of causality'; I shall be content simply to exclude it, as 'metaphysical', from the sphere of science (Popper, 1972: 60–61).

It is necessary to note, however, that Popper, in discarding the principles of causality, does not mean the scientists should cease to strive for general laws and coherent theoretical systems.

It would not be appropriate to end the argument here, however. It must still be referred to the study of power relations. Take for example Simon who, in his *Models of Man*, articulates opinions about most things including power relations, and who, in spite of his mechanistic approach (Mintzberg, 1977) prefers to regard power relations as asymmetrical.

> This definition involves an asymmetrical relation between influencer and influencee. Now we are wary, in the social sciences, of asymmetrical relations. They remind us of pre-Humeian and pre-Newtonian notions of causality. By whip and sword we have been converted to the doctrine that there is no causation, only functional interrelation, and that functional relations are perfectly symmetrical (Simon, 1957: 65).

Simon continues his argument to conclude that power relations, after all said and done (by Hume), are indeed causal and asymmetrical. He feels that he could solve the problem by introducing a variable of time.

> We might say that if A and B are functionally related and if A precedes B in time, then A causes B. There is no logical obstacle to this procedure (Simon, 1957: 67).

There are indeed, however, logical obstacles; at least if one keeps in mind the long and detailed argumentation presented by Hume with its principle of habit and its principle of experience that produce what we think about relations. A temporal frequence does not imply causality, even if the appearance of A precedes the appearance of B. There are a number of phenomena to be found which are correlated without necessarily being causally linked.

13. Later in the text I shall discuss the way in which our conceptualisation of power – both as an object of research and as a phenomenon in our everyday actions and interactions – is embedded within the ideology which has governed Western thought and action since the Middle Ages, i.e. to dominate, control and rule over our environment including the people living in it (Nietzsche, *La Généalogie de la Morale* (1887) 1964; the total works of Foucault).

14. The formulation or consideration of a purpose in terms of a *process* must be seen against the background of a broader discussion on the level of the theory of science. The problem could be summed up as follows: if one works inductively (which I do not) one can present a *hypothesis*, e.g.: Are all swans white or not? The task of the *purpose* is then to verify whether the hypothesis is true or false or, to be more precise, to determine the proximity of the hypothesis to the truth. As Reichenbach (1930: 186, in Popper, *The Logic of Scientific Discovery*, 1972: 29–30) says:

> We have described . . . the principle of induction, as the means whereby science decides upon truth. To be more exact, we should say that it serves to decide upon probability. For it is not given to science to reach either truth or falsity . . . but scientific statements can only attain continuous degrees of probability whose unattainable upper and lower limits are truth and falsity.

This presupposes the 'existence' of *absolute* and *universal* truths. This is rejected however by Popper as he writes:

> Now it is far from obvious, from a logical point of view, that we are justified in inferring universal statements from singular ones, no matter how numerous; for any conclusion drawn in this way may always turn out to be false: no matter how many instances of white swans we may have observed, this does not justify the conclusion that all swans are white (Popper, 1972: 27).

The purpose of this study is not to 'go out' and test an already constructed model, nor is it to verify whether power is white or black. Rather my purpose is to understand the phenomenon of power as it is thought of in theory, and manifested in practice, i.e. in action. It could thus be said that my purpose is a project, i.e. a process, in which I gradually explore, understand and describe. At the other end of the process (a process never ends) I shall suggest an alternative way in which to conceptualise the explored phenomenon.

15. For a detailed review of Foucault's work and its application here I refer the reader to Chapter Three. The argument in Chapters Five, Six and Seven is based partly upon that which has been written there, and partly upon other thoughts which will be presented in due course in the text.

16. *Multiplicity*, here, conveys the idea that the discourse reproduces itself by constantly finding new objects. An object is only legitimised, however, when it becomes the *object* of a discourse. Thus the object is *produced* by the discourse which makes a statement about it. This implies that a discourse reproduces itself precisely by making statements about and by producing its object(s) (Foucault, 1971a). The discourse of organisations, for example, produces and multiplies its object in the sense that this is reflected in the multiplicity of organisation theories — different schools of thought, different perspectives and methods, different ideologies, different levels of analysis, etc. — which in turn give rise to additional statements and theories, either entirely new ones, or in the form of criticisms of these and/or of complementary additions to already existing ones. The snowball rolls on and the discourse of organisations is nourished by its own object.

17. The concept *logic of action* is borrowed from Karpik (1978) and is considered in detail in Daudi and Alvesson, 1983. This article has been the main source of inspiration for the argument which I shall conduct on the first method-dimension.

CHAPTER THREE

1. Many researchers have devoted much attention to this attitude amongst social scientists. Reality is not something which is 'out there' but is rather, trivial though it may seem, omnipresent. This trite assertion is nonetheless of significance for the method which one chooses and for what, on the whole, one sees in the empirics. Authors such as Schutz (1962, 1964, 1966, 1967); Goffman (1959, 1963, 1967, 1969); Garfinkel (1967); Cicourel (1964) have

led a potent argument against the separation made in research situations between the subject and the object.

2. By 'unique' knowledge in this context, I mean knowledge which emerges as a result of 'new' combinations between various phenomena, a knowledge which throws new light on certain objects. In connection with this, insight into epistemological problems could be said to be of particular importance in the social sciences since the production of a 'unique' or new knowledge often goes hand in hand with the development of adequate methods.

3. Thomas (1966) writes in this regard that if people define situations as being real they will have real consequences. This is fundamental in the interactional perspective where the attention is focused on the processes by means of which the members of society define their situations and identities. The researcher must thus come close to those whom he/she is studying and describe their situation as they themselves conceive of it. Further, the interactional perspective must be seen as a predecessor of a social action perspective or theory. A central idea within this perspective is that the researcher should strive to *understand* those whom he/she is studying. He should strive to see the world through their eyes, put himself into their position and see how the world presents itself to them. Furthermore, he should try to imagine the ideas, conceptions, motives and goals which govern people's actions. With a knowledge of the way in which reality presents itself to people, and of the thoughts, impulses and wishes which people have, the researcher is able to see that they act as they do because they are striving to realise their goals and wishes as much as possible according to their experience of the situation. This form of research aimed at understanding, derives its origins from Weber's *Verstehende*. The demand for an action perspective has arisen from a dissatisfaction with the current methods of research and analysis. For further discussion see Blumer (1966); Rex (1961); Simmel (1964). But naturally also Mead (1936, 1967) and Goffman (1961a,b, 1969). See also Cuff and Payne (1979).

4. The principle of exclusion, as a foundation of the structuring of the world around us, seems to be deeply rooted in Western thought. Gödel's *Incompleteness Theorem* (1931), showed that 'Principia Matematica' is based on such principles. I discussed Gödel's *Incompleteness Theorem* in a previous article (Daudi, 1981, *Dialogue in the Tower of Babel*). Gödel's theorem, which is based upon an ancient and simple intuition, has apparently had tremendous implications for mathematics. He had, as his point of departure, a philosophical paradox which he has subsequently translated into mathematical terms: Epimenides' paradox. Epimenides was a Cretan who made an immortal statement: *All Cretans are liars*. Another way of expressing this statement is: *This statement is false*. This is contrary to the 'accepted' dichotomy of true and false statements. Gödel's idea was to explore the mathematical argument with the aid of the mathematical argument itself: Introspective mathematics, which proved to be a potent concept and which led to Gödel's *Incompleteness Theorem*. What the theorem says and how this is proved are two different matters. Barker (1969) writes that 'Gödel's theorem can be compared to a pearl, while the method of proof can be compared to an

oyster. The pearl may be admired for its simplicity and its purity; whereas the oyster is a complex living organism which gives birth to the beauty – the pearl.' Gödel published his theorem in an article in the year 1931 (1962): 'On Formally Undecidable Propositions in "Principia Matematica" and Related Systems'. The pearl, writes Barker (1969), in Gödel's theorem is that: *all consistent axiomatic formulations of number theory include undecidable propositions*. But it is difficult to see the pearl in the theorem since it is carried by the oyster, i.e. the proof. The proof of Gödel's *Incompleteness Theorem* rests on the fact that the mathematical statement in it is self-referring, in the same way as Epimenides' paradox is a linguistic self-referring statement. It seems to be relatively simple to talk about language in linguistic terms. It is not, however, as easy to conceive of the way in which a statement of numbers can make a statement about itself. Yet it is precisely this that appears to be the strength of Gödel's theorem. Mathematical statements, at least if one concentrates on statements of number theory, are concerned with the characteristics of whole numbers. The problem is that neither the whole numbers nor their characteristics are statements (axioms). This implies that a statement of number theory does not describe another statement of number theory; it is only a statement of number theory. Gödel realised that there was more to this problem than meets the eye. He intuitively believed that a statement of number theory could deal with another statement of number theory (perhaps even itself). What is needed is for the numbers to stand for the statements. One can codify the numbers which, in fact, is what Gödel did. The 'Gödel numbering' is a system where the numbers stand for symbols and sequences of symbols. In this way each statement of number theory is given a Gödel number, i.e. a code, with the help of which the statement can be referred to; an interesting trick which allows for the understanding of these statements of number theory on two different levels: as statements of number theory and as statements about statements of number theory. He experimented with Epimenides' paradox and finally arrived at the following: *This statement of number theory has no proof.* He preferred the latter to a more direct translation of Epimenides which would have read as follows: 'This statement of number theory is false.' Gödel's work is an essential link in the combined efforts of mathematicians to explain what proof is. By proof, one means demonstrations *within a fixed system of assertions*, for example mathematical proposition. That system to which Gödel had the word *proof* to refer to, are the number-theory argumentations which constitutes the *Principia Matematica*, the opus by Bertrand Russell and Alfred North Whitehead.

Gödel's proposition can be rewritten as follows: *This statement of number theory does not have any proof in the system of 'Principia Matematica'* (Hofstadter, 1979).

This is Gödel's proposition but not Gödel's theorem. In the same way, Epimenides' proposition is not the observation that 'Epimenides' proposition is a paradox.' The point is that Epimenides' statement creates a paradox in that it is neither true nor false whereas Gödel's proposition is unverifiable (within 'Principia Matematica') but true!

The conclusion would therefore be that the system of 'Principia

Matematica' is incomplete. There exist statements of number theory which are true but whose truth cannot be demonstrated since their methods of proof are too weak.

But could one falsify Gödel's theorem within other systems than that of 'Principia Matematica'? This is not the case. We recall the title of Gödel's article: 'On Formally, Undecidable Propositions in "Principia Matematica" and Related Systems'. The very phrase 'and Related Systems' solved Gödel's problem. Others could have improved 'Principia Matematica' and ousted Gödel's theorem if he had pointed out imperfections only in the works of Russell and Whitehead.

But it was impossible to throw out Gödel's theorem since this stood up against any axiomatic system whatsoever based on the 'Principia Matematica'. Thus Gödel has demonstrated that *verifiability is a weaker concept than that of truth*, and this is the case no matter which axiomatic system may be involved.

5. The physical environment and its role in the individual's experiences and interpretations of his/her world, has been discussed extensively by Whyte (1955), Suttles (1968) and Goffman (1959). In addition to this Hall (1969a) speaks of the distance between people, and the implications which this distance might have on interaction and communication. He discusses 'How space communicates', and asserts that 'not only is a vocal message qualified by the handling of distance, but the substance of a conversation can often demand special handling of space. There are certain things that are difficult to talk about unless one is within the proper conversational zone' (Hall, 1969a: 162).

6. Crozier and Friedberg (1977) argue in *L'acteur et le système*, for the idea that organisations are *human artefacts* and are therefore susceptible to external influences and are changeable. But the thought stretches beyond that. In the phenomenological–existential tradition it is considered meaningful to proceed from the assumption that society is a human product, and vice-versa. The existentialists lay the responsibility on the individual and argue that 'Man is what man makes himself to be' (Sartre, 1943). Sartre uses three sentences to characterise the being of man: 'L'être est soi' (being is itself) or 'L'être est en soi' (being is in itself), 'L'être est ce qu'il est' (being is what it is) and finally 'L'être-en-soi est' (being-in-itself is). The first sentence holds that 'L'être' is not created, neither by God nor by itself. All creations are human creations. 'L'être-en-soi' (being-in-itself), is beyond all passivity and activity: it is beyond affirmation and negation.

7. This is based on Sartre's ontological investigations (1943). The concepts of nothingness, consciousness, freedom and being-for-itself (L'être-pour-soi), converge to the same fundamental human reality. Man is never, according to Sartre, identical to what he was or to what he strives to become. He is always at a distance in relation to himself, whether we focus on his past, present, or future. To be conscious is to choose at the right moment. By choosing, we are simultaneously choosing what we shall become. One must, says Sartre, be conscious in order to choose and one must choose in order to be conscious. Choice and consciousness are one and the same thing.

8. The argumentation can be found in Plato's 'seventh letter', paragraph 31d. It treats the relationship between the philosopher and the Prince, or between the thinker and the politician, and the sum of it all is that the art of ruling over others goes via the art of ruling over oneself (*Phaedrus*, 1973).

9. Symbolic interactionism as it is known today, might be said to be an American product, even though it has been strongly influenced by the European sociological tradition (which stems from Weber) and also by phenomenology and existentialism. That this school (symbolic interactionism) is associated with Chicago is due to the fact that George Herbert Mead lectured at the university of Chicago between 1894 and 1931. Herbert Blumer (one of Mead's students), and Everett Hughes and his colleagues (all principally linked to the university in Chicago) have, on the one hand, attempted to prove the sociological relevance of Mead's thoughts and, on the other hand, argued for the empirical value of the ideas in symbolic interactionism (Hughes, 1961).

10. The problem at issue here is that of the relation between subject and object in epistemological terms. The world which exists independently of us does not exist externally to us. A world about which we have knowledge can only exist if we exist within it, as a part of it. Israel (1979: 31) writes: 'with the discovery of Max Planck of the quantum, physics was plunged into an epistemological crisis. If one carries out certain experiments with light the result will best be explained with the aid of wave motion. This applies, for example, to interference phenomena. Other experiments, for example those examining radiation from bodies, imply that light radiation is conceived of as being discontinuous and thus as particles, so called light quantum or photons. Does light have the character of a wave, or does it consist of photons, i.e. particles. What are we actually speaking about when we speak of "light"?' It was epistemological questions of this kind that confronted quantum physics and that Nigel Bohr, among others, tried to answer. The answer was to come with Werner Heisenberg's discovery of the uncertainty principle. He showed, by experiment, that if one were to attempt to locate, with high precision, the position of a particle at a given moment, one would not be able to learn much about its momentum. Also, inversely, if one were to determine its motion with an equally high precision, it would be impossible to know of its position. It is important, in this context, to emphasise that the fallibility of the measurement does not depend on the measuring instrument, but is rather a consequence of the fact that it is we who carry out the measurements. A more extensive discussion on epistemological problems in quantum physics may be found in Rosenfeld (1964) and in Bohr (1967). I have discussed this problem extensively in a metaphor – *Dialogue in the Tower of Babel* (1981).

11. I refer here primarily to the methods directly derived from the models of the natural sciences and which also have their classics in the social sciences. Comte and Durkheim are two of these. 'Treat social facts as if they were things', says Durkheim. He means that researchers should study social facts which he differentiates from facts about individuals. According to Durkheim, social facts are qualities of communities and they arise like chemical reactions. Durkheim's intention was to demonstrate that social facts differ from

psychological facts and then to define the specific type of phenomenon which sociologists should analyse.

12. It was no mere coincidence that Vincennes was turned into a battlefield between gauchists and communists. This was no doubt precisely what the government intended when they appointed the teaching staff at Vincennes. This was comprised not only of a number of leftist-intellectuals, but also of a significantly large group of teachers with strong communist sympathies and ditto approaches. The battle which broke out between these two groups was largely a result of the polarisation which took place between the groups in question: while the leftist-intellectuals appealed for freedom and the emancipation of thought, the communists appointed themselves as the guardians of the interests of the proletariat. The former were experienced by the latter as the force of anarchy in the hands of the bourgeoisie. The latter were regarded by the former as inhibiting forces of order in the hands of a political ideal, without any value for intellectual thought. Foucault did not partake in these battles. At least not on the terms of the positions taken by the antagonists.

13. Among the first of the new philosophers are André Glucksmann (1975) and Bernard-Henri Levy (1977). These attacked 'the marxist doctrine and the totalitarian social order which is its result'. Nietzsche's ideas occupied a prominent position in this argument. His standpoint as advocate for freedom (rather than fascism and totalitarianism) was rediscovered. This was partly due to Foucault's interpretations of Nietzsche, but also due to his rehabilitation.

14. Friedrich Nietzsche was born on 15 October 1844. His sister Elisabeth, who was later to play a significant part in his life, or rather, after his death, was born two years later. He studied in Leipzig under the philologist Ritschl. He valued the subject highly since it provided him with opportunities to penetrate the Greco-Latin antiquity; but the great fascination came neither from Ritschl nor from philology – it came from his discovery of Schopenhauer (Granier, 1969). However, it was not the latter's theses on the absurdity of existence and on ascetism as a cure which fascinated him the most. Through these studies a theme began to take shape: the struggle for truth (Granier, 1969). This was to be a guiding theme in Nietzsche's work as a whole. His career as a university professor in philology in Basel did not last long. *La Naissance de la tragédie*, which he published in 1871 undermined his career in the academy. Because of this, and due also to his failing health (he was already a sick man at the age of 30), he left his post and lived on his pension. During this time feelings of antipathy towards him emerged and developed due to his criticism of the German Academy and of the Hegelian state and its professed educative role (Andler, 1958). Between 1878 and 1888 he wrote and published nine works and, in addition to this, a number of notes, essays and fragments; some of which were not published until after his death. (1878 *Humain, trop humain* – 1885 *Ainsi parlait Zarathoustra* – 1886 *Par-delà le bien et le mal* – 1887 *La Généalogie de la morale* – 1888 *Le cas Wagner*; *Le crépuscule des idoles*; *L'Antechrist*; *Nietzsche contre Wagner* – *Ecce Homo* was written 1888–89 but was not published until 1908). During this period Nietzsche was able,

time and time again, to raise himself and to write once again, in spite of the repeated aggressive attacks of his illness. But on 3 January 1889, in Torino on Piazza Alberto, he fell ill for good and died eleven years later, 25 August 1900 in Weimar, seriously mentally ill.

A number of intrigues and power games, primarily by Nietzsche's sister, have totally modified and falsified the picture of him handed down to posterity. One can read about this in Granier (1969), Andler (1958) and Blondel (1980). But later, serious critics have been able to re-establish the truth and thus give Nietzsche the restoration he deserves. Karl Schlechta is among those who has worked scrupulously in re-establishing the truth concerning Nietzsche's posthumous (and falsified) works.

The work primarily referred to is *La Volonté de Puissance* (Wille zur Macht) (29th edition, Paris, 1948). The first edition was falsified, compiled and produced by Elisabeth Förster-Nietzsche. It was based upon Nietzsche's fragmentary posthumous notes. She claimed that there *de facto* existed a 'Nietzsche's system' which she gave the pompous title of 'Volonté de Puissance' (Will zur Macht). In addition to this she declared that the natural fate of this 'system' was to become the philosophy of national socialism. She also created a grotesque picture of her brother's personality and works in a thick pensum. For this fraud she was, unfortunately, rewarded with an honoris-causa doctorate (Granier, 1969)! But now everything 'is back in order': the last editions of Nietzsche's work, and the flora of publications which were a result of the debate, have restored the authentic meaning to the texts.

There is nothing in Nietzsche's philosophy in which the fascist and nazi 'ideologies' can find support (Granier, 1969; Andler, 1958; Blondel, 1980; Baroni, 1961; Heidegger, 1961), to name but a few.

15. The search for the origin of things is a running theme in Nietzsche's work. The theme is more explicitly expressed, however, in *La généalogie de la morale* (1887–1964). He defines his work as a scrutiny of the origin of moral premises (Origin or Herkunft). He asks himself, ironically; 'Can God be held responsible for the origin of the Devil?' In *Humain, trop humain* (1879–1943), Nietzsche continues to scrutinise not only morals, but also ascetism, justice and punishment.

16. 'Will to knowledge' appears as a notion in Nietzsche's posthumous essays (1934). He sees it as a necessary phase in man's *Selbstüberwindung* in which he raises himself, no thanks to externally determined factors, but through his own internal strength. This theme is also treated in *Volonté de Puissance* (1948), while *Zarathoustra* (1885–1968) – Nietzsche's mouthpiece – says that 'the will to truth' (le vouloir véridique), must free itself from its bonds and its Gods, its fears and its serfdom (Nietzsche, 1968: 219).

17. Foucault (1971b), in 'Nietzsche, la généalogie, l'histoire', tries to answer the question of why Nietzsche has gradually taken over the position formerly held by Marx in the French intellectual debate:

> It was Nietzsche who specified the power relations as the general focus, shall we say, of philosophical discourse – whereas for Marx it was the

production relation. Nietzsche is the philosopher of power, but he managed to think power without confining himself within a political theory to do so.

CHAPTER FOUR

1. The overestimation of the rationality of organisations is often extreme. Their effectiveness is taken for granted. One speaks of comparisons and analogies since the organisation is associated with a given ideal. This ideal can appear to be acceptable as a model if one is content with merely observing the turn-out or output, as it is promised 'by the model'. Some examples of this point of view can be found in the following works: Reinhard Bendix (1956), *Work and Authority in Industry*. Other classical examples have been discussed by D.S. Pugh, D.J. Hickson and C.R. Hinings (1971), *Writers on Organizations*. In the same book other contiguous theories are discussed, including those of Weber, Woodward, Cyert and March, Simon, the Hawthorne study, the Human Relations Movement but also Argyris, Herzberg, Likert, McGregor, and Blake and Mouton. The point is that beyond the optical illusion of the models there exists a reality of the organisation. The pattern is in fact formed by individuals whose actions constitute the intra-organisational processes. To force these processes into rational models without any empirical relevance is merely a technocratic dream. 'But reality has never been and neither will it ever be like that dream and the fiction' (Crozier and Friedberg, 1977).

2. Many interesting studies have been made of the university environment. Some of these have particularly emphasised the political aspect of the university organisation. March and Olsen (1976), and Holdaway et al. (1975) are some examples.

3. It is perhaps necessary to emphasise here that where I claim to describe the processes in an organisation as political actions, my description differs from, for example, a Marxist perspective which would see the processes in an organisation merely as a reflection of the ongoing class struggle. See for example, Zey-Ferrell (1981), 'Introduction to critiques of dominant perspectives', in Zey-Ferrell and Aiken (1981), *Complex Organizations: Critical Perspectives*. My use of the notion of the political dimension is to draw attention to the strategical actions taken by the actors within the framework of power relationships in organisations.

4. Weber's work to which I refer here is that which was translated into English by Parsons and Henderson: *The Theory of Social and Economic Organization* (Weber, 1947).

5. For some reason Crozier chooses in principle to ignore all research on power that has taken place since Machiavelli and Marx. These are of interest to be sure, but that does not allow us to neglect the many classical works on this subject, such as: Weber (1947), Michel, Lipset et al. (1956), Dahl (1957), and above all the total works of Foucault.

6. The concepts of 'coalition' and of the formation of coalitions have been the objects of many studies, both theoretical and empirical. Among the writers whose works have had a certain preponderance in the studies of organisations

are: Caplow (1968); Gamson (1964); Komorita and Chertkoff (1973); Lawler and Youngs (1975); Murnighan (1978); and Stryker (1972).

CHAPTER FIVE

1. The definition appearing in Bennis et al. seems representative of the way that power studies have been orientated in organisation theory. This definition is to be found in the article: 'Authority, power and the ability to influence', *Human Relations*, 11: 143–156; it reads as follows: 'Authority is the potentiality to influence based on a position, whereas power is the actual ability of influence based on a number of factors including, of course, organizational position' (Bennis et al., 1958: 144).

2. Hobbes and Machiavelli are perhaps two of the most significant thinkers to have paved the way for the emergence of a political theory by shifting the focal point in the discussion from God to that which is 'here and now' (the Actual). The ideas of interest, action and 'The Power of Man' have been developed by Hobbes primarily in *Leviathan* (1651), which has been republished in 1958 by Schneider, and in 1962 by M. Oakshott. The concept of 'The Power of Man' is also mentioned in *The Element of Law* (1650) published in 1889 by F. Tönnies, also in *English Works*, published by Sir William Molesworth (1839).

   Hobbes argues 'metaphysically' for the concepts of *interest* and *honour*, which means that they may be used even externally to Hobbes' discourse. We must bear in mind, however, that Hobbes' conception of power is causal. He writes: 'Power and Cause are the same thing. Correspondent to cause and effect are POWER and ACT; nay, those and these are the same things' (Hobbes, *English Works*, X, 1839: 127).

   Moreover, Hobbes maintains, power can be expressed metaphorically in terms of movement (motion). In this sense, and disengaged from the metaphysical discussion, Hobbes suggests that both interest and honour (the striving for these) might be seen as the motion of Power. He spreads the idea, via his metaphorical 'State of Nature', of a metaphilosophical discourse: *science*. To do this he parenthesises any conceivable value of the history of society, especially the history of political philosophy. This is rejected as vulgar, false and irrelevant (*The Elements of Law*). It shall, he says, be replaced by science, the premises of which are composed of the praxis of the discourse which, in turn, forms the basis for the possibility of reason (For *reason . . .* is nothing but reckoning, *Leviathan*, 1958: 46).

   > By this it appears that reason is not, as sense and memory, born with us, nor gotten by experience only, as prudence is, but attained by industry: first in apt imposing of names, and secondly by getting a good and orderly method in proceeding from the elements, which are names, to assertions made by connection of one of them to another, and so to syllogisms, which are the connections of one assertion to another, till we come to a knowledge of all the consequences of names appertaining to the subject in

hand; and that is it men call SCIENCE. And whereas sense and memory are but knowledge of fact, which is a thing past and irrevocable, *Science* is the knowledge of consequences and dependence of one fact upon another, by which out of that we can presently do, we know to do something else when we will, or the like another time; because when we see how any thing comes about, upon what causes and by what manner, when the like causes come into our power, we see how to make it produce the life effects. (Hobbes, *Leviathan*, 1958: 49)

Hobbes conducts an absolutistic argument when working with the idea of a philosophical science whose object would be some kind of linguistic truth: the logical propositions. In order to do this, however, Hobbes is literally 'forced' to exercise power over the discourse. According to Hobbes there must first be order in the social theory if one is to find order in the social reality. The former might be accomplished by the establishment of some sort of metadiscourse, as in mathematics or in geometry, about which everyone is in agreement and on the basis of which one might articulate theories and statements. 'The first author of speech was God himself', writes Hobbes (*Leviathan*, 1958: 37). He maintains that we can reconstruct order 'through contract and convention'. Man must refrain from acting as if he were God. He must surrender to a ruler who has sole right over the discourse. Hobbes' solution for society seems more like a fiction than something that is realisable. This fiction seems nevertheless to have left visible tracks in modern political theories that have as their common denominator the concept of power (Zeraffa, 1976; Blais, 1974, etc.).

3. The social sanctions referred to here are those which Hobbes, in *Leviathan*, calls *common power* and which could be said to be the equivalent in social contexts of what Adam Smith's *invisible hand* is in economic contexts. According to Macpherson, Hobbes' 'state of nature [is] a hypothetical state in which men with . . . natures formed by living in civilized society, would necessarily find themselves if there were no common power able to overgive them all' (Macpherson, 1962: 18–19).

4. Crozier and Friedberg (1977) have developed the idea of organisational members being involved in a game-like process where a limited number of winning strategies are focalised. If the members are to attain these strategies they must partake in the game; but in order to be able to play they must respect the rules of the game.

5. Situations in which actions are impelled by a logic of their own have been the object of numerous studies. Sceptics and technocratic dreamers call these processes metaphysical phenomena which take place on the borders of rationality. To more realistic researchers, who do not give priority to models at the expense of reality, these processes are empirical, of relevance to reality, and a part of every day life. According to Weick (1976), decisions can often be made without this implying that one is able, from an analytical standpoint, to tie the various activities together to form a 'rational process'. It is a question of *loosely composed decision processes* and *loosely connected systems*. The activities in these processes have their own dynamics which are not dependent

upon, for instance, the intentions of the decision-makers. Robinson and Majak (1967) might also be recommended in this context. There are also studies that have devoted attention to political events whose development seems to have followed its own course rather than being the result of 'rational deliberations'. Giovanitti and Freed (1962) present the example of the American atom bomb attack against Japan. Even if President Truman and his colleagues had wanted to call off the attack on Japan, this would not have been possible since the technical preparations were so far advanced. In fact, up until the last minute they sat discussing the pros and cons of the attack. Similar phenomena have been studied in different contexts: in the military arms race by Schilling (1967) and in local government politics by Coleman (1957), Long (1958), and Olsen (1970), to mention but a few.

Loosely coupled decision processes are usually related to studies of *organised anarchy*. In Cohen et al. (1972) these are situations where decision-making may be likened to a mosaic of various types of ongoing organisational activities, including those which do not seem to have anything to do with the actual decision. According to Cohen and March (1974) and March and Olsen (1976) the decision process can be likened to a *garbage can* into which participants throw various types of problems and solutions as they arise. The mixture of garbage in a specific can depends on which cans are available, which designations are to be found on the alternative cans, which types of garbage are being produced at the time, and, in addition to this, the speed with which the garbage is fetched and removed from the site.

6. Dahl readily sees power as a question of *cause and effect*. From the point of view of method he has as his basis John Stuart Mill's 'Method of difference': If party B does x when party A does y but not when party A does y^1, then A has power over B'. The extent of power depends on the specific probability that B does x (instead of x^1) when A does y versus when A does y^1. This constitutes an extreme and exaggerated mechanistic view of a phenomenon which is actually highly abstract and evasive.

7. The reason that I have chosen to take up the definitions of these authors in particular is that they have a common denominator inasmuch as they see power as a dimension of people's interactions – as opposed to others who insist upon regarding power as a structural characteristic which stands entirely on its own and which is independent of the actors involved in interactions.

8. Both influence and authority, which is perhaps an expression of the primitive conceptualisation of power, have, since Weber, been related to power yet without any distinction between form and content. As a result great confusion prevails in the literature as regards the relations between these concepts. Peabody (1964) has reviewed these, and comes to the conclusion that researchers have considered authority and influence in three different ways: (1) there are those who would place them on a par with each other, (2) there are others who say that power is equal to influence and that authority is a special case of power, (3) a third wing sees authority and influence as two separate dimensions.

Peabody himself gives the designation of authority to all the forms, contents and manifestations of power in organisations. This is, to my mind, a primitive way of conceptualising power. At another end we have, for example, Lawrence and Lorsch (1967), who refer to all types of power in organisations as influence.

9. The representatives of this view are numerous; among others a number of sociologists with political schooling might be mentioned. For example: Hunter (1953); Pellegrini and Coates (1956); Schulze (1958). Even pluralists such as Dahl (1957) might be said to uphold this view. Those who relate power to the structures as one of their particular characteristics are, above all, the Marxists or those who, methodologically speaking, approach power studies from a Marxist perspective – Clegg (1977, 1979a,b); Carchedi (1977); Williams (1960).

10. It would perhaps be appropriate to give a short specification of the notions *interdependent and dependent relations*. I use interdependency when referring to two or more interactors. I use the term dependent relations when speaking, as is the case in this instance, from the point of view of one of the parties. Emerson (1962, 1972b) and Blau (1964) are perhaps the ones to have discussed the most extensively the aspect of dependency in what they call 'the power-depending theory'. According to them, power is a function of dependency. This implicates a causal reasoning which has, to my mind, too little if any relevance in social contexts. One might, in the best of cases, speak of multi-causality, but hardly of simple causal relationships. Moreover, they associate dependency with 'power bases', which has been strongly criticised by, for instance, Gergen (1969) and Homans (1974). To associate dependency with 'power bases' is to implicate the view of both power and the 'creation' of dependency as attributes.

11. Bacharach and Lawler (1980: 44) present a valuable review of statements in this field and suggest a compilation with emphasis on the contrast between the concepts of authority and influence:

> Authority is the static, structural aspect of power in organizations; influence is the dynamic, tactical element.
> Authority is the formal aspect of power; influence is the informal aspect.
> Authority refers to the formally sanctioned right to make final decisions; influence is not sanctioned by the organizations and is, therefore, not a matter of organizational rights.
> Authority implies involuntary submission by subordinates; influence implies voluntary submission and does not necessarily entail a superior–subordinate relationship.
> Authority flows downward and is unidirectional; influence is multidirectional and can flow upward, downward, or horizontally. The source of authority is solely structural; the source of influence may be personal characteristics, expertise, or opportunity. Authority is circumscribed, that is the domain, scope and legitimacy are typically ambiguous.

12. Among the authors who argue for the significance of power for the understanding of organisations are: Blau (1964); Berle (1967); Bachrach and Baratz (1962); Bourricaud (1961); Cartwright (1959, 1965); Clegg (1975, 1979a,b); Crozier (1964a,b); Crozier and Friedberg (1977); Dahl (1957,

1968); Emerson (1962); Etzioni (1961, 1969); French and Raven (1960); Gamson (1968); March (1966); Parsons (1956, 1960, 1965); Wrong (1968).

Among earlier works the most important are: Barnard (1938); Bierstedt (1950, 1963); Lasswell and Kaplan (1950); Newmann (1950). The works of Max Weber remain classics while the entire works of Foucault might be seen as the most original contributions in this field. His work is of particular interest for this study.

13. The idea comes from Nietzsche, *La Généalogie de la Morale* (1964) (written and published 1887). Foucault is, to a great extent, influenced by Nietzsche. I attempt to elucidate this relationship in Chapters Three and Six. The problem posed by Nietzsche in the book concerns the *value* of established values and the social and cultural conditions rendering possible their development and acceptance. In order to discuss these values, Nietzsche goes 'over to the other side of the mirror' and looks at the *opposition, the outer territory* of the values; at everything that appears against the background of their mere existence.

14. Action as a concept and as a phenomenon in man's existence is the object of the cogitations of various categories of thinkers and philosophers: from Aristotle 'L'étique à nicomaque' to the contemporary advocates of, on the one hand, analytic philosophy (primarily Anglo-Saxon) and, on the other hand, the continental philosophy (primarily French/German). I have stressed the point that I base my argument on the French/German tradition. The two traditions are not, however, irreconcilable. Nevertheless, it might be appropriate to give some indications here with regard, primarily, to my standpoint in relation to the discourse of action.

Ricoeur (1977) differentiates between the philosophy of action and the science of action. This differentiation is due to certain disciplines within the social sciences also having their own discourses of action. As far as the philosophy of action is concerned, it is *ethics* which is in the centre. The teachings of Aristotle culminate in a practical philosophy, and the discourse of action, in this sense, becomes an 'ethico-practical discourse'. For Kant, for example, 'the criticism of the practical reason' is constituted by that theory (or those principles) which determines the *will*. Yet the principle which would be able, *a priori*, to determine will, is *moral*. This implies that the theory of the practical reason is reduced to the relation between *freedom* and *moral*. The continental version of the philosophy of action is not content with merely being an epistemology of the science of action; i.e. of behavioural science for psychologists, and of social conditions for sociologists. The philosophy of action that is represented by Heidegger, Sartre, Merleau-Ponty, Ricoeur, etc., is concerned with that which precedes the actual ethic; a 'conceptual' analysis is then suggested; i.e. an analysis of the concept which endues the action with a meaning from the point of view of the actor. These concepts are intention, interest/motive, finality, responsibility. To these Sartre adds: freedom and will. The Anglo-Saxon tradition is concerned rather with the 'post-ethic', so to speak, of action and its analysis is directed towards the 'propositional' level, i.e. the linguistic sentences which state (or the linguistic sentences argue for) an action. In this tradition, Anscombe (1958) and von Wright (1971) are the main figures. Wittgenstein's work forms one of the bases of the Anglo-Saxon approach in general and of 'action language' and 'action semantics' in particular.

15. Much attention has been devoted within both the analytic and the phenomenological/existential schools of philosophy to the concept of intention. Anscombe (1957), who represents the former and who works in the tradition of Wittgenstein, has conducted a sort of 'mosaic-discussion' of the concept in a philosophical text; 'intention', without any introduction, and without a conclusion, but with a potent 'topographic logic' (Ricoeur, 1977: 41). The concept of intention seems to be treated by Anscombe as a grammatic type, in the sense that 'the base' of the intentions is not a proof but a motive: not an answer to the question 'why should anything be true?', but 'why should anything be good, pleasant, desirable, etc.?'. According to Sartre the concept can only be seen in relation to man's being and his consciousness.

16. The idea here is similar to what Anscombe sees as the answer to the question: 'Why should anything be good?'. The difference between Anscombe's and Sartre's approaches lies in that Sartre goes one step further back and discusses the origin of the question itself.

CHAPTER SIX

1. The concept of *deconstruction* is used here in the confined sense of the discursive context. By the deconstruction of the discourse I mean the analysis of the same against the background of its own origin. This set aside, one might say that deconstruction is a method which has, in the main, been developed as a reaction against the tendencies within structuralist thought that imply that the discourse produces statements about itself (Derrida, 1967). Jacques Derrida is perhaps the major representative of this 'antistructuralist criticism'. Derrida shows in his book, *Glas* (1974) how Hegel's text, with its totalitarian tone – as opposed to Genet's text – 'constitutes a loop' which becomes a parody of itself. I personally get the same feeling when reading Levy (1977), *La barbarie à visage humain*; the message of the text, *the constitutive*, is one big antitotalitarian scream, the purpose of which is to warn us against the sneaking, destructive taming and objectivising collectivism whereby our individualism, our dignity, and, in short, our essence as beings is kneaded to an unrecognisable lump. The *constituent*, however, the text *per se*, is so totalitarian and its message consequently propounded with such force, that the liberating effect of the message is transformed into a threatening monster. But the method of deconstruction is also used, to a large extent, in literary contexts, as for example in Sollers and Barthes (see also Bloom, 1973, 1975, 1976, 1977). Seen from a broader perspective it is evident that both Foucault and Nietzsche have contributed, with their critical examinations of Western thought, to the development of the method of deconstruction: Foucault discloses the identity of our thinking and Nietzsche explores the ultimate origin of our morals. One might say that what deconstruction boils down to is a conscious reading of the text, but which must, naturally, be critical. The

criticism is not to be aimed at the logic or internal consistency of the text but rather at the mentality with which it is permeated, or at the original premises of the text. There is one problem, however, that is still taken up for debate by the advocates of this method: how are others to read the texts of the *deconstructors*? For further acquaintance with this subject see *Deconstruction: Theory and Practice*, Christopher Norris (1982). Norris presents a well-thought-out summary of the difficult work of Derrida along with de Man's (1969, 1979) contribution to the development of this approach.

2. Dahl (1957) writes that scientists have not yet formulated a statement of the concept of power that is rigorous enough to be of use in the systematic study of this important social phenomenon. Hickson et al. (1971); Tedeschi (1974) and many others, maintain that a major problem, as regards the study of power in organisations, is that people do not dare to discuss it, or they avoid discussing it. To this one might add the predisposition of the researchers towards positivism, and their preferences for working with variables that are quantifiable and measurable.

3. The concept of *rationality* is highly controversial within the social sciences. It came to light primarily in the discourse of the Enlightenment philosophers of the 18th century. These believed in the reasoning capacity of man and further developed Descartes' search for the truth. Today the concept is used in different ways and in various contexts, and also in daily speech. Normally, one speaks of rationality as if it were a God-given absolute; a set of criteria in relation to which a judgement is made as to whether an action is in some way 'right' or 'wrong'. The concept is used in the social sciences of today as *a priori* assumption for the explanation of certain economical and political phenomena (e.g. Downs, 1957; Krupp, 1966) on the one hand, and, on the other hand, as a basis upon which to compare modes of thought of people in different cultures (e.g. Wilson, 1970). Simon (1947) attempted to introduce, by suggesting the concept of 'limited rationality', a theory which would be closer to the empirical reality. Simon and his colleagues developed this theory as a reaction against the exaggerated assumptions of a total rationality which was to be found in traditional political economics. They felt that it had no empirical relevance. The majority of organisation theorists, at least among those who have treated the concept in their statements, further develop Weber's (1947) two principal typologies: rational behaviour in relation to a goal and rational behaviour in relation to a value. Recently, some organisations researchers, e.g. Crozier and Friedberg (1977), have begun to speak of a rationality of the individual. This means that each individual acts, no matter how he/she may do so, in accordance with his/her own rationality; i.e. own motives, own interest. A contiguous concept might be the logic of action of the individual (Karpik, 1978; Daudi and Alvesson, 1983). The fact remains, however, that the concept is highly controversial and is imbued with different meaning. Garfinkel (1974) has found more than fourteen different interpretations of the concept within the social sciences.

4. Dahl is no doubt one of the strongest *authorities of delimitation* (instances de délimitation) as regards the production and dissemination of the primitive discourse of power. His definition and conceptualisation of power is to be

found in the writings of many other researchers of power. He sums up his overall idea as follows:

> What is the intuitive idea we are trying to capture? I stand on a street corner and say to myself, 'I command all automobile drivers on this street to drive on the right side of the road'; suppose further that all the drivers actually do as I 'command' them to do, still, most people will regard me as mentally ill if I insist that I have enough power over automobile drivers to compel them to use the right side of the road. On the other hand, suppose a policeman is standing in the middle of an intersection at which most traffic moves as he orders it to do, then it accords with what I conceive to be the bedrock idea of power to say that the policeman acting in this particular role evidently has the power to make automobile drivers turn right or left rather than go ahead. My intuitive idea of power, then, is something like this: A has power over B to the extent that he can get B to do something that B would not otherwise do (Dahl, 1957: 203).

Although this does intimate the existence of a power relation it does not provide us with a definition or an understanding of the phenomenon of power. Dahl maintains that power manifests itself in the form of changes in behaviour. If the cause lies with A and the change of behaviour with B, then we say that A has power over B. This implicates numerous assumptions, the most essential of which being that (1) power is associated with an individual; it is his/her own property, and that (2) there exists a causal relationship between A and B. This, in turn, implicates a fundamentally mechanistic view of power. Dahl goes on to discuss the difficulties concerned with the concept of power. Most probably because he is not quite satisfied with his own definitions. A mechanistic conceptualisation of power can only lead to some kind of 'no-man's land' which puts an end to all future understanding of the concept.

> A thing to which people attach many labels with subtly or grossly different meanings in many different cultures and times is probably not a thing at all but many things, there are students of the subject, . . . who think that because of this the whole study of 'power' is a bottomless swamp (Dahl, 1957: 201).

5. In a previous article, 'Power as organizing concept' (Daudi, 1984), I have discussed some aspects of the eternal dichotomy that has characterised the research of power since the time of the Hebrew prophets up until today. In this long-lasting polemics power has been, time and time again, conceptualised as an attribute and as a property due to the prevailing ideology and ritual which sees in power a means of coercion, dominance and repression. On the conservative side power has been portrayed as if it were the exercise of a necessary and legitimate authority, while the critics depict it as if it were a misuse and oppression of human potential (Daudi, 1980).

The functionalists. Talcott Parsons and his pupil Kingsley Davis can, with all certainty, be regarded as the leading functionalists who have provided the most detailed presentations of their notions of the distribution of power. Both attack the problem from a perspective which encompasses society as a whole and considers the problem to be 'a necessary trait in every properly functioning society' (Gamson, 1968). Davis (1949: 367) sums up the functionalist view as follows: 'Social inequality is thus a consciously developed pattern, whereby society ensures that the most important functions are consciously assumed by the most important people.' This is then the essence of the standpoint adopted by the functionalists: the distribution of power, and subsequently inequality, is something which emerges from the needs of society and not from the needs and desires of the individual.

Parsons' view of the subject differs from that of Davis in form rather than in content. He assumes, in every human society, a presence of collectively embraced values. Inasmuch as the values originate in the society's needs, and inasmuch as the fundamental needs of society are more or less alike, these values then also tend to be the same throughout the world. That which differs from one society to the next is the relative order of rank of these values. Effectivity may be evaluated higher in one society than stability, whereas in another society the reverse may be true, but, every society is forced to evaluate both effectivity and stability. Parsons (in Bendix, 1956: 92–126) maintains that the stratification system in each society is an expression of the system of values in that society. The positions which people occupy (and the remunerations which they receive) are a function of the extent to which their qualities, achievements and possessions correspond to the standards established by their society. Since people, with necessity, differ in these respects, inequality is inevitable.

Many authors have attempted to constitute a theory of organisations on the basis of the general functionalist theory. Parsons (1956) and Merton (1957) might be mentioned here, among others. They use two classic concepts: the 'normative integration' of action, and 'role' concepts. This approach was, at the time, valuable, as it rendered possible a better interpretation than the one provided by the rational model. Perhaps their greatest contribution was in showing how individuals are shaped by the norms and standards of their roles, and how these roles are then reinforced by expectations. It is less certain, however, as to whether this approach would be of value in the focusing of power relations in organisational contexts. The functionalist theory seems to be based upon a conceptualisation of roles that is far too mechanistic. It is precisely on this point that it has been most widely criticised. Crozier and Friedberg (1977: 83–86) say, for example, that organisational actors seldom meet up to the expectations which they have of each other, as regards their respective roles. It might be added here that the possibility to deviate from the expectations and norms associated with these roles is, in fact, in the context of power relations, a 'source of power' which serves to expand the individual's space of action. The predicament of being 'closed in' in a role implies that the actor is clearly in a weak position *vis à vis* the others, since his actions then become entirely predictable.

The conflict theorists. In contrast to the functionalists, they have the individual and the various groups in society as their point of departure when they consider the problem of the distribution of power. It is here a matter of the needs and desires of the individual, rather than the needs of society as a whole. The difference between the two schools comes most clearly to the fore in the attitudes of their members towards power as a phenomenon.

The dualism in the approaches of these schools is relatively obvious. While the functionalists emphasise those interests which are shared by the members of a given society, the conflict theorists underline the interests which separate them. While the one school lays emphasis upon the shared advantages that emerge through social relations, the other school stresses the elements of domination and exploitation. Whereas the one group emphasises consensus as a basis for the social entity, the other group underlines force. Whereas the one group considers human societies to be systems, the other sees them as stages of the ongoing power struggle. Dahrendorf (1959) points out that society, like Janus, has two faces, and that the functionalists and the conflict theorists are quite simply looking at two sides of the 'same reality'.

The pluralists and the elitists. The radical and the conservative ideals are perhaps most apparent in the pluralist and the elitist theories. The discussion is primarily held on an ideological level, but in both cases the concept of power holds a central position. The pluralists have generally political scientists affiliation while the elitists are mainly represented by sociologists. During the 1960s potent polemics put these two blocks in opposition to each other. The point of departure for these polemics was probably the debate developed in the United States around 'The Community Power Debate' and which was articulated in, among others, Dahl's book *Who Governs?* and in Mill's book *The Power Elite.* Other pluralist studies have been carried out by, for example, Long and Belknap (1956) and Sayre and Kaufman (1960). Among the elitists we may mention Hunter (1953); Pelligrini and Coates (1956) and Schulze (1958). The elitists maintain that a ranked power structure is to be found in all human institutions as an integrated part of their essence. This postulate is naturally rejected by the pluralists who claim that:

> Nothing categorial can be assumed about power in any community. . . . If anything, there seems to be an unspoken notion among pluralist researchers that at the bottom nobody dominates in a town, so that their first question is not likely to be, 'who runs this community?' The first query is somewhat like, 'Have you stopped beating your wife?', in that virtually any response short of total unwillingness to answer will supply the researchers with a 'power elite' along the lines presupposed by the stratification theory (Polsby, in Bachrach and Baratz, 1962: 948).

Another elitist postulate rejected by the pluralists is that power structures tend to be stable through time:

> Pluralists hold that power may be tied to issues, and issues can be fleeting or persistent, provoking coalitions among interested groups and citizens, ranging in their duration from momentary to semi-permanent . . . to presume that the set of coalitions which exists in the community at any given time is a timelessly stable aspect of structure is to introduce systematic inaccuracies into one's description of social reality (Bachrach and Baratz, 1962: 940).

The third objection to the elitist model is that it places 'reputed' power on a par with actual power:

> If a man's major life work is banking, the pluralists presume he will spend his time at the bank, and not in manipulating community decisions. This presumption holds until the banker's activities and participations indicate otherwise. . . . If we presume that the banker is 'really' engaged in running the community, there is practically no way of disconfirming this notion, even if it is totally erroneous. On the other hand, it is easy to spot the banker who really does run community affairs when we presume he does not, because his activities will make this act apparent. (Bachrach and Baratz, 1962: 949)

The pluralists, in contrast to the elitists, concentrate on the exercising of power, rather than on the sources of power:

> Power to them means 'participation in decision making' and can be analysed only after 'careful examination of a series of concrete decisions'. (Bachrach and Baratz, 1962: 950)

They maintain that the power structure cannot merely be studied on the basis of the actual decisions made. *Non-decisions* must also be taken into consideration, since power may be manifested, within certain groups, more in that which they are able to prevent; that is, the production of non-decisions, than in that which they are able to actualise. They regard power as an extremely controversial and evasive phenomenon for which neither the elitists nor the pluralists have been able to provide a satisfactory explanation:

> The concept of power remains elusive despite the recent and prolific outpourings of case studies on community power. Its elusiveness is dramatically demonstrated by the regularity of disagreement as to the locus of community power between the sociologists and the political scientists. Sociologically oriented researchers have consistently found that power is highly centralized, while scholars trained in political science have just as regularly concluded that in 'their' communities power is widely diffused. Presumably, this explains why the later group styles itself 'pluralist', its counterpart 'elitists'. (Bachrach and Baratz, 1962: 947)

6. Power researchers with positivist preferences and research ideals, have, over the years, developed a number of measuring indices or variables to be focused on the 'actual' observable effect of power. Dahl (1957: 203) mentions some of these variables: 'the base of Power; the means of Power; the amount of Power; the scope of Power'. In his literature review, Cartwright (1965: 4) discerned three main categories: 'the agent exerting influence, the method of exerting influence, the agent subjected to influence'. There are, of course, a number of other variables, but they do not notably differ from those mentioned above. After a thorough review of 'Statements about Power' Gustafsson (1979: 340) states: 'It seems impossible to identify any theories of power in the real sense of the word.'

7. Gustafsson (1979: 71) writes in this context that:

Although the causes of power might lie in that the possessor of power has 'control' over various resources, various values, it is manifested in the form of behavioural changes. As a consequence of the general scientific hypothesis that nothing emerges from nothingness nor disappears into nothingness – which Bunge (1967, I, s 295) calls 'the principle of non magic' – we search for a cause for every behavioural change. If the cause of a change in behaviour of B lies with A then we say that A has had power over B. This outlook forms the basis of Dahl's view of power, according to which A has power over B to the extent that he is able to persuade B to act in a way that he otherwise would not do. In this way Dahl ignores the causes of power and the actual process of influence and instead devotes his attention to the *measurement* of the empirically observable power – that is, established influence. The approach is therefore highly empirical. Nonetheless, it suffers from weaknesses.

Dahl goes on to present an operational definition of 'the amount of power' so as finally to shape the concept of power empirically and statistically (Dahl, 1957: 205). The definition depicts a *static* power relation, yet causal. This mode of thought illustrated here by Dahl's model is not isolated but rather fairly widespread among researchers of power.

8. The period between the 16th and 17th centuries is identified by Foucault as a turning point, particularly in England, with regard to the emergence of a new form for the will to find the truth. While the *rationalism* of Descartes was predominant on the continent, an entirely different philosophical outlook was gradually to emerge in England. Europe was soon divided, philosophically speaking, into two large, almost geographically delimited, parts. The other philosophy, in contrast to rationalism, was called *empiricism*. The basic idea of empiricism is that *reason*, ratio, is not in itself a source of knowledge. Typical of the English empiricism is that it is much simpler in its argument than the rationalism of the continent. It refrains from subtle discussion and cogitations, and deals, instead, with the problems in a self-evident manner. But empiricism has had (and indeed still does have) a great deal of success as regards the tackling of concrete and material problems, and this has been (and still is) of much use for the 'practical sciences'. Also typical for the English empiricism, however, is that it has, since the beginning of its career, 'warned against the sources of error' with regard to knowledge. These admonitions may still be felt and experienced today, and they often have an inhibiting effect on the creative production of knowledge. Francis Bacon scanned these warnings in his work on the theory of knowledge, *Novum Organon*, which was a criticism of Aristotle's 'Organon'. Bacon warns, in the first instance, against the four different types of prejudices which inevitably lead the knowledge astray. These are the sources of error from the philosophical tradition (he has in mind the philosophy of Aristotle); the source of error from language; the sources of error from human attitudes and, finally, those prejudices and sources of error which arise from one's personal experiences. One must free oneself from these prejudices; one must, according to the empiricists, become objective by disregarding one's own opinion. It is a

confounding thought that these admonitions are still alive today and are even taken seriously in social contexts. The theories of knowledge according to empiricism were further specified in Locke's *Essay Concerning Human Understanding* (1690). *Reason* is for Locke a *tabula rasa*; that is, an erased table upon which experiences from immediate observations are to be written (Francois Chatelet, vol. 2, 1972).

9. In *Criticism and Growth of Knowledge* (Imre Lakatos and Alan Musgrave, 1979, eds.) a number of thinkers deal with and discuss Popper's *The Logic of Scientific Discovery* (1959a) and Kuhn's *Structure of Scientific Revolution* (1962), as well as the ways in which these have influenced (and do influence) the production of scientific knowledge in the Western world.

In his article 'Falsification and the Methodology of Scientific Research Programmes' (1970, revised in 3rd edition 1974: 91–96), Imre Lakatos ardently attacks the reductionist mode of thought whose contributions to the development of science he considers worthless. 'They do not add up to a genuine research programme and are, on the whole, worthless.' He comments on Meehl's *Theory Testing in Psychology and Physics* (1967) and Lykken's *Statistical Significance in Psychological Research* (1968), who also attack the reductionism of knowledge production.

> After reading Meehl (1967) and Lykken (1968) one wonders whether the function of statistical techniques in the social sciences is not primarily to provide a machinery for producing *phoney corroborations and thereby a semblance of 'scientific progress'* where, in fact, there is nothing but an increase in *pseudointellectual garbage*. Meehl writes that 'in the physical sciences, the usual result of an improvement in experimental design, instrumentation, or numerical mass of data, is to increase the difficulty of the "observational hurdle" which the physical theory of interest must successfully surmount; whereas, in psychology and some of the allied behaviour sciences the usual effect of such improvement in experimental precision is to provide an easier hurdle for the theory to surmount.' Or, as Lykken put it: 'Statistical significance (in psychology) is perhaps the least important attribute of a good experiment; it is never a sufficient condition for claiming that a theory has been usefully corroborated, that a meaningful empirical fact has been established, or that an experimental report ought to be published.' It seems to me that theorizing condemned by Meehl and Lykken may be *ad hoc*. Thus the methodology of research programmes might help us in devising laws for stemming this *intellectual pollution* which may destroy our cultural environment even earlier than industrial and traffic pollution destroys our physical environment. (Imre Lakatos, 1974: 176)

10. I refer, in the main, to the philosophies of action as *one* tradition, despite the specific differences between them: *the existentialists* with, for example, Sartre; *the pragmatists* with, for example, Peirce (1935–58) and Dewey (e.g. 1938); and *the analytic philosophers* with the tradition inspired and initiated by Wittgenstein (1953, 1961). As representative of this latter tradition one might mention Louch (1966); Taylor (1964, 1967); Anscombe (1958); Hampshire

(1959); Ryle (1949), etc. The analytic approach differs from the first two in that it 'ignores' the continental philosophy of the 1800s and its argument against rationalism and empiricism. In spite of these differences, however, there is still general agreement on one matter: namely the deviation from Descartes' ontological duality between body and soul, from the method which was deemed capable of leading man to the ultimate truth as well as from the view according to which true knowledge is that knowledge which in a clear and complete manner grasps a *determined* reality (see Peirce's collected papers from 1869 in Hartshorne and Weiss, 1931–1935, vols I–VI, and in Burk's 1958 vols VII–VII; see also Sartre, 1943, 1960, 1983).

11. In the previous chapter I attempted to give a 'description' of the concept of freedom, which as such is contrary to the meaning of the concept. I have also argued for the idea that when speaking of freedom in general, we are in fact only able to speak of our own freedom in particular. Sartre outlines how we might conceive of freedom as a concept; a concept to explain and discuss.

> To be sure, I could not describe a freedom which would be common to both the other and myself; I could not therefore contemplate an essence of freedom. On the contrary, it is freedom which is the foundation of all essences by surpassing the world toward his own possibilities. But actually the question is *my* freedom. Similarly when I described consciousness, I could not discuss a nature common to certain individuals but only my particular consciousness, which like my freedom is beyond essence, or – as we have shown with considerable repetition – for which *to be* is to have been. I discussed this consciousness so as to touch it in its very existence as a particular experience – the *cogito*. Husserl and Descartes, as Gaston Berger has shown, demand that the *cogito* release to them a *truth as essence*: with Descartes we achieve the connection of two simple natures; with Husserl we grasp the eidetic structure of consciousness.[3] But if in consciousness its existence must percede its essence, then both Descartes and Husserl have committed an error. What we can demand from the *cogito* is only that it discover for us a factual necessity. It is also to the *cogito* that we appeal in order to determine freedom as the freedom which is *ours*, as a pure factual necessity; that is, as a contingent existent but one which I *am not able* not to experience. I am indeed an existent who *learns* his freedom through his acts, but I am also an existent whose individual and unique existence temporalizes itself as freedom. As such I am necessarily a consciousness [of] freedom since nothing exists in consciousness except as the nonthetic consciousness of existing. Thus my freedom is perpetually in question in my being; it is not a quality added on or a *property* of my nature. It is very exactly the stuff of my being: and as in my being, my being is in question, I must necessarily possess a certain comprehension of freedom. (1977: 438–439)

Note [3], Gaston Berger: 'Le Cogito chez Husserl et chez Descartes' 1940.

12. A number of interesting attempts are to be found that at least acknowledge the relational dimension of power: these are Bittner (1965), Goldman (1976),

Benson (1977), Burrell and Morgan (1979), Wrong (1979) and, above all, Giddens (1979), who deals with the necessity of relating the concept of power to the concept of action. He does not, however, mean by this that power is reflected in actions and that our analysis must therefore be directed towards these. On the other hand he claims that power might be considered as being 'the transformative capacity of human action' (Giddens, 1979: 92) and this is of some relevance here. He argues, furthermore, for the fruitfulness of focusing on the relational aspects of power: 'power is between'.

13. A concept which might be regarded as contiguous to that of *negative dynamics* is that of counter-intuitive *effects* or *perverse effects* (Forrester, 1970). This is really no more than a 're-discovery' of 'the unexpected effects' which Merton (1936) discussed in his well-known article 'the unanticipated consequences of purposive social action'. At the present time a number of contributions in this field are to be found, for example, in France with Sainsaulieu (1965); Sainsaulieu and Kergoat (1968); Grémion (1977).

14. I refer here to the traditional theory of organisations; i.e. the classical and neo-classical schools, but also to a certain extent the school inspired by systems theory. (See for example, Berg and Daudi, 1982; Clegg and Dunkerley, 1980; Alvesson, 1983; Jackson and Morgan, 1978). In recent years, that is from the middle of the 1970s, interesting tendencies have developed which embrace the concepts of action (Weick, 1976; Crozier and Friedberg, 1977), and psychodynamics (de Board, 1978; Berg, 1979; Lévy, 1969; Lourau, 1969, 1970) and, from a broader perspective, the history of organisation as a phenomenon, i.e. as a form of organisation against the background of the socio-political, economic and cultural aspects. This tendency is illustrated by Karpik (1972a,b,c, 1977, 1978) (see also Daudi and Alvesson, 1983). These modern tendencies do not treat the phenomenon of power in an explicit manner but they do, on the other hand, conceptualise the organisational processes in the light of the actions, personal logic and rationality of the individuals. They may thus be said to be fruitful tendencies opening up new perspectives.

15. Apart from his interest for the criteria of a good theory, Kuhn also devotes some attention to the choosing by the researcher of one theory in preference to another. He has written a note (6) in connection with the quoted excerpt that reads as follows:

> (6) The last criterion, fruitfulness, deserves more emphasis than it has yet received. A scientist choosing between two theories ordinarily knows that his decision will have a bearing on his subsequent research career. Of course he is especially attracted by a theory that promises the concrete successes for which scientists are ordinarily rewarded (note (6) in Kuhn, 1977: 322).

16. Kuhn's (1977) concept of simplicity should not be taken literally as 'simple' or 'easy'. In that case the models 'A–B' might also be described as 'easy', yet they do not throw much light on the nature of power. What Kuhn means by simplicity is rather a quality of a theory which, through the elucidation and

explanation of an otherwise diffuse phenomenon, makes it simple, i.e. understandable.

17. This sentence was said by Plato to Dionysios, the ruler of Cyracusa. Instead of giving him normative advice as to how he *ought* to reorganise the state and govern his people, he speaks to him of the fundamental principles of government. According to Plato, insight into these principles, and into his own actions, is more important for the ruler who wishes to change his mode of government than are normative models as to how he should rule. Plato also explores the role of the 'philosopher' in relation to the 'Prince'. In our terms what is designated here is the relationship between the theoretician (the scholar) and the practician. Should the scholar tell the practician what he *ought* to do, or should he be content with describing the way things *are*. The practician may come to his own conclusions and adapt the research result to his own situation. (Plato: *The Phaedrus*, and letters VII and VIII, 1973).

18. M.C. Escher, Dutch artist (1902–72) has created some of the most intellectually stimulating (and confounding) pictures in the history of mankind. The principal message of most of what Escher drew, painted or sculpted was to point to the various paradoxes upon which our conceptions of the world are based. His work was admired by mathematicians for he could, by means of the visual arts, illustrate more clearly than with calculations, the limitations of mathematics (see Gödel's theory) (Bruno, 1976, *The Magic Mirror of M.C. Escher*; Maurits, 1972, *The World of M.C. Escher*).

19. The graphic way of discussing Escher's 'Print gallery' is taken from Hofstadter, 1979: 715–716). It can also be found in Daudi (1981: 16–21) with reference to Hofstadter (1979).

CHAPTER SEVEN

1. The argument in this chapter has two main sources: on the one hand, an article with the same title – 'The discourse of power or the power of discourse' (Daudi, 1983), and, on the other hand, 'Power and knowledge' (Daudi, 1980). The discussion often demands more thorough explanations and commentary than has been allowed by this limited space. Moreover, I consider this chapter to be a set of reflections and loose ends that reach beyond the confines of this thesis. I have therefore endeavoured to be concise; sometimes at the expense of a certain measure of precision. The interested reader may turn to the articles referred to above.

Bibliography

Aaron, R.I. (1941–42), 'Hume's theory of universals', *Proceedings of the Aristotelian Society*, Vol. 49, London.

Abell, P. (ed.) (1975), *Organizations as Bargaining and Influence Systems*, London, Heinemann.

Abell, P. (1977), 'The many faces of power and liberty: revealed preference autonomy and teleological explanation', *Sociology*, 11, 3–24.

Aiken, H.D. (1948), *Hume's Moral and Political Philosophy*, New York.

Aldrich, H.E. (1975), 'An organization–environment perspective on co-operation and conflict in the manpower training system', in A.R. Negandhi (ed.), *Inter-Organization Theory*, Kent, Ohio, Kent State University Press.

Aldrich, H.E. (1979), *Organizations and Environments*, Englewood Cliffs, N.J., Prentice-Hall.

Allen, V.L. (1975), *Social Analysis*, London, Longman.

Allison, G. (1971), *The Essence of Decision. Explaining the Cuban Missile Crisis*, Boston, Little Brown.

Alvesson, M. (1983), *Organisationsteori och teknokratiskt medvetande*, Stockholm, Natur & Kultur.

Amidt, M. (1967), 'Le relativisme culturaliste de Michel Foucault', *Les Temps Modernes*, No. 248, 1271–1298.

Andler, C. (1958), *Nietzsche, sa vie et sa pensée*, 3 vols, Paris, NRF, Gallimard.

Anscombe, G.E.M. (1958), *Intention*, Oxford, Basil Blackwell.

Argyris, C. (1964), *Integrating the Individual and the Organization*, New York, Wiley.

Argyris, C. (1965), *Organization and Innovation*, Homewood, Ill., R.D. Irwin.

Argyris, C. (1970), *Intervention Theory and Method*, Reading, Mass., Addison-Wesley.

Argyris, C. (1972), *The Applicability of Organizational Sociology*, Cambridge, Mass., Harvard University Press.

Aristotle (1943), B. Jowett, *Politics*, New York, Modern Library. *Politique d'Aristote*, R. Weil (ed.), (1966), Paris.

Aron, R. (1964), *La lutte des classes*, Paris, Seuil.

Asch, S.E. (1952), *Social Psychology*, Englewood Cliffs, N.J., Prentice-Hall.

Bacharach, S.B. and Lawler, E.J. (1980), *Power and Politics in Organizations*, San Francisco, Jossey-Bass.

Bacharach, S.B. and Lawler, E.J. (1980), *Power Tactics in Bargaining*, Ithaca, New York, New York State School of Industrial and Labor Relations, Cornell University.

Bachrach, P. and Baratz, M.S. (1962), 'Two faces of power', *American Political Science Review*, 56, 947–952.

Bachrach, P. and Baratz, M.S. (1963), 'Decisions and nondecisions: an analytical framework', *American Political Science Review*, 57, 632–642.

Bachrach, P. and Baratz, M.S. (1971), *Power and Poverty*, Oxford University Press.

Bakan, D. (1967), *On Method*, San Francisco, Jossey-Bass.

Baldridge, J.V. (1971), *Power and Conflict in the University*, New York, Wiley.

Barker, S.F. (1969), *Philosophy of Mathematics*, Englewood Cliffs, N.J., Prentice-Hall.

Baroni, C. (1961), *Nietzsche éducateur. De l'homme au surhomme*, Paris, Buchet-Chastel.

Barry, B. (1974), 'Review article: exit, voice, and loyalty', *British Journal of Political Science*, 4, 79–107.

Barthes, R. (1964), *Essais Critiques*, Paris, Seuil.

Baudrillard, J. (1977), *Oublier Foucault*, Paris, Galilée.

Baumgartner, T., Burns, T.R. and Deville, P. (1982), 'Work, politics and social structuring under capitalism', in *Power, Conflict and Exchange in Social Life*, Institute of Sociology, Uppsala University.

Beer, M. (1976), 'On gaining power and influence for OD', *Journal of Applied Behavioral Science*, 12(1), 44–51.

Bem, S.L. and Bem, D.J. (1970), 'Training the woman to know her place: the power of a nonconscious ideology', in D.J. Bem (ed.), *Beliefs, Attitudes, and Human Affairs*, Monterey, Wadsworth Publishing Company.

Benacerraf, P. and Putman, H. (1964), *Philosophy of Mathematics – Selected Readings* (in Gödel, 1931), Englewood Cliffs, N.J., Prentice-Hall.

Bendix, R. (1956), *Work and Authority in Industry*, New York, Wiley.

Bennis, W.G. (1966), *Changing Organizations*, New York, McGraw-Hill.

Bennis, W. (1975), 'Practice vs. theory', *International Management*, 30(10).

Benson, J.K. (1977), 'Organizations: a dialectical view', *Administrative Science Quarterly*, Vol. 22, 1–21.

Berelson, B. and Steiner, G.A. (1964), *Human Behavior: an Inventory of Scientific Findings*, New York, Harcourt, Brace & World.

Berg, P.O. and Daudi, Ph. (1982), *Traditions and Trends in Organization Theory, a Book of Readings*, Lund, Studentlitteratur.

Berger, P.L. (1963), *Invitation to Sociology: A Humanistic Perspective*, New York, Doubleday Anchor.

Berger, P.L. and Luckmann, T. (1966), *The Social Construction of Reality: a Treatise in the Sociology of Knowledge*, New York, Doubleday.

Berle, A.A. (1967), *Power*, New York, Harcourt, Brace & World.

Bernstein, R.J. (1971), *Praxis and Action*, Philadelphia, University of Pennsylvania Press.

Bierstedt, R. (1950), 'An analysis of social power', *American Sociological Review*.

Bierstedt, R. (1963), *The Social Order: an Introduction to Sociology*, New York, McGraw-Hill.

Bion, W.R. (1968), *Experiences in Groups*, London, Tavistock.

Bittner, E. (1965), 'The concept of organization', *Social Research*, 32, 239–255.

Blais, A. (1974), 'Power and causality', *Quality and Quantity*, 8, 45–64.

Blake, R. and Mouton, J.S. (1968), *Corporate Excellence Through Grid Organization Development*, Houston, Gulf.

Blau, P.M. (1955), *The Dynamics of Bureaucracy*, Chicago, University of Chicago Press.

Blau, P.M. (1964), *Exchange and Power in Social Life*, New York, Wiley.

Blau, P. and Schoenherr, R. (1971), *The Structure of Organizations*, New York, Basic Books.

Blondel, E. (1980), *Nietzsche: le cinquième évangile?*, Paris, ed. Les Bergers et Les Mages.

Bloom, H. (1973), *The Anxiety of Influence: a Theory of Poetry*, New York and London, Oxford University Press.

Bloom, H. (1975), *A Map of Misreading*, New York and London, Oxford University Press.

Bloom, H. (1976), *Poetry and Repression*, New Haven, Conn., Yale University Press.

Bloom, H. (1977), *Wallace Stevens: the Poems of Our Climate*, Ithaca, N.Y., Cornell University Press.

Blot, J. (1975), 'Michel Foucault: Surveiller et punir', *Nouvelle Revue Française*, No. 276, 89–92.

Blumer, H. (1954), 'What's wrong with social theory?', *American Sociological Review*, 19, 3–10.

Blumer, H. (1956), 'Sociological analysis and the "variable" ', *American Sociological Review*, 21, 683–690.

Blumer, H. (1966), 'Sociological implications of the thought of George Herbert Mead', *American Journal of Sociology*, 71, 535–544.

Bohr, N. (1967), *Atomteori och naturbeskrivning*, Stockholm, Aldus.

Bottomore, T.B. (1966), 'Equality or elites', in T.B. Bottomore (ed.), *Elites and Society*, Harmondsworth, Penguin.

Boulding, K.E. (1956), 'General system theory – the skeleton of science', *Management Science*, 3, 197–208.

Bourdieu, P. (1979), *La distinction: critique social du jugement*, Paris, Minuit.

Bourricaud, F. (1961), *Esquisse d'une théorie de l'autorité*, Paris, Plon.

Bradshaw, A. (1976), 'A critic of Steven Lukes' Power: a radical view', *Sociology*, X, 121–127.

Braybrooke, D. and Lindblom, C.E. (1963), *A Strategy of Decision, Policy Evaluation as a Social Process*, New York, Free Press of Glencoe.

Brochier, J.L. (1975), 'Entretien sur la prison: le livre et sa méthode' (intervju med M. F.), *Magazine littéraire*, No. 16.

Brunet, O. (1965), *Philosophie et Esthétique chez David Hume*, Paris, Nizet.

Bruno, E. (1976), *The Magic Mirror of M.C. Escher*, New York, Random House.

Brunschvigg, L. (1949), *L'Expérience humaine et la causalité physique*, Paris, Presse Universitaire Française.

Bunge, M. (1967), *Scientific Research I & II*, Berlin, Springer Verlag.

Burke, W. (1976), 'Organizational development in transition', *Journal of Applied*

Behavioral Science, 12(1).

Burns, T. and Buckley, W. (1974), 'The prisoner's dilemma game as a system of social domination', *Journal of Peace Research*, no. 11, 221–228.

Burns, T. and Stalker, G.M. (1961), *The Management of Innovation*, London, Tavistock.

Burrell, H. and Morgan, G. (1979), *Sociological Paradigms and Organizational Analysis*, London, Heinemann.

Butler, R.J. (1976), 'Relative deprivation and power', *Human Relations*, 29, 623–641.

Caplow, T. (1968), *Two Against One*, Englewood Cliffs, N.J., Prentice-Hall.

Carchedi, G. (1977), *On the Economic Identification of Social Classes*, London, Routledge & Kegan Paul.

Cartwright, D. (1959), 'A field theoretical conception of power', in D. Cartwright (ed.), *Studies in Social Power*, Ann Arbor, University of Michigan Press.

Cartwright, D. (1965), 'Influence, leadership and control', in J.G. March (ed.), *Handbook of Organizations*, Chicago, Rand McNally.

Castoriadis, C. (1975), *L'Institution imaginaire de la société*, Paris, Seuil.

Chalumeau, J-L (1971), *La pensée en France de Sartre à Foucault*, Paris, Nathan.

Châtelet, F. (ed.) (1972), *La Philosophie*, vol. 2, Paris, Marabou.

Chenu, M.D. (1950), 'Introduction à l'étude de Saint Thomas d'Aquin', *Publications de l'Institut d'Études médiévales de Montréal*, 11, Montréal-Paris.

Child, J. (1969), *The Business Enterprise in Modern Industrial Society*, London, Collier-Macmillan.

Child, J. (1972a), 'Organization structure, environment and performance: the role of strategic choice', *Sociology*, 6, 1–22.

Child, J. (1972b), 'Organization structure and strategies of control', *Administrative Science Quarterly*, 17, 163–177.

Child, J. (1973), 'Organization: a choice for man', in J. Child (ed.), *Man and Organization*, London, George Allen & Unwin.

Cicourel, A. (1958), 'The front and back of organizational leadership', *Pacific Sociological Review*, 1, 54–58.

Cicourel, A. (1964), *Method and Measurement in Sociology*, New York, Free Press.

Cicourel, A. (1968), *The Social Organization of Juvenile Justice*, New York, John Wiley.

Cicourel, A. (1973), *Cognitive Sociology*, London, Cox & Wyman.

Clegg, S.R. (1975), *Power, Rule and Domination*, London, Routledge & Kegan Paul.

Clegg, S. (1977), 'Power, organization theory, Marx and critique', in S. Clegg and D. Dunkerley (eds), *Critical Issues in Organizations*, London, Routledge & Kegan Paul.

Clegg, S. (1979a), *The Theory of Power and Organization*, London, Routledge & Kegan Paul.

Clegg, S. (1979b), 'The sociology of power and the university curriculum', in M. Pusey and R. Young (eds), *Ideology, Domination and Knowledge*, Canberra, ANU Press.

Clegg, S. and Dunkerley, D. (eds), (1977), *Critical Issues in Organizations*,

London, Routledge & Kegan Paul.

Clegg, S. and Dunkerley, D. (1980), *Organization, Class and Control*, London, Routledge & Kegan Paul.

Cohen, M.D. and March, J.G. (1974), *Leadership and Ambiguity: The American College President*, New York, McGraw-Hill, Carnegie Commission on the Future of Higher Education.

Cohen, M.D., March, J.G. and Olsen, J.P. (1972), 'A garbage can model of organizational choice', *Administrative Science Quarterly*, 17(1), 1–25.

Cohen, P.S. (1970), *Modern Social Theory*, London, Heinemann.

Coleman, J.S. (1957), *Community Conflict*, New York, Free Press.

Collin, R. (1975), *Conflict Sociology: Toward an Explanatory Science*, New York, Academic Press.

Corvez, M. (1968), 'Le structuralisme de Michel Foucault', *Revue Thomiste*, t. 68, no. 1, 101–124.

Crémant, R. (1969), *Les matinées structuralistes*, Paris, Laffont.

Cressey, D.R. (1965), 'Prison organizations', in J.G. March (ed.), *Handbook of Organizations*, Chicago, Rand McNally.

Crozier, M. (1961), 'De la bureaucratie comme système d'organisation', *Archives Européenes de Sociologie*, 2, 18–52.

Crozier, M. (1964a), 'Pouvoir et organisation', *Archives Européenes de Sociologie*, 5, 52–64.

Crozier, M. (1964b), *Le phénomène bureaucratique*, Paris, Seuil.

Crozier, M. (1973), 'L'Influence dell'informatica sul guverno delle imprese', in F. Rosito (ed.), *Razionalita sociale e tecnologia della informazione*, Milan, Ed. Communita.

Crozier, M. (1976), 'Comparing structures or comparing games', in G. Hofsted and M. Sami-Kassem (eds), *European Contributions to Organization Theory*, Amsterdam, Van Gorkum.

Crozier, M. and Friedberg, E. (1977), *L'Acteur et le système*, Paris, Seuil.

Crozier, M. et al. (1974), *Où va l'administration française?*, Paris, Ed. d'Organisation.

Cuff, E.C. and Payne, G.C.F. (eds) (1979), *Perspectives in Sociology*, George Allen & Unwin.

Cyert, R.M. and March, J.G. (1963), *A Behavioural Theory of the Firm*, Englewood Cliffs, N.J., Prentice-Hall.

Cyert, R.M., Simon, H.A. and Trow, D.B. (1956), 'Observation of a business decision', *Journal of Business*, 237–248.

Dahl, R.A. (1957), 'The concept of power', *Behavioural Science*, 2, 201–215.

Dahl, R.A. (1961), *Who Governs?*, New Haven, Conn., Yale University Press.

Dahl, R.A. (1963), *Modern Political Analysis*, Englewood Cliffs, N.J., Prentice-Hall.

Dahl, R.A. (1965), 'Cause and effect in the study of politics', in D.J. Lerner (ed.), *Cause and Effect*, New York, Free Press, 79–98.

Dahl, R.A. (1968), 'Power', *International Encyclopedia of the Social Science*, vol. 12, New York, Macmillan, 405–415.

Dahrendorf, R. (1959), *Class and Class Conflict in Industrial Society*, Stanford, Calif., Stanford University Press.

Daix, P. (1968), 'Structure du structuralisme, II: Althusser et Foucault', *Les lettres françaises*, no. 1239, 7–11.

Dalton, M. (1959), *Men who Manage*, New York, Wiley.

Daudi, Ph. (1980), *Maktfenomenet i Organisationer 11*, Lund, Department of Business Administration, University of Lund, Sweden.

Daudi, Ph. (1981), *Dialogue in the Tower of Babel*, Lund, Department of Business Administration, University of Lund, Sweden.

Daudi, Ph. (1983), 'The discourse of power and the power of discourse', *Journal of World Policy*, IX(2), 317–325.

Daudi, Ph. (1984), 'Power, relationships as organizing concept', Lund, Department of Business Administration, University of Lund, Sweden.

Daudi, Ph. and Alvesson, M. (1983), *Handlingslogik, organisation och teknologisk kapitalism: en inledning till en integrerad organisationsteori, 1*, Lund, Department of Business Administration, University of Lund, Sweden.

Davis, K. (1949), *Human Society*, New York, Macmillan.

Davis, K. (1957), *Human Relations in Business*, New York, McGraw-Hill.

De Board, R. (1978), *The Psychoanalysis of Organizations*, London, Tavistock.

Delacampagne, C. and Maggiori, R. (1980), *Philosopher, les interrogations contemporaines*, Paris, Fayard.

Deleuze, G. (1967), 'Un nouvel archéologue', *La Quinzaine Littéraire*, 1–17.

Deleuze, G. (1972a), 'Les intellectuels et le pouvoir' (intervju med Michel Foucault), *L'Arc*, no. 49.

Deleuze, G. (1972b), 'Un nouvel archiviste', *Critiques*, no. 274, 195–209.

Deleuze, G. (1975), 'Entretien', *Nouvelles littéraires*, 17–3.

Derrida, J. (1963), 'Cogito et histoire de la folie', *Revue de métaphysique et de morale*, no. 4, 460–494.

Derrida, J. (1967), *De la grammatologie*, Paris, Les Éditions de Minuit.

Derrida, J. (1972), *Marges*, Paris, Les Editions de Minuit.

Derrida, J. (1974), *Glas*, Paris, Galilée.

Descartes, R. (1966), *Les passions de l'âme*, Paris, Vrin.

Dewey, J. (1931), 'Qualitative thought', in *Philosophy and Civilization*, New York, Minton, Balch & Co.

Dewey, J. (1931), 'Philosophy of freedom', in *Philosophy and Civilization*, New York, Minton, Balch & Co.

Dewey, J. (1938), *Logic: The Theory of Inquiry*, New York, Henry Holt.

Dewey, J. and Bentley, A.F. (1949), *Knowing and the Known*, Boston, The Beacon Press.

Douglas, J.D. (1970), *The Relevance of Sociology*, New York, Appleton-Century-Crofts.

Downs, A. (1957), *An Economic Theory of Democracy*, New York, Harper & Row.

Eisenstadt, S.N. (1965), *Essays on Comparative Institutions*, New York, Wiley.

Elger, A.J. (1975), 'Industrial organizations, a processual perspective', in J.B. McKinley (ed.), *Processing People: Cases in Organizational Behaviour*, London, Holt, Rinehart & Winston, 91–149.

Emerson, R.M. (1962), 'Power–dependence relations', *American Sociological Review*, 27, 31–40.

Emerson, R.M. (1970), 'Power–dependence relations' in M. Olsen (ed.), *Power in Societies*, New York, Macmillan, 44–53.

Emerson, R.M. (1972a), 'Exchange theory, Part I: A psychological basis for social exchange', in J. Berger, M. Zelditch and B. Anderson (eds), *Sociological Theories in Progress*, vol. 2, Boston, Houghton Mifflin.

Emerson, R.M. (1972b), 'Exchange theory, Part II: Exchange relations, exchange networks, and groups as exchange systems', in J. Berger, M. Zelditch and B. Anderson (eds), *Sociological Theories in Progress*, vol. 2, Boston, Houghton Mifflin.

Etzioni, A. (1959), 'Authority, structure and organizational effectiveness', *Administrative Science Quarterly*, 4, 43–67.

Etzioni, A. (1961a), *A Comparative Analysis of Complex Organizations* (2nd edn 1975), Glencoe, Ill., Free Press.

Etzioni, A. (ed.), (1961a), *Complex Organizations: A Sociological Reader*, New York, Holt.

Etzioni, A. (1969), *A Sociological Reader on Complex Organizations*, New York, Holt, Rinehart & Winston.

Fayol, H. (1949), *General and Industrial Management*, London, Pitman.

Feyerabend, P. (1974), 'Consolations for the specialist', in I. Lakatos and A. Musgrave (eds), *Criticism and the Growth of Knowledge*, Cambridge University Press, 197–230.

Feyerabend, P. (1978), *Science in a Free Society*, London, Lowe & Brydone Ltd.

Filmer, P. et al. (1972), *New Directions in Sociological Theory*, London, Collier-Macmillan.

Fontana, M. (1977), 'Vérité et pouvoir' (intervju med Michel Foucault), *L'Arc*, no. 70.

Forrester, J. (1970), *Urban Dynamics*, Cambridge, Mass., MIT Press.

Foucault, M. (1954), *Maladie mentale et personnalité*, Paris, P.U.F.

Foucault, M. (1961–72), *Histoire de la folie à l'âge classique*, Paris, P.U.F.

Foucault, M. (1963a), *Naissance de la clinique*, Paris, P.U.F.

Foucault, M. (1963b), *Raymond Roussel*, Paris, P.U.F.

Foucault, M. (1966), *Les mots et les choses*, Paris, Gallimard.

Foucault, M. (1967), 'Nietzsche, Freud, Marx', *Cahiers du Royaumont*, Paris, Minuit.

Foucault, M. (1969), *L'archéologie du savoir*, Paris, Gallimard.

Foucault, M. (1970), 'Qu'est'ce qu'un auteur?', *Bulletin de la Societé Française de philosophie*, LXIV, 73–104.

Foucault, M. (1971a), *L'ordre du discours*, Paris, P.U.F.

Foucault, M. (1971b), 'Nietzsche, la généalogie, l'histoire', in M. Foucault (ed.), *Hommage à Jean Hyppolite*, Paris, P.U.F.

Foucault, M. (1972), *The Archaeology of Knowledge*, London, Tavistock and New York, Pantheon.

Foucault, M. (1973a), *Ceci n'est pas une pipe*, Montpellier, Fata Morgana.

Foucault, M. (1973b), *Moi, Pierre Rivière, ayant égorgé ma mère, ma soeur et mon frère . . .*, Paris, Gallimard/Julliard.

Foucault, M. (1975), *Surveiller et punir*, Paris, Gallimard.

Foucault, M. (1976a), *La volonté de savoir*, vol. 1, *Histoire de la sexualité*, Paris, Gallimard.

Foucault, M. (1976b), *Les machines à guérir (aux origines de l'hôpital moderne)* (La politique de la santé au XVIIIe), in M. Foucault (ed.), *Dossiers et documents d'architecture*, Paris, Institut de l'environment.

Foucault, M. (1984), *L'usage des plaisirs*, vol. 2, *Histoire de la sexualité*, Paris, Gallimard.

Foucault, M. (1984), *Le souci de soi*, vol. 3, *Histoire de la sexualité*, Paris, Gallimard.

Fox, A. (1966), *Industrial Sociology and Industrial Relations*, Research Paper 3, Royal Commission on Trade Unions and Employers Associations, London, HMSO.

Fox, A. (1974), *Beyond Contract: Work, Power and Trust Relations*, London, Faber & Faber.

Fox, A. (1976), 'The meaning of work', Block 3, Unit 6, *People and Work*, OU Course DE 351, Milton Keynes, Open University Press.

French, J.R.P. and Raven, B.H. (1959), 'The bases of social power', in D. Cartwright (ed.), *Studies in Social Power*, Ann Arbor, University of Michigan Press.

Friedlander, F. and Brown, L. (1974), 'Organization development', *Annual Review of Psychology*, 24, 313–341.

Friedman, G. (1947), *Problèmes humains du machinisme industriel*, Paris, Gallimard.

Friedman, N. (1967), *The Social Nature of Psychological Research*, New York, Basic Books.

Gamson, W.A. (1964), 'Experimental studies of coalition formation', in L. Berkowitz (ed.), *Advances in Experimental Social Psychology*, vol. 1, New York, Academic Press.

Gamson, W.A. (1968), *Power and Discontent*, Homewood, Ill., Dorsey Press.

Gamson, W.A. (1974), 'Power and probability', in J.D. Tedeschi (ed.), *Perspective on Social Power*, Chicago, Aldine.

Gamson, W.A. (1975), *The Strategy of Social Protest*, Homewood, Ill., Dorsey Press.

Gans, H.J. (1968), 'The participant–observer as a human being: observations on the personal aspects of field work', in Horward S. Berker et al. (eds), *Institutions and the Person*, Chicago, Aldine.

Garfinkel, H. (1967), *Studies in Ethnomethodology*, Englewood Cliffs, N.J., Prentice-Hall.

Garfinkel, H. (1974), 'The origins of the term "ethnomethodology" ', in R. Turner (ed.), *Ethnomethodology*, Harmondsworth, Penguin.

Gasparini, G. (1976), *Tecnologia, ambiente e struttura – Temi e modelli per una sociologia dell'organizzatione*, Milano, F. Angeli.

Gergen, K.J. (1969), *The Psychology of Behavior Exchange*, Reading, Mass., Addison-Wesley.

Gerth, H.H. and Mills, W.C. (1960), *From Max Weber: Essays in Sociology*, New York, Oxford University Press.

Giddens, A. (1971), *Capitalism and Modern Social Theory*, Cambridge, Cambridge University Press.

Giddens, A. (1973), *The Class Structure of the Advanced Societies*, London, Hutchinson.

Giddens, A. (1974), 'Elites in the British class structure', in P. Stanworth and A. Giddens (eds), *Elites and Power in British Society*, Cambridge, Cambridge University Press, 1–22.

Giddens, A. (1976), *New Rules of Sociological Method*, London, Hutchinson.

Giddens, A. (1979), *Central Problems of Social Theory*, London, Macmillan.

Giovanitti, L. and Freed, H. (1962), *The Decision to Drop the Atomic Bomb*, New York, Holt, Rinehart & Winston.

Glaser, B. and Strauss, A. (1968), 'Awareness contexts and social interaction', *Administrative Science Quarterly*, 29, 669–679.

Glucksmann, A. (1975), *La cuisinière et le mangeur d'hommes*, Paris, Seuil.

Glucksman, A. (1977), *Les maîtres penseurs*, Paris, Grasset.

Goffman, E. (1959), *The Presentation of Self in Everyday Life*, Garden City, N.Y., Doubleday Anchor.

Goffman, E. (1961a), *Asylums; Essays on the Social Situations of Mental Patients and other Inmates*, Anchor Books, Doubleday & Co.

Goffman, E. (1961b), *Encounters: Two Studies in the Sociology of Interaction*, Bobbs-Merril.

Goffman, E. (1963), *Behavior in Public Places*, New York, Free Press.

Goffman, E. (1967), *Interaction Ritual*, Garden City, N.Y., Doubleday Anchor.

Goffman, E. (1969), *Strategic Interaction*, Philadelphia, University of Pennsylvania Press.

Goldman, P. (1976), 'Ideology, bureaucracy and sociology: a critique of bourgeois organization theory and research', *Annual Meeting of the American Sociological Association*, New York.

Gouldner, A.W. (1954), *Patterns of Industrial Bureaucracy*, Glencoe, Ill., Free Press.

Gouldner, A.W. (1955), 'Metaphysical pathos and the theory of bureaucracy', *American Political Science Review*, 49, 496–507.

Gouldner, A.W. (1965), *Wildcat Strike*, New York, Free Press.

Gouldner, A.W. (1971), *The Coming Crisis of Western Sociology*, London, Heinemann.

Gouldner, F.H. (1970), 'The division of labor: process and power', in M.N. Zald, (ed.), *Power in Organizations*, Nashville, Vanderbilt University Press.

Granier, J. (1969), *Le problème de la vérité dans la philosophie de Nietzsche*, Paris, Seuil.

Grémion, P. (1976), *Le pouvoir périphérique*, Paris, Seuil.

Grémion, C. (1977), *Décision et indécision dans la haute administration*, thèse de doctorat d'Etat, Paris.

Guedez, A. (1972), *Foucault*, Paris, Éditions Universitaires.

Gulick, L. and Urwick, L. (eds), (1937), *Papers on the Science of Administration*, New York, Institute of Public Administration.

Gustafsson, C. (1979), *Om utsagor om makt*, Åbo, Stiftelsen för Åbo Akademi.

Habermas, J. (1971a), *Knowledge and Human Interests*, London, Heinemann.

Habermas, J. (1971b), *Toward a Rational Society*, London, H.E.B.

Habermas, J. (1973), *La technique et la science comme "ideologie"*', Paris, Gallimard.

Habermas, J. (1976), *Legitimation Crisis*, London, Heinemann.

Hage, J. and Aiken, M. (1970), *Social Change in Complex Organizations*, New York, Random House.

Hall, E.T. (1969), *The Silent Language*, New York, Doubleday Anchor.

Hamilton, E. (1940), *Mythology*, Gerard & Co.

Hampshire, S. (1959), *Thought and Action*, London, Chatto & Windus.

Harsanyi, J.C. (1959), 'A bargaining model for the co-operative *n*-person game', in A.S. Tucker and R.D. Luce (eds), *Contributions to the Theory of Games*, IV, Princetown.

Harsanyi, J.C. (1962a), 'Measurement of social power, opportunity cost, and the theory of two-person bargaining games', *Behavioral Science*, I, 67–80.

Harsanyi, J.C. (1962b), 'Measurement of social power in *n*-person reciprocal power situations', *Behavioral Science*, II.

Harsanyi, J.C. (1962c), 'Models of the analysis of balance of power in society', in E. Nagel et al. (eds), *Logic Methodology and Philosophy of Science*, Stanford, Ill., Stanford University Press.

Harsanyi, J.C. (1977), *Rational Behaviour and Bargaining Equilibrium in Games and Social Situations*, New York, Cambridge University Press.

Hayden, V.W. (1973), 'Foucault decoded: notes from underground', *History and Theory*, 12(1).

Hearn, F. (1978), 'Rationality and bureaucracy: Maoist contributions to a marxist theory bureaucracy', *Sociological Quarterly*, 19, 37–44.

Hector, J. (1972), 'Michel Foucault et l'histoire', *Synthèses*, no. 309–10.

Hegel, G.W.F. (1974), *La Constitution de l'Allemagne*, Paris, ed. Champ libre.

Heidegger, M. (1961), *Nietzsche*, vols I and II, P. Fullingen, Günther Nestle.

Heidegger, M. (1962), *Being and Time*, New York, Harper & Row.

Heller, C.S. (1969), *Structured Social Inequality*, Ontario, Collier-Macmillan.

Hicks, H. and Gullet, C.R. (1975), *Organization: Theory and Behavior*, New York, McGraw-Hill.

Hickson, D.J. et al. (1971), 'A strategic contingencies theory of intra-organizational power', *Administrative Science Quarterly*, 6, 216–229.

Hinings, C.R. et al. (1974), 'Structural conditions of intra-organizational power', *Administrative Science Quarterly*, 19(1), 22–43.

Hirschman, A.O. (1972), *Exit, Voice and Loyalty*, Cambridge, Mass., Harvard University Press.

Hobbes, T. (1839), *The English Works* (11 vols), Sir W. Molesworth (ed.), London.

Hobbes, T. (1928), *The Elements of Law*, F. Tönnies (ed.), Cambridge, Cambridge University Press. (1st edn 1650 in two volumes: *On Human Nature* och De Corporare Politico.)

Hobbes, T. (1958), *Leviathan*, H.W. Schneider (ed.), New York, Bobbs-Merrill (1st edn. 1651).

Hofstadter, D.R. (1979), *Gödel, Escher, Bach: An Eternal Golden Braid*, Harmondsworth, Penguin.

Holdaway, E.A. et al. (1975), 'Dimensions of organizations in complex societies: the educational sector', *Administrative Science Quarterly*, 20, 37–58.

Homans, A.C. (1974), *Social Behavior: Its Elementary Forms*, New York, Harcourt Brace Jovanovich.

Hughes, H.S. (1961), *Consciousness and Society*, New York, Random House.

Hume, D. (1938), *An Abstract of a Treatise of Human Nature*, J.M. Keynes and P. Straffa (eds), Cambridge, Cambridge University Press.

Hume, D. (1951), *Enquiries concerning the Human Understanding and concerning the Principles of Morals*, Oxford, L.A. Selby Bigge.

Hunter, F. (1953), *Communty Power Structure*, University of North Carolina Press.

Husserl, E. (1967), *Ideas*, London, Allen & Unwin.

Husserl, E. (1969), *Formal and Transcendental Logic*, The Hague, Martinus Nijhoff.

Hyman, H. (1949), 'Inconsistencies as a problem of attitude measurement', *Journal of Social Issues*, 5, 40–41.

Hyman, H. (1954), *Interviewing in Social Research*, Chicago, University of Chicago Press.

Israel, J. (1979), *Om relationistisk socialpsykologi*, Göteborg, Korpen.

Jackson, H.J. and Morgan, C.P. (1978), *Organization Theory: A Macro Perspective for Management*, Englewood Cliffs, N.J., Prentice-Hall.

Jacques, E. (1970), 'A contribution to a discussion on Freud's "group psychology and the analysis of the ego" ', in E. Jacques (ed.), *Work, Creativity and Social Justice*, London, Heinemann.

Jacques, E. (1976), *A Central Theory of Bureaucracy*, London, Heinemann.

Johannisson, B. (1980), *Den organisatoriska smaltdegeln*, Stockholm, Liber Tryck.

John of Salisbury (1927), *The Stateman's Book*, New York, Knopf.

Kaplan, A. (1964), 'Power in perspective', in R.L. Kahn and E. Boulding (eds), *Power and Conflict in Organization*, London, Tavistock.

Karpik, L. (1972a), 'Sociologie, économie, politique et buts des organizations de production', *Revue Française de Sociologie*, 13, 299–324.

Karpik, L. (1972b), 'Les politiques et les logiques d'action de la grande entreprise industrielle', *Sociologie du Travail*, 13, 82–105.

Karpik, L. (1972c), 'Multinatonal enterprises and large technological corporations', *Revue Economique*, 23, 1–46.

Karpik, L. (1977), 'Technological capitalism', in S. Clegg and D. Dunkerley (eds), *Critical Issues in Organizations*, London, Routledge & Kegan Paul.

Karpik, L. (1978), 'Organizations, institutions and history', in L. Karpik (ed.), *Organizations and Environment: Theory, Issue, and Reality*, Beverly Hills, Sage.

Katz, D. and Kahn, R.L. (1966), *The Social Psychology of Organizations*, New York, Wiley.

Kaufman, H. and Jones, V. (1954), 'The mystery of power', *Public Administration Review*, 14.

Keller, S. (1963), *Beyond the Ruling Class: Strategic Elites in Modern Society*, New York, Random House.

Kergoat, D. (1970), 'Emergence et création d'un système d'action collective à travers une expérience d'autogestion en mai 68', *Sociologie du travail*, no. 3, 276–292.

Komorita, S.S. and Chertkoff, J. (1973), 'A bargaining theory of coalition formation', *Psychological Review*, 80, 149–162.

Kremer-Marietti, A. (1974), *Foucault*, Paris, Seghers.

Kristeva, J. (1969), *Séméiotiké: Recherches pour une sémanalyse. Essais*, Paris, Seuil.

Krupp, S.R. (1961), *Pattern in Organization Analysis: A Critical Examination*, New York, Holt, Rinehart & Winston.

Kuhn, T.S. (1962), *The Structure of Scientific Revolution*, Chicago, University of Chicago Press.

Kuhn, T.S. (1977), *The Essential Tension*, Chicago, University of Chicago Press.

Kuty, O. (1973), *Le pouvoir du malade: analyse sociologique des unités de rein artificiel*, thèse de doctorat, Paris, Université René Descartes.

Lacharite, N. (1970), 'Archéologie du savoir et structures du langage scientifique', *Dialogue*, t. 9, no. 1.

Laing, R.D. (1959), *The Divided Self*, London, Tavistock.

Laing, R.D. (1961), *The Self and Others*, London, Tavistock.

Laing, R.D. (1967), 'Sanity and madness – on the invention of madness', *New Statesman*, 16–26.

Laing, R.D. (1967), *The Politics of Experience*, Harmondsworth, Penguin.

Laing, R.D. (1970), *Knots*, Harmondsworth, Penguin.

Laing, R.D. and Cooper, D.G. (1964), *Reason & Violence*, London, Tavistock.

Laing, R.D. and Esterson, A. (1964), *Sanity, Madness and the Family*, London, Tavistock.

Lakatos, I. and Musgrave, A. (1970), *Criticism and the Growth of Knowledge*, Cambridge, Cambridge University Press (2nd edn, 1974).

Lasswell, H.D. and Kaplan, A. (1950), *Power and Society*, New Haven, Conn., Yale University Press.

Lawler, E.J. and Youngs, G.A. (1975), 'Coalition formation: an integrative model', *Sociometry*, 38(1), 1–17.

Lawrence, P.R. and Lorsch, J.W. (1967), *Organization and Environment: Managing Differentiation and Integration*, Boston, Harvard University Press.

Lecourt, D. (1972), *Pour une critique de l'épistémologie (Bachelard, Canguilhem, Foucault)*, Paris, Maspero.

Lehman, W.E. (1969), 'Toward a macrosociology of power', *American Sociological Review*, 34(4), 453–465.

Lehman-Haupt, C. (1969), 'Thoughts for the end of the year', *New York Times*, 31 December, s. 23, in D.L. Phillips (1971), *Knowledge From What?*, Chicago, Rand McNally.

Lenski, G. (1966), *Power and Privilege*, New York, McGraw-Hill.

Leroy-Ladurie, E. (1973), *Le territoire de l'historien*, Paris, Gallimard.

Lévy, A. (1969), *Les paradoxes de la liberté dans un hôpital psychiatrique*, Paris, ed. de l'Epi.

Levy, B.-H. (1977), *La barbarie à visage humain*, Paris, Grasset.

Likert, R. (1960), *New Patterns of Management*, New York, McGraw-Hill.

Likert, R. (1967), *The Human Organization: Its Management and Values*, New York, McGraw-Hill.

Lindblom, C.E. (1959), 'The science of "muddling through"', *Public Administration Review*, 19(2), 78–88.

Lindblom, C.E. (1965), *The Intelligence of Democracy*, New York, Free Press.

Lindblom, C.E. (1968), *The Policy-Making Process*, New York, Prentice-Hall.

Lipset, S. (1960), *Political Man*, London, Heinemann.

Lipset, S.M., Trow, M. and Coleman, J. (1956), *Union Democracy*, New York, Doubleday.

Locke, J. (1960), *Two Treatises of Government*, Laslet (ed.), Cambridge, Cambridge University Press.

Locke, J. (1972), *Essai concernant l'entendement humain*, Paris, Vrin.

Long, N.E. (1958), 'The local community as an ecology of games', *American Journal of Sociology*, 64(3), 251–261.

Long, N.E. and Belknap, G. (1956), 'A research program on leadership and decision-making in metropolitan areas', Governmental Affairs Institute Publication.

Louch, A.R. (1966), *Explanation and Human Action*, Berkeley and Los Angeles, University of California Press.

Lourau, R. (1969), *L'instituant contre l'institué*, Paris, ed. Antrhopos.

Lourau, R. (1970), *L'analyse institutionnelle*, Paris, ed. de Minuit.

Luce, R.D. and Raiffa, H. (1957), *Games and Decisions*, New York, Wiley.

Lukes, S. (1973), *Emile Durkheim: His Life and Work*, London, Allen Lane.

Lukes, S. (1974), *Power: A Radical View*, London, Macmillan.

Lupton, T. (1963), *On the Shop Floor*, Oxford, Pergamon.

Lykken, P. (1968), 'Statistical significance in psychological research', *Psychological Bulletin*, 70, 151–159.

Machiavelli, N., *Le Prince*, Paris, Garnier-Flammarion, no. 317.

McGregor, D. (1966), *Leadership and Motivation*, Cambridge, Mass., MIT Press.

McMullen, R. (1969), 'Michel Foucault', *Horizon*, 11–8, 36–39.

Macpherson, C.B. (1962), *The Political Theory of Possessive Individualism*, Oxford, Clarendon Press.

Macpherson, C.B. (1973), *Democratic Theory, Essays in Retrieval*, Oxford, Clarendon Press.

de Man, P. (1969), 'The rhetoric of temporality', in C.S. Singleton (ed.), *Interpretation: Theory and Practice*, Baltimore, Md., Johns Hopkins University Press.

de Man, P. (1979), *Allegories of Reading: Figural Language in Rousseau, Nietzsche, Rilke, and Proust*, New Haven, Conn., Yale University Press.

(Manus) 'The Laws of Manus' (1886), band 25, in *Sacred Books of the East*, Max Müller, Oxford, Clarendon Press.

March, J.G. (1955), 'An introduction to the theory of influence', *American Political Science Review*, 49, 431–453.

March, J.G. (ed.) (1965), *Handbook of Organizations*, Chicago, Rand McNally.

March, J.G. (1966), 'The power of power', in D. Easton (ed.), *Varieties of Political Theory*, New York, Prentice-Hall.

March, J.G. and Olsen, J.P. (1976), *Ambiguity and Choice in Organizations*, Oslo, Universitetsforlaget.

March, J.G. and Simon, H.A. (1958), *Organizations*, New York, Wiley.

Margolin, J.-C. (1967), 'L'homme de Michel Foucault', *Revue des sciences humaines*, t. 32.

Maslow, A.H. (1954), *Motivation and Personality*, New York, Harper.

Maslow, A. (1966), *The Psychology of Science*, New York, Harper & Row.

Maurits, E.C. (1972), *The World of M.C. Escher*, New York, Harry N. Abrams.

Mead, G.H. (1936), *Movements of Thought in the Nineteenth Century*, Chicago, University of Chicago Press.

Mead, G.H. (1967), *Mind, Self and Society*, Chicago, University of Chicago Press.

Mechanic, D. (1962), 'Sources of power of lower participants in complex organizations', *Administrative Science Quarterly*, 7, 349–364.

Meehl (1967), 'Theory testing in psychology and physics: a methodological paradox', *Philosophy of Science*, 34, 103–115.

Merleau-Ponty, M. (1971), *Existence et dialectique*, Paris, P.U.F.

Merton, R.K. (1936), 'The unanticipated consequences of purposive social action', *American Sociological Review*, 1, 894–904.

Merton, R.K. (1949), *Social Theory and Social Structure*, Glencoe, Ill., Free Press (2nd edn, 1957).

Merton, R.K. (1957), 'The role-set: problems in sociological theory', *British Journal of Sociology*, 8, 106–120.

Michels, R. (1949), *Political Parties*, Chicago, Free Press (*Les parties politiques*, 1913).

Mills, C.W. (1940a), 'Methodological consequences of the sociology of knowledge', *American Sociological Review*, 5, 316–330.

Mills, C.W. (1940b), 'Situational actions and vocabularies of motive', *American Sociological Review*, 5, ss. 904–913.

Mills, C.W. (1956), *The Power Elite*, London, Oxford University Press.

Mills, C.W. (1959), *The Sociological Imagination*, London, Oxford University Press.

Mintzberg, H. (1977), Review of Simons, 'The new science of management decision' (rev. edn, 1977), *Administrative Science Quarterly*, 22(2).

Mintzberg, H. (1983), *Power In and Around Organizations*, Englewood Cliffs, N.J., Prentice-Hall.

de Monthoux, P.G. (1981), *Doktor Kant och den oekonomiska rationaliseringen*, Göteborg, Korpen.

Mooney, J.D. (1930), 'The scalar principle', in J.D. Mooney and A.C. Reily (eds), *The Principles of Organization*, New York, Harper & Row.

Mooney, J.D. and Reiley, A.C. (1931), *Onward Industry!*, New York, Harper.

Mosca, G. (1939), 'Elementi di scienza politica' (English version, *The Ruling Class*, New York, McGraw-Hill).

Mouloud, N. (1969), *Langage et structure*, Paris, Payot.

Mulder, M. (1971), 'Power equalization through participation?', *Administrative Science Quarterly*, March, pp. 31–38.

Murnighan, J.K. (1978), 'Models of coalition behavior: game theoretic, social psychological, and political perspectives', *Psychological Bulletin*, 85, 1130–1153.

Nagel, J.H. (1968), 'Some questions about the concept of power', *Behavioral Science*, 13, 129–137.

Nathanson, M. (1963), *Philosophy of the Social Sciences: A Reader*, New York, Random House.

Nathanson, M. (1970), *The Journeying Self: a Study in Philosophy and Social*

Role, Reading, Mass., Addison-Wesley.

Neumann, von J. and Morgenstern, O. (1944), *Theory of Games and Economic Behavior*, Princeton, Princeton University Press.

Nicolaus, M. (1966), 'Remarks at ASA convention', *American Sociologist*, 4, 154–156.

Nietzsche, F. (1934), *La volonté de puissance*, Paris, NRF, Gallimard.

Nietzsche, F. (1950), *Le gai savoir*, Paris, NRF, Gallimard.

Nietzsche, F. (1964), *La généalogie de la morale*, Paris, Mercure de France.

Nietzsche, F. (1968), *Ainsi parlait Zarathoustra*, Paris, Aubier.

Nord, W. (1975), 'The failure of current applied behavioral science: a Marxian perspective', *Journal of Applied Behavioral Science*, 4, 557–578.

Norman, H.M. and Sims, J.H. (1956), 'Power tactics', *Harvard Business Review*, Nov.–Dec., pp. 25–29.

Norris, C. (1982), *Deconstruction: Theory and Practice*, London and New York, Methuen.

Nunnally, J.C. (1967), *Psychometric Theory*, New York, McGraw-Hill.

Olsen, J.P. (1970), 'Local budgeting, decision-making or a ritual act?', *Scandinavian Political Studies*, 5, 85–118.

Olsson, G. (1980), *Birds in Egg/Eggs in Bird*, Pion, London.

Olsson, G. (1982), '–/–', *Substance*, 35, (XI), no. 2.

Parkin, F. (1971), *Class Inequality and the Political Order*, London, McGibbon & Kee.

Parkin, F. (1976), 'System contradiction and political transformation: the comparative study of industrial societies', in T.R. Burns and W. Buckley (eds), *Power and Control: Social Structures and their Transformation*, London, Sage.

Parsons, T. (1949), *The Structure of Social Action*, New York, Free Press of Glencoe.

Parsons, T. (1956), 'Suggestions for a sociological approach to the theory of organizations', *Administrative Science Quarterly*, 1, 63–85, 225–239.

Parsons, T. (1960), *Structure and Process in Modern Societies*, Chicago, Free Press.

Parsons, T. (ed.), (1965), *Theories of Society*, New York, Free Press of Glencoe.

Parsons, T. and Shils, E.A. (eds) (1951), *Toward a General Theory of Action*, Cambridge, Mass., Harvard University Press.

Parsons, T. and Smelser, N.J. (1956), *Economy and Society*, New York, Free Press of Glencoe.

Peabody, R.L. (1964), *Organizational Theory Superior–Subordinate Relationships in Three Public Service Organizations*, New York, Atherton.

Peaucelle, J.-L. (1969), 'Théorie des jeux et sociologie des organisations', *Sociologie du travail*, no. 1, 22–43.

Peirce, C.S. (1931–35), *Collected Papers of Charles Sanders Peirce*, Vol. I–VI (C. Hartshorne and P. Weiss, eds), Cambridge, Mass., Harvard University Press.

Peirce, C.S. (1958), *Collected Papers of Charles Sanders Peirce*, Vol. VII–VIII, (A.W. Burks, ed.), Cambridge, Mass., Harvard University Press.

Pellegrini, R. and Coates, C.H. (1956), 'Absentee-owned corporation and community power structure', *American Journal of Sociology*, 61, 413–419.

Perrow, C. (1963), 'Goals and power structure: a historical case study', in E. Friedson (ed.), *The Hospital in Modern Society*, Chicago, Free Press of Glencoe.

Perrow, C. (1970), 'Departmental power and perspectives in industrial firms', in M. Zald (ed.), *Power in Organization*, Nashville, Tenn., Vanderbilt University Press.

Perrow, C. (1973), 'The short and glorious history of organizational theory', in *Organizational Dynamics*, (also in P.O. Berg and Ph. Daudi (eds), *Traditions and Trends in Organization Theory*, 1982).

Pettigrew, A. (1973), *The Politics of Organizational Decision Making*, London, Tavistock.

Pfeffer, J. (1978), 'The micropolitics of organizations', in M.W. Meyer (ed.), *Environments and Organizations*, San Francisco, Jossey-Bass.

Pfeffer, J. (1981), *Power in Organizations*, London, Pitman.

Pfeffer, J. and Salancik, G.R. (1974), 'Organizational decision-making as a political process: the case of a university budget', *Administrative Science Quarterly*, 19, 135–151.

Platon, *La république*, Paris, Garnier-Flammarion, No. 90.

Polsby, N. (1960), 'How to study community power: the pluralist alternative', *Journal of Politics*, 22, 174–184.

Polsby, N. (1963), *Community Power and Political Theory*, New Haven, Conn., Yale University Press.

Popper, K.R. (1959a), *The Logic of Scientific Discovery* (6th edn, 1972), London, Hutchinson.

Popper, K.R. (1959b), 'Testability and "ad-hocness" of the contraction hypothesis', *British Journal for the Philosophy of Science*, 10.

Popper, K.R. (1972), *The Logic of Scientific Discovery*, 6th edn, London, Hutchinson.

Pugh, D. (1969), 'Organizational behavior: an approach from psychology', *Human Relations*, no. 22, 345–354.

Pugh, D.S. et al. (1968), 'Dimensions of organization structure', *Administrative Science Quarterly*, 13, 65–105.

Pugh, D.S., Hickson, D.J. and Hinings, C.R. (1971), *Writers on Organizations*, Harmondsworth, Penguin.

Ramström, D. (1963), *Administrative Processer*, Stockholm, Bonniers.

Raven, B.H. (1974), 'A comparative analysis of power and power preference', in J.T. Tedeschi (ed.), *Perspectives on Social Power*, Chicago, Aldine.

Rex, J. (1961), *Key Problems of Sociological Theory*, London, Routledge & Kegan Paul.

Rhenman, E. and Stymne, B. (1965), *Företagsledning i en föränderlig värld*, Stockholm, Aldus.

Ricoeur, P. (1969), *Le conflit des interprétations*, Paris, Seuil.

Ricoeur, P. (1977), *La sémantique de l'action*, Paris, Centre National de la Recherche Scientifique.

Riecken, H.W. (1962), 'A program for research on experiments in social psychology', in N.F. Washburne (ed.), *Decisions Values and Groups*, vol. 2, New York, Pergamon, 25–41.

Robinson, J.A. and Majak, R.R. (1967), 'The theory of decision-making', in J.C. Charlesworth (ed.), *Contemporary Political Analysis*, New York, Free Press.

Roethlisberger, F.G. and Dickson, W.J. (1939), *Management and the Worker*,

Cambridge, Mass., Harvard University Press.

Rosanvallon, P. (1976), *L'âge de l'autogestion*, Paris, Seuil.

Rose, S. et al. (1977), *L'Idéologie deldans la science*, Paris, Le Seuil.

Rosenfeld, L. (1964), 'Komplementaritetssynpunkter konsolideras og udbygges', in *Niels Bohr*, Copenhagen, J.H. Schultz.

Rosenthal, R. (1966), *Experimental Effects in Behavioral Research*, New York, Appleton-Century-Crofts.

Rousseau, J.J. (1964), *Oeuvres complètes*, M. Raymond and B. Cagnegin (eds), Paris, Bibliothéque de la Pléiade.

Ryle, G. (1949), *The Concept of Mind*, London, Hutchinson.

Sacks, H. (1974), 'On the analysability of stories by children', in I.R. Turner (ed.), *Ethnomethodology*, Harmondsworth, Penguin.

Said, E. (1975), *Beginnings: Methods and Intentions*, New York, Basic Books.

Sainsaulieu, R. (1965), 'Pouvoir et strategie de groupes ouvriers dans l'atelier', *Sociologie du travail*, 2, 162–174.

Sainsaulieu, R. and Ackermann, W. (1970), L'étude sociologique du changement technique: pour une analyse stratégique', *Bulletin du CERP*, 19, 1–22.

Sainsaulieu, R. and Kergoat, D. (1968), 'Milieu de travail et modèle d'action', *Analyse et Prévision*, 4(6), 781–807.

Salaman, G. (1979), *Work Organizations: Resistance and Control*, London, Longman.

Salaman, G. and Thompson, K. (eds) (1973), *People and Organizations*, London, Longman.

Salaman, G. and Thompson, K. (1978), 'Class culture and the persistence of an elite: the case of army officer selection', *Sociological Review*, 26, 283–304.

Sartre, J.-P. (1943), *L'être et le néant*, Paris, Gallimard.

Sartre, J.-P. (1960a), *Critique de la raison dialectique*, Paris, Gallimard.

Sartre, J.-P. (1960b), *Esquisse d'une théorie des émotions*, Paris, Herman.

Sartre, J.-P. (1964), *Les mots*, Paris, Gallimard.

Sartre, J.-P. (1977), *Being and Nothingness*.

Sartre, J.-P. (1983), *Cahiers pour une morale*, Paris, Gallimard.

Sayre, W.S. and Kaufman, H. (1960), *Governing New York City*, Beverly Hills, California, Russell Sage.

Schegloff, E. (1968), 'Sequencing in conversational openings', *American Anthropologist*, 70.

Schelling, T. (1960), *The Strategy of Conflict*, Cambridge, Mass., Harvard University Press.

Schilling, W.R. (1967), 'The H-bomb decision: how to decide without actually choosing', in W.R. Welson (ed.), *The Politics of Science*, Oxford, Oxford University Press.

Schmidt, S. and Kochan, T. (1972), 'The concept of conflict', *Administrative Science Quarterly*, 17, 359–370.

Schople, J. and Layton, D.B. (1974), 'Attribution of interpersonal power', in J.T. Tedeschi (ed.), *Perspectives on Social Power*, Chicago, Aldine-Atherton.

Schulze, R. (1958), 'Economic dominants and community power structure', *American Sociological Review*, 23, 3–9.

Schumacher, E.F. (1977), *A Guide for the Perplexed*, London, Abacus.

Schutz, A. (1953), 'Common-sense and scientific interpretations of human actions', *Philosophy and Phenomenological Research*, 14, 1–37.

Schutz, A. (1954), 'Concept and theory formation in the social sciences', *Journal of Philosophy*, LI, 257–273.

Schutz, A. (1962), *Collected Papers*, vol. 1, M. Natanson (ed.), The Hague, Martinus Nijhoff.

Schutz, A. (1964), *Collected Papers*, vol. 2, A. Broderson (ed.), The Hague, Martinus Nijhoff.

Schutz, A. (1966), *Collected Papers*, vol. 3, I. Schutz (ed.), The Hague, Martinus Nijhoff.

Schutz, A. (1967), *The Phenomenology of the Social World*, Evanston, Ill., Northwestern University Press.

Schwartz, M.S. and Schwartz, C.G. (1955), 'Problems in participant observation', *American Journal of Sociology*, no. 60, 343–354.

Searles, H. (1978), *L'Effort pour rendre l'autre fou*, Paris, Gallimard.

Selznick, P. (1949), *TVA and the Grass Roots*, Berkeley, University of California Press.

Selznick, P. (1957), *Leadership in Administration*, Evanston, Ill., Row, Peterson.

Serres, M. (1968), *Hermès ou la communication*, Paris, P.U.F.

Shapley, L.S. (1953), 'A value for *n*-person games', in H.W. Kuhn and A.W. Tucker (eds), *Contributions to the Theory of Games, II*, Princeton, Ill., Princeton University Press.

Shapley, L.S. and Shubik, M. (1954), 'A method for evaluating the distribution of power in a committee system', *American Political Science Review*, 787–792.

Silverman, D. (1968), 'Formal organizations or industrial sociology: towards a social action analysis of organizations', *Sociology*, 2, 221–238.

Silverman, D. (1970), *The Theory of Organizations*, London, Heinemann.

Silverman, D. (1972), 'Some neglected questions about social reality', in P. Filmer, M. Phillipson, D. Silverman and D. Walsh (eds), *New Directions in Sociological Theory*, Collier-Macmillan.

Silverman, D. (1975), 'Accounts of organizations: organizational "structures" and the accounting process', in J.B. McKinlay (ed.), *Processing People: Cases in Organizational Behaviour*, London, Holt, Rinehart & Winston.

Silverman, D. and Jones, J. (1976), *Organizational Work*, London, Collier-Macmillan.

Simmel, G. (1950), *The Sociology of Georg Simmel*, New York, Free Press.

Simon, H.A. (1947), *Administrative Behavior*, New York, Free Press (2nd edn, 1957).

Simon, H.A. (1953), 'Notes on the observation and measurement of political power', *Journal of Politics*, 15, 500–516.

Simon, H.A. (1957), *Models of Man, Social and Rational*, New York, Wiley.

Simon, H.A. (1968), 'The future of information processing technology', *Management Science*, 619–624.

Simon, H.A. (1969), *The Science of the Artificial*, Cambridge, Mass., MIT Press.

Simon, H.A. (1973a), 'Applying information technology to organization design', *Public Administration Review*, 268–278.

Simon, H.A. (1973b), 'Organization man: rational or self-actualizing', *Public*

Administration Review, 346–353.

Simon, H.A. (1977), *The New Science of Management Decision*, rev. edn, New York, Prentice-Hall.

Simon, H.A. and Stedry, A.C. (1968), 'Psychology and economics', in G. Lindzey and E. Aronson (eds), *The Handbook of Social Psychology*, Reading, Mass., Addison-Wesley.

Skolimowski, H. (1983), 'Power: Myth and reality', *Alternatives, A Journal of World Policy*, 9(1), 25–49.

Snyder, R.C. and Paige, G.D. (1958), 'The United States decision to resist aggression in Korea: the application of an analytic scheme', *Administrative Science Quarterly*, 3, 342–378.

Storer, N.W. (1966), *The Social System of Science*, New York, Holt, Rinehart & Winston.

Stryker, S. (1972), 'Coalition behavior', in C.G. McClintock (ed.), *Experimental Social Psychology*, New York, Holt, Rinehart & Winston.

Summers, W.G. (1903), *What Social Classes Owe to Each Other*, New York, Harper & Row.

Suttles, G. (1968), *The Social Order of the Slum: Ethnicity and Territory in the Inner City*, Chicago, University of Chicago Press.

Tannenbaum, R. and Massarik, F. (1950), 'Participation by subordinates in the managerial decision-making process', *Canadian Journal of Economics and Political Science*, 16, 408–418.

Taylor, C. (1964), *The Explanation of Behaviour*, New York, Humanities Press.

Taylor, C. (1967), 'Relations between cause and action', *Proceedings of the Seventh Inter-American Congress of Philosophy*, Quebec, Les Presses de l'Université Laval.

Taylor, F.M. (1907), 'On the art of cutting metals', *Transactions of the American Society of Mechanical Engineers*, 28.

Taylor, F.M. (1911), *Principles of Scientific Management*, New York, Harper.

Taylor, R. (1966), *Action and Purpose*, Englewood Cliffs, N.J., Prentice-Hall.

Tedeschi, J.T. (1970), 'Threats and promises', in P. Swingle (ed.), *The Structure of Conflict*, New York, Academic Press.

Tedeschi, J.T. (1972), *The Social Influence Process*, Chicago, Aldine.

Tedeschi, J.T. (ed.) (1974), *Perspectives on Social Power*, Chicago, Aldine-Atherton.

Tedeschi, J.T. and Bonoma, T.V. (1972), 'Power and influence: an introduction', in J.T. Tedeschi (ed.), *Social Influence Processes*, Chicago, Aldine-Atherton.

Tedeschi, J.T., Schlenker, B.R. and Bonoma, T.V. (1973), *Conflict, Power, and Games*, Chicago, Aldine-Atherton.

Thibault, J.W. and Kelley, H.H. (1959), *The Social Psychology of Groups*, New York, Wiley.

Thomas, L.V. (1978), *Mort et pouvoir*, Paris, Payot.

Thomas, W.I. (1966), 'On social organization and social personality', in M. Janowitz (ed.), *Selected Papers*, Chicago, University of Chicago Press.

Thompson, J.D. (1956), 'Authority and power in "identical" organizations', *American Journal of Sociology*, 62, 290–301.

Thompson, J.D. (ed.) (1966), *Approaches to Organizational Design*, Pittsburgh,

University of Pittsburgh Press.

Thompson, J.D. (1967), *Organizations in Action*, New York, McGraw-Hill.

Tiryakian, E.A. (1965), 'Existential phenomenology', *American Sociological Review*, 30, 674–678.

Touraine, A. (1966), *Sociologie de l'action*, Paris, Seuil.

Touraine, A. (1978), *La voix et le regard*, Paris, Seuil.

Turner, R. (1962), 'Role-taking: process versus conformity', in M.R. Arnold (ed.), *Human Behavior and Social Process: an Interactionist Approach*, Boston, Houghton Mifflin.

Veljko, R. (1980), 'Positive and negative power: thoughts on the dialectics of power', *Organization Studies*, 1(1), 3–19.

Vickers, Sir G. (1965), *The Art of Judgement*, London, Chapman & Hall.

Votaw, D. (1966), 'What do we believe about power?', *California Management Review*, no. 8.

Wahl, F. (ed.) (1968), *Qu'est-ce que le structuralisme*, Paris, Seuil.

Walker, C.J. and Guest, R.H. (1952), *The Man on the Assembly Line*, Cambridge, Mass., Harvard University Press.

Walton, R.E. and McKersie, R.B. (1965), *A Behavioral Theory of Labor Negotiations*, New York, McGraw-Hill.

Warner, M. (1977), *Organizational Choice and Constraint*, Weastmead, Saxon House.

Weber, M. (1930), *The Protestant Ethic*, Allen & Unwin.

Weber, M. (1947), *The Theory of Social and Economic Organization*, New York, Free Press.

Weick, K.E. (1968), 'Systematic observational methods', in Lindzey and Aronson (eds), *Handbook of Social Psychology*, vol. II, Reading, Mass., Addison-Wesley.

Weick, K.E. (1969), *The Social Psychology of Organizing*, Reading, Mass., Addison-Wesley.

Weick, K. (1976), 'Educational organizations as loosely coupled systems', *Administrative Science Quarterly*, 21, 1–19.

Weinberg, J.R. (1977), *Ockham, Descartes and Hume*, London, University of Wisconsin Press.

Whyte, W.F. (1955), *Street Corner Society*, Chicago, University of Chicago Press.

Whyte, W.F. (1969a), 'Reflections on my work', in I.L. Horowitz (ed.), *Sociological Self-Images*, Beverly Hills, Calif., Sage Publications.

Whyte, W.F. (ed.) (1969b), *Organizational Behavior*, Homewood, Ill., Irwin.

Whyte, W.H. (1956), *The Organization Man*, New York, Simon & Schuster.

Williams, G.A. (1960), 'The concept of "egemonia" in the thought of Antonia Gramsci: some notes on interpretation', *Journal of the History of Ideas*, 21, 586–599.

Wilson, T.P. (1970), 'Conceptions of interaction and forms of sociological explanation', *American Sociological Review*, 35, 697–710.

Winstanley, G. (1944), *Selections from His Works*, L. Hamilton (ed.), London, Cresset Press.

Wittgenstein, L. (1953), *Philosophical Investigations*, New York, Macmillan.

Wittgenstein, L. (1961), *Tractatus Logico-Philosophicus*, London, Routledge & Kegan Paul.

Wright, G.H. von (1971), *Explanation and Understanding*, New York, Cornell University Press.

Wrong, D.H. (1961), 'The oversocialized conception of man in modern society', *American Sociological Review*, 2, 184–193.

Wrong, D.H. (1968), 'Some problems in defining social power', *American Journal of Sociology*, 73(6), 673–681.

Wrong, D.H. (1979), *Power: Its Forms, Bases and Uses*, Oxford, Blackwell.

Zald, M.N. (1962), 'Power balance and staff conflict in correctional institutions', *Administrative Science Quarterly*, no. 7, 22–49.

Zald, M.N. (1970), 'Power in organizations', Nashville, Tenn., Vanderbilt University Press (special issue of *Administrative Science Quarterly*, 14(4), 1969).

Zaleznik, A. (1971), 'Power and politics in organizational life', in A. Zaleznik, *Developing Executive Leaders*, Cambridge, Mass., Harvard University Press (also in H.J. Leavitt and L.R. Pondy (1973) *Readings in Managerial Psychology*, Chicago, University of Chicago Press).

Zeraffa, M. (1976), *Fictions: The Novel and Social Reality*, Harmondsworth, Penguin.

Zey-Ferrell, M. (1981), 'Critiques of dominant perspectives', in P.O. Berg and Ph. Daudi (eds) (1982), *Traditions and Trends in Organization Theory*, Part II, Lund, Studentlitteratur.

Zey-Ferrell, M. and Aiken, M. (1981), *Complex Organizations: Critical Perspectives*, Glenview, Ill., Scott, Foresman.

Index